Complete Middle Egyptian

Teach® Yourself

Complete Middle Egyptian

A New Method for Understanding Hieroglyphs: Reading Texts in Context

Richard Bussmann

First published in Great Britain in 2017 by John Murray Learning.
An Hachette UK company.

British Library Cataloguing in Publication Data: a catalogue record for this title is available from the British Library.

Library of Congress Catalog Card Number: on file.

Paperback 9781473609792

eBook 9781473615724

3

Typeset by MPS Limited.

Printed and bound in Great Britain by CPI Group (UK) Ltd, Croydon, CR0 4YY.

John Murray Learning policy is to use papers that are natural, renewable and recyclable products and made from wood grown in sustainable forests. The logging and manufacturing processes are expected to conform to the environmental regulations of the country of origin.

Carmelite House

50 Victoria Embankment

London EC4Y 0DZ

www.hodder.co.uk

Also available in ebook

Contents

Acknowledgements

This course is the result of many helping hands. I would like to thank, first of all, Faye Newton, the development editor of this course. A novice to Middle Egyptian, Faye has been a great test reader and offered invaluable, constructive feedback throughout the project. A very big thank you also goes to the students of my classes, who commented on the course as it was developing. Their thoughts and critique had a great impact on the book. I am most grateful to John Tait, former Amelia Edwards Professor in Egyptology at University College London. His comments on Egyptian grammar and English wording have greatly helped me to handle some difficult aspects of the book. Joseph Clayton kindly took over the proofreading of the hieroglyphs and the transliteration, offering meticulous feedback far beyond the correction of individual mistakes, and the course has benefited enormously from his comments. I thank Elli Petrocheilou for her accurate drawings of the hieroglyphs and the maps for the course.

Many thanks also go to the team from Hodder for their guidance and help, especially Victoria Roddam, James Hobbs and Cecilia Bembibre, who initially approached me with the idea of writing this book. Professor Dr Ludwig Morenz and Dr Gianluca Miniaci have kindly granted me permission to use their photos (in Units 4 and 9). I am grateful to Serge Rosmorduc for the permission to use his hieroglyphic font JSesh for this book.

About the author

I have always been fascinated by ancient languages and cultures. In my Greek class at school, I remember looking at a monumental inscription of a Hittite king. The language of the inscription is similar to ancient Greek and was written with images. I found it enthralling to decipher this inscription and gradually understand the similarities between ancient Greek and this much older language from which Greek had developed. This made me curious about the world before the Greeks, particularly the ancient Egyptian language and Egyptian hieroglyphs.

I decided to study Egyptology, Near Eastern studies, and the Old and New Testament at Heidelberg, Berlin and Göttingen universities. I soon noticed that the translation of a text was not simply about 'what the ancient Egyptians said', but that it required a deep understanding of the context of their texts and language. Parallel to learning the ancient languages, I started excavating in Egypt. I enjoyed recording the pots and pebbles that people like me had handled thousands of years ago. I learned much from the material culture that I had not read about in texts, for example how ordinary ancient Egyptians lived and died and how they might have experienced their landscape.

In my current research, I combine language and archaeology. I co-direct an excavation project in Middle Egypt and lead a project that studies the earliest Egyptian hieroglyphs used on seals. *Complete Middle Egyptian* is a course that reflects in many ways this research interest. It emerged from teaching ancient Egyptian language and archaeology, first at University College London and now at Cologne University. I hope that the book conveys something of my fascination for deciphering archaic scripts, reading texts in their archaeological context and discovering an unknown world of people who lived in the remote past.

How this book works

Complete Middle Egyptian uses a new method for learning hieroglyphs. The two key ideas, developed for how modern languages are taught, are that contextual learning and learning by discovery help with a deeper understanding of the language – and, simply put, are more fun.

With the discovery method, you are asked to discover patterns in a new text, first on your own and then once the grammar is explained and reinforced with different types of exercises – from classical transliteration and translation over simple matching exercises, to pronunciation practices. Contextual learning means that each unit in this course is structured around a different theme. From the beginning, you will read coherent passages of original texts reproduced here in the form in which they were carved on a tomb or temple wall. If you study the photos, drawings and maps while you are doing the language exercises, you will understand the historical and archaeological relevance of the texts discussed. In this way, learning signs, words and grammar will automatically lead you into core tenets of the ancient Egyptian culture. And the good thing is that your brain absorbs grammar much better when language content is linked to themes and context.

The course begins with funerary inscriptions and royal self-presentation, and then highlights aspects from the world of kings and officials, before looking at key ideas of Egyptian religion and finally exploring fiction and power exercised through the written word. Each theme corresponds to a level in the grammar, progressing from signs, words and phrases to sentences and advanced forms of the verb and finally to reading longer passages of texts. This structure means that that you will need to complete a unit in order to understand the next, so starting with Unit 1 is essential. The final part of the course offers a review of the grammar, a key to the exercises, an Egyptian–English vocabulary and a sign list for your reference. Throughout the course, you can look up the meaning of the most frequently used signs on the inside front and back covers of the book.

Each unit, apart from the first, has the following structure:

- It begins with an **introduction** to the theme, followed by one or two questions that lead you from there into the theme and language content of the unit.
- The **Vocabulary builder** lists the relevant words for a unit and includes exercises to help you learn the signs and words.
- The **focus text** introduces the new grammar of the unit. Once you have familiarized yourself with the new words, you can start reading the focus text and try to answer the content questions that follow.
- The **Language discovery** section looks at the grammar in greater detail. First, you are asked to study the focus text again, concentrating on the grammar. Next, you find an explanation of the grammar and you are offered some exercises to consolidate your knowledge.
- The **Explore** section brings together all that you have learned in the unit. It asks for your detective skills because here you can explore a new text using what you have already learned. Don't worry if you find it a bit challenging at times and if you make mistakes. This is a normal part of every discovery!
- Then have a look at the **Drawing hieroglyphs** section. Drawing helps you to recognize which lines in the shape of a hieroglyph are important and aids your learning of the signs.
- In the final **Test yourself** section, you can check with a few quick exercises that you have understood the grammar points of the unit.

Throughout the units, **insight** boxes in the margins offer additional information on a particular word or phrase in a hieroglyphic text, so do check what they have to say.

This course offers a complete overview of Middle Egyptian in the sense that it introduces the most relevant grammatical structures and up to 400 words and 300 hieroglyphic signs. If you wish to become a professional Egyptologist, try the following two textbooks:

- James P. Allen, *Middle Egyptian: An Introduction to the Language and Culture of Hieroglyphs*, 3rd edition, Cambridge 2014. You may find this course challenging, but it includes keys to the exercises, so is suitable for self-study.
- Alan H. Gardiner, *Egyptian Grammar: Being an Introduction to the Study of Hieroglyphs*, 3rd edition, Oxford 1955. The authoritative mother of all Middle Egyptian grammar textbooks, 'the Gardiner' is outdated here and there, but still is the most comprehensive and detailed review of the Middle Egyptian language, and best used with a teacher.

The discovery method

There are many philosophies and approaches to language learning, some practical, some quite unconventional, and far too many to list here. Perhaps you know of a few, or even have some techniques of your own. In this book we have incorporated the discovery method of learning, a sort of do-it-yourself approach to language learning. What this means is that you will be encouraged throughout the course to engage your mind and figure out the language for yourself, through identifying patterns, understanding grammar concepts, noticing words that are similar to English, and more. This method promotes language awareness, a critical skill in acquiring a new language. As a result of your own efforts, you will be able to retain more of what you have learned, use it with confidence, and, even better, apply those same skills to continuing to learn the language (or, indeed, another one) on your own after you have finished this book.

Everyone can succeed in learning a language – the key is to know how to learn it. Learning is more than just reading or memorizing grammar and vocabulary. It is about being an active learner, learning in real contexts, and, most importantly, using what you have learned in different situations. Simply put, if you figure something out for yourself, you are more likely to understand it. And when you use what you have learned, you are more likely to remember it.

And because many of the essential but (let's admit it!) challenging details, such as grammar rules, are introduced through the discovery method, you will have more fun while learning. Enjoy yourself!

Learn to learn

Here's how to become a successful language learner:

1 **Make learning a habit.**

Study a little every day; between 20 and 30 minutes is ideal. Give yourself short-term goals for example working out how long you will spend on a particular unit and keeping to this time limit, to create a study habit. Try to make your environment conducive to learning – one that is calm, quiet and free from distractions. As you study, do not worry about your mistakes or the things you can't remember or understand. Languages settle gradually into the brain. Just give yourself enough time and you will succeed.

2 **Maximize your exposure to the language.**

Try to find signs and words in inscriptions of objects on display in the Egyptian gallery of a museum. Look up images of inscribed objects on the Internet and see whether you can make out bits and pieces in the inscription.

3 **Learn vocabulary in context.**

Do this by reading again and again the hieroglyphic text in which it occurs. Create stories around individual hieroglyphs to memorize the meaning of the word in which they are used. Cover up the English side of the vocabulary list and see whether you remember the meaning of the word. Do the same for the hieroglyphs. Create flash cards, drawings and mind maps. Write Egyptian words on post-it notes and stick them to objects around your house.

4 **Experiment with grammar rules.**

Sit back and reflect on how the rules of Middle Egyptian compare with your own language or other languages you may already know.

5 **Use known vocabulary to practise new grammar structures.**

Change individual elements of a text so for example say *I* instead of *you* or negate a sentence, and see how the changes would affect the hieroglyphs, transliteration and translation.

6 **Read texts out loud.**

Read aloud the transliteration of a text, even if you are not asked for it in an exercise.

7 **Learn from your errors.**

Making errors is part of any learning process, so don't be too worried about making mistakes. Reflect on why you have made a mistake to understand better the rules of Middle Egyptian. Note the seriousness of errors: many errors are not serious as they do not affect meaning.

8 **Learn to cope with uncertainty.**

Hieroglyphic texts record a lived experience different from our modern world. Translations may sound archaic or strange and still be correct. Give them the time to sink into your mind and think about how you might say a similar sentence in English.

9 **Don't give up if you don't understand.**

If at some point you feel you don't understand what a text is talking about, try to guess what it is about and keep following it.

10 **Don't overuse your dictionary.**

Resist the temptation to look up every word you don't know. Read the same passage several times, concentrating on trying to get the gist of it. If, after the third time, some words still prevent you from making sense of the passage, look them up in the dictionary.

The history and language of ancient Egypt

When you read through this course, you will find that many Egyptian hieroglyphs depict natural phenomena, such as the sky, plants or animals. The ancient Egyptians clearly had a strong sense of the landscape they were living in, and it may be best to outline the context for this book by taking it from here.

Have a closer look at the hieroglyph 𓈋. The sign depicts the sun disc between two mountains and means *horizon*. The mountains represent the desert plateaus on both sides of the valley through which the river Nile flows. The Egyptians lived close to the river, where there was cultivable land. The area to the east, between the valley and the Red Sea (see map), is rocky and was inhabited by nomadic Bedouin. Since the Egyptians considered it hostile, the hieroglyph 𓈉, which depicts a mountainous landscape, means *foreign land*. The sign 𓈂 is used in the word for *eternity* and might depict the endless, sandy desert plain of the Sahara, which begins behind the Western plateau.

The ancient Greek historian Herodotus probably visited Egypt in antiquity, in around 450 BCE. He famously called it a 'gift of the Nile' because life in Egypt largely depended on the Nile. If you sail the Nile upstream from the Mediterranean, as Herodotus might have done, you will first pass through the Nile Delta, called Lower Egypt. This fertile area is fed by several arms of the river which branch off the main river just north of Cairo. From Cairo, your journey will continue through the Nile valley. In Middle Egypt, the cultivable floodplain on both sides of the river is up to 20 km wide. In contrast, Upper Egypt, further south, is characterized by a narrow strip of cultivation, which provides less agricultural hinterland for the communities who lived in this area. The rapids of Aswan, the so-called First Cataract, will interrupt your journey, before you can continue south. In Lower and Upper Nubia, you pass a series of more cataracts and see little or no cultivable land along the riverbanks. Finally, you will reach Khartoum at the confluence of the White Nile and the Blue Nile, the main tributaries of the Nile.

In prehistory, the climate in north-eastern Africa was wetter, and people and animals inhabited what is a desert today. As a more arid climate arose during the Neolithic period, *c.*8000 to 4300 BCE, many people gave up their nomadic lifestyle and started settling permanently in and near the Nile valley and the Delta. Before the Aswan High Dam was built in the 1960s, fertile sediments were washed down every year from the Ethiopian highlands and were spilled over the fields. Once people had managed to exploit sufficiently the fertile soil, agriculture became the backbone of the Egyptian economy. The ancient Egyptian state – its kings, officials, craftsmen and peasants – ultimately rested on this wealth.

However, the annual inundation was not entirely controllable and it often destroyed settlements on the floodplain. This had an impact on what we know about ancient Egypt today. Archaeologists focused much of their attention on the better-preserved remains on the desert slopes in the Nile valley, particularly monumental tombs and their inscriptions. In contrast, settlements – apart from their inscribed stone temples – were deemed aesthetically unappealing and yielded less written material; for a long time they were badly explored. For this reason, there is a bias in the recorded texts from ancient Egypt towards inscriptions and papyri from temples and tombs.

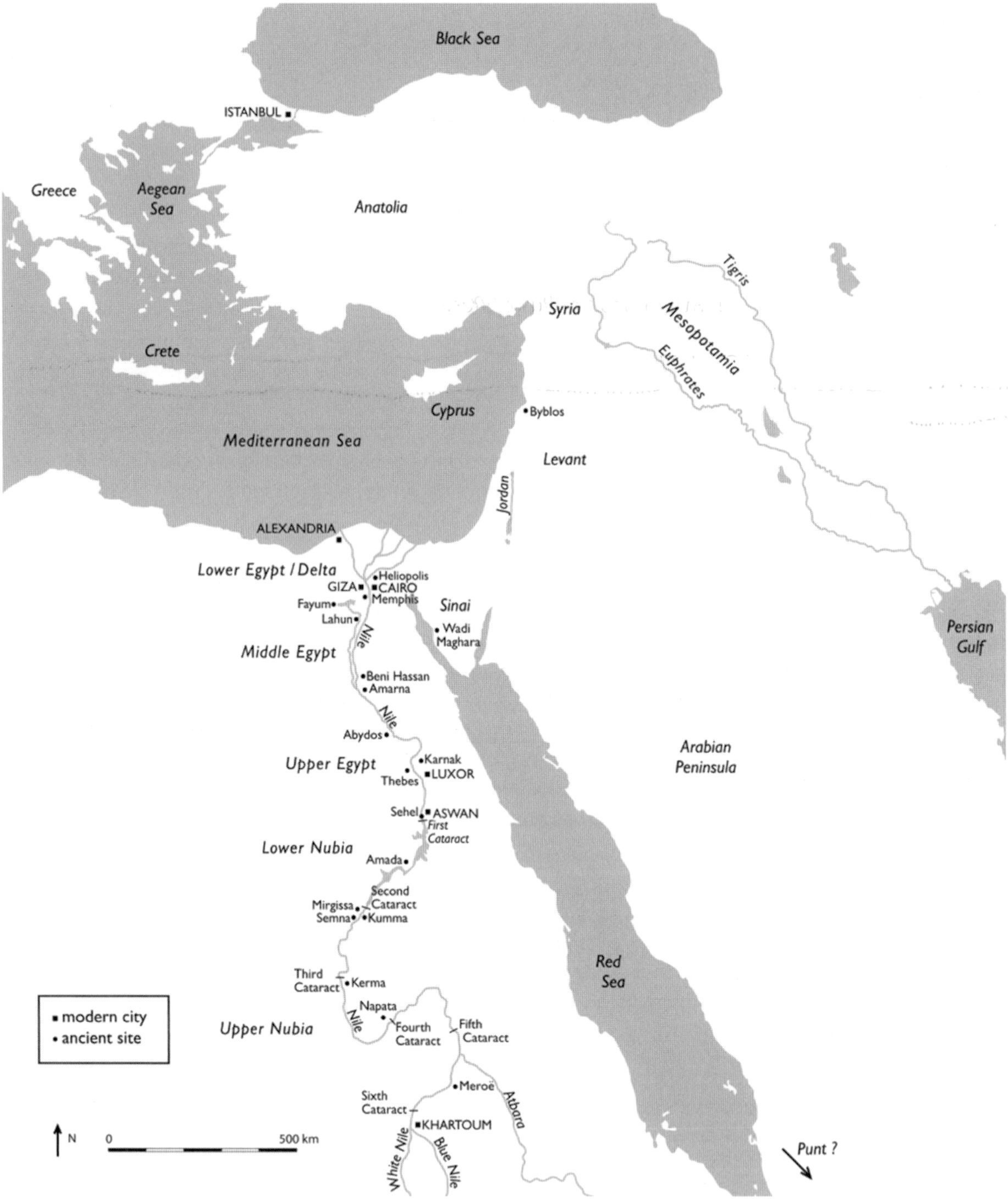
Black Sea
ISTANBUL
Greece
Aegean Sea
Anatolia
Tigris
Syria
Mesopotamia
Euphrates
Crete
Cyprus
Byblos
Mediterranean Sea
Levant
Jordan
ALEXANDRIA
Lower Egypt / Delta
Heliopolis
GIZA
CAIRO
Memphis
Fayum
Lahun
Sinai
Wadi Maghara
Nile
Middle Egypt
Beni Hassan
Amarna
Nile
Abydos
Karnak
Upper Egypt
Thebes
LUXOR
Sehel
ASWAN
First Cataract
Lower Nubia
Amada
Second Cataract
Mirgissa
Semna
Kumma
Persian Gulf
Arabian Peninsula
Red Sea
Third Cataract
Kerma
Napata
Nile
Fourth Cataract
Fifth Cataract
Upper Nubia
Meroë
Sixth Cataract
KHARTOUM
Atbara
White Nile
Blue Nile
Punt ?
modern city
ancient site
N
0
500 km

How the hieroglyphs were deciphered

Egyptian hieroglyphs are among the most iconic features of ancient Egypt, rivalled only by the pyramids, the bust of Nefertiti and the death mask of Tutankhamun. In medieval times and during the Renaissance, Arabic and European travellers and scholars were fascinated with what the signs might reveal about the wisdom and knowledge of a very old age. At that time, ideas about the age of the earth – and the position of ancient Egypt and the Biblical stories within human history – varied greatly.

Towards the end of the 18th century, when the Enlightenment era in Europe drew to a close, the French Revolution resulted in battles between France and the British Empire for control over Egypt. The decipherment of hieroglyphs fell into this political and intellectual climate. The French troops discovered a large stone slab reused in the walls of a fort at Rashid/Rosetta, a town at the Mediterranean coast. One side of the stone carried an inscription in three different scripts: hieroglyphs, Demotic – an abbreviated version of hieroglyphs – and Greek. The Rosetta Stone, as it is known today, was eventually brought to the British Museum. One of the copies made of the inscriptions reached the young French scholar François Champollion. In 1822, Champollion explained in a letter to the French Academy that hieroglyphs were not mere images representing ideas, but rendered the sound of the ancient Egyptian language. His discovery, based on previous attempts of others and later corrected and expanded, made it possible for the first time to read ancient Egyptian texts on their own terms rather than only through the lens of Greek and Biblical interpretation.

Once hieroglyphs were deciphered, the demand in Europe for fresh inscriptions from Egypt increased. It blended into the competition of European nation leaders for ancient Egyptian monuments to be displayed in their new national museums. Scholars were thus able to study new inscriptions and papyri and gradually revealed the grammar of the Egyptian language. The flipside of this development was an unprecedented flowering of the antiquity market. Inscribed stone slabs and other objects were offered on the market and are displayed in museum galleries today, with little information about their original find context. It took archaeology almost another century to progress from treasure hunting to the scientific documentation of inscriptions, objects and the natural environment. Current agendas in Egyptology move towards advanced interpretation of this evidence and embrace critical discussions of the Western dominion over the study of ancient Egypt, including the role that Egyptian heritage should play within and outside Egypt.

The story of decipherment is ultimately rooted in the origins of writing in Egypt. Hieroglyphs emerged between 4000 and 3000 BCE, when communities in north-eastern Africa became more hierarchical and one of the earliest states on the globe developed in Egypt based on centralized control, a written administration and sacred kingship. Phonetic script, that is, a visual code that represents the sound of the Egyptian language, appeared for the first time on labels from around 3300 BCE. The labels were attached to vessels and recorded the place of origin of the goods contained in them. They belonged to the burial equipment of a local ruler at Abydos, the later burial ground of the earliest Pharaohs.

We can distinguish two major types of scripts from fairly early on. The first is hieroglyphs used on stone monuments and typically carved into hard surfaces, often accompanying artistic representations probably executed by the same craftsmen as the hieroglyphs. The second script, which we call hieratic, was handwritten and was derived from hieroglyphs. Hieratic was written with ink on papyrus and other flat surfaces. After 3000 BCE, hieroglyphs and hieratic spread beyond the sphere of kings and courtiers and were used for tomb and temple decoration, letters, documents, literature, religious texts and medico-magical instructions.

The texts of this course are taken from the period from *c.*3000 to 1000 BCE, spanning the Old, Middle and New Kingdoms, when Egypt was united under one Pharaoh. In the Old Kingdom (*c.*2700–2300 BCE), the Pharaohs controlled the heartland of Egypt from the Mediterranean coast to the First Cataract. In the

Middle Kingdom (*c.*2050–1750 BCE), they expanded their control into Lower Nubia. The New Kingdom (c.1500–1070 BCE) saw the emergence of an empire that stretched from Upper Nubia over the Levant – that is, modern Israel and Palestine – to parts of Syria. This period is sometimes called the first global age in world history because the societies of North Africa, the eastern Mediterranean and the Near East were interacting with one another much more closely than ever before.

Egypt after the New Kingdom

After the end of the New Kingdom, Egypt was mostly dominated by rulers of foreign origin, first the Libyans from the West, then the Nubians from the South and the Assyrians and Persians from the East, and finally the Greeks from the North. Alexander the Great conquered Egypt and in 330 BCE founded Alexandria, which became the leading intellectual capital of the entire Mediterranean world for the next thousand years. After Alexander's death, rule of Egypt was handed over to his general Ptolemy, and the years between 303 and 30 BCE are known as the Ptolemaic period.

In 30 BCE, Egypt was incorporated into the Roman Empire. When the Empire split in 395 CE, Egypt became part of its eastern successor, the Byzantine Empire, whose capital was at Constantinople, modern Istanbul. At this time, Egypt had become predominantly Christian. Christianity flourished until well after the Arab conquest in 640 CE, before Islam gradually replaced it from around 800 CE onwards. Today, up to 90 per cent of the Egyptian population is Muslim.

There is much overlap between the different scripts and phases of the Egyptian language, which were used during the same period. Broadly speaking, hieroglyphs and hieratic prevailed from the Old to the New Kingdom. Middle Egyptian, which had developed from Old Egyptian, became typical of monumental inscriptions in the Middle Kingdom and remained so, with some alterations, until the last hieroglyph was carved into a temple wall in 392 CE. Middle Egyptian is the language that you will learn on this course.

During the New Kingdom, Late Egyptian replaced Middle Egyptian in documentary and literary texts. After the New Kingdom, hieratic remained in use for some religious texts, but was more and more replaced by Demotic. This script was derived from hieratic and had its heyday in the Ptolemaic and Roman periods. Its use on a monumental stone slab, such as the Rosetta Stone, is an exception, since most Demotic texts were written on papyrus. The last known inscription in Demotic is a visitor graffito in the temple of Philae dating to 452 CE.

Alexander the Great introduced Greek as the language for the administration of his empire. Greek played this role for a thousand years, until after the Arab conquest. Latin never quite settled in Egypt, even not during the Roman period. Rather, the Egyptians started writing their own language with Greek letters and added a few characters to express sounds typical of the Egyptian language. This script is called Coptic. The earliest Coptic words were used in contexts of the declining Pharaonic culture, such as magical texts and mummy labels, but ultimately Coptic was to become the script of Egyptian Christianity. It was used for the translation of Biblical texts into Egyptian, in the local administration and for the management of monasteries. The last dated Coptic text, a poem, was written in the 13th century CE. How long Coptic was still spoken in rural areas is difficult to say, but it was perhaps into the early 17th century. Much earlier than this, after the Arab conquest in 640, Arabic, which does not originate in the ancient Egyptian language, gradually replaced Greek and Coptic and is the official language of Egypt today. Other languages, such as Turkish, French and English, also played an important role in various periods of Egyptian history, until Egypt became independent again in the 20th century.

Different from the cuneiform script used to write texts in Sumerian, Akkadian and Ugaritic, among others, and unlike the Latin script used to notate many languages of the modern Western world, the Egyptian scripts – hieroglyphs, hieratic, Demotic and Coptic – were closely tied to the Egyptian language and hardly ever used for writing non-Egyptian languages.

Egyptian historical periods

Below is a summary of the most common terms used for the various periods of Egyptian history. The Greek–Egyptian priest Manetho, who lived in the Ptolemaic period, divided the Pharaonic past into dynasties, some of which represent a distinct family. Egyptologists have started to criticize Manetho's dynasties for being exclusively royal and often meaningless in local contexts, but they still refer to the dynasties for writing Egyptian history, as does this book.

8000–4300 BCE	Neolithic	
4300–3300 BCE	Predynastic	
3300–2700 BCE	Early Dynastic	Dynasty 1–2
2700–2200 BCE	Old Kingdom	Dynasty 3–6
2200–2050 BCE	First Intermediate Period	Dynasty 7–11
2050–1750 BCE	Middle Kingdom	Dynasty 11–13
1750–1550 BCE	Second Intermediate Period	Dynasty 14–17
1550–1070 BCE	New Kingdom	Dynasty 18–20
1070–664 BCE	Third Intermediate Period	Dynasty 21–25
664–332 BCE	Late Period	Dynasty 26–31
332–30 BCE	Ptolemaic Period	
30 BC–395 CE	Roman Period	
395–640 CE	Byzantine Period	
Since 640 CE	Islamic Period	

1 Pronunciation and transliteration

In this unit you will learn how to:

- **pronounce ancient Egyptian**
- **read transliteration**
- **transliterate simple hieroglyphs**
- **transliterate simple words**
- **draw frequently used hieroglyphs.**

The sound of the ancient Egyptian language

This book invites you on a journey into ancient Egypt, 5,000 years back in time, to the origins of Pharaonic civilization. You will be able to explore what life was like then along the Nile, through original historical texts. *Complete Middle Egyptian* introduces you to both the hieroglyphic script and the language in which most hieroglyphic texts were written.

Did you know that we can understand not only what hieroglyphic texts are saying, but also how the ancient Egyptian language sounded, even though it has died out as a spoken language? Imagine being able to speak like an ancient Egyptian. This is what you will learn in this unit.

How did Egyptologists work out how ancient Egyptian sounds? There are several sources that help with the answer to this question. Firstly, the last phase of Egyptian – Coptic – has survived in the liturgy of the Egyptian Church up to the present day. This is similar to how Latin continues to be used in the Western Church. Secondly, a bit closer in time to Pharaonic Egypt, ancient travellers wrote down the Egyptian names they encountered using Greek letters. And, finally, ancient Egyptian belongs to a large family of languages spoken today in North Africa and the Near East.

With the help of these sources, Egyptologists have reconstructed the sounds of ancient Egyptian. To render these sounds in writing, Egyptologists transliterate hieroglyphic texts with Roman letters prior to translation. The letters include *b* (as in bar), *p* (as in path), *f* (as in foot), *m* (as in moon), *n* (as in never), *h* (as in have), *z* (as in zero), *s* (as in sister), *k* (as in kiln), *g* (as in give), *t* (as in tip) and *d* (as in dust). The consonant *r* was pronounced like the 'rolling' r in Italian, using the tip of the tongue, but you can pronounce it like an English r (as in river).

You will not find vowels (a, e, i, o, u) used in transliteration. This is because hieroglyphs record the consonants only; vowels were inferred in speech. Arabic is a modern script that works in a similar way. For example, the Arabic word 'salaam', *peace*, is written with the three letters s-l-m only. Arabic speakers know the word 'salaam' and so do not need to see the vowels written; they recognize the word from just its consonants.

Today, we can only speculate about which vowels were used and how they sounded in ancient times. Since we cannot pronounce transliteration coherently without vowels, a short 'e' sound is added between the consonants. For example, you would pronounce the Egyptian word *nfr* (meaning *good, beautiful*) nefer, with the emphasis placed on the first syllable, i.e. néfer. Another example is *bnr sweet*, pronounced béner.

1 Read the words in transliteration aloud. You can use the English approximation of the pronunciation written in brackets for help if you need to.

a *nfr* (néfer) *good, beautiful*

b *bnr* (béner) *sweet*

c *pn* (pen) *this*

d *st* (set) *it*

e *Kmt* (kémet) *Egypt*

f *gs* (ges) *side*

g *mn* (men) *to endure*

h *tp* (tep) *head*

i *dpt* (dépet) *boat*

j *hp* (hep) *law*

k *zp* (zep) *occasion*

LANGUAGE INSIGHT

Names of places, deities, kings and individuals, for example *Kmt Egypt*, are capitalized in transliteration, just as in English.

Congratulations! You have just spoken your first words in Egyptian.

LETTERS WITH ADDITIONAL DOTS AND STROKES

The following section introduces letters that are written with additional dots and strokes in transliteration. The simplest are *š* (as in *sh*ine), *ṯ* (as in *ch*eap, pronounced *tj*eep), and *ḏ* (as in *j*am, pronounced *dj*am). Words using these signs are, for example, *dšr red* pronounced déshér, *nṯr god* pronounced nétjer, and *ḏd to speak* pronounced djed.

Ancient Egyptian has a few sounds that English does not have. To pronounce them, most Egyptologists simplify a little and use a more familiar sound in English. You can do that, too. The letter *q*, for example, represents a k-sound produced deep in the throat. Most Egyptologists find it easier to pronounce it as a simple k (as in *k*iln). The word *qrs burial*, therefore, is pronounced kéres. Similarly, the letter *ḥ* (h with a dot) notates a strong h-sound. Egyptologists usually pronounce it as a simple h (as in *h*ave), for example *ḥm servant*, pronounced hem. The sound *ḫ* (h with a crescent) is sounded as in German ma*ch*en, whereas *ẖ* (h with an understroke) is sounded softer as in German i*ch*. Egyptologists simplify and pronounce both as kh (as in Lo*ch* Ness). Examples are *nḫt strong*, pronounced nékhet, and *ẖnm to unite*, pronounced khénem.

2 Try to match the words in transliteration with their correct pronunciation, as shown in the first example. Then read the words in transliteration aloud.

a *šs linen*	djet
b *ḏt eternity*	heh
c *qbb cool*	tjez
d *ḫt wood*	shes
e *ṯz knot*	peh
f *ẖt belly*	medj
g *ḥḥ million*	ménekh
h *zš scribe*	khet
i *pḥ to reach*	kébeb
j *mnḫ excellent*	khet
k *mḏ ten*	zesh

DARK AND BRIGHT VOWELS

We have seen that no vowels are used in transliteration. However, some consonants have a strong vowel component and, in fact, are sometimes pronounced like vowels.

The letter *w* is either pronounced w (as in *w*ater), when used at the beginning or in the middle of a word, or oo (as in p*oo*r) in final position. The word *wḏ decree* is pronounced wédj, *swr to drink* séwer, and *mnw monument* ménoo.

The letters *j* and *y* stand for the sounds y (as in *y*es), usually when used at the beginning of a word, or ee (as in b*ee*), when used in the middle or at the end. Examples are *jnk I*, pronounced yének, *bjn bad*, pronounced been, and *mry beloved*, pronounced méree. The difference between the two letters is that *y* indicates a long and *j* a short y and ee, but in practice Egyptologists pronounce them the same.

As they can be pronounced as a consonant or a vowel, *w*, *j* and *y* are called semi- or half-consonants. When any two of them appear side by side within a word, they are connected in pronunciation, for example *njwt town*, pronounced néeoot.

3 Match the words in transliteration with their correct pronunciation, as in the previous exercise. Then read them aloud.

a *wbn to rise*	rédee
b *wr great*	wében
c *wsr strong*	yénee
d *ḫrw voice*	wer
e *fdw four*	hézee
f *rwd stair*	fédoo
g *rdj to give*	khéroo
h *jnj to bring*	réwed
i *ḥzj to praise*	wéser

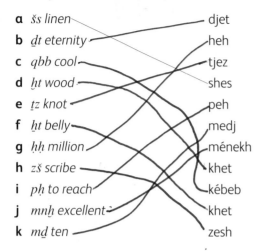

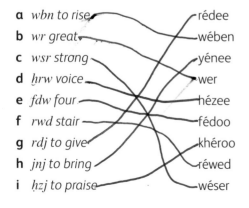

LANGUAGE INSIGHT

Some Egyptologists also pronounce *w* in initial or central position as oo, for example óoben, instead of wében, or róod instead of réwed. Similarly, when *j* or *y* stand at the beginning of a word, some prefer to pronounce them ee instead of y, for example éenee, instead of yénee. There is no strict rule for the correct pronunciation, partly because we do not know exactly, how the words sounded in the mouth of an ancient Egyptian.

SPECIAL LETTERS

There are two signs in transliteration that have no equivalent in Roman letters. The sign *ꜣ* (two superimposed crescents) renders a sound called alef. It demarcates a break in the flow of the voice. In English, for example, you can pronounce 'theatre' without a break between the syllables 'the' and 'atre' or interrupt them, making it sound like 'the'atre'. 'Theatre' would be written without an alef and 'the'atre' with an alef in Egyptian. Egyptologists simply pronounce alef as a long aa (as in bath), for example *pꜣ that* pronounced paa.

The sign *ꜥ* (a hook in superscript) notates an a- or e-sound called ayin. It is produced deep in the throat and is difficult for English speakers to imitate adequately. Again, Egyptologists simply pronounce it as a long aa, as in *wḏꜥ to judge* wédjaa.

When *ꜣ* and *ꜥ* are doubled or used side by side within a word, you interrupt the voice. For example, *mꜣꜥ true* and *mꜣꜣ to see* are both pronounced máa-aa.

4 Match the words in transliteration with their correct pronunciation and read them aloud.

a *zꜣ son* — áaped
b *tꜣ land* — aadj
c *ꜣpd bird* — zaa
d *ꜥq to enter* — méshaa
e *ꜥḏ to be safe* — aa-aa
f *mšꜥ army* — aak
g *ꜥꜣ big* — taa

SUMMARY OF SOUNDS

Well done. Now you know all the sounds of ancient Egyptian and how to pronounce them. The following table summarizes the sounds in 'alphabetical' order. The alphabet is a modern arrangement that helps Egyptologists find words in the dictionary.

ꜣ aa	*m* m	*z* z	*t* t
j, y y, ee	*n* n	*s* s	*ṯ* tj
w w, oo	*r* r	*š* sh	*d* d
ꜥ aa	*h* h	*q* k	*ḏ* dj
p p	*ḥ* h	*g* g	
b b	*ḫ* kh	*k* k	
f f	*ẖ* kh		

Your first hieroglyphs

Now have a look at how the sounds you have learned were expressed in hieroglyphs. The hieroglyphs introduced in this section represent animals or parts of the human body and are transliterated with one individual letter. In many cases, we know why a sign was chosen to render a specific sound. You will find the explanations below.

hieroglyph	transliteration	explanation
𓂋	*r*	The sign represents a human mouth. The Egyptian word for mouth is 'raa'. As it begins with an r, the human mouth was chosen to stand for the sound *r*.
𓂝	ʿ	The human forearm represents the sound ʿ because the Egyptian word for forearm is 'aa'.
𓃀	*b*	This sign represents the lower part of a human leg and a foot. It indicates the place at which somebody stands. As the Egyptian word for place is 'boo', the leg and foot were chosen to represent the sound *b*.
𓅓	*m*	The Egyptian word for owl 'mooladj' begins with an m. For this reason, the owl represents the sound *m*.
𓆓	*ḏ*	The cobra represents the sound *ḏ* because the Egyptian word for cobra 'djet' begins with a dj.
𓆑	*f*	The sound *f* is represented by a horned viper because the Egyptian word for viper 'fee' begins with an f.

5 Match the hieroglyphs with their correct transliteration and pronunciation, as shown.

a 𓅓	*ḏ*	f
b 𓂋	*f*	m
c 𓆓	*r*	aa
d 𓃀	*m*	r
e 𓆑	*b*	dj
f 𓂝	ʿ	b

6 Now transliterate a group of signs, as shown in the first example. Read the hieroglyphs from left to right.

a 𓆓𓆑 *ḏf*

b 𓅓𓂋

c 𓂋𓂝

d 𓂝𓃀

e 𓆓𓂋

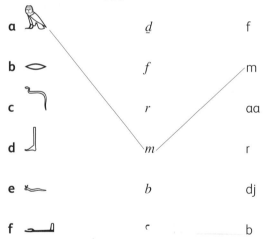

MORE SOUND SIGNS

The following group of sound signs represents made objects or natural phenomena. Like the signs above, each represents one sound and is transliterated with one letter.

hieroglyph	transliteration	explanation
𓈖	*n*	The ripple of water represents the sound *n*. We do not know exactly why.
𓊪	*p*	The small rectangle depicts a simple stool or seat. It stands for the sound *p* because the Egyptian for seat 'pe' begins with a p.
𓊃	*z*	This hieroglyph depicts a door bolt with a seal. The Egyptian word for a door bolt is 'ze'; hence the door bolt stands for the sign *z*.
𓏏	*t*	This sign shows a loaf of bread. The Egyptian word for bread is 'ta', which is why the hieroglyph for bread was chosen to render the sound *t*.
𓎡	*k*	This hieroglyph is a basket with a handle. For unknown reasons, it stands for the sound *k*.
𓋴	*s*	The sound *s* is expressed with a hieroglyph representing a folded cloth. Again, it is not clear why.
𓎛	*ḥ*	The sign represents a twisted wick. It renders the sound *ḥ* because the first letter of the Egyptian word for wick 'haat' is an h.

7 Compare the words in hieroglyphs below with their transliteration and try to figure out how the hieroglyphs are arranged and the order to read to them in. For example, in the first case, the hieroglyph for *p* is placed over the hieroglyph for *f*, and the transliteration is *pf*. Hence the hieroglyphs are read from top to bottom.

a 𓊪𓆑 *pf that*

b 𓎡𓅓 *km complete*

c 𓆓𓏏𓂧 *ḏt eternity*

d 𓈖𓏏𓆑 *ntf he*

e 𓎛𓊃 *ḥz praise*

f 𓃀𓈖𓂋 *bnr sweet*

8 Now, try to transliterate the words in the column on the right, by using the words in the left column to help you. The first example is done for you.

a 𓊪𓆑 *pf that* — 𓊪𓈖 *pn* this

b 𓆓𓏏𓂧 *ḏt eternity* — 𓆓𓋴 ____________ self

c 𓈖𓏏𓆑 *ntf he* — 𓈖𓏏𓎡 ____________ you

d 𓎡𓅓 *km complete* — 𓎡𓏏 ____________ other

e 𓂋𓈖 *rn name* — 𓂋𓂝 ____________ sun

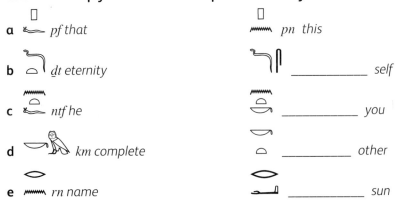

Drawing hieroglyphs

A great way to learn hieroglyphs – and one that is a lot of fun, too – is by drawing them. You will find it easier to recognize the underlying shape and characteristic features of a sign when you know how to draw it. Once you can draw a sign, you will feel confident in recognizing it in a new text. This will help you when you come to decipher original texts because the way hieroglyphs were drawn can vary, just as handwriting varies in English.

The signs below are used frequently in hieroglyphic texts, including those in the next unit. You can either develop your own style of writing hieroglyphs or follow the step-by-step guidelines below. Play with them and try to write your name in hieroglyphs.

1 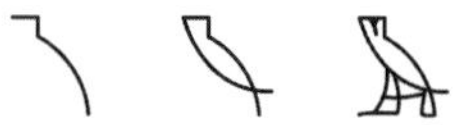

2 

3 

Test yourself

1 Pronounce the following letters: *b, t, š, ḏ, r, ꜣ, ꜥ, ẖ*

2 Read the following words out loud: *nts, ptr, ṯn, bw, mꜣꜥ, ḥzj, ẖzj, wḏꜣ*

3 Match the hieroglyphs with their correct transliteration.

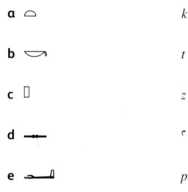

a  *k*

b  *t*

c  *z*

d  *ꜥ*

e  *p*

4 Transliterate the following words.

a  ___________ *he*

b  ___________ *name*

c  ___________ *and*

d 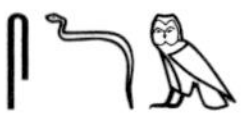 ___________ *to listen*

5 Write the following words in hieroglyphs, placing the signs either side by side or one over the other.

a *nf* (*this*) one over the other: 𓈖𓆑

b *ntf* (*he*) one over the other:

c *mḏ* (*ten*) side by side:

d *nm* (*who?*) side by side:

e *ḏs* (*self*) side by side:

SELF-CHECK

	I CAN
○	pronounce ancient Egyptian
○	read transliteration
○	transliterate simple hieroglyphs
○	transliterate simple words
○	draw frequently used hieroglyphs

2 Offerings for the afterlife

In this unit you will learn how to:
- **translate a simple offering formula**
- **read hieroglyphs in the correct direction**
- **transliterate multi-sound signs with and without complements.**

REQUESTING AN OFFERING

The ancient Egyptians are famous for their funerary culture. Inscriptions on stone slabs and tomb walls record the requests of the dead for food in the afterlife. In fact, when you visit the gallery of an Egyptian museum, you will notice that many hieroglyphic inscriptions begin with the group of signs *ḥtp dj njswt* (*an offering which the king gives*). This opening phrase is then followed by the name of a deity, for example Ptah-Sokar-Osiris, a god formed from Ptah, Sokar and Osiris, who were originally three separate deities. The *ḥtp* (*offering*), a word sometimes also spelled *ḥtpt* with an additional , included drinks and food. They were given *n k3 n* (*to the ka-soul of*) the deceased who was declared *m3ʿ-ḫrw*, literally *true of voice*, once he had passed a moral interrogation in the afterlife. In the inscriptions, the deceased asked the king for offerings, but in reality family members placed food and drinks in the tomb during the funeral and later at funerary feasts. According to Egyptian belief, each human being had a *ka-soul*, an *akh-soul* and a *ba-soul*. The terms are difficult to translate adequately because they have no direct equivalents in English.

1 How would you interpret the phrase *true of voice*?

2 What do you notice about the direction in which the hieroglyphs are written in the photograph?

Vocabulary builder

THE OFFERING FORMULA

1 Read each word in transliteration aloud.

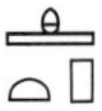	*ḥtp*	*offering*
	*njswt*	*king*
	*dj*	*to give*
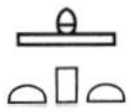	*ḥtpt*	*offering* (written with additional *t*)
	*ḏfꜣ*	*food*
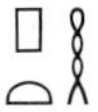	*Ptḥ*	*Ptah*
	*Zkr*	*Sokar*
	*Wsjr*	*Osiris*
	*n kꜣ n*	*to the ka-soul of*
	*mꜣꜥ-ḫrw*	*justified*

2 Go through the vocabulary from the offering formula again and identify all the examples of the hieroglyphic signs which represent these letters: *r*, *ꜥ*, *ḏ*, *f*, *n*, *z*, *t*, *k*, and *ḥ*. You were introduced to these signs in the previous unit.

3 Speculate as to what these new signs depict by matching them with their correct description.

a		*ḥtp*	pair of arms
b		*dj*	oar
c		*kꜣ*	triangular loaf of bread
d		*mꜣꜥ*	loaf on a mat
e		*ḫrw*	pedestal

NEW EXPRESSIONS

4 The following words will help you understand the rest of the offering formula of Sobekemhab. Read them aloud.

	*Sbk*	*Sobek*
	*m*	*in*
	*ḥb*	*festival*
	*ʿnḫ n njw.t*	*officer of the town regiment*
	*=f*	*he; his*

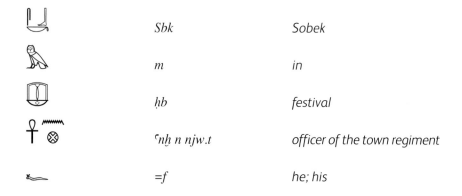

LANGUAGE INSIGHT

The word *=f* means *he* after verbs and *his* after nouns. In transliteration, it is attached to the verb or noun with an equals sign.

THE STELA OF SOBEKEMHAB

Egyptologists call an inscribed stone slab, either round-topped or rectangular, a 'stela' (pronounced 'stéela'). The stela discussed in this unit belongs to an official called *Sbk-m-ḥb* who lived around 1800 BCE. His name means *Sobek-(is)-in-festival*. This could indicate that Sobekemhab was from the Fayum, where the god Sobek was worshipped. Sobekemhab held the low-ranking military title *ʿnḫ n njwt officer of the town regiment*. The individuals depicted on the stela are smelling the scent of a lotus flower. The inscriptions on the stela of Sobekemhab are typical of many others, so if you understand the pattern of the hieroglyphs you will be surprised at how many other examples you will be able to read next time you visit an Egyptian museum.

Go through the text and answer the following questions.

1 Which part of the stela contains the offering formula?

a The inscription on the upper two lines
ḥtp dj njswt Ptḥ-Zkr-Wsjr dj=f ḥtpt
ḏfꜣ n kꜣ n ꜥnḫ n njwt Sbk-m-ḥb mꜣꜥ-ḫrw
An offering that the king gives to Ptah-Sokar-Osiris. May he give an offering and food for the ka-soul of the officer of the town regiment Sobekemhab, justified.

b The inscription in front of the man on the upper left
ꜥnḫ n njwt Sbk-m-ḥb — *the officer of the town regiment Sobekemhab*

c The inscription in front of the man on the lower left
jt=f Bbj mꜣꜥ-ḫrw — *his father Bebi, justified*

d The inscription in front of the woman on the upper right
nbt pr Snwt mꜣꜥt-ḫrw — *the mistress of the house Senut, justified*

e The inscription above the woman on the upper right
ḥmt=f *his wife*

f The inscription in front of the woman on the lower right
nbt pr Nbw-m-rsj (the name is difficult to make out)
the mistress of the house, Nebuemresi

2 Read the text again and answer these questions.

a Which deity does Sobekemhab address in the offering formula?

b Where is Sobekemhab's name and title written on the stela?

c Where is Sobekemhab depicted on the stela, and where is his wife?

d How do ancient Egyptians say *May he give*? Find the term in the transliteration.

3 Read out the transliteration of the inscription.

> **LANGUAGE INSIGHT**
> The translation of the opening phrase of the offering formula is still debated. The interpretation adopted here is that the king gives an offering to Ptah-Sokar-Osiris and that this offering will be passed on to the deceased in the netherworld. However, the word *to* is not written before the name of Ptah-Sokar-Osiris on this stela, and generally not in the offering formula. Therefore others would translate the beginning of inscription (a) *an offering that the king gives and Ptah-Sokar-Osiris* or *an offering that the king gives of Ptah-Sokar-Osiris.*

Language discovery

1 Compare the word order of the hieroglyphic text on the stela with the transliteration. In which direction do you think the inscriptions a–f of the stela (marked grey) are written?

a from right to left

b from left to right

c top down and left to right

d top down and right to left

2 Compare these words with how they are written on the stela. How are the hieroglyphs arranged below?

a 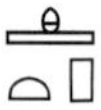 *ḥtp*

In this example, the sign 𓏏 *t* is placed in the bottom left corner, 𓊪 *p* in the bottom right corner and 𓊵 above these two signs. Since the word is transliterated *ḥtp*, the hieroglyphs are read from the top down and from left to right.

b 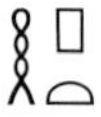 *Ptḥ*

c  *ḏf3*

d  *Zkr*

3 The hieroglyphs in the inscription have been executed in quite a low quality. Try to find the following words on the stela. Refer to the vocabulary builder to help you.

a *food* **b** *Ptah* **c** *offering* (*ḥtpt*) **d** *king*

e *give* **f** *festival* (x 2) **g** *for the ka-soul of* **h** *justified* (x 2)

4 Unlike English, Egyptian words can be written in more than one way. Study the inscription of the stela again. How is the word *ḥtp* ***offering*** **written in it?**

THE ARRANGEMENT OF HIEROGLYPHS

Hieroglyphs were, ideally, arranged in squares to make them visually appealing. Large signs like fill a full square, medium-sized signs like a half-square and small signs like a quarter of a square. Within a square the signs are read from top to bottom. Hieroglyphs representing animated beings, such as animals and human beings, always face the reader. When they look left, for example, the reading direction is from left to right.

Two squares, read from left to right: → 

Two squares, read from right to left:  ←

Some signs that take up a half-square can be drawn in both a vertical and a horizontal position. An example is the arrangement of the signs in the word *mꜣʿ-ḫrw* *justified* on the stela of Sobekemhab. This is written in two different ways in separate inscriptions on the stela.

 (inscription a) and  (inscription b, written without the hieroglyph of the arm; for an explanation see paragraph on 'Complementing signs' further down in this unit)

5 In which direction do you read the hieroglyphs on the following temple blocks?

a A block with the name of Ramses I in his temple at Abydos

a

b A block of Thutmosis III in the temple of Elkab. The original temple of Thutmosis III was dismantled and a new building erected from stone blocks taken from his temple. Since the inscriptions of Thutmosis III did not matter for the later temple, the block was turned upside down. This is how it is depicted in the photo.

b

MULTI-SOUND SIGNS

In unit 1, you learned how to recognize a series of single-sound signs. Ancient Egyptian also contains a number of multi-sound signs, which represent a string of consonants and are transliterated with two or three letters. Examples in this unit are:

ḥtp *dj* *m3ʿ* *ḫrw*

k3 *ḥb* *ʿnḫ*

COMPLEMENTING SIGNS

Egyptian scribes could add single-sound signs to multi-sound signs to help with their correct reading. For example, the group combines the multi-sound sign *ḥtp* with the two single-sound signs *t* and *p*. It is translated *ḥtp* rather than *ḥtptp* because the single-sound signs repeat two sounds from the 'mother sign' for clarification. Other examples of how *ḥtp* can be written are without any complement or with only one, for example . Single-sound signs that help the reader decode how to pronounce multi-sound signs are called 'phonetic complements'.

6 The following words combine multi- and single-sound signs. Find the signs that function as phonetic complements.

a *ḥb* **b** *m3ʿ* **c** *njwt* **d** *ʿnḫ*

Explore

Now try to apply what you have learned to a similar example. Take a closer look at the following offering formula and answer the questions.

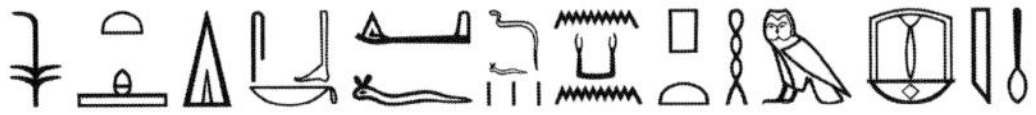

1 **Is the text written from left to right or from right to left?**

2 **Where do the individual words of the offering formula start and end? Draw a line to separate one word from the next, using the vocabulary builder if you need to.**

3 **Transliterate the offering formula.**

4 **Now translate.**

5 **Phonetic complements help you read unknown signs. The following groups combine a new sign with two phonetic complements that you know. Follow the example to work out which letters the multi-sound signs , and represent.**

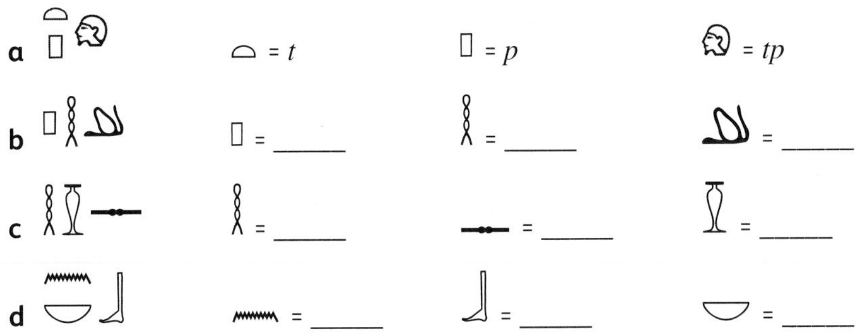

Drawing hieroglyphs

1 **The following two hieroglyphs are typical of the offering formula. Try to draw them. It will help with memorizing the signs.**

a 

b 

2 **Now try to copy the inscription in the Explore section in hieroglyphs. Look up the signs that you learned how to draw in the first unit.**

Test yourself

1 Judging from the signs representing animated beings, which words do you think are written from right to left and which ones from left to right?

a 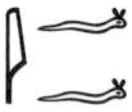

b 

c 

d 

2 Choose the correct transliteration of these multi-sound signs with complements.

a  *m3ʿ* or *m3ʿʿ*

b 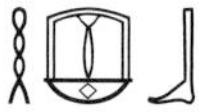 *ḥb* or *ḥḥbb*

c 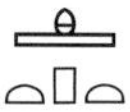 *ḥtp* or *ḥtpt*

d 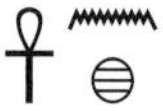 *ʿnḫ* or *ʿnḫ n njw.t*

3 Translate the phrases from the offering formula. Read the hieroglyphs from left to right.

a 

b 

c 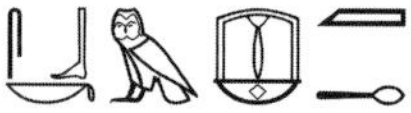

d 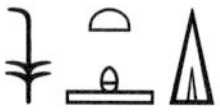

SELF-CHECK

	I CAN
○	translate a simple offering formula
○	read hieroglyphs in the correct direction
○	transliterate multi-sound signs with and without complements

3 Family and household

In this unit you will learn how to:

- **express family relationships**
- **read an extended offering formula**
- **recognize the gender of Egyptian nouns**
- **specify the meaning of a noun using an adjective.**

KINSHIP

The owner of a tomb stela was often depicted with his family. Ideally, this included his *ḥm.t* (*wife*), even if a wedding had not been celebrated formally. An important aspect of marriage was to ensure the handing down of property from *jt* (*father*) and *mw.t* (*mother*) to their *z3* (*son*) or *z3.t* (*daughter*). Egyptian kinship terms describe broader social roles than their English equivalents. A *sn* (*brother*), for example, can be a brother as well as somebody of peer status, such as an uncle or a brother-in-law. Similarly, *z3* can mean son or grandson, and *jt* can mean father, grandfather or teacher. Older women seem to have been held in particularly high esteem within Egyptian families.

What do you notice about the way male and female kinship terms are written in transliteration?

Vocabulary builder

1 Go through the vocabulary below and try to read out the words.

FAMILY

male			**female**		
	*z3*	*son*		*z3.t*	*daughter*
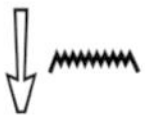	*sn*	*brother*	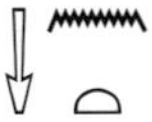	*sn.t*	*sister*
	*ḥm*	*husband*		*ḥm.t*	*wife*
	*jt*	*father*		*mw.t*	*mother*

2 Go through the words above and try to work out which letters the following signs represent.

a  (goose)

b  (section of a canal)

c  (reed)

3 The sign (arrow) stands for the two letters *sn* and the sign  (vulture) for the three letters *mwt*. Look closely at the hieroglyphs and the transliterations in the vocabulary list. What do you think the purpose is of the single-sound signs and in these words?

a 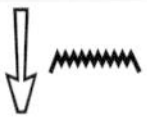

b 

4 Imagine the following family. Sue and Stephen are the parents of Tom, Lisa and Peter. Tom and his wife Barbara have two children, Max and Kate. Describe the family from Tom's perspective, using the correct Egyptian words. Add *=f his* as in the first example and translate.

a Sue: *mw.t=f his mother*

b Stephen: ______________________

c Lisa: ______________________

d Peter: ______________________

e Barbara: ______________________

f Max: ______________________

g Kate: ______________________

NEW EXPRESSIONS

Here are some more words commonly used in the offering formula.

	*Wsjr* (óoseer)	*Osiris*
	*nb* (neb)	*lord; every*
	*Ḏdw* (djédoo)	*Busiris*
	*nṯr* (nétjer)	*god*
	*ꜥꜣ* (aa-aa)	*great*, also written
	*ꜣbḏw* (áabdjoo)	*Abydos*
	*ḫ.t* (khet)	*thing*
	*nfr* (néfer)	*good*
	*wꜥb* (waab)	*pure*
	*jmꜣḫy* (eemáakhee)	*the revered*

LANGUAGE INSIGHT

The name of the god Osiris is written either  or  (see Unit 2).

5 Find the following signs in the words above and choose their correct transliteration from the two options given.

a 	column	*ꜥꜣ* or *zꜣ*
b 	cloth wound around pole	*ꜥꜣ* or *nṯr*
c 	placenta	*ḫ* or *ẖ*
d 	windpipe	*ꜣb* or *nfr*
e 	basket	*nb* or *mwt*
f 	leg, vessel, water	*nfr* or *wꜥb*
g 	reed column	*ḏd* or *dḏ*

h		chisel	*ꜣb* or *ꜥb*
i		chicken quail	*y* or *w*
j		cross-section of Nile valley	*ḫꜣs* or *ḏw*
k		spiral cord	*jḫꜣm* or *jmꜣḫ*

The stela of Senwosret

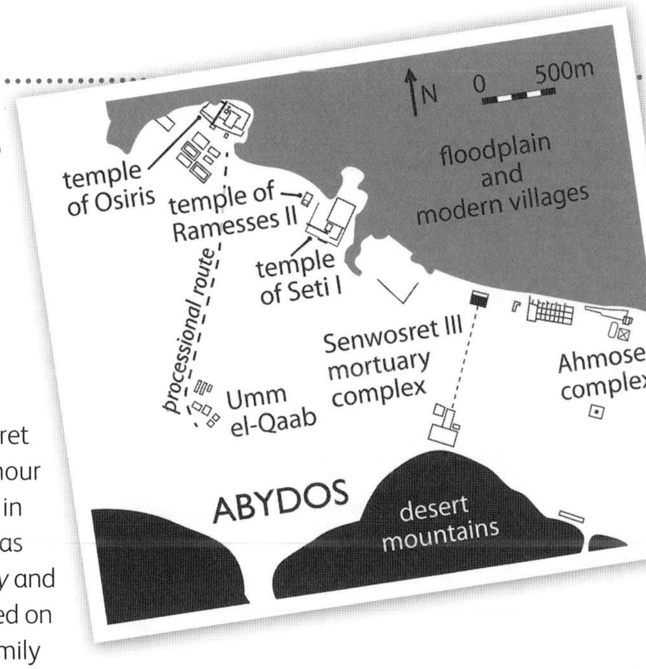

Names can tell you interesting stories about a family, when you know how to read between the lines. The owner of the stela below was a carpenter called *Senwosret*. He was named after a king of the Middle Kingdom, who was very possibly his employer. He was the only member in his family to have this privilege. His father bears the name of the ram-headed god *Khnumu*. Senwosret called his daughter *Zat-Khnumu* to honour her grandfather, which was a tradition in Egyptian families. Senwosret's sister was called *Zat-Kherty* and his brothers *Kherty* and *Za-Kherty*. His grandfather is not depicted on the stela, but if we assume that the family followed the same naming traditions, we can guess that he was called *Kherty*. Kherty is the name of an earth god. Senwosret was married to *Zat-Hathor*, Hathor being a popular goddess among women. The remaining two names on the stela are difficult to read. They belong to Senwosret's mother and another brother. The stela was probably found at Abydos, where the god Osiris was worshipped. Like other officials and skilled craftsmen, Senwosret may have set up the stela in a memorial chapel along the route of a procession for Osiris. Since none of the names refer to Osiris, it is unlikely that the family lived at Abydos.

You will work through the inscriptions on the stela in more detail as you progress through the rest of the unit. First, however, have a look at the visual arrangement and try to answer these questions.

1 What is represented in front of the seated couple?

2 Are the inscriptions written from left to right or from right to left?

3 The hieroglyphs in the lower part are less formally arranged than in the upper part. What might this tell you about the way the stela was manufactured?

4 **Look at the stela. What does this group mean?**

 ____________________

5 **How often is the name**  *Zj-n-Wsr.t* ***Senwosret*** **(spelled** *Wsr.t-z-n* **in hieroglyphs) written on the stela?**

6 **Where are the following names written on the stela?**

 *Khnumu*

 *Kherty*

 *Zat-Khnumu*

 *Zat-Kherty*

 *Zat-Hathor*

 *Za-Kherty*

Language discovery

1 **List all the male and female kinship terms mentioned in the inscription.**

male	female
____________________	*sn.t*
____________________	____________________
	____________________
	____________________

CULTURE INSIGHT

You may have noticed that the arrangement of some of the hieroglyphs on the stela differs from what you learned in the vocabulary builder. Each stonecutter made choices depending on space constraints and his visual preferences.

2 **Find the female kinship terms in the hieroglyphs on the stela. What is the final hieroglyph in each case?**

3 **Find the following phrases in the upper part of the stela and answer the question. Is the word order in transliteration and translation the same, or inverted?**

nṯr ꜥꜣ *great god*

ḫ.t nb.t *every thing*

4 The groups below mean *justified*; see Unit 2. Which family members are labelled *mꜣꜥ-ḫrw* and which *mꜣꜥ.t-ḫrw* on the stela?

sn=f	________________
________________	________________
________________	

GENDER

Egyptian nouns are either masculine or feminine. Feminine words have the ending ⌓ separated in transliteration with a full stop *.t*. Masculine words have no specific ending. Some masculine nouns like *jt* (*father*) end in *t*.

> **LANGUAGE INSIGHT**
> Middle Egyptian does not have an article. You decide from context whether, for example, *jt* is best translated as *father*, *a father* or *the father*.

5 Look at the ending of the following nouns and decide whether they are masculine or feminine.

a *nṯr* (m / f)	**b** *ḫ.t* (m / f)	**c** *kꜣ* (m / f)	**d** *ḥm.t* (m / f)
e *ḥtp.t* (m / f)	**f** *Ptḥ* (m / f)	**g** *jt* (m / f)	**h** *njswt* (m / f)

6 Complete the table below, writing the correct form of the male and female equivalents into the gaps.

male			**female**		
	*nṯr*	*a god*		________	________
	*nb*	*the lord*	________	________	*the lady*
________	________	*brother*	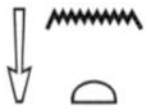	________	________

ADJECTIVES AND NOUNS

Adjectives specify the meaning of nouns, for example *the great god* rather than any *god*. Egyptian adjectives follow the noun they specify. In English translation, you reverse the Egyptian word order.

	*nṯr*	*ꜥꜣ*
	god	*great* → *great god*

Egyptian adjectives change their form according to the gender of the noun, which is different from English. When the noun is feminine, they take a feminine ending *.t*.

masculine:  *nṯr ꜥꜣ great god*

feminine:  *ẖ.t nb.t everything*

The *t* of feminine adjectives was often omitted by the writer, for the sake of brevity. This means that when you read hieroglyphs you will not always see the sign where you would expect to. Translating the *.t*, whether it is expressed in hieroglyphs or not, will help the reader understand the grammar.

 *ẖ.t nb.t nfr.t wꜥb.t every good and pure thing*

As the example above shows, several adjectives can follow a noun in Egyptian, connected by *and* in the English translation.

> **LANGUAGE INSIGHT**
> The word *nb* means *lord*, and with the feminine ending *nb.t lady*. However, when it is used as an adjective after a noun, it means *every* or *any*.

7 Match the nouns with the correct adjective, to write the following expressions in transliteration:

a *the great god*	*nṯr*	*ꜥꜣ.t*
b *great lady*	*nb.t*	*nb.t*
c *every mother*	*mw.t*	*nfr*
d *a pure offering*	*ḥtp.t*	*ꜥꜣ*
e *his revered father*	*jt=f*	*jmꜣḫy*
f *the good festival*	*ḥb*	*wꜥb.t*

8 Transliterate the following phrases, as shown. Remember that the *.t* ending of adjectives is sometimes omitted in hieroglyphs.

a  *nṯr nfr*

b 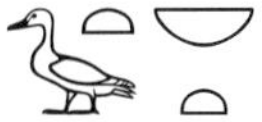

c 

d 

e 

f 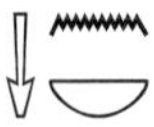

9 What do the phrases in exercise 8 mean? Try a translation.

Explore

There is a lot you can learn from looking at recurrent patterns in inscriptions, without understanding all the details straight away. You can work out the meaning of the offering formula on the stela of Senwosret by using the inscription in the previous unit and other examples. You will see how easy it is to decipher hieroglyphs on your own.

1 Compare the beginning of the offering formulas for Sobekemhat (Unit 2) and Senwosret, and then answer the questions.

(1) 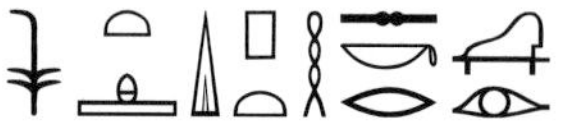

(2) 

a Which parts are identical?

b What do you think the part after *ḥtp dj njswt* means in the second formula?

c Look up any new words in the vocabulary builder.

d Transliterate inscription (2).

e Translate inscription (2). Here, *nb* means *lord of*.

> **LANGUAGE INSIGHT**
>
> The sign represents a crossroad. When it is added to the end of place names, such as *3bḏw Abydos*, it is not pronounced and not transliterated. You see the same sign being used at the end of the word *Ḏdw Busiris*. It is written here with an additional stroke and a , which is exceptional after a place name. Again, the group in remained mute in speech and is not transliterated.

2 Now compare the remaining part of the offering formulas.

(1) 

(2) 

a Which parts are identical?

b Transliterate the final part of inscription (2), starting from *n k3 n*. The seated man indicates that *Zj-n-Wsr.t* (literally *Man-of-the-strong-goddess*) is a male name. It is silent when spoken and is not transliterated. The Egyptian word for *man* is *zj*, although only *z* is usually written in hieroglyphs.

c Translate the final part of inscription (2).

d Can you guess the general meaning of the words in the middle part of the formula of Senwosret between *dj=f* and *n k3 n*?

3 For the remaining part of the offering formula of Senwosret, compare a few more examples and answer the questions.

pr.t-ḫrw tꜣ ḥnq.t kꜣ ꜣpd šs mnḫ.t

a voice offering, bread and beer, ox and fowl, linen and alabaster

pr.t-ḫrw tꜣ ḥnq.t ḫ.t nb.t nfr.t wꜥb.t prj.t m-bꜣḥ nṯr ꜥꜣ

a voice offering, bread and beer, all good and pure things that come before the great god

pr.t-ḫrw tꜣ ḥnq.t kꜣ ꜣpd ḫ.t nb.t nfr.t wꜥb.t ꜥnḫ.t nṯr ꜥꜣ jm

a voice offering, bread and beer, ox and fowl, all good and pure things of which a great god lives

a Read the three examples aloud.

b Which group of hieroglyphs is used in all three examples?

c Can you speculate what a *voice offering* might be?

d Among the phrases following *pr.t-ḫrw tꜣ ḥnq.t*, find those that are used in one example only.

e Now go back to the offering formula of Senwosret and transliterate the part between *dj=f* and *n kꜣ n.*

f Translate your transliteration.

AUTHOR'S NOTE

Well done. Step by step, you have managed to understand the individual parts of the stela – first the visual layout, then the names and kinship terms and finally the offering formula. The only sections we have not looked at are the title, where it says *Senwosret carpenter* next to the offering table, and the area where the names of the mother and one of the brothers are written. This part is difficult to make out on the original stela. The way in which Senwosret's stela is structured is typical of many other examples. Next time you visit an Egyptian gallery, try to recognize the elements you have learned in this unit. You will be astonished at how many inscriptions you can read!

Drawing hieroglyphs

1 Here are a few more hieroglyphs for you to try to draw.

a 

b 

c 

d 

2 Write the following phrases in hieroglyphs.

a *z3=f*

b *jt* (use a seated man as a silent sign at the end to indicate that *jt* is a male person)

c *mw.t* (use a seated woman as a mute sign at the end to indicate that *mw.t* is a female person)

Test yourself

1 Translate these phrases into Egyptian and transliterate.

a *his mother* ________________

b *his brother* ________________

c *daughter* ________________

d *father* ________________

e *his wife* ________________

f *a husband* ________________

g *his sister* ________________

2 Choose m or f, depending on whether the word is masculine or feminine.

a  (m / f)

b  (m / f)

c  (m / f)

d  (m / f)

3 Match the phrases in transliteration with their correct translation.

a *zꜣ nb*	*great lord*
b *ḥtp.t nfr.t*	*every son*
c *nb ꜥꜣ*	*every great mother*
d *mw.t nb.t ꜥꜣ.t*	*good offering*

4 What does the following offering formula mean in English?

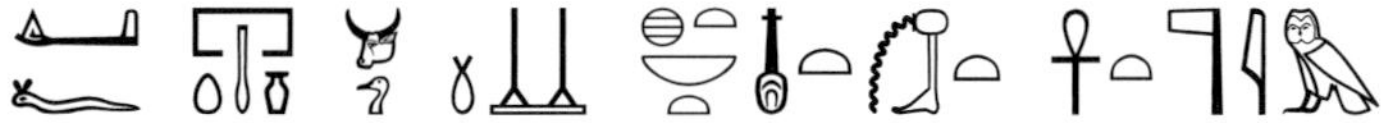

SELF-CHECK

	I CAN
○	express family relationships
○	read an extended offering formula
○	recognize the gender of Egyptian nouns
○	specify the meaning of a noun using an adjective

4 Egypt and the Sinai

In this unit you will learn how to:

- **recognize the king in a scene**
- **read royal titles and epithets**
- **understand labels in a scene expressing action**
- **recognize the singular, plural and dual of Egyptian nouns**
- **tell the difference between classifiers and picture signs.**

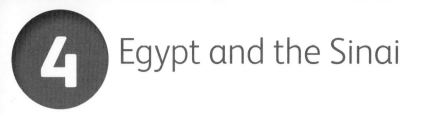

SACRED KINGSHIP

Ancient Egyptian kingship was deeply rooted in the world of the gods. The reigning *njswt-bjt* (*king of Upper and Lower Egypt*) was a *nṯr nfr* (*perfect god*) and a *nṯr ꜥꜣ* (*great god*). According to Egyptian mythology, he was identified with the falcon-god *Ḥrw* (*Horus*) and held the title *zꜣ-Rꜥ* (*son of Ra*). The king ruled over *tꜣ.wj* (*the two lands*). By this, Egyptians meant the Nile valley, i.e. Upper Egypt, and the Nile Delta, i.e. Lower Egypt. See also the map on page xiv. The two parts of the country were represented by *nb.tj* (*the two ladies*), Upper Egypt by the vulture goddess Nekhbet and Lower Egypt by the cobra goddess Wadjet. Royal display in ancient Egypt, such as the rock inscriptions of the Sinai shown above, portrays a symbolic world. Owing to its strong association with the gods, Egyptian kingship is defined as a variety of sacred authority. The reigning kings or queens were not treated as gods, but some were deified after they had died.

1 Why was Egypt represented by two goddesses instead of only one?

2 There are many hieroglyphs representing birds. Which ones can you recognize in the text above?

Vocabulary builder

ROYAL TITLES AND EPITHETS

1 Work through these words in hieroglyphs and then find the words in the introductory text. Then read them aloud.

	*Ḥrw*	*Horus* (falcon god; also a royal title)
	*Rꜥ*	*Ra* (sun god)
	*nb.tj*	*Two Ladies* (royal title)
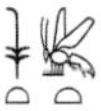	*njswt-bjt*	*king of Upper and Lower Egypt* (royal title)
	*W3ḏ.t*	*Wadjet* (cobra goddess representing Lower Egypt)
	*t3*	*land*
	*ꜥnḫ*	*life*
	*ḏ.t*	*eternity*
	*mry*	*beloved of*
	*dj*	*given; to give* (see Units 2 and 3)

LANGUAGE INSIGHT

The word *dj to give* is written either with a forearm offering a triangular loaf of bread (see Units 2 and 3) or, in an abbreviated form, with the loaf of bread only: .

2 Exercise your knowledge from the previous unit and find all the feminine words in the vocabulary list above.

3 Which words in the list above are written with these new signs?

a  (column in the form of a papyrus plant) *w3ḏ*

b  (strip of land with three grains of sand) *t3*

c  (sandal strap) *ꜥnḫ*

d  (hoe) *mr*

e 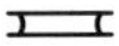 (canal) *mr*

4 Here are a few more words for this unit. Read them aloud.

	*ḫꜥ.w*	*crowns*
	*sqr*	*to strike down*
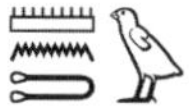	*mnṯ.w*	*Mentu-Bedouin* (an ethnic group living in the Sinai)
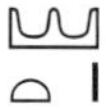	*ḫꜣs.t*	*foreign land*
	*dꜣr*	*to smite*
	*s.t*	*throne*

5 Go through the words in exercise 4 again and use them to identify the correct transliteration of the following new signs.

a  (rays of sun above hill): *ḫꜥ* or *ṯ*?

b  (hand): *d* or *ḫꜥ*?

c  (vulture): *ꜣ* or *ṯ*?

d  (unclear): *mn* or *sqr*?

e  (outline of desert mountain): *ḫꜣs* or *ḏw*?

f  (gaming board): *n* or *mn*?

g  (hobble): *ṯ* or *n*?

h  (seat): *st* or *sqr*?

6 Look at how the word *dꜣr* is written in hieroglyphs. What do you notice about the final *r*?

EGYPT AND THE SINAI

The Sinai is the rocky peninsula located between the Egyptian Nile Delta and modern Israel. It has been a zone of interaction between these two regions from early history. Egyptian kings were particularly interested in the natural resources of the Sinai, such as turquoise and copper.

In the Fifth Dynasty, King Sahura (*c.* 2480–2465 BCE, pronounced Sáahooráa) inscribed the rocks that flank the entrance to the turquoise mines of the Wadi Maghara, an Arabic name meaning *Valley of the Caves*. His large inscription, shown below, conveyed a strong message of his supremacy. Framed by two sceptres and the stars of the sky, Sahura is depicted with a mace striking down a Mentu-Bedouin who belongs to a semi-nomadic tribe living in this area. Behind him is a jackal standard and two further representations of him. In the first representation he is wearing the crown of Lower Egypt, often coloured in red, while in the second he is wearing the white crown of Upper Egypt – just like the main figure in the scene. The crowns and the gesture of striking down an enemy were typical of Egyptian royal display until the Roman period.

TRANSLITERATION

(1) Line running above the scene and continuing down between the two figures on the left: *Ḥrw Nb-ḫꜥ.w njswt-bjt Sꜣḥw-Rꜥ dj ꜥnḫ ḏ.t*

(2) In front of the head of the king: *nṯr ꜥꜣ*

(3) Column on the right: *sqr mnṯ.w ḫꜣs.wt nb.wt*

(4) Column behind the smiting king: *dꜣr ḫꜣs.wt nb.wt*

Have a look at the visual arrangement of the inscription and then consider the following questions.

1 What would you say left a stronger impression of royal power on ancient viewers, the imagery or the hieroglyphs?

2 What can you possibly deduce from your answer to question 1 about the level of reading skills in ancient Egypt?

3 The mace is depicted four times in the entire scene. Can you see where?

4 Read the transliteration and try to pronounce it.

5 Where are the names and titles of Sahura written in the hieroglyphic inscription?

6 Try to translate the Horus name *Nb-ḫꜥ.w* and the formula *dj ꜥnḫ ḏ.t* in line (1).

7 What do the two signs in front of the head of the king (2) mean?

8 Which direction are the hieroglyphs in column (4) written in?

9 Can you deduce the general meaning of columns (3) and (4) from the scene they accompany?

Language discovery

1 Which royal titles are mentioned in the inscription of Sahura?

2 Find the word *sqr* ***to strike down*** in the hieroglyphs of the inscription. What function do you think the final sign plays in the meaning of the word?

3 Go back to the inscription and add the translation of the following words:

word	item hieroglyph represents	translation
a 𓅃	falcon	________ (falcon god)
b 𓇳	sun	________ (sun god)
c 𓈉	foreign land	________
d 𓋹	sandal strap	________

4 Compare the second and third column for each word in exercise 3. How does the word in the final row, d, differ from the words in rows a, b and c?

5 Can you guess, from looking at the hieroglyphs, which word in Sahura's inscription is written in the plural?

6 Have a look again at the entire inscription. What information do columns (3) and (4) add to the imagery?

ROYAL NAMES AND TITLES

From the Old Kingdom onwards, Egyptian kings had five names, each connected with a specific title.

 The oldest and most prestigious title is *Ḥrw Horus*. It usually precedes a rectangle interpreted as the enclosure and façade of a palace. The Egyptian word for this rectangle is *serekh*.

 The title *Two Ladies* is written with the hieroglyphic sign of a cobra and vulture both placed on the *nb*-basket, an abbreviated spelling for *nb.tj*.

 The title *Ḥrw-nbw Golden Horus* linked the king again to Horus. It is written with the hieroglyph of the falcon *Ḥrw* placed on a collar, meaning *nbw gold*.

 The title *zꜣ-Rꜥ Son of Ra* precedes a name encircled by an oval cartouche. The cartouche represents a knotted rope symbolizing protection.

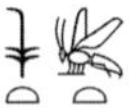 Another name written in the cartouche is introduced by the title *njswt-bjt King of Upper and Lower Egypt*.

7 Learn how to decode the sequence of royal names and titles. Have a look at those for King Senwosret I and answer the questions.

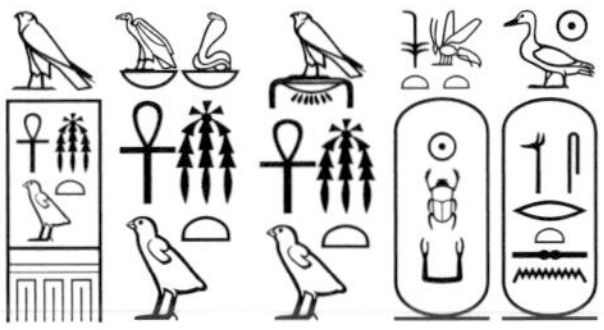

a Which column contains the Horus title?

b Which titles precede the two cartouches?

c The Horus name of Senwosret I is *ꜥnḫ-mswt*, literally meaning *who-lives-of-births*. What are his Two Ladies and the Golden Horus names?

d What is the Son of Ra name? Refer to Unit 3 if you need to.

PICTURE SIGNS

Hieroglyphs can be used as picture signs, as well as to represent sounds. As a picture sign, a hieroglyph means what it represents. For example, the sign of the sun disc means *Ra* (= the sun god), the Egyptian word for which is *rꜥ*. Picture signs, also called 'ideograms', regularly take an additional stroke, although it is occasionally missed off.

	*Rꜥ*	*Ra*
	*Rꜥ*	*Ra*

When a picture sign represents a feminine word, it is often complemented by a hieroglyph representing the feminine ending *.t* and a single stroke.

 *ḫ3s.t* *foreign land*

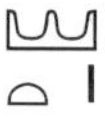 *ḫ3s.t* *foreign land*

CLASSIFIERS

Egyptian scribes sometimes added a classifier to the end of a word to indicate its general meaning and help the reader establish where a word ended. Classifiers remained mute in speech and so are not transliterated. Another term for classifier is 'determinative'.

 *sqr striking down* = 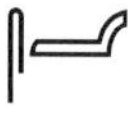 *sqr* +  STRIKING

hieroglyphs	transliteration	translation	classifier
	*sqr*	*to strike down*	 STRIKING
	*d̠.t*	*eternity*	 (ENDLESS) LAND
	*W3d̠.t*	*Wadjet*	 COBRA (GODDESS)

LANGUAGE INSIGHT

Hieroglyphs and art are closely integrated in ancient Egypt. In the inscription of Sahura, for example, the mace is used as a classifier in the hieroglyphs and depicted at a larger scale in the hand of the king.

LANGUAGE INSIGHT

The feminine ending ⌓ is almost always placed before the classifier. The spelling of *W3d̠.t* in the inscription of Sahura is therefore unusual.

8 You can often infer the general meaning of a word from its classifier, whenever it has one, as in the first example here (underlined). What do you think the general meaning is of the other words?

a  a word referring to a male individual (here: the name of a man)

b  ______________________

c  ______________________

d 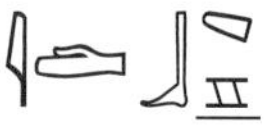 ______________________

e 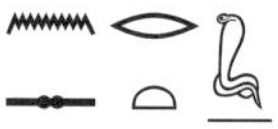 ______________________

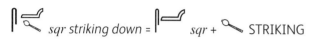

CLASSIFIER VERSUS PICTURE SIGN

Many hieroglyphs can be used as either a picture sign *or* a classifier. It means that you have to decide from the context whether a sign was pronounced in ancient times and is therefore transliterated, or was used as a reading aid only and so is not transliterated. A simple rule is that a classifier is always preceded by a word whose meaning it illustrates. In contrast, a picture sign is a standalone word. With a little practice, you will find it easier to distinguish one from the other.

	used as classifier	used as picture sign
𓈉 FOREIGN LAND	𓎡𓈙𓈉 *Kš Kush*	𓈉𓏏𓏤 *ḫ3s.t foreign land*
𓊖 TOWN	𓍋𓃀𓇥𓊖 *3bḏw Abydos*	𓊖𓏏𓏤 *njw.t town*

In some cases, a picture sign takes both a stroke and a classifier.

𓇾 LAND 𓇾𓈇𓏤 *t3 land*

9 Try to work out how these signs are used. Choose *pic* for picture sign or *class* for classifier.

a 𓈉	𓈉𓏏𓏤 *ḫ3s.t*	*foreign land*	pic – class
b 𓈉	𓊪𓃹𓏏𓈉 *Pwn.t*	*Punt*	pic – class
c 𓇳	𓆄𓅱𓇳 *šw*	*light*	pic – class
d 𓇳	𓇳𓏤 *Rꜥ*	*Ra*	pic – class
e 𓈘	𓈘𓂋𓏤 *mr*	*canal*	pic – class
f 𓈘	𓇅𓅨𓈘 *W3ḏ-wr*	*sea*	pic – class

NUMBER OF NOUNS

Egyptian nouns can be set in the plural or dual. The plural expresses many items and is usually translated with an English noun ending in –s or –es. The dual expresses two items and is translated with *two* followed by the counted noun. You decide from the context whether a translation with a definite or an indefinite article works better. Egyptians doubled or tripled the element of a noun, in hieroglyphs, to express its number. There are several ways in which this was done.

(a) by multiplying a picture sign:

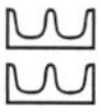 *two foreign lands*  *foreign lands*

(b) by multiplying the classifier:

 *two sons*  *the sons*

(c) by using two or three strokes added to the end of the word:

 *the two gods*  *gods*

(d) by multiplying a core sign of the word:

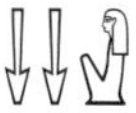 *two sisters* 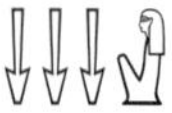 *the sisters*

10 How would you translate the words in the second column? Follow the first example.

a  *son*  *two sons*

b  *god*  __________

c  *mother*  __________

d  *land*  __________

In speech, the plural and dual had specific endings. Whenever you see a word in hieroglyphs set in the plural or dual, you add these endings in transliteration using a full stop. The plural ending of masculine nouns is *.w* (pronounced oo) and the dual ending *.wj* (ooee). For feminine nouns, the ending is *.wt* (oot) in the plural and *.tj* (tee) in the dual.

MASCULINE NOUNS

singular	plural	dual

nṯr (nétjer)	*nṯr.w* (nétjeroo)	*nṯr.wj* (nétjerooee)
the god	*the gods*	*two gods*

FEMININE NOUNS

singular	plural	dual
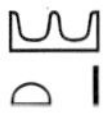	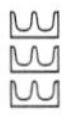	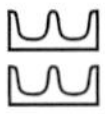
ḫ3s.t (kháset)	*ḫ3s.wt* (khásoot)	*ḫ3s.tj* (khástee)
a foreign land	*foreign lands*	*two foreign lands*

Since the endings were pronounced in speech, the plural was sometimes expressed with a simple sound sign in hieroglyphs rather than by multiplying an element.

 *ḫʿ.w* (kháaoo) *crowns*

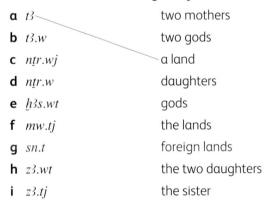

11 Watch out for the endings, as you match the words with their correct translation.

a *t3*	two mothers
b *t3.w*	two gods
c *nṯr.wj*	a land
d *nṯr.w*	daughters
e *ḫ3s.wt*	gods
f *mw.tj*	the lands
g *sn.t*	foreign lands
h *z3.wt*	the two daughters
i *z3.tj*	the sister

12 Read the Egyptian words in the previous exercise aloud.

13 Combine hieroglyphs, transliteration and translation. Complete the table, using the correct endings in transliteration as shown in example a.

a		*tꜣ land*		*tꜣ.wj two lands*
b		*ḫꜣs.t* _____		_____ _____
c		_____ _____		_____ *two sons*
d		_____ *lady*		_____ _____

LABELS EXPRESSING ACTION

Egyptian images often include labels that describe the action depicted. The labels begin with a verb set in the infinitive. The Egyptian infinitive usually has no particular ending and is translated either with the English infinitive (*to do*) or the gerund ending in –ing (*doing*). In the inscription of Sahura, for example, *dꜣr* is the infinitive of the verb *dꜣr*. The label *dꜣr ḫꜣs.wt nb.wt* can thus be translated as *smiting all foreign lands.*

14 Translate the verbs of the labels, inferring their meaning from the scene they accompany, as in the first example.

a	*dꜣr*	king smites an enemy	*smiting*
b	*sqr*	kings strikes down an enemy	__________
c	*ḏd*	deity speaks to the king	__________
d	*mꜣꜣ*	governor inspects the fields	__________

Explore

King Neuserra (*c.*2445–2410 BCE, pronounced Néeooseráa) cut a similar inscription into the rock near the one of his predecessor Sahura. The hieroglyphs of the inscription have a clear shape but are less formally arranged than one would expect. The bottom left corner is not preserved. Have a look at the entire composition first and try to understand which inscription belongs where. Then answer these questions.

1 Where is the Horus name of king Neuserra written?

2 What does the phrase below the Horus name mean?

3 The name in the cartouches reads *Nj-wsr-Rˁ* **Neuserra, literally *Strength-belongs-to-Ra.* Where else is it written in the inscription?**

4 Find the other royal titles in the inscription.

a King of Upper and Lower Egypt

b Son of Ra

c Two Ladies

d Golden Horus

5 **How often are the following phrases used in the inscription?**

a *nb tꜣ.wj*

b *nṯr ꜥꜣ*

c *nṯr nfr*

d *ḫꜣs.wt*

6 **Translate the phrases in question 5.**

7 **Try to transliterate and translate all hieroglyphs in the label written above the Bedouin. Use the inscription of Sahura to help you.**

8 **Try to guess what might have been depicted in the bottom left corner, based on the label** *dꜣr ḫꜣs.wt nb.wt* **written above the destroyed area.**

9 **Look at the inscription above the figure in the centre. Which deity is the king** *mry* ***beloved of*?**

Drawing hieroglyphs

1 **Follow the steps to draw the following hieroglyphs typically used in royal titles.**

a 

b 

2 **Now write in hieroglyphs the titles and names of Sahura from the first inscription.**

Test yourself

1 What are typical attributes of the king depicted in a scene?

2 List the five titles of the king in the transliteration.

3 Classifier or picture-sign? Decide how the signs  and are used in the following words?

a  *Ḏdw* *Busiris*

b  *njw.t* *town*

c 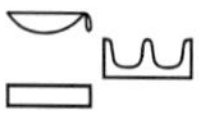 *Kš* *Kush*

d 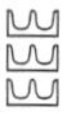 *ḫꜣs.wt* *foreign lands*

4 Match the hieroglyphs with their correct transliteration and correct translation.

a		*nṯr*	*god*
		nṯr.wj	*two gods*
b		*ḫʿ.w*	*two crowns*
		ḫʿ.tj	*crowns*
c		*s.tj*	*a seat*
		s.t	*two seats*
d	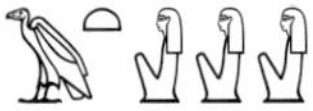	*mw.tj*	*two mothers*
		mw.wt	*the mothers*

5 How do you translate the label  placed next to the depiction of the king striking down an enemy?

SELF-CHECK

I CAN

- recognize the king depicted in a scene
- read royal titles and epithets
- understand labels in a scene expressing action
- recognize the singular, plural and dual of Egyptian nouns
- tell the difference between classifiers and picture signs

5 The temples of Thebes

In this unit you will learn how to:

- **read royal building inscriptions**
- **use prepositions**
- **express possession**
- **interpret two nouns set side by side**
- **recognize weak verbs.**

THEBES AND AMUN

The religion of ancient Egypt was closely intertwined with the political history of the country. When Egypt was reunited at the beginning of the New Kingdom, the kings of the new dynasty made their home town 𓌀𓏏𓊖 *W3s.t* (*Thebes*) the religious capital of the country. Every town in ancient Egypt had its own deity and the patron god of Thebes was 𓇋𓏠𓈖𓀭 *Jmn* (*Amun*). In the New Kingdom, Amun was merged with Ra to become Amun-Ra, a deity that combined the power of the sun god with the Theban origins of Amun. The names Amun and Amun-Ra can appear side by side in inscriptions, suggesting that they refer to one single deity only. The preserved remains of the 𓊹𓉗𓏏 *ḥw.t-nṯr* (*temple*) of Amun at Thebes date back to the early Middle Kingdom. With the rise of Thebes in the New Kingdom, the building was massively enlarged and today is one of the biggest and best-preserved temples of the Pharaonic period. On a trip to Egypt, you can visit its statues, sanctuaries, columned halls and obelisks, shown in the photo. The ancient Egyptians called large buildings, such as the temple of Amun, a 𓏠𓈖𓏌𓏌𓏌 *mnw* (*monument*). This noun is derived from the verb *mn to endure*, and, in fact, many temples in Egypt do endure up to the present day.

1 Can you remember what the sign 𓊖 represents given that it is used as a classifier in the word *Thebes*?

2 Since *nṯr* means *god*, what might *ḥw.t-nṯr* mean translated word for word?

Vocabulary builder

ROYAL BUILDING INSCRIPTION

1 Read these new words aloud.

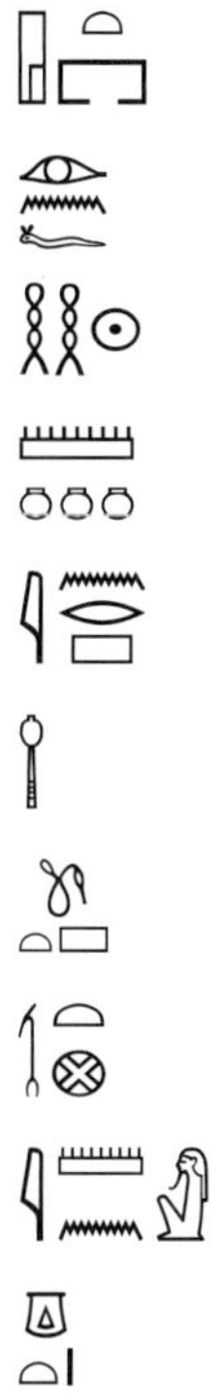

ḥw.t	enclosure
jrj.n=f	he made (it)
nḥḥ	eternity
mnw	monument
jnr	stone
ḥḏ	bright
rwd.t	strength
W3s.t	Thebes
Jmn	Amun
ns.t	throne

> **LANGUAGE INSIGHT**
>
> The word *mnw monument* looks as if it is plural because of the triple use of the sign *nw*. The Egyptians saw a monument as consisting of several individual structures and, for this reason, made it appear like a plural noun in hieroglyphs. Since *mnw* often refers to an individual building, it is better translated with the singular, unless it is clear from the context that it refers to many buildings, in which case you translate *monuments*. Similarly, *ḏf3 food* is a collective term for many pieces to eat. Therefore it has plural strokes but is translated with the singular in English.

2 Go through the new classifiers in the left-hand column. Then match them with the word they classify, as shown.

a STONE BLOCK
b SUN, TIME
c SETTLEMENT
d STONE BLOCK
e BUILDING
f GOD

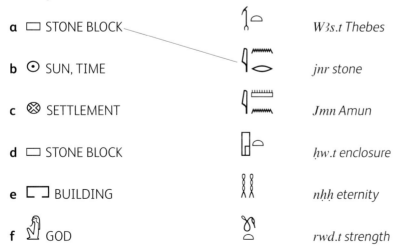

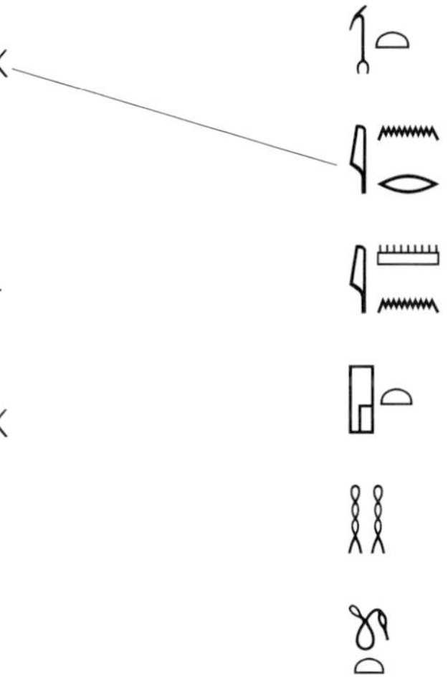

W3s.t Thebes
jnr stone
Jmn Amun
ḥw.t enclosure
nḥḥ eternity
rwd.t strength

3 Find these new signs within the new words introduced in the vocabulary builder. Choose whether they function as a picture sign or sound sign.

a	 (plan of enclosure)	*ḥwt*	picture – sound
b	 (human eye)	*jr*	picture – sound
c	 (pot)	*nw*	picture – sound
d	 (mace)	*ḥḏ*	picture – sound
e	 (bow string)	*rwd*	picture – sound
f	 (sceptre)	*wꜣs*	picture – sound
g	 (gaming board)	*mn*	picture – sound
h	 (pot stand)	*ns*	picture – sound

4 Read through these new words, which you will also need for this unit.

	*šps* (shépes)	*noble*
	*jmj-wrt* (éemee-wéret)	*west bank*
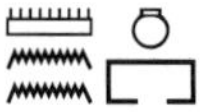	*mnnw* (menénoo)	*fortress*

THE FUNERARY TEMPLE OF AMENHOTEP III

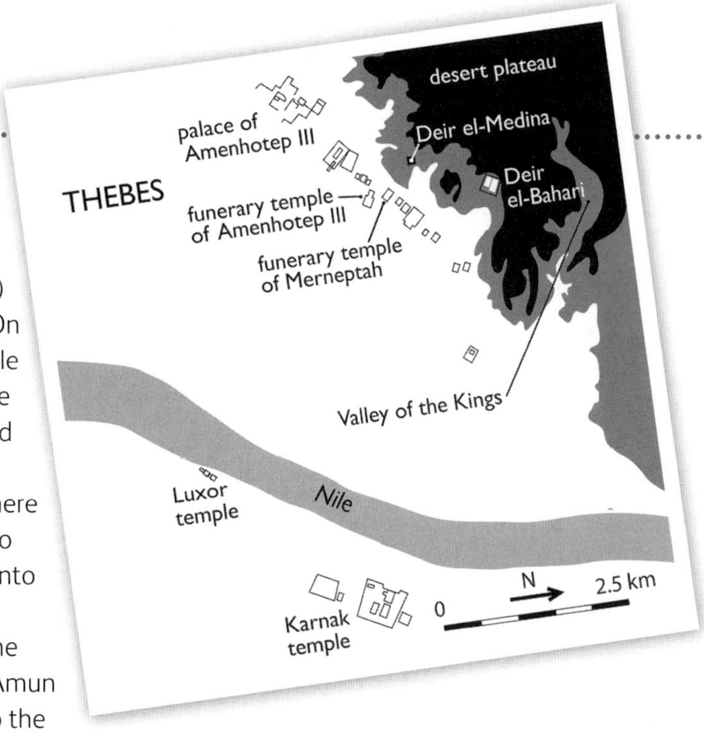

In his long reign of almost 40 years, king Amenhotep III (1388–1350 BCE) redesigned Thebes on a grand scale. On the east bank he built the Amun temple at Luxor and parts of the Amun temple at Karnak. On the west bank he erected a palace, a tomb in the Valley of the Kings, and a large funerary temple, where the deceased king received offerings to live on in the afterlife. Thebes turned into a gigantic cultic stage during popular festivals celebrated on both sides of the river. On these occasions, a statue of Amun was carried from the Karnak temple to the West bank and visited the funerary temples of Amenhotep III and other kings.

Amenhotep III recorded the building of his funerary temple on a granite stela, from which the passage, reproduced here, is taken. The inscription of the stela was partially erased after Amenhotep III had died. King Seti I (1323–1279 BCE) restored the stela. Later, king Merneptah (1213–1203 BCE) removed it from its original location into his own funerary temple, where it was found by the archaeologist Flinders Petrie. Merneptah's inscription, carved on the reverse side, mentions the people of Israel for the first time in history outside the Bible. Because of this, the stela has become famous as the *Israel Stela,* but its original purpose was to celebrate Amun and the deeds of Amenhotep III.

Study the hieroglyphs and depictions on the stela and try to answer the questions.

1 Who do you think the figure is, making offerings in the upper section of the stela?

2 Who is the god receiving the offerings? Try to find his name in the central column.

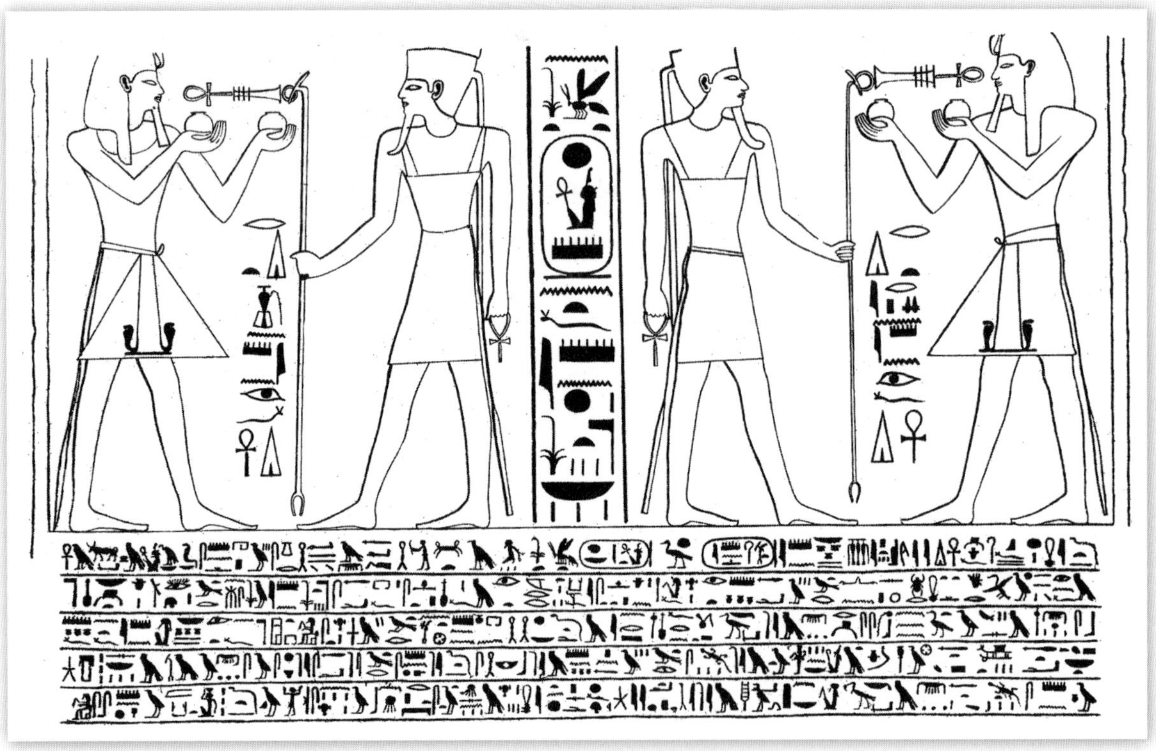

3 Find the following passage in the original inscription on the stela.

jrj.n=f m mnw=f n jt=f Jmn nb ns.wt tꜣ.wj

jrj.t n=f ḥw.t-nṯr šps.t ḥr jmj-wrt n Wꜣs.t

mnnw n nḥḥ r ḏ.t m jnr ḥḏ nfr n rwd.t

> **LANGUAGE INSIGHT**
>
> The word *jt father* is written in the hieroglyphs of this text as 𓏏 rather than 𓇋𓏏. It means that you do not see a hieroglyph for the weak consonant *j* where you would expect one.

4 Where is the name *Amun* written in the passage?

5 Where does it say in the passage that the funerary temple was located *on the West bank of Thebes?*

6 Read the transliteration aloud.

> **LANGUAGE INSIGHT**
>
> The Egyptians had two different words for *eternity*, and they distinguished the meaning of each in writing. The two words are often combined in a text, as in the final line of the passage. One of them is 𓆓𓏏𓇾 *ḏ.t*. The classifier of this word represents a flat strip of land because *ḏ.t* refers to the idea of a linear endlessness. In contrast, 𓎛𓇳𓎛 *nḥḥ*, written less accurately as 𓎛𓎛𓇳 in the passage above, looks like the beginning of a repetitive pattern: 𓎛𓇳𓎛𓇳𓎛𓇳𓎛, etc. Different from *ḏ.t*, it expresses the idea of cyclical repetition. The initial *n* in this group is often omitted in hieroglyphs, making the word look like *ḥḥ* instead of *nḥḥ*. However, the Egyptians knew that the group 𓎛𓇳𓎛 stood for *nḥḥ*. The combination of both words in the phrase *nḥḥ r ḏ.t*, sometimes reduced to *nḥḥ ḏ.t*, is similar to the English *forever and ever*.

Language discovery

1 Find the Egyptian equivalents in the transliterated passage.

a as his monument

b for his father

c for him

d on the West bank

e to eternity

f out of stone

2 Compare the Egyptian expressions of possession with their English translation and answer the questions.

a Which Egyptian word is the equivalent of English *of*?

jmj-wrt n Wꜣs.t	West bank of Thebes
mnw n nḥḥ r ḏ.t	a fortress of eternity to eternity (= an eternal fortress)
jnr ḥḏ nfr n rwd.t	bright beautiful stone of strength (= sandstone)

b Which hieroglyph is used for this word in the inscription?

c How is possession expressed in the following Egyptian phrases?

nb ns.wt	lord of the thrones
ns.wt tꜣ.wj	the thrones of the two lands
ḥw.t-nṯr	enclosure of the god

d Go back to the hieroglyphic passage. How does the word order of *ḥw.t-nṯr* differ in transliteration from the word order in hieroglyphs?

3 Study the word-for-word translation of this group of hieroglyphs, then look at the options that follow it. Which phrase would you say makes a better English translation to convey the meaning of the writer?

Jmn nb ns.wt tꜣ.wj
word for word: *Amun – lord – thrones – two lands*

a Amun of the lord of the thrones of the two lands

b Amun, lord of the thrones of the two lands

c Amun and the lord of the thrones of the two lands

d Amun or the lord of the thrones of the two lands

4 Have a closer look at the spelling of *jrj* in the inscription.

a How is the final *j* of *jrj* in *jrj.n=f* and *jrj.t* written in the hieroglyphic text?

b *jrj.t* in the second line is the infinitive of *jrj*. How does the form differ from the infinitives you looked at in the previous unit?

c How would you translate *jrj.t*?

PREPOSITIONS

Prepositions are 'small words' preceding a noun, such as *in, to, on* or *against*. Together, preposition and noun express the circumstance under which something happens, such as the time, location or reason for an action, for example 'I sleep *on the floor*'. The most common prepositions in Egyptian are *m, n,* and *r*; another preposition is *ḥr*. Each Egyptian preposition can have several meanings in English. You will learn some of them in this unit and others as we progress through the course. Context helps you decide which translation makes the best sense.

hieroglyph	transliteration	translation
	*n*	*for; to*
	*r*	*to, towards*
	*m*	*in; as; out of*
	*ḥr*	*on*

The preposition *n* means *to* and *for*, expressing the object or person benefiting from an action.

	*n jt=f*	*for his father*
	*n kꜣ*	*to the ka-soul*

The preposition *r* indicates a direction and is translated with *to* or *towards*.

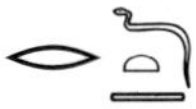	*r ḏ.t*	*to eternity*

The preposition *m* expresses location in time and space (*in*), identity (*as*) and substance (*out of*).

	*m 3bḏw*	*in Abydos* (location)
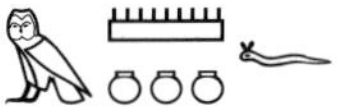	*m mnw=f*	*as his monument* (identity)
	*m jnr*	*out of stone* (substance)

The preposition *ḥr* often means *on*.

	*ḥr jmj-wrt*	*on the west bank*

You can replace the noun after a preposition with a pronoun. When the noun is masculine, the pronoun *=f him* is used.

	*n z3*	*for the son*
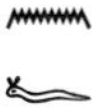	*n=f*	*for him*

5 Match the prepositions with their correct noun or pronoun, as shown.

a *for Ptah*	*m*	*3bḏw*
b *out of stone*	*n*	*=f*
c *towards Thebes*	*ḥr*	*ḥw.t-nṯr*
d *at Abydos*	*m*	*Ptḥ*
e *in the temple*	*r*	*jnr*
f *on him*	*m*	*W3s.t*

6 Transliterate and translate.

a  **b**  **c**  **d**  **e** 

POSSESSION

The Egyptians use the connector *n* between two nouns to express possession, similar to *of* in English. The connector looks like the preposition *n*, which you have learned above. In the context of a sentence, it is usually simple to decide whether the best translation is with *of, to* or *for*.

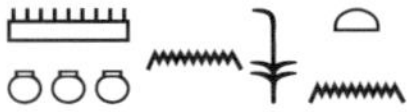 *mnw n njswt* *monument of the king*

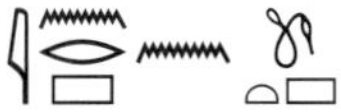 *jnr n rwd.t* *stone of strength*

Alternatively, the Egyptians simply set two nouns side by side.

 *nb W3s.t* *lord of Thebes*

The word order is often reversed in hieroglyphs, whenever the possessor is a deity or king. The purpose of this was to honour deities and kings by placing them upfront in writing. However, the group was pronounced and is transliterated with the king or deity being placed *after* the thing they are possessing. A hyphen in transliteration indicates that the words belong closely together and can be switched in the written hieroglyphs. They are often better translated with a single word in English. This switching is called 'honorific transposition'.

 *ḥw.t-nṯr* (not *nṯr ḥw.t*) *enclosure of the god* (= *temple*)

In the honorific transposition, the word *njswt king* is usually written simply .

 *z3-njswt* (not *njswt z3*) *son of the king* (= *prince*)

7 Translate these expressions of possession.

a *nb.t W3s.t*

b *z3-Rʿ*

c *jt n mw.t*

d *mnw ḏ.t*

e *ḥm.t-njswt*

8 Write the phrases a–e from the previous exercise in hieroglyphs, by combining the correct groups below.

a 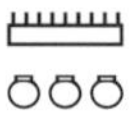 b  c  d  e  f 

g  h  i 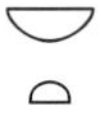 j  k 

The second noun can be replaced with the pronoun *=f*, translated in this position with *his*.

	*zꜣ-Rꜥ*	*son of Ra*
	*zꜣ n Rꜥ*	*son of Ra*
	*zꜣ=f*	*his son*

9 Complete the table, using the correct transliteration and translation of possession, as shown.

a	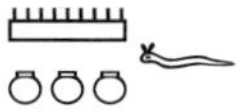	*mnw=f*	*his monument*
b	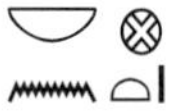	*nb n njw.t*	____________
c		____________	*throne of Horus*
d		*sn=f*	____________
e		____________	*the father of the king*
f		____________	____________

COMMENT AND PAIR

When you translate an Egyptian text, one task is to work out how individual words relate to each other. In the previous section, for example, you learned that two nouns set side by side in Egyptian express possession and are therefore connected with *of* in translation. Apart from possession, two nouns can also mean that they are a pair or that the second noun comments on the first. When you interpret them as a pair, you add *and* or *or* in the translation. If you think the second noun comments on the first, you add a comma before it. Context helps you decide which interpretation fits best. Sometimes several options work well.

	*Jmn nb=f*	*Amun, (namely) his lord* (comment)
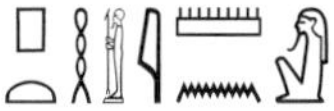	*Ptḥ Jmn*	*Ptah and Amun* (pair)
		Ptah or Amun (pair)

10 Go through the following phrases, each formed from nouns set side by side, and transliterate.

a 

b 

c 

d 

11 Now translate the phrases from the previous exercise. Try to establish whether the phrases express most likely possession, pair or comment.

WEAK VERBS

Egyptian verbs can be grouped in different classes according to their form. Those ending in –*j* are called weak verbs because the final *j* was pronounced in speech, but usually not written in hieroglyphs. Some forms of weak verbs have a distinct set of endings. Their infinitive, for example, ends in *.t* separated in transliteration with a full stop. By convention, English verbs are quoted in the infinitive, such as in vocabulary lists.

base of verb		infinitive		
	*jrj*	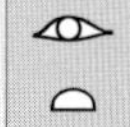	*jrj.t*	*to make, making*
	*mrj*	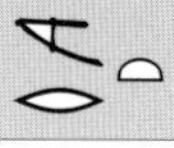	*mrj.t*	*to love, loving*

12 Distinguish strong from weak verbs by selecting the correct answer.

a *sqr to smite* strong or weak?

b *dj to give* strong or weak?

c *d3r to smite* strong or weak?

d *sꜥḥꜥ to erect* strong or weak?

e *sḏm to listen* strong or weak?

f *jnj to bring* strong or weak?

13 Choose 'correct' or 'incorrect', depending on whether the forms of the infinitives are correct. For example, a is 'incorrect' because the infinitive of strong verbs does not end in *.t*.

a  *sqr.t* correct incorrect ✓

b 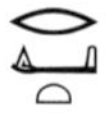 *rdj.t* correct incorrect

c  *d3r.t* correct incorrect

d 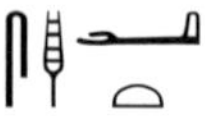 *s:ꜥḥꜥ.t* correct incorrect

e  *sḏm.t* correct incorrect

f 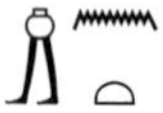 *jnj.t* correct incorrect

Explore

Before the reign of Amenhotep III, one of his ancestors, the famous king Thutmosis III, erected several temples and shrines at Thebes. His inscriptions are similar in style to the one you have just studied for Amenhotep III, reproduced below for convenience. The following two examples A and B were cut into stone blocks erected in the rear part of the great Amun temple at Karnak. This area was called *Akhmenu* and was built by Thutmosis III.

Learn more about the pattern of royal building inscriptions by comparing the inscriptions and answering the following questions.

Inscription of Amenhotep

(1) 

(2) 

(3) 

Inscription A

(1) 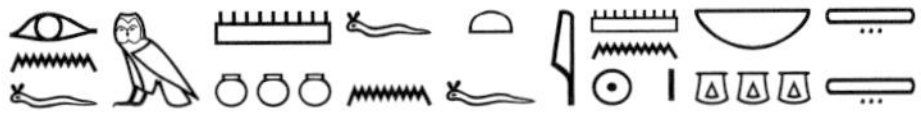

(2) 

(3) 

1 **Compare line (1) of inscription A with line (1) of the inscription of Amenhotep III. Which parts are identical?**

2 **Transliterate and translate line (1), using the inscription of Amenhotep III to help you if you need it.**

3 **Which part in line (2) differs from line (2) in the inscription of Amenhotep III?**

4 **What does line (2) mean? The new expressions in this line are the feminine noun**  *ḥrj.t-jb* **(héreet-eeb)** ***sanctuary*** **and**  *m m3w.t* **(em-máaoot)** ***as something new.***

5 **According to line (3), which material is the building of Thutmosis III built from?**  *ʿnw* **means** ***Tura.*** **It is the name of the site of a limestone quarry near Cairo.**

Inscription B

(1) 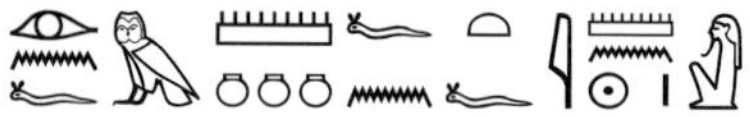

(2) 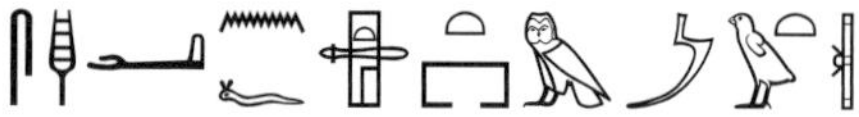

(3) 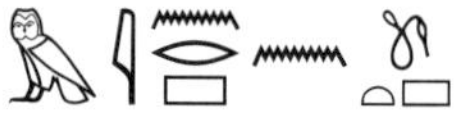

6 Which phrase is lacking in line (1) of inscription B compared to line (1) of inscription A?

7 Transliterate line (2). *s:ꜥḥꜥ* **(se-áahaa) means *to erect*, and** **is a combined spelling of** **.**

8 Translate line (2).

9 What does line (3) say?

Drawing hieroglyphs

1 Follow the steps to draw the following signs.

a 

b 

2 Write the first line of Amenhotep's building inscription in hieroglyphs.

Test yourself

1 To whom is a building with this inscription dedicated?

2 Translate these phrases, deciding which meaning of the prepositions used fits best.

a 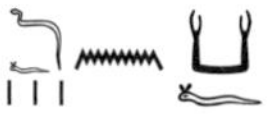 *ḏfꜣ n kꜣ=f*

b  *ḥw.t-nṯr m jnr*

c  *mnw nḥḥ r ḏ.t*

d  *Jmn m njw.t*

3 Choose the correct transliteration and translation.

a 

jt=f his father

jt his father

b 

W3s.t-nb Thebes of the lord

nb W3s.t lord of Thebes

c 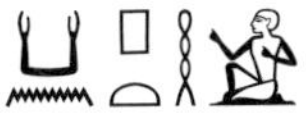

k3 n Ptḥ the ka-soul and Ptah

k3 n Ptḥ the ka-soul of Ptah

d 

njswt-z3.t daughter of the king

z3.t-njswt daughter of the king

4 Which one is likely to be the best translation of this phrase?

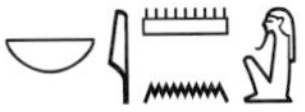 *nb Jmn*

a *the lord and Amun* (pair)

b *the lord, Amun* (comment)

c *the lord of Amun* (possession)

5 How does the infinitive of *jnj to bring* look in transliteration?

SELF-CHECK

	I CAN
●	read royal building inscriptions
●	use prepositions
●	express possession
●	interpret two nouns set side by side
●	recognize weak verbs

6 Tomb and memory

In this unit you will learn how to:

- **read a biographical text**
- **recognize attached pronouns**
- **express action in the past**
- **translate verbal sentences.**

REMEMBRANCE IN LOCAL COMMUNITIES

High officials were keen to be remembered in their local communities. They built large tombs, sometimes true mausoleums, comprising an underground burial chamber and an accessible chapel above ground. The burial chamber contained the mummy and coffin of the deceased and was sealed after the burial ceremony. On several days of the year, friends and family came to visit the chapel. While they offered food to the deceased, they gazed at the walls which were *s:mnḫ* (*embellished*) with scenes of their ancestor and his dependents. The accompanying inscriptions recorded his *rn* (*name*), titles and biography. Affluent people allotted a piece of land to a funerary priest, whose duty it was to maintain the provision of food to his deceased patron. In the time of the Old and Middle Kingdoms, some provincial governors built an additional *ḥw.t-k3* (*ka-chapel*) for their *twt* (*statue*). Their statues joined the statues of deities during temple processions, a privilege that the entire community was able to witness. Funerary culture thus spun webs of relationships among the living, which were sustained by public memory, religious festivals and economic arrangements.

1 Why would you say Egyptian funerary culture means more than a belief in the afterlife?

2 What do you notice about the transliteration of the Egyptian word for *to embellish*?

Vocabulary builder

TOMB AND MEMORY

1 Read these new words aloud.

	*s:rwd*	*to establish*
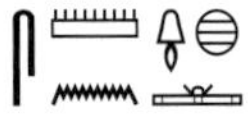	*s:mnḫ*	*to embellish*
	*s:mꜣʿ*	*to put in order*
	*qd*	*to build*
	*s:ʿḥʿ*	*to erect*
	*wḥm*	*to repeat, to report*
	*rn*	*name*
	*ḥw.t-kꜣ*	*ka-chapel*
	*twt*	*statue*
	*pꜣ.t*	*offering bread*
	*šps*	*noble*
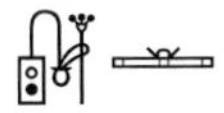	*zš*	*inscribed*

2 Some of the verbs in the list above are 'causative verbs'. Try to figure out what this might mean by answering these questions.

a Look at the transliteration of these verbs. How are those listed in the right column derived from those in the left column?

mnḫ to be excellent	*s:mnḫ* to make excellent, to embellish
mꜣʿ to be correct	*s:mꜣʿ* to make correct, to put in order
rwd to be firm	*s:rwd* to make firm, to build
ʿḥʿ to stand	*s:ʿḥʿ* to make something stand, to erect

b Now study the translations. How does the added *s:* change the meaning of the verbs?

c If  *ʿnḫ* means *to live*, how would you translate  *s:ʿnḫ*?

NEW EXPRESSIONS

Here are a few more words you need for this unit.

	*jrj.w* (éereeoo)	*belonging to (him)*
	*šms* (shémes)	*to follow*
	*m-ḫnw* (em-khénoo)	*in, inside* (literally *in the interior of*)
	*wḫꜣ* (wékhaa)	*hall*
	*wḫꜣ* (wékhaa)	*column* (final *ꜣ* not written)
	*mꜣṯ* (maatj)	*granite*
	*ḏs* (djes)	*own, self*

INSIGHT

The sign 𓏏 usually stands for *t*, but sometimes replaces 𓍿 and is transliterated *ṯ*.

3 Have a look at these new signs, taken from the new vocabulary, and speculate as to what they might represent by matching them with their correct description.

a		*qd*	writing equipment
b		*šps*	leg (and hoof) of an ox
c	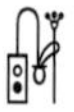	*zš*	mast
d		*pꜣ*	noble person on chair
e		*wḥm*	man building a wall
f		*mnḫ*	pintail duck flying
g		*ꜥḥꜥ*	pot above waterlines
h		*šms*	circle with lines (placenta?)
i		*m-ḫnw*	chisel
j		*ḫ*	crook with package

4 Which words in the vocabulary builder are written with these new classifiers listed below?

a SEALED PAPYRUS SCROLL, ABSTRACT IDEA (5x)

b  BREAD

c  STATUE

d WOOD

KHNUMHOTEP AT BENI HASSAN

If you go on a Nile cruise, you'll pass many sites that look like Swiss cheese. Each 'hole' is, in fact, the entrance to a rock tomb, like those shown in the photo. One such site is the cemetery of Beni Hassan. The upper row of rock tombs was reserved for governors and higher-ranking administrators. Below them, further down the desert slope, were the mud-brick tombs of lower-ranking officials, many of which have vanished today. The tombs of commoners are not preserved.

Khnumhotep was a provincial governor at Beni Hassan in the reign of Senwosret II (1882–1872 BCE). The scenes in his tomb chapel show Khnumhotep going hunting with his sons, craftsmen working for him and rows of men bringing offerings to him and his wife. The passage below is taken from his biography. It is written below the wall scenes, complementing them with details about the deeds and achievements of Khnumhotep during his life.

1 Scan the text and decide whether Khnumhotep is describing the procession of statues or the erection of columns.

(5) (4) (3) (2) (1)

This transliteration is arranged according to how the words appear in the columns:

(1) *s:rwd.*

(2) *n=j rn n jt=j s:mnḫ.n=j ḥw.wt-*

(3) *kꜣ jrj.w šms.n=j twt.w*

(4) *=j r ḥw.t-nṯr s:mꜣꜥ.n=j n=sn*

(5) *pꜣ.t=sn*

2 What did Khnumhotep *s:mnḫ* ***embellish*** **for his father?**

3 Compare the hieroglyphs with the transliteration. Does the end of a column coincide with the end of a word?

4 What do you notice about the way *ḥw.t-nṯr* is written in the hieroglyphic text?

5 Now look at the expression of *ḥw.wt-k3 ka-chapels*. How is it written in hieroglyphs?

6 Read out the transliteration of the entire text.

Language discovery

1 Work out how *I*, *my*, *their* and *them* are expressed in the biography of Khnumhotep.

a How is the sign 𓀀 transliterated?

b How is the group 𓋴𓈖𓏥 transliterated?

c Go back to the text and make a list of the following words:

verbs with 𓀀	nouns with 𓀀	noun with 𓋴𓈖𓏥	preposition with 𓋴𓈖𓏥
____________	____________	____________	____________
____________	____________		
____________			
____________			

d What is the meaning of *=j* and *=sn*? Try to match the phrases in transliteration with their correct translation.

šms.n=j	*their ka-chapel*
jt=j	*for them*
ḥw.t-k3=sn	*my father*
n=sn	*I followed*

2 Investigate how the Egyptians expressed past tense.

a Make a list of all the verbs used in Khnumhotep's biography.

b Which letter in the transliteration sits between these verbs and their attached pronouns?

c Which hieroglyph is used for this letter?

3 The word order in an Egyptian sentence differs from word order in English. Do these sentences in Khnumhotep's biography begin with a verb or with a noun?

s:rwd.n=j rn n jt=j

s:mnḫ.n=j ḥw.wt-k3 jrj.w

šms.n=j twt.w=j r ḥw.t-nṯr

s:m3ꜥ.n=j n=sn p3.t=sn

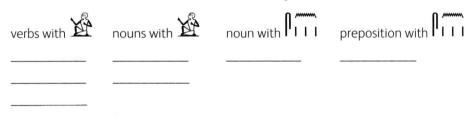

ATTACHED PRONOUNS

In transliteration, attached pronouns are connected to a preceding noun, a verb or a preposition with an equals sign. After nouns, they express possession. When following a verb, they say who is acting. After prepositions, they replace the person or thing that the preposition introduces.

The translation will usually come naturally to you, but, if in doubt, you may find the systematic table below useful. Note that Egyptian distinguishes between masculine and feminine in the second person singular, but does not have a separate word for *it*, which is expressed with the masculine or, more often, the feminine pronoun.

		after nouns	after verbs	after prepositions
Singular				
1st person	*=j*	*my*	*I*	*me*
2nd person masc	*=k*	*your*	*you*	*you*
2nd person fem	*=ṯ*	*your*	*you*	*you*
3rd person masc	*=f*	*his, its*	*he, it*	*him, it*
3rd person fem	*=s*	*her, its*	*she, it*	*her, it*
Plural				
1st person	*=n*	*our*	*we*	*us*
2nd person	*=ṯn*	*your*	*you*	*you*
3rd person	*=sn*	*their*	*they*	*them*

4 Find the correct translation for the attached pronouns. The first example is done for you.

a *jt=f his father* *jrj.n=f he made* *n=f for him*

b *jt=j* ________ *s:ꜥḥꜥ.n=j* ______ *n=j* _______

c *rn=s* ________ *šms.n=s* ______ *r=s* ________

d *nṯr=sn* ______ *qd.n=sn* ______ *ḥr=sn* _____

e *twt=k* ______ *s:ꜥnḫ.n=k* _____ *n=k* _______

In hieroglyphs, the first person *=j* is written with a sign that represents the speaker. It means that when a man speaks, the hieroglyph of the seated man is used. For a female speaker, it is the hieroglyph of a seated woman. Kings use a hieroglyph representing a king, and so on. Sometimes, *=j* is simply written with the single sound sign 𓇋. Since *j* is a weak consonant, you'll even find that it is dropped in hieroglyphic writing, which regularly happened in the Old Kingdom. If this is the case, you can decide from the context whether a sentence makes more sense if you infer it and then include it in your translation.

The sound *ṯ* can be written with 𓏏 and 𓍿, and the sound *s* with 𓋴 and 𓊃. This is because these sounds were originally more clearly distinguished in speech and therefore rendered with separate hieroglyphs. Over time, the two different t- and s-sounds were pronounced similarly and their hieroglyphs used interchangeably.

Singular		
I, me, my	*=j*	 or  or  or 
you, your	*=k*	
you, your	*=ṯ*	 or 
he, him, his; it, its	*=f*	
she, her; it, its	*=s*	 or 
Plural		
we, us, our	*=n*	
you, your	*=ṯn*	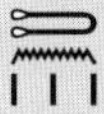 or  or also without plural strokes 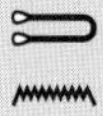 or 
they, them, their	*=sn*	 or 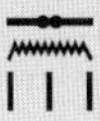 or also without plural strokes 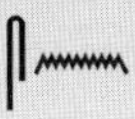 or 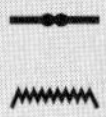

LANGUAGE INSIGHT

In other grammar textbooks, you may find the term 'suffix pronoun' used instead of 'attached pronoun'.

5 Transliterate and translate the hieroglyphs by completing the table.

a	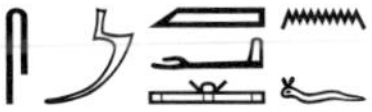	*s:mꜣꜥ.n=_____*	*_____ put in order*
b		*_____=sn*	*_____ ka-chapel*
c	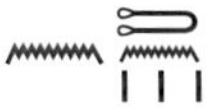	*n=_____*	*for _____*
d		*_____=_____*	*_____ town*
e		*wḥm.n=_____*	*_____ _____*
f		*_____=_____*	*_____ name*
g		*_____=n*	*_____ _____*

6 For each of these phrases, indicate whether a king, man or woman is speaking or if it has not been indicated.

LANGUAGE INSIGHT

The word *ḏs self, own* always takes an attached pronoun. *ḏs=k* means *yourself, your own*, *ḏs=f himself, his own*, etc.

a 

b 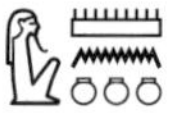

c 

d 

e 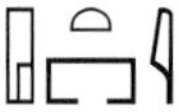

7 Now try a transliteration and translation of the phrases in exercise 6.

PAST TENSE

Past tense in Egyptian is expressed by adding — to a verb, transliterated with an *.n* and pronounced as en. The full stop in the transliteration is intended to help the reader understand where the verb ends.

 *s:rwd.n=k* *you established*

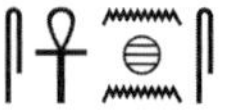 *s:ꜥnḫ.n=s* *she kept alive*

8 How would you say the following phrases in Egyptian? Use transliteration.

a *they erected*

b *he built*

c *you* (plural) *embellished*

d *you* (feminine singular) *made*

e *I repeated*

EGYPTIAN SENTENCES

Many Egyptian sentences begin with a verb followed by a series of words expressing who is doing what to whom. It is useful to introduce a few grammar terms here, which will help you understand how Egyptian sentences function and how they differ from English sentences.

The person acting is called the 'subject' in a sentence, and the activity the subject performs is expressed by the 'predicate'. In the sentence *He built a ka-chapel for his statue*, the subject is *he* and the predicate is *built*. Standard English sentences begin with the subject, whereas in Egyptian the predicate comes first. For a translation, you can begin by rendering a text word for word before rearranging the words into coherent sentences, as shown below.

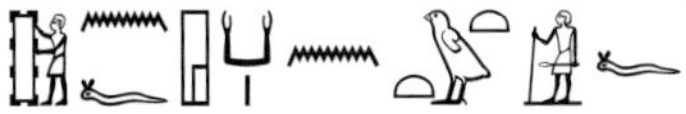

qd.n=f ḥw.t-kꜣ n twt=f

Built he ka-chapel for statue his (word-for-word translation)

→ *He built a ka-chapel for his statue.* (coherent sentence)

In the Egyptian sentence above, the subject is *=f he* and the predicate is *qd.n built*. Phrases that express for whose benefit something is done are called the 'indirect object'. In the example above, the indirect object is *for his statue*. In Egyptian sentences, the indirect object is always introduced by *n* translated with *for* or *to*. It can be followed by a noun, such as *n twt=f*, or by an attached pronoun, for example *n=f*.

9 Translate these sentences from Khnumhotep's biography.

a 

b 

c 

d 

10 Complete the transliteration of the following sentences.

a 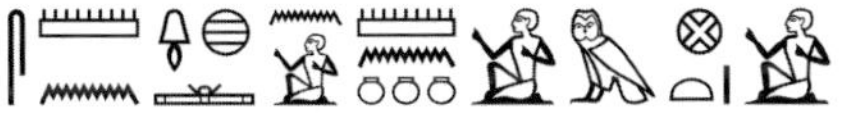 *s:mnḫ.n=j* _____ = _____ *m* _____ = _____

b  _____ *zꜣ* _____ _____ *jt* _____

c  _____ = _____ _____ = _____ *ḥw.t-nṯr*

11 Now translate the sentences in exercise 10. Try a word-for-word translation first and then arrange the words to form coherent sentences in English.

Explore

Khnumhotep built not only a tomb but also a house or chapel in his town. Archaeologists believe that the town was located in the floodplain at the foot of the desert hill, shown in this photo, but it has not been found so far. The biography of Khnumhotep, which we studied above, sheds light on what the town might have looked like. Among the other houses made of mud bricks, Khnumhotep's building must have stood out given its building materials. Read the text in hieroglyphs and then answer the questions.

1 Can you find in the text what materials the *wḫ3.w columns* of the building were made of?

(1) 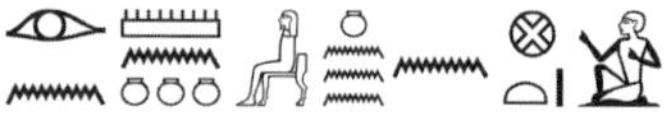

(2) 

(3) 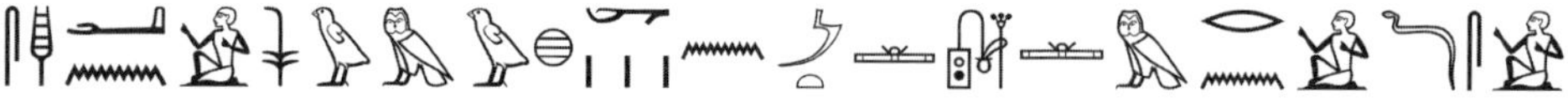

(4) 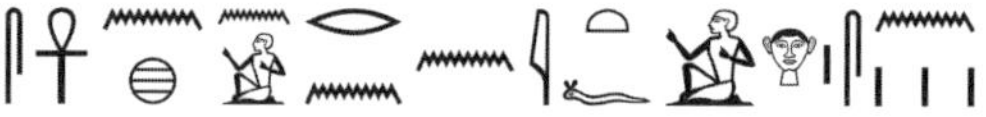

(5) 

2 Try to work out the content of the text. Don't worry if you cannot understand all the details.

a Which line tells the reader that the building was located *in the town*?

b What was *inscribed* on the *columns* of the building?

c What did Khnumhotep do with the *rn name* of his father?

d How would you interpret the final line? *jrj.t=j* means *what I did.*

3 Now concentrate on the grammar.

a Compare the first phrase in lines (2) to (5) and transliterate them.

b Assuming line (1) follows the same pattern, what word would you infer after *jrj.n* in line (1)?

c Transliterate and translate the entire text. Line (3): *sw* means *it.*

4 The following words and phrases include s- and t-sounds and are written in several different ways. Transliterate and pronounce them.

a  or  or  *to keep alive*

b 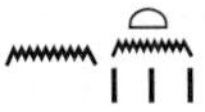 or 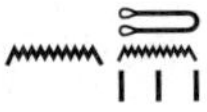 *you*

c  or  or  or  *granite*

Drawing hieroglyphs

1 Draw the following hieroglyphs from Khnumhotep's inscription.

a  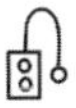 

b    The arms and triangular whip are not always depicted.

c   

d   

2 Practise drawing some more hieroglyphs by writing lines (1) to (3) of the inscription from the Explore section in hieroglyphs.

Test yourself

1 Match the hieroglyphs with their correct transliteration and translation.

a 	*nṯr=n*	*for you*
b 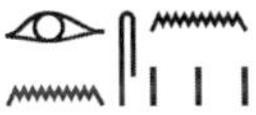	*ḥw.t-k3=j*	*our god*
c 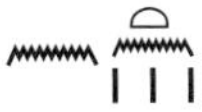	*r=s*	*himself*
d 	*n=ṯn*	*my ka-chapel*
e 	*twt=j*	*towards it*
f 	*šms.n=ṯ*	*they made*
g 	*jrj.n=sn*	*you followed*
h 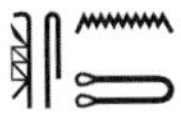	*ḏs=f*	*my statue*

2 Which of these phrases expresses the past tense?

a 

b 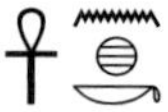

c 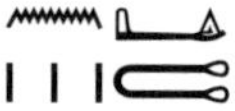

d 

3 Translate the following sentences into Egyptian by placing the transliterated words in the correct order.

a *I repeated the good name of my fathers. =j =j jt.w wḥm.n n nfr rn*

b *He made a monument for the king for eternity. =f mnw jrj.n n njswt r ḏ.t*

SELF-CHECK

	I CAN
○	read a biographical text
○	recognize attached pronouns
○	express action in the past
○	translate verbal sentences

7 Royal self-fashioning

In this unit you will learn how to:

- **read typical royal names**
- **modify the meaning of adjectives**
- **translate verbal adjectives**
- **make a statement using a noun.**

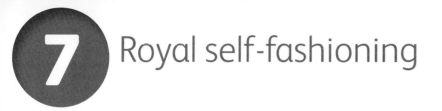

ROYAL NAMES

At first glance, royal names seem to make timeless statements about the qualities of a king, but take a closer look and you can see that there are fashions and trends reflecting political and social change. A fairly constant feature in names was to include a reference to the sun god. For example, Mentuhotep III, who reigned in about 2000 BCE, was called *S:ʿnḫ-kꜣ-Rʿ* (*Who-makes-the-ka-soul-of-Ra-live*), as you can see in the picture, and 600 years later Thutmosis III had the name *Mn-ḫpr-Rʿ Stp-n-Rʿ* (*Enduring-is-the-manifestation-of-Ra Whom-Ra-has-chosen*). In contrast, or *Mꜣʿ.t* (*Ma'at*), the goddess of justice, who wears a feather or is symbolized by one, became widely popular in royal names only in the New Kingdom. Royal names of this period abound with terms like *nḫt* (*strong*), *ḫpš* (*strength*) and *ḥwj* (*to smite*). Viewed together, these words conjure up an image of a law-and-order kingship based on the military and the temples. In fact, the New Kingdom was the peak of Egypt's imperial control in Nubia and the Near East. It was also the time when temples such as those at Thebes became truly monumental.

1 Why do you think the sign ☉ is placed at the front in the cartouches of the king?

2 Which signs might be classifiers meaning *force*?

Vocabulary builder

ROYAL NAMES AND EPITHETS

1 Read these new words aloud.

	*nḫt*	*strong*. The sign  can be used as picture sign or as a classifier *FORCE*.
	*ḫꜥj*	*to appear*
	*Mꜣꜥ.t*	*Ma'at*, also written 
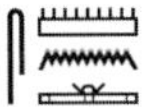	*s:mn*	*to make enduring, to establish*
	*hp*	*law*
	*ḫpš*	*strength*
	*ḥwj*	*to smite* (*w* and *j* not written in hieroglyphs)
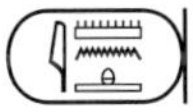	*Jmn-ḥtp*	*Amenhotep*
	*ḥqꜣ*	*ruler*
	*wr*	*great*
	*pw*	*he is, she is, it is*
	*njswt*	*king*
	*wsr*	*strong*
	*nṯrj*	*divine*
	*wꜣḥ*	*to endure*
	*ḫrp*	*to guide;*  used as classifier *FORCE*
	*pḥtj*	*strength*
	*ḏsr*	*sacred*
	*Mn-ḫpr-Rꜥ Stp-n-Rꜥ*	*Enduring-is-the-manifestation-of-Ra Whom-Ra-has-chosen*

2 Familiarize yourself with the words and group them according to their meaning and form.

a names of deities used in royal names: ______, ______, _______

b adjectives expressing sacredness: ______, ______

c words expressing strength: ______, ______, _______, ______

d nouns for somebody in power: ______, ______

3 Try to match the new signs, introduced in the word list, with their correct transliteration.

a  (arm with brush) *wsr*

b  (arm with stick) *ḏsr*

c  (head and neck of jackal) *wr*

d  (head of leopard) *wꜣḥ*

e  (sceptre) *nḫt*, also classifier *force*

f  (swab) *ḫt*

g  (adze and block of wood) *pḥ*

h  (sparrow) *ḫrp*

i  (crook) *ḫpš*

j  (foreleg of ox) *stp*

k  (piece of wood) *ḥqꜣ*

4 Learn more about the conventions of hieroglyphic writing.

a Why do you think the signs in the second column have the same function as those in the first?

  *k3* *bull*

  *M3ʿ.t* *Ma'at*

  *nḫt* *strong;* classifier FORCE

  *dj* *to give*

b When a word ended in *–j/–y*, Egyptian scribes could choose different ways of rendering this ending in hieroglyphs. Which options are used in the following words?

(i)  *jry* (éeree) *made*

(ii)  *nṯrj* (nétjeree) *divine*

(iii)  *ḫʿj* (kháaee) *to appear*

(iv)  *pḥtj* (péhtee) *strength*

c In royal names, titles and formulas, some words you have already learned are written differently from when they are used independently. How would you describe the difference in the following examples?

used independently

 *W3s.t Thebes*

 *njswt king*

 *njswy.t kingship*

 or  or  *jt father*

part of a title or formula

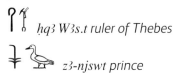

 *ḥq3 W3s.t ruler of Thebes*

 *z3-njswt prince*

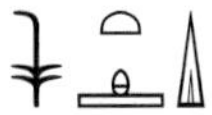 *ḥtp dj njswt an offering that the king gives*

 *njswy.t n Rʿ the kingship of Ra*

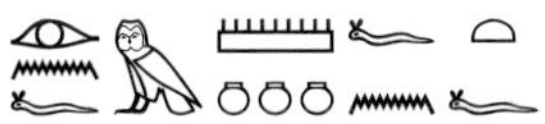

jrj.n=f m mnw=f n jt=f he made it as a monument for his father

LANGUAGE INSIGHT

In the spelling of the word *jt*, the 'superfluous' *f* was perhaps included because *jt=f* was a standard expression and over time the entire expression was understood to mean simply *jt*. The initial  is sometimes omitted in the hieroglyphs.

5 You will need these words for the focus text and the Explore section.

	*s:grḥ* (se-géreh)	*to pacify*
	*Sṯṯjw* (Sétjteeoo)	*'Asiatics'*; Bedouin from the Levant
	*mj* (mee)	*like*
	*p.t* (pet)	*sky*

LANGUAGE INSIGHT

The sign can stand for *g*, as in *s:grḥ to pacify*, and for *ns*, as in *ns.t throne*.

MARRIAGE AND EMPIRE

Amenhotep III (see Unit 5) married a woman called Tiy whose parents were not of royal status. Perhaps for this reason, Amenhotep felt a need to promulgate his marriage more widely. The inscription below is taken from a series of large scarabs, each approximately the size of the palm of your hand. We do not know where most of these were found, whether in tombs of nobles, a royal palace, or burials and the houses of commoners. Perhaps Amenhotep distributed them among the highest officials who contested his power.

The final lines of the inscription, not reproduced below, say that *His Southern frontier is at Kari and his Northern frontier at Naharina*. Naharina literally means *the two rivers* and refers to the Euphrates and Tigris in Mesopotamia, which is modern Iraq. Whether Amenhotep really controlled an area as far away as that is difficult to say. The historical value of the scarabs lies in the light they shed on the long-term changes of political reality and imagination. Mesopotamia appears on the radar of royal self-presentation for the first time in the 18th Dynasty. It reflects the growing scale of international interaction during the time of the Egyptian 'empire'.

1 Try to match the inscription below with the hieroglyphs on the scarab.

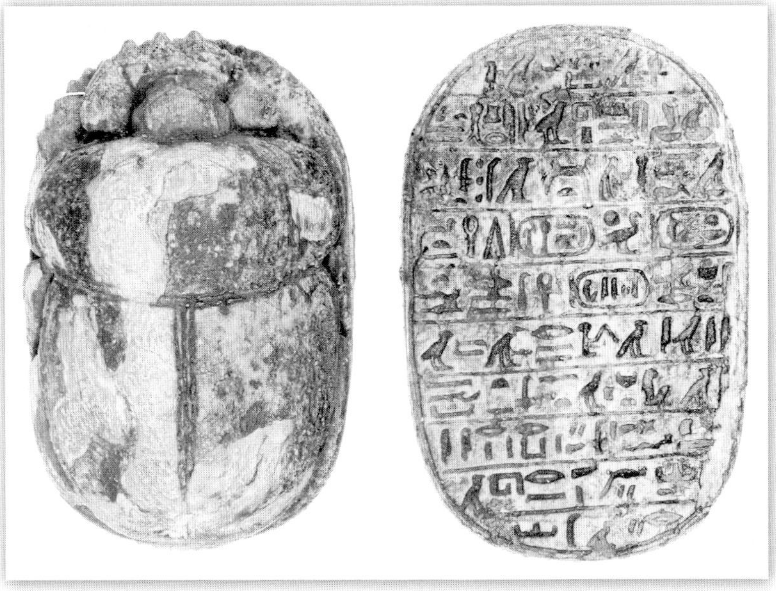

2 Which part of the inscription speaks about Amenhotep III and which one about Tiy?

 (1)

 (2)

 (3)

 (4)

 (5)

 (6)

 (7)

 (8)

 (9)

3 **Which deities does Amenhotep III mention in his *njswt-bjt* and *z3-Rꜥ* names?**

4 **Can you read the title in front of Tiy's name?**

5 **Where is *Tjy ꜥnḫ.tj* *Tiy, may she live* written in the inscription?**

6 **What do you think the sound is of the sign 𓏲?**

Language discovery

1 **The meaning of Egyptian adjectives can be modified with a noun. Investigate how this works in the following example.**

- **a** Which name of Amenhotep III in the inscription contains the phrase *ꜥ3-ḫpš*?
- **b** Does the adjective or the noun come first in this phrase?
- **c** How would you translate the phrase?

2 **Have a closer look at how the verbs in Amenhotep's names are translated.**

- **a** Complete the transliteration of lines 1 to 3. Use the vocabulary builder to help you.
  - **(1)** *ꜥnḫ Ḥrw K3-nḫt Ḫꜥj-m-M3ꜥ.t*
  - **(2)** *nb.tj* ___________ ___________
  - **(3)** *Ḥrw-nbw ꜥ3-ḫpš* ___________
- **b** Try to complete the gaps in this English translation for lines 2 and 3, following the example of line 1.
  - **(1)** *May live Horus Strong-Bull Who-appears-with-Ma'at,*
  - **(2)** *Two Ladies* ___________ ___________,
  - **(3)** *Golden Horus Great-of-strength* ___________ .

3 **Lines 7 to 9 make statements using a noun. Have a go at translating them by answering the questions.**

- **a** Complete the transliteration of lines 7 and 8 first.
  - **(7)** *rn* ______ ______ = ______ *Ywj3* *The name of her father is Yuya.*
  - **(8)** ______ ______ ______ *Ṯwj3* *The name of the mother is Tjuya.*
- **b** Which word is added in translation, apart from *the* and *of*?
- **c** Now try a transliteration of line 9 by yourself.
- **d** How would you translate line 9?

LANGUAGE INSIGHT

In standard Middle Egyptian, 𓈖 *n of* agrees in gender and number with the preceding noun. After feminine nouns, it takes the form 𓈖𓏏 *n.t*, and after nouns in the plural the form 𓏌𓏤 *n.w*. Over time, simple *n* was used in all instances.

AUTHOR NOTE

You may have noticed that you will often need to interpret an Egyptian expression and then rephrase it to match English grammar. Additionally, ancient Egyptian spoken language does not always map directly on to the written script, for example when nouns are switched for honorific reasons or when vowel endings are missing in hieroglyphs. What would be clear in a conversation with an ancient Egyptian thus becomes a matter of trying several options in the translation of the written word. Ultimately, a good translation is not a simple mechanical transfer from one language to another, but is informed by understanding and interpretation.

MODIFYING THE MEANING OF ADJECTIVES

In Egyptian, you can use a noun to modify the meaning of an adjective. For example, a king is not only *njswt ꜥꜣ a great king*, but *njswt ꜥꜣ pḥtj a king great of strength*, i.e. *a king great in view of his strength* or simply *a very strong king*. The word order in Egyptian is noun – adjective – noun. When translating this type of phrase, it is a good idea to start with word for word first and, if necessary, find a more fluent wording.

	word by word	fluent
njswt ꜥꜣ pḥtj	*a king great of strength*	*a very strong king*

4 Place the Egyptian words in correct order and then transliterate them word for word, as shown.

a *the king great of strength:* 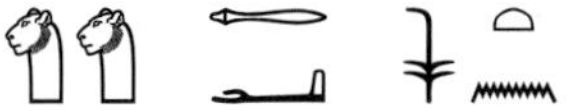 → *njswt ꜥꜣ pḥtj*

b *a king strong of arm (arm = ꜥ):*  → ___________

c *Zat-Hathor (Zꜣ.t-Ḥw.t-Ḥrw) true of voice:*  → ___________

d *Ptah beautiful of face (face = ḥr):*  → ___________

5 Find a fluent translation for the phrases in exercise 4.

6 The names of queen Hatshepsut include examples of adjectives modified by a noun. Have a go at their transliteration and translation.

a 

b 

VERBAL ADJECTIVES (PARTICIPLES)

Verbal adjectives are adjectives whose meaning is derived from a verb. Examples in English are appear*ing*, lov*ing* and lov*ed*. Verbal adjectives, also called 'participles', can describe that somebody is acting (active voice) or is acted upon (passive voice). In English, the active forms end in *–ing* and the passive forms in *–ed*, although irregular verbal adjectives in English have special forms in the passive voice, such as giv*en* instead of giv*ed*.

Egyptian verbal adjectives end in *–w*, *–j* or *–y* or show no ending. You can translate them either with an English *–ing* or *–ed* form, depending on whether active or passive voice makes more sense in a specific context. As a rule of thumb, Egyptian scribes almost always wrote the *w*-ending in hieroglyphs, when the verbal adjective expressed passive voice, but the ending is also used for the active voice.

hieroglyphs	transliteration	translation
	*s:mnw*	establishing or established
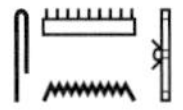	*s:mn*	establishing or established
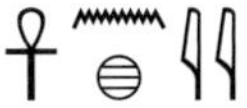	*ꜥnḫy*	living
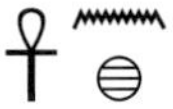	*ꜥnḫ*	living
	*ḫꜥj*	appearing

7 Translate these verbal adjectives, following the first example.

	transliteration	active voice	passive voice
a 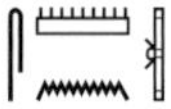	*s:mn*	establishing	established
b 	_____	_____	_____
c 	____	_____	_____
d 	_____	_____	_____
e 	_____	_____	_____
f 	_____	_____	_____

Sometimes, as in the inscription of Amenhotep III above, a more convenient option is to use a separate clause introduced by *who* or *which*. Since verbal adjectives do not indicate a specific setting in time, you need to decide from context whether past, present or future would fit best for your translation.

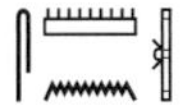	*s:mn*	who/which established or who/which was established
		who/which establishes or who/which is established
		who/which will establish or who/which will be established

8 Translate the verbal adjectives in the previous exercise with *who* and *which* clauses.

If the ending of a verbal adjective is not written in hieroglyphs, you often cannot recognize it from the form alone and therefore distinguish it from other forms of the verb, for example the infinitive. As usual, context helps you. Like normal adjectives, verbal adjectives follow a noun and agree with it in gender and number. In the names of Amenhotep III, for example, the verbal adjectives follow the title of the king *Horus Establishing-laws*, i.e. *the Horus Who-establishes-laws*. More often than not, several translations of a phrase are possible and you need to choose which one you think works best.

The one verbal class that shows clearer variation of forms in writing is the weak verbs. For example, the ending *y* regularly indicates passive voice, as in *jry made*. Also, verbal adjectives of weak verbs can show a duplication of the second letter, with the final *–j* being dropped, for example *jrr making* or *made*.

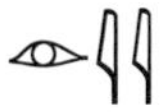	*jry*	*made*
	*jrj*	*making* and *made*
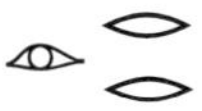	*jrr*	*making* and *made*
	*jrr* or *jrj* (could be either)	*making* and *made*

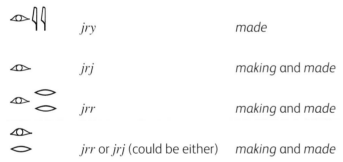

The duplicated form *jrr*, which can also be written with the ending *–w*, expresses habitual and continuous action in the past, present or future, in the active and passive voice. In contrast, simple *jrj* describes an action as happening without such implication, but is most typically used to say that a past action is completed. Therefore it is usually translated with *who has made*. These nuances will have existed for other verbs, too, but are not expressed in the hieroglyphs. Note that the duplicated form of *dj to give* is written  or  *giving* or *given* and transliterated as *dd*.

9 Transliterate and translate these verbal adjectives of weak verbs.

a 

b 

c 

The plural forms can have the ending *.w* and *.yw* in the masculine as in  *dd.w giving* or *given*. The feminine ending of verbal adjectives for both the singular and plural is *.t*, for example  *s:mn.t establishing* or *established*, sometimes also written with the plural strokes, such as 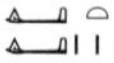 *dd.t which are given*. However, the plural strokes and the endings *.w*, *.yw* and *.t* are regularly omitted in hieroglyphs. In order to help the reader understand the grammar better, you can add them in the transliteration, just as you do with normal adjectives.

10 Complete the transliteration by using the correct form of the verbal adjective.

a 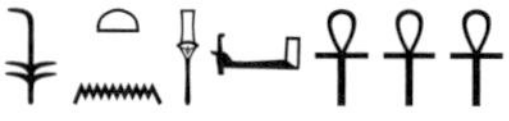 *njswt* ______ *ʿnḫ.w*

b  *njswt* ______ *m s.t-Ḥrw*

c 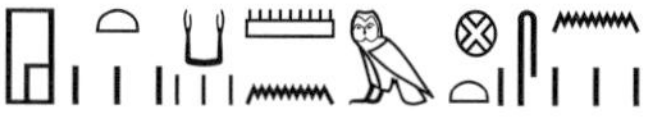 *ḥw.wt-k3* ______ *m njw.t=sn*

d  *ḥw.t-nṯr* ______ *m jnr*

e  *z3.t* ______ *rn n jt=s*

f  *hp.w* ______ *m t3.wj*

11 Translate the phrases in exercise 10. Try both active and passive voice and then decide which option makes better sense.

STATEMENTS USING A NOUN

When the Egyptians want to say *A is B*, they can set *A* and *B* side by side without an equivalent of *is*. In the example from Amenhotep's scarab, the first noun *rn* takes the additional expression of possession *n jt=s of her father*.

 *rn n jt=s Ywy3* *The name of her father is Yuya.*

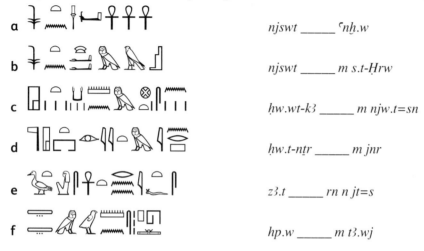

From a grammatical point of view, you could also translate the phrase with *The name of her father Yuya*, *The name of her father and Yuya* or *The name of her father or Yuya*. However, in the context of Amenhotep's inscription it is probably best to translate it with *The name of her father is Yuya*. The construction ***A B*** *A is B* is common in short statements, involving the name of an individual. It can also express past tense, depending on context: *The name of her father was Yuya.*

12 What do you think these sentences mean? In your translation, add a form of *to be*, where necessary.

a  *Ṯwjꜣ rn=ṯ*

b  *jt=j Ptḥ*

c  *Jmn-ḥtp nb=n*

d  *Jmn-Rꜥ njswt nṯr.w*

To express *He (she, it) is A*, the Egyptians use *pw* after the noun *A*. Again, the sentence can refer to the past or present.

 *ḥm.t=f pw* *She is (was) his wife.*

Adjectives depending on the noun and expressions of possession usually follow *pw*.

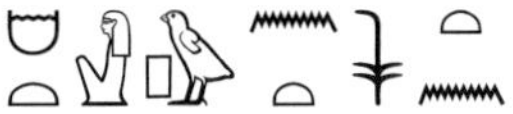 *ḥm.t pw n.t njswt* *She is (was) the wife of the king.*

 *ḥm.t pw wr.t* *She is (was) the great wife.*

13 Place the words in hieroglyphs in the correct order and transliterate.

a 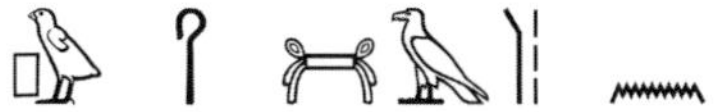 *He is a ruler of the Asiatics.*

b  *He was his strong son.*

c  *She is a wife of the king; her name is Tiy.*

d 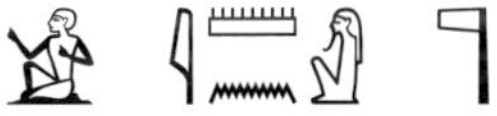 *Amun is my god.*

14 Now have a go yourself. Transliterate and translate these statements using a noun.

a 

b 

c 

d 

Explore

If you visit the cities of Europe and the United States – London, Paris, Rome, New York – you will come across obelisks that originally belonged to the temples of ancient Egypt. Obelisks are usually made from one single block of stone inscribed with a royal name and just a few formulaic phrases. They are powerful markers of royal presence and were also held in high esteem as a currency of imperial claims after Pharaonic times. The Roman emperors Constantius II and his successor Theodosius I removed an obelisk of Thutmosis III from Karnak to Alexandria, and from there to Constantinople, the capital of the Byzantine empire and modern Istanbul. This is where the obelisk still stands today (pictured). The obelisks in other cities have their own stories to tell, about competing nation states in 19th-century Europe and their claims to power over Egypt at the time. Using what you have learned in this unit, go through the titles and names of Thutmosis III written on the obelisk of Istanbul shown below.

1 Which of the five royal titles is missing?

2 Transliterate and translate the names of Thutmosis one at a time.

- **a** Begin with the Horus name. Use the scarab of Amenhotep III as a guide.
- **b** Next, try the *njswt-bjt* name. Use the vocabulary builder to help you.
- **c** The Golden Horus name consists of two phrases. Treat them one after the other.
- **d** The Two Ladies name begins with *who endures of*. Complete the remaining part.

The following lines are taken from a hymn dedicated to King Senwosret III. The original text was handwritten on papyrus and was found at an ancient town, which today is referred to as Lahun. The first line says *wr.wj nb n njw.t=f How great is the lord of his town*. The lines after that are indented on the papyrus and introduced with *jsw Indeed, …* Don't worry if you don't understand all the hieroglyphs and words straight away. In this section, we are asking you to try something different and see whether you can apply your knowledge to a new text, much as an Egyptologist would do. The questions below are designed to help you.

3 We can only speculate about the occasions for which the hymn was composed. What do you think is more likely, a one-off occasion or a ritual purpose?

4 Why do you think lines 2 and 3 were indented?

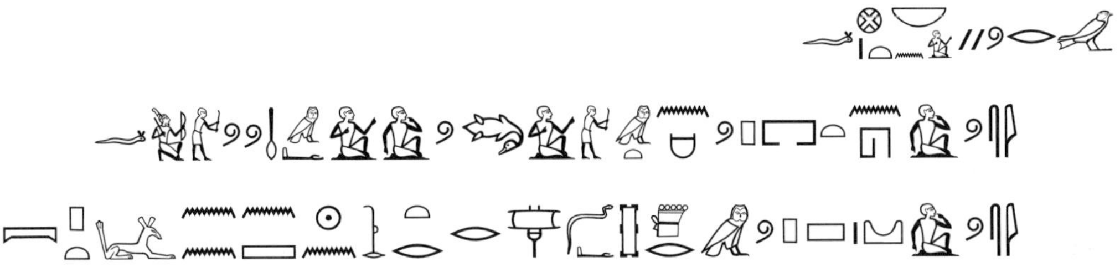

(1)

(2)

(3)

5 Try to figure out the meaning of a new sign typical of hieratic handwriting on papyrus.

a Which sign stands for *w* in *wr.wj* in line 1 and *jsw* in lines 2 and 3?

b Which sign would you expect here instead?

6 Read out the transliteration of lines 2 and 3 below and try to match it with the hieroglyphs. Some signs are used as sound signs, others as picture signs and others again as classifiers.

(2) *jsw nh.t pw nḥm.t snḏw m-ꜥ ḫrw=f*

(3) *jsw ḏw pw mḏr ḏꜥ r tr n nšnn p.t*

7 Have a look at the new words in the text. They will help you to answer the next few questions.

(2) *nh.t a shelter, nḥm to protect, snḏw the fearful, m-ꜥ from, ḫrw foe*

(3) *ḏw mountain, mḏr to resist, ḏꜥ storm, tr time, nšnn raging, p.t sky*

8 Investigate the sentence patterns in lines 2 and 3. Make use of the grammar you have learned in this unit.

a Which word appears in the first half of all lines, apart from *jsw*?

b Now translate the first three words of each line.

9 Have a closer look at line 2, which contains another grammar phenomenon you have learned in this unit.

a Which form is *nḥm.t*: past tense, infinitive or a verbal adjective?

b Why does it have a feminine ending?

c Translate *nḥm.t*.

d Translate the line beginning with *nḥm.t*.

10 Now have a go at translating line 3 by yourself. It has the same structure as line 2.

Drawing hieroglyphs

1 Here are a few more hieroglyphs that you can learn how to draw.

a 

b 

2 If you wish to practise your drawing skills further, copy lines 1 and 6 of Amenhotep's inscription in hieroglyphs.

Test yourself

1 Find a fluent wording for the translation of these royal names, which include an adjective modified with a noun.

a Horus name of Thutmosis II:  *K3-nḫt Wsr-pḥtj*

b Horus name of Pepi II:  *Nṯrj-ḫʿ.w*

c Horus name of Antef II:  *W3ḥ-ʿnḫ*

2 Translate these royal names that include a verbal adjective.

a  (Horus name of Mentuhotep III, see illustration at beginning of this unit)

b  (Horus name of Ramses II)

3 Translate the following statements that use a noun.

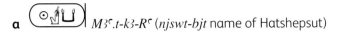

a  *M3ʿ.t-k3-Rʿ (njswt-bjt* name of Hatshepsut)

b 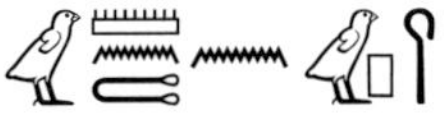 *ḥq3 pw n mnṯ.w*

SELF-CHECK

	I CAN
○	read typical royal names
○	modify the meaning of adjectives
○	translate verbal adjectives
○	make a statement using a noun

8 Corridor to Africa

In this unit you will learn how to:

- **read historical inscriptions**
- **translate numbers and dates**
- **express different tenses**
- **make a descriptive statement.**

THE FIRST CATARACT

Km.t (*Egypt*) was a hub of exchange between the Near East, the Mediterranean and Africa. The archaeologist William Adams famously called Nubia, the area between modern Aswan and Khartoum, the 'corridor to Africa'. Ancient Egyptians saw Nubia as inferior to Egypt and called its southern part, the area also known as Upper Nubia, *K3š ẖzj.t* (*wretched Kush*). However, Nubia was home to the highly developed Kerma culture (2,200–1,500 BCE), the Napatan kingdom (800–300 BCE), and the empire of Meroe (300 BCE–350 CE). In fact, you could describe Nubia and Egypt as twin civilizations, one depending on the developments of the other. In administrative terms, the Egyptian *t3š* (*border*) was located at the First Cataract, in ancient times a rapid south of modern Aswan, shown in the photo above. When the level of the Nile was at its lowest, it was almost impassable by boat. One might assume that this border divided people into those living north and those living south of it. However, as in many modern societies, geography does not always map on to the culture. Archaeological evidence shows that the entire area around the First Cataract, from Lower Nubia right to the southern area of Upper Egypt, was a zone of ethnic interaction, just as it is today.

1 What can you deduce from the classifiers in the words for *Egypt* and *Kush*?

2 What do you think the classifier × could possibly signify in the word ?

Vocabulary builder

1 Read these new words aloud.

	*ḥm*	*Majesty*
	*wḏ*	*to decree; stela* (inscribed with a decree)
	*mr*	*canal*
	*pn*	*this*
	*m m3w.t*	*as something new*
	*w3j.t*	*road, passage*
	*wḏ3*	*to travel*
	*ḫntj*	*to sail upstream* (= *to sail south*)
	*m-ḫt*	*after*
	*s:ḫr*	*to make somebody fall, to smite*
	*K3š*	*Kush*
	*ḫzj*	*wretched*
	*s:wsḫ*	*to make broad, to extend*
	*t3š*	*border*
	*Km.t*	*Egypt*
	*rdj* (rédee)	*to cause; to give*
	*jyj* (éeyee)	*to come* (*m from*)

INSIGHT

K3š (*Kush*), and names of countries generally, is a feminine noun even if it does not have a *.t* ending. Thus, *wretched Kush* is written 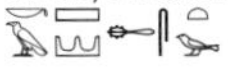 *K3š ḫzj.t* rather than *K3š ḫzj* in Egyptian.

LANGUAGE INSIGHT

The verb *rdj* is the longer stem of *dj*, both meaning *to give* and *to cause*. Whenever *rdj* / *dj* is followed by another verb, it usually means *to cause (that somebody does something)*, whereas when it is followed by an indirect object introduced with *n to, for*, there is a good chance that it means *to give*.

2 Word types and classes of verbs help you understand and translate Egyptian sentences. Group the new words in the vocabulary of this unit according to the categories below.

a nouns: ______, ______, ______, ______, ______, ______, ______, ______

b adjective: ______

c weak verbs: ______, ______, ______

d causative verbs: ______, ______

e regular verbs with two or three letters: ______, ______

3 Complete this table to learn how to compare the spelling of words you already know with alternative ways of writing those words.

	known	new	transliteration	translation
a	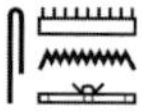	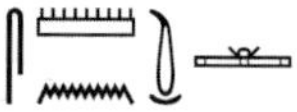	*s:mn*	__________
b			__________	*name*
c			*dj, rdj*	__________

4 Here is a list of new signs used in this unit. Try to complete the transliteration of the signs by studying the vocabulary list.

a  (canal) *m*___

b  (path with shrubs) *w*___ ___

c  (fire drill) ___*ꜣ*

d 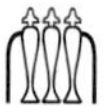 (jars in a rack) ___ *n* ___

e  (cup) *w* ___*ḫ*

f  (kiln) *t* ___

g  (crocodile scales) ___ *m*

h  (launderer's club) ___ *m*

i  (reed with legs) ___ *y*

5 Try to guess what these new classifiers relate to, by looking at their shape and the words in which they are used. Match them with their correct meaning.

a  *BAD*

b  *ENEMY*

c  *SAILING*

d  *STELA*

THE CANAL INSCRIPTION OF SENWOSRET III

In the later Middle Kingdom (*c.*1800 BCE), Egyptian kings exhibited an increased interest in exploiting the natural resources of Lower Nubia, particularly the gold mines in the Eastern Desert. The island of Sehel is located in the First Cataract and had long been a stopover for expeditions to Nubia. Beginning in the Old Kingdom, kings and officials inscribed their names and titles on the surfaces of the granite blocks lying on the island. In one of them, Senwosret III (1870–1831 BCE) describes the digging of a canal. In the accompanying image, he is depicted standing opposite the goddess Satet. Satet is one of the main deities of Elephantine, the next biggest town in the area.

1 First, look at the depiction of Senwosret III. Which crowns is he wearing?

2 What does the label written next to his name say?

3 In which line below the depiction is the name (*rn*) of the canal written?

Language discovery

1 Try to figure out how the numbers in the inscription work by answering these questions.

a Which year of the reign of Senwosret is the inscription dated to, according to the first line?

b The lower three lines record the (4) length, (5) width and (6) depth of the canal measured in 𓂣 *mḥ* (*cubits*, *c*.50 cm). Where are the numbers written in these lines?

c How long, wide and deep was the canal? Try to work out which hieroglyph stands for which number.

2 Tenses are less clearly expressed in Egyptian than in English. Have a look at the forms of the verbs used in the inscription of Senwosret.

a Complete the transliteration of the sentences and phrases. Look up the new signs and verbs in the vocabulary if you need to.

i ______-*kꜣ.w-Rꜥ*	*May-the-ka-souls-of-Ra-appear* (name of Senwosret III)
ii ______ *ḥm=f*	*His Majesty decreed*
iii ______ *mr*	*that a canal will be made*
iv *m-ḫt* ______ *ḥm=f*	*after the travelling of His Majesty*
v *m* ______	*while sailing south*
vi *r* ______ *Kꜣš ẖzj.t*	*in order to smite wretched Kush*

> **LANGUAGE INSIGHT**
> The ending 𓏏 after 𓁹 stands for *.tw*. This element indicates passive voice; compare for example *jrj=f he makes* and *jrj.tw=f he is made.*

b Concentrate on the phrases i–iii first. Which Egyptian verbs express past tense and which ones future tense?

c Which of the phrases iv–vi say that something has happened, is happening or will happen?

3 The name of the canal *Nfr-wꜣj.wt-Ḫꜥj-kꜣ.w-Rꜥ ḏ.t* **introduces a new sentence type. Have a go at the translation to see whether you can identify a pattern.**

a Translate the sentence first, word for word.

b Now try to turn your word-for-word translation into a coherent sentence by adding a form of the verb *to be*, where you think it might be needed.

NUMBERS

The Egyptians counted in single units, tens, hundreds, thousands, ten thousands and millions. Here are the hieroglyphs used to express these numbers.

	one		thousand		million
	ten		ten thousand		
	hundred		hundred thousand		

Egyptian numbers usually follow the words counted and are arranged from highest to lowest. The counted word is often written in the singular, but we translate it in the plural in English.

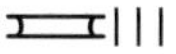 *mr 3* *three canals*

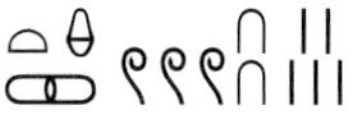 *tꜣ 325* *325 loaves of bread*

In the offering formula you will often find the preposition *m* used after the number 1,000 (*ḫꜣ*), literally meaning *one thousand of*. You can omit *of* in the translation.

 *ḫꜣ m kꜣ ꜣpd* *one thousand oxen and fowl*

4 Transliterate and translate the following:

a 

b  (the upper sign means *zp times*)

c 

d 

DATES

The dates in Egyptian inscriptions combine the regnal year of the king with the season, month and day of the calendar year. The Egyptian year had 365 days. It was grouped into three seasons, each having four months of 30 days, plus five additional days at the end of the year. The seasons were called *ꜣḫ.t inundation*, *pr.t growing* and *šmw harvest*. Originally they coincided with the agricultural seasons, but over the centuries they migrated across the year because the Egyptian calendar had no leap year. You will sometimes also find the translation *winter* for *pr.t* and *summer* for *šmw*, although this is misleading.

Season	*ꜣḫ.t* inundation				*pr.t* growing				*šmw* harvest				---
Days	30	30	30	30	30	30	30	30	30	30	30	30	5

Dates are expressed in this form: *regnal year: number – month: number, season, number of day – under His/Her Majesty XY*. The Egyptian words used to express dates are:

-  *rnp.t-zp regnal year* (literally year of (cattle) counting)
-  *ꜣbd month*
- 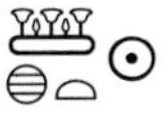 *ꜣḫ.t inundation*,  *pr.t growing* (winter), 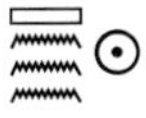 *šmw harvest* (summer)
- 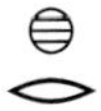 *ḫr under*

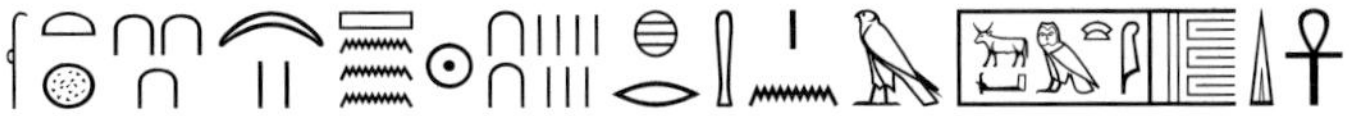

rnp.t-zp 3 ꜣbd 3 pr.t 26

ḫr ḥm n njswt-bjt Nbw-ḫpr-Rꜥ zꜣ-Rꜥ Jnj-jt=f dj ꜥnḫ mj Rꜥ ḏ.t

Regnal year 3, month 3 of growing, (day) 26

under the majesty of the king of Upper and Lower Egypt Nebu-kheper-Ra, son of Ra Intef given life like Ra forever

LANGUAGE INSIGHT

Egyptologists have suggested different transliterations for *rnp.t-zp*. You will find *ḥꜣ.t-zp* and *ḥsb* in the literature, both derived from spellings in texts of the late first millennium BCE and from Coptic. Whatever the correct transliteration, there is agreement that it means *regnal year* from the Middle Kingdom onwards.

The full pattern is not always used. In the inscription of Senwosret III above, for example, only the regnal year is indicated.

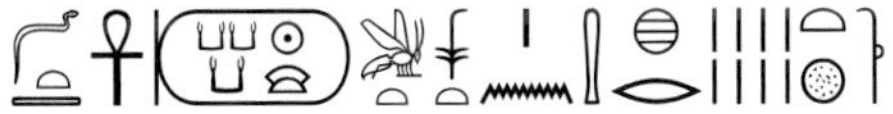

rnp.t-zp 8 ḫr ḥm n njswt-bjt Ḫꜥj-kꜣ.w-Rꜥ ꜥnḫ ḏ.t

Regnal year 8 under the majesty of the king of Upper and Lower Egypt Khai-kau-Ra who lives forever

5 Translate the following dates, but transliterate them first to help with your translation.

a 

b 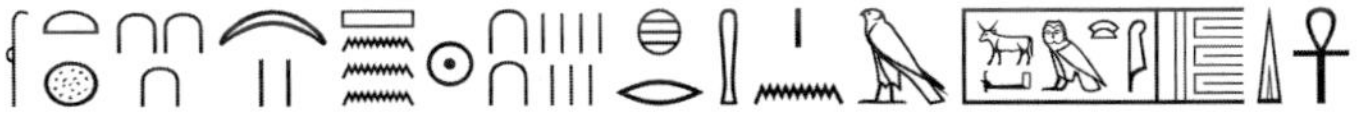

c 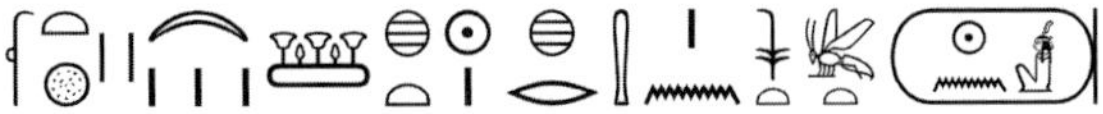

Nj-Mꜣꜥ.t-Rꜥ Ra-belongs-to-Ma'at is the name of king Amenemhat II (1911–1877 BCE)

LANGUAGE INSIGHT

The group *dj ꜥnḫ* is typical after royal names. It is variously understood as either *who gives life*, meaning that the king is a life-giving source, or *(who is) given life*, which refers to depictions of the king receiving life from the gods.

PAST, PRESENT AND INTENDED FUTURE

In Unit 6 you learned that the Egyptians attached *.n* to the end of a verb to express past tense, for example *s:wsḫ.n=f he extended*. However, verbs can also be used without *.n* to express past tense, present tense or the intended future in English. Intended future is different from simple future as the action is projected only, not definite. This is usually translated with *may*.

 *wḏ=f* *he decreed, he decrees, he may decree*

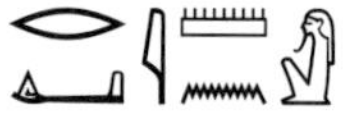 *rdj Jmn* *Amun gave, Amun gives*

The forms of some verbs show variation in different tenses. For example, the stem *rdj* is used for past and present tense, whereas the shorter stem *dj* is used for the intended future.

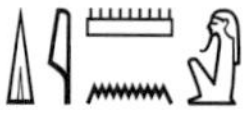 *dj Jmn* *Amun may give*

Which tense is most appropriate in translation depends on context and interpretation. In the narration of a tale, for example, you would normally use past tense in English. In a royal inscription, you could interpret the form *wḏ=f* as recording history (*he decreed*) or making a timeless statement (*he decrees*).

6 Transliterate these sentences.

a 

b 

c 

d 

7 Translate the sentences in exercise 6 with the following tenses.

a 6a with intended future

b 6b with present tense

c 6c with past tense

d 6d with intended future (*m ḥtp in peace*, i.e. *in safety* or simply *safe*)

In most cases, Egyptian verbs have no particular form to indicate the tense, apart from *.n* for past tense. However, there are a few rules that help with recognizing the tense. One is the use of the intended future after *rdj to cause*, *wḏ to decree* and other words that imply future action. The intended future is then translated with *that*.

 *wḏ ḥm=f jrj.tw mr*

His Majesty decreed that a canal be made.

8 What are these sentences saying? Find the verbs *wḏ* and *rdj* and use the intended future in your translation for the verbs that follow them.

a 

b 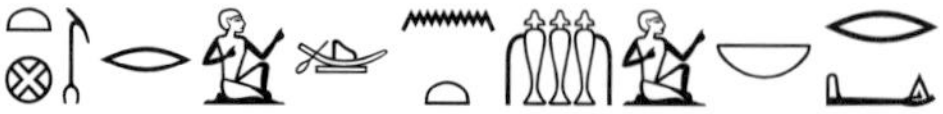

RELATIVE TENSES

You can express action in absolute terms, as in the examples above, as well as relative to the main tense of the sentence. Typical examples in English are *while trying, by doing, after having returned* and *in order to make*. Similarly, in Egyptian, you use a preposition followed by the infinitive to express relative tenses. Popular prepositions are *m in*, *ḥr on*, *r towards*, and *m-ḫt after*.

	*m jyj.t*	*while going*	relative present
	*ḥr rdj.t*	*while giving*	relative present
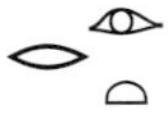	*r jrj.t*	*in order to make*	relative future
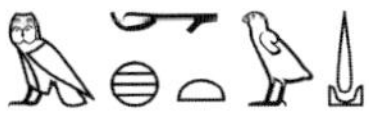	*m-ḫt wḏ3*	*after having travelled*	relative past

Both *m* and *ḥr* express the relative present. The difference is that *m* is typically used with verbs of motion, such as *going, sailing, travelling, coming*, etc., whereas *ḥr* is used with other verbs.

The infinitive can be followed by a noun or an attached pronoun and is then often better translated with a separate clause in English.

m-ḫt ḫntj ḥm=f	*after the travelling South of His Majesty* → *after His Majesty had travelled South*
r s:ḫr.t=sn	*in order to smite them*

LANGUAGE INSIGHT

Like the infinitive of weak verbs, the infinitive of causative verbs with two letters ends in ⌓ *.t*, for example  *s:ḫr.t smiting.*

9 Complete the transliteration and then translate. Since you do not know the context of these sentences, you can translate them with past tense, present tense or intended future.

a 

_____=*f ḥr* _____-*Ḥrw* _____ _____ *ḫ3s.t nb.t*

b 

_____ *ḥm=f* _____ _____ *m* _____ *r K3š*

c  (*jz* tomb)

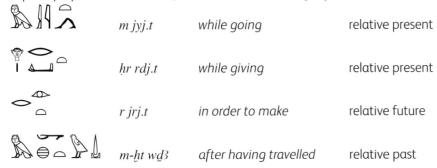

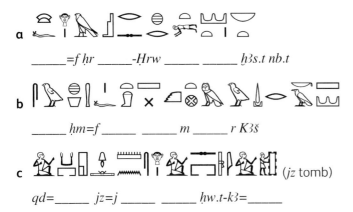

*qd=*_____ *jz=j* _____ _____ *ḥw.t-k3=*_____

DESCRIPTIVE STATEMENTS

In English, descriptive statements combine a form of the verb *to be* and an adjective. An example of this would be 'She *is tall*'. There is nothing special about this type of statement in English, but in Egyptian it follows a specific word order. Descriptive statements begin with an adjective in Egyptian followed by the subject, whereas in English the subject comes first, followed by the form of *to be* and the adjective.

 *wr mnw njswt*

Word-for-word translation: *Great monument king.*

Fluent translation: *The monument of the king is great.*

Descriptive statements are tenseless in Egyptian. Decide from the context which form of *to be* fits best: present tense *is* or past tense *was*. The Egyptian adjective always takes the masculine singular form in descriptive statements.

 *nfr wꜣj.wt*

Word-for-word translation: *Good roads.*

Fluent translation: *The roads are (were) good.*

Word order and the masculine singular form of *nfr* tells you that this phrase does not mean *the good roads* because this would require *nfr* to go after *wꜣj.wt* and take the feminine plural form.

Keep an eye on word order in Egyptian. Since the Egyptians did not use full stops, word order helps you establish where a sentence begins and ends. For example, only word order can tell you that the example above – *wr mnw njswt* – makes a coherent statement and is not a string of unrelated words.

10 Why does word order matter? Look at these phrases and sentences and see what a difference it makes to translation. Then match the phrases in transliteration with their correct translation.

a *Kꜣš ḫzj.t*	*Kush is wretched.*
b *ḫzj Kꜣš*	*wretched Kush*
c *nḫt ḥqꜣ.w n.w ḫꜣs.wt*	*The rulers of the foreign countries were strong.*
d *ḥqꜣ.w nḫt.w n.w ḫꜣs.wt*	*the strong rulers of the foreign countries*
e *ʿꜣ mnw ḥḏ nfr jnr*	*The monument of bright beautiful stone is great.*
f *ʿꜣ mnw n jnr ḥḏ nfr*	*The bright monument is great and the stone is beautiful.*

11 Transliterate and translate, keeping word order in mind.

a  (*r* more than)

b 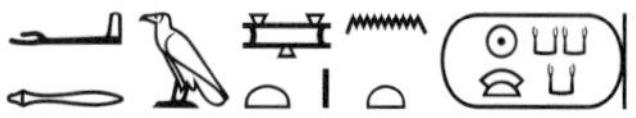

Explore

In the New Kingdom, Pharaohs extended their control into Upper Nubia and Egyptians started settling there permanently. Egyptian-style temples served as the arenas of royal display. The text below is inscribed on a stela of Amenhotep II (1427–1400 BCE). The stela originally stood in the temple of Amada dedicated to the Egyptian gods Amun and Ra-Horakhti. The deities are depicted in a barge in the upper part of the stela. This might indicate that the cult in the temple involved processions on the River Nile. Amenhotep II says that he has enlarged an earlier temple built by Thutmosis III at the site. The tone of the inscription is otherwise violent. As a demonstration of his power, Amenhotep hanged six captives head down from the top of the walls of Thebes, when he returned from a campaign in Syria, and a seventh at Napata, the capital of Upper Nubia.

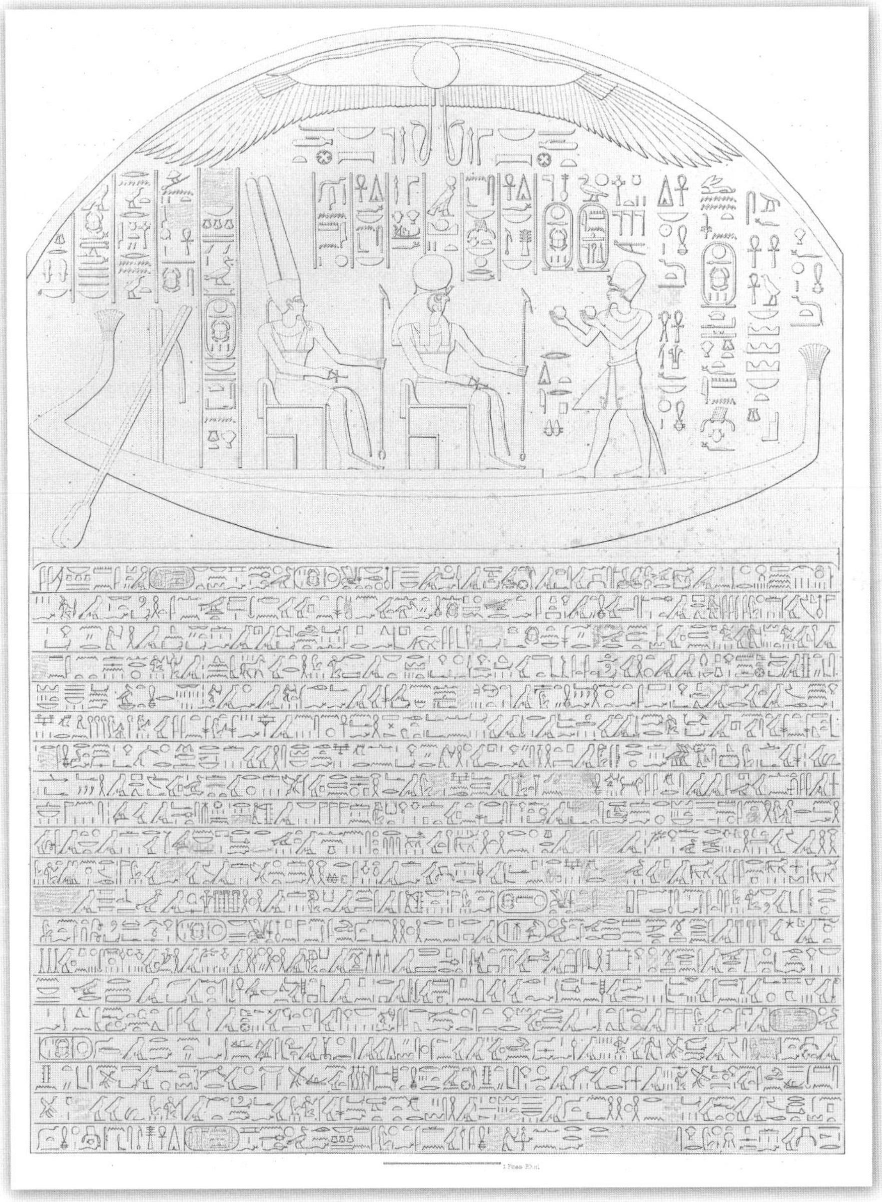

Read the passage below taken from the stela and answer the questions.

1 Which year in the reign of Amenhotep is the text dated to?

2 In which line does the inscription speak about the stela on which it is written?

3 Where does it say that the *tꜣš.w Km.t* borders of Egypt were extended?

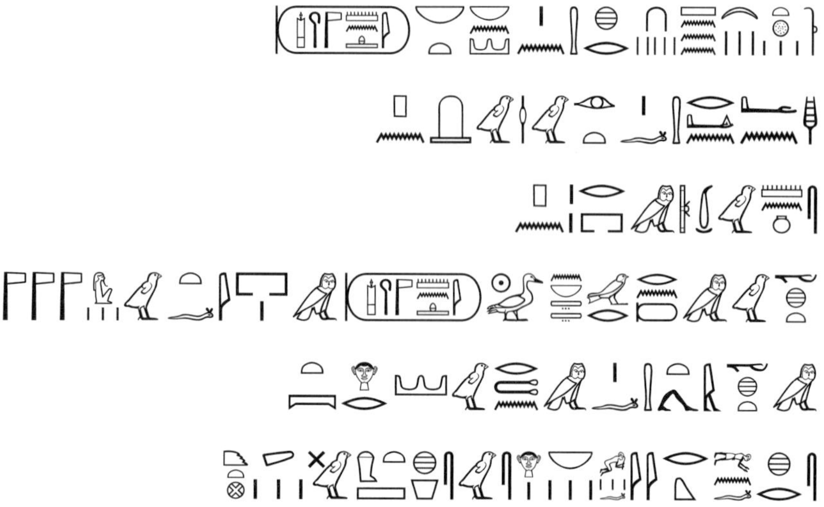

(1)
(2)
(3)
(4)
(5)
(6)

4 This is a longer passage of text that combines many of the things you have already learned. Try to transliterate and translate it step by step, using the following questions and annotations to guide you.

- **a** Begin with the date and name of Amenhotep II in the first line. The final sign in the cartouche means *Jwnw Heliopolis*, today a suburb of Cairo where a temple for the sun god Ra was located.
- **b** Continue with line 2. The first word is which means *ꜥḥꜥ.n then.*
- **c** Transliterate as much as you can of line (3).
- **d** The first word of line 3 is a verbal adjective ending in *.w*. Given that it follows *this stela*, do you think it expresses active or passive voice in the context of this text?
- **e** Translate line 3. The phrase *rꜣ-pr* means *temple*.
- **f** Transliterate line 4. The first word is a form of the verb *ḫtj to inscribe* (*m with*). The word *pr* means *house* or, just like *rꜣ-pr*, *temple*.
- **g** Translate line 4. Notice that it has a similar structure to line (3).
- **h** Transliterate and translate line 5. The final two words mean *Rṯnw ḥrj.t Upper Syria*.
- **i** The new word in line 6 is *rqy.w enemies*. Transliterate and translate the line.

Drawing hieroglyphs

1 Exercise your drawing skills and try to draw the following hieroglyphs, which are used in the words *ḫntj*, *s:ḫr* and *wꜣj.t*. Follow the step-by-step guide.

a 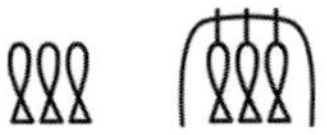

b 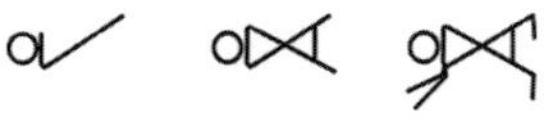

c 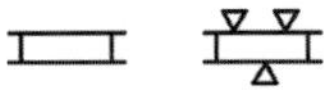

2 Now try to write the upper three lines of the Sehel inscription of Senwosret by yourself.

Test yourself

1 Transliterate and translate.

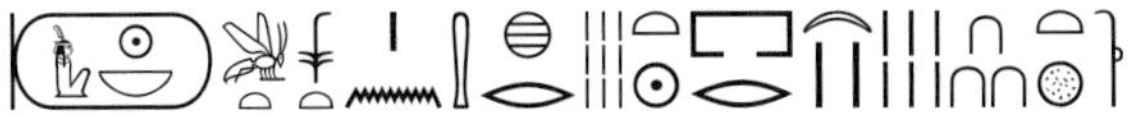

2 Translate these sentences, using the correct tense for the verbs underlined.

a *rdj.n Jmn-ḥtp jrj.tw mr m mꜣw.t*

b *wḏ=f ḫntj=sn r Kꜣš ḫzj.t r dꜣr ḥqꜣ.w*

c *jrj.n n=f ḥm=f mnw pn ḫr s:wsḫ tꜣš.w Km.t*

3 Match the hieroglyphs and their transliteration with their correct translation.

a 

nfr rn wr n ḥm=f

the beautiful and great name of His Majesty

The great name of His Majesty is beautiful.

His Majesty has a great, beautiful name.

b 

nb=j pw ḏsr ḫꜥ.w

The crowns of my lord are sacred.

He is my lord with sacred crowns.

the sacred crowns of my lord

SELF-CHECK

	I CAN
●	read historical inscriptions
●	translate numbers and dates
●	express different tenses
●	make a descriptive statement

9 Religious life

In this unit you will learn how to:

- **read simple prayers**
- **create adjectives from nouns and prepositions**
- **make a statement that expresses circumstances**
- **recognize different types of sentences.**

ENCOUNTERING THE GODS

The ancient Egyptians created images to represent their gods on earth, for example little figurines, temple statues, and depictions on temple and tomb walls. Of all these forms, the temple statues were the most exclusive and magnificent. They were made of metal and precious stones and must have left a strong impression on the ancient Egyptians, who would rarely come across these materials in their daily lives. However, temple statues were kept in the inner part of the temples, hidden from public view. Commoners had few opportunities to see the temple statue of a deity. They would usually give *jꜣw* (*praise*) to the gods at the outer enclosure walls of large temples, hoping that the gods would listen to their *njs* (*prayer*), as the carving in the photo shows.

An occasion where people could approach a god directly was a public procession, when the statues were carried out of the temple. The procession of *Jmn-Rꜥ ḫntj Jp.t-s.wt* (*Amun-Ra, Foremost of Luxor*), the best example that we know about, was particularly spectacular, a joyful and exciting event for the participants. Whereas prayers and processions are fairly formalized ways of interacting with the gods, archaeologists have also found small community shrines crowded with simple votive objects and personal jewellery. This shows that people from all levels of society could enjoy a close relationship with their gods outside the large, state-run temples.

1 Look at the hieroglyphs for *jꜣw* and *njs*. What do their classifiers tell you about the body gestures which the Egyptians used, when they approached the gods?

2 Which adjective means *foremost* in Egyptian?

Vocabulary builder

1 Read these new words aloud.

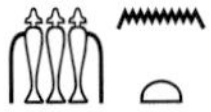	*ḫnt*	*front*
	*Jp.t-s.wt*	Luxor
	*jꜣw*	*praise*
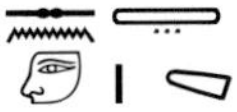	*sn-tꜣ*	*to pray*, literally *to kiss the ground*
	*sḏm*	*to hear, to listen to*
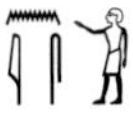	*njs*	*prayer*
	*mꜣꜥ*	*just person*
	*tp*	*head*
	*jb*	*heart* (perhaps meaning *guts*, but traditionally translated as *heart*)
	*ẖr*	*under* (often in the sense of *loaded with something* or *carrying something*)
	*ḥꜣtj*	*heart* (exact difference between *jb* and *ḥꜣtj* not clear)
	*nn*	*not*
 or 	*grg*	*falsehood*
	*jm=*	*in*; form of the preposition *m* before an attached pronoun, e.g.  *jm=sn in them*
	*sḏm-ꜥš*	*servant*
	*ḥꜣ.t*	*front*

LANGUAGE INSIGHT

The word *jꜣw praise* can be written in different ways: with the seated or standing man praying ; with phonetic complements ; and without plural strokes  and .

LANGUAGE INSIGHT

The word *mꜣꜥ* means *true, just* (see Unit 2) when used as an adjective. However, it can also be used as a noun without changing its form or taking additional endings, either in hieroglyphs or in transliteration. In the English translation, you need to add *one* or *person* and an article so that it makes sense, for example *the just one* or *a just person*. This rule also works for other adjectives, for example 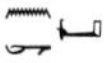 *nḫt* meaning *strong* as an adjective and *a strong one* or *a strong person* as a noun. Ideally, but not necessarily, a scribe would add the classifier of a seated man when the word was used as a noun, as in 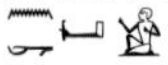.

	*nfrw*	*beauty, perfection*
	*dwꜣ*	*praise*
	*ḥtp*	*to go down* (used of the sun)
	*nḥy*	*request*
	*snmḥ*	*prayer*
	*ḥr*	*face*
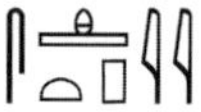	*s:ḥtpj*	*to satisfy* (with an offering)
	*rꜥ nb*	*every day*

2 Two of the new words in the vocabulary list look identical to words you have already learned, but have a different meaning. Add the two meanings to the list below to make sure that you try both translations whenever you come across these words in a text.

		transliteration	known meaning	new meaning
a		*ḥtp*	__________	__________
b		*ḥr*	__________	__________

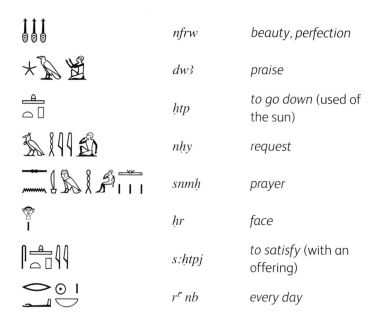

3 Study the vocabulary and use it to work out the correct transliteration of these new signs.

a (socle): *m* or *d*?

b (heart): *ḥꜣt* or *jb*?

c (foreleg and head of a lion): *ḥꜣt* or *ḥꜣtj*?

d (arms in gesture of negation): *nm* or *n*?

e (pick and basin): *gr* or *grg*?

f (ear): *ḏm* or *sḏm*?

g (butcher knife): *nm* or *mḥ*?

h (domed structure): *jpt* or *swt*?

i (man in praying gesture): *jꜣw* or *jwꜣ*?

j (two strokes): *w* or *j*?

k (head): *ḥr* or *tp*?

l (star): *dwꜣ* or *dꜣw*?

4 There are a few words in this unit that you know already, but which are written in a new way. Compare the known and the new spelling and try to work out what the words mean. Then complete the table.

	known	new	transliteration	translation
a	,	or	________	________
b		or	________	________

THE PRAYER OF MERI-WASET

Mry-Wꜣs.t (*Meri-Waset*) lived during the late New Kingdom in a village that we know as Deir el-Medina today. The village is located in the cliffs of the Theban west bank and is shown in the photo. It was built to accommodate the skilled craftsmen for the royal tombs located in the Valley of the Kings; see the map in Unit 5. Meri-Waset held the title of *sḏm-ʿš m s.t Mꜣʿ.t servant in the Place of Truth*, which was typical among the craftsmen. The phrase *Place of Truth* is perhaps the ancient name of Deir el-Medina, or it refers to the royal tomb or the cemetery more generally. Be this as it may, Meri-Waset recorded one of his prayers on a stela, which we are going to look at. On the stela, he is depicted praying to a barge, which is carried by several *wʿb*-priests, whose titles are written on their robes. These low-ranking *purification* priests assisted with temple rituals and were employed on a rotating basis throughout the year. One of their duties was to help with temple processions, for example during the so-called *Beautiful Feast of the Valley*. During these processions, the statues of deities from temples on the east bank were carried over to the west bank, where Meri-Waset and others could put forward their prayers and ask questions of the god. The statue would 'reply' by moving and leaning towards an answer with the help of the priests carrying it.

The inscriptions on the stela are rearranged below, to help you recognize the hieroglyphs more easily. Read through them carefully and then try to answer these questions.

1 What is line (10) in which the title and name of Meri-Waset is written saying? Try a transliteration and a translation.

2 According to the label written in front of the barge, which deity is Meri-Waset praying to?

Label written in the column in front of the barge from left to right:

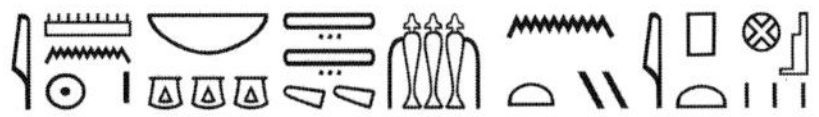
(1)

Labels in front of Meri-Waset:

(2)

(3)

Meri-Waset's prayer written above him:

(4)

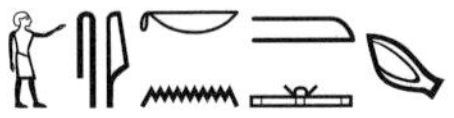
(5)

(6)

(7)

(8)

(9)

Meri-Waset's name and title in the final column:

(10)

3 What is Meri-Waset doing? In order to answer the question, transliterate and translate the label written in front of him. In the transliteration, add the ending *.t* **of** *rdj.t*, **which is omitted in hieroglyphs.**

Language discovery

1 Revisit lines 1 and 6 of the prayer of Meri-Waset and try to work out how the Egyptians created adjectives from prepositions and nouns.

a Compare the hieroglyphs in both these lines with their transliteration and translation.

(1) *Jmn-Rꜥ nb ns.wt tꜣ.wj ḫntj Jp.t-s.wt Amun-Ra, lord of the thrones of the two lands who is related to the front of Luxor.*

(6) *jnk mꜣꜥ ḥrj-tp tꜣ I am a just person who is on the head of the earth.*

> **LEARNING INSIGHT**
> Ancient scribes made mistakes, just as we do today. On the stela of Meri-Waset, the phrase  is a typo. The correct form is  and means *jnk I am.*

b What do you notice about the ending in the transliteration of *ḫntj* and *ḥrj*?

c How is this ending written in the hieroglyphs of *ḫntj* as compared to *ḥrj*?

d How are these two adjectives translated?

e Try to find a better wording for the translation of these adjectives.

2 Go back to lines 8 and 9 of the hieroglyphic text and investigate how the Egyptians used phrases with a preposition in these sentences. What do you have to add in the English translation to make them into complete sentences?

(8) *jb=j ẖr mꜣꜥ.t*	*My heart __________ under truth.*
(9) *ḥꜣtj=j nn grg jm=f*	*My heart, not __________ falsehood in it.*

3 The sentences in lines 4, 5 and 7 begin with a verb. Look up any new words in the vocabulary list and then have a go at their translation and transliteration.

ADJECTIVES ENDING IN –*j*

The Egyptians added the ending –*j* to nouns and prepositions to create new adjectives. In hieroglyphs, this ending is often written with the dual strokes \\. Since –*j* is a semi-consonant, it is sometimes omitted in the original hieroglyphs, but should be added to the transliteration. An English equivalent would be the adjective *cloudy,* derived from the noun *cloud.* However, a literal translation with –*y* of adjectives in –*j* often sounds awkward in English or is even impossible, for example '*fronty*' derived from the noun *front.* A good way of finding a better translation in English is to translate the word provisionally with *who is* or *which is* for prepositions and *who is related to* or *which is related to.* Then review your translation and the context and look for a more adequate wording in English.

Adjective ending in –*j* derived from a preposition

	*ḥr*	*upon*
 ,  or 	*ḥrj*	*who* or *which is upon* → *upper* or often simply *upon*

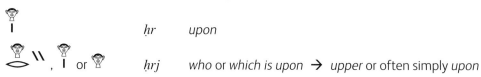

Adjective ending in –*j* derived from a noun

 *ḫnt* *front*

 or 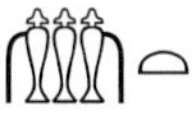 *ḫntj* *who* or *which is related to the front* → *foremost*

LANGUAGE INSIGHT

The ending –*j* is called a 'nisbe'. It is a typical feature of Near Eastern languages such as Arabic, Hebrew, or Akkadian, a language spoken in ancient Mesopotamia.

4 Follow the examples of *ḥrj* and *ḫntj* above and fill in the gaps in this table to uncover the meaning of these adjectives ending in –*j*.

a		________	*god*
		*nṯrj*	________ → ________
b		*njw.t*	________
	 or 	________	________ → ________
c		*ẖr*	________
		________	*who* or *which is under* → *lower*

5 Now have a look at these examples of adjectives ending in –*j* in context. Try to find a fluent translation, after you have transliterated the phrases.

a 

b 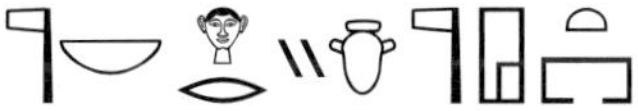

c 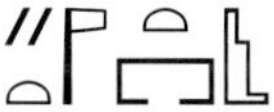

d  Note:  *jmn.tjw the Westerners* (= the dead)

STATEMENTS EXPRESSING CIRCUMSTANCES

Statements that describe the circumstances of somebody or something are called adverbial sentences. Examples in English are *My bike is in the shed* and *My bike was in it*. Like English ones, Egyptian adverbial sentences begin with the subject followed by an adverbial phrase – that is, a preposition combined with a noun or pronoun (*in the shed* and *in it*). The only difference from English is that the form of *to be* is not written in Egyptian. You need to infer it. In your translation, choose the past or present tense from the verb – whatever you think is most appropriate to the specific context. In the following examples, the adverbial phrase is underlined to help you find it in the transliteration and translation.

	*Jmn m ḥꜣ.t*	*Amun is (was) at the front.*
	*Jmn jm=s*	*Amun is (was) there* (literally *at it*).

Circumstantial statements are negated with *nn not*. This negation is placed at the beginning of the sentence in Egyptian. The following examples are translated with the present tense to keep them simple, but past or future tense is also possible.

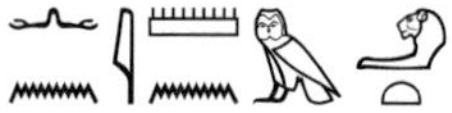	*nn Jmn m ḥꜣ.t*	*Amun is (was) not at the front.*
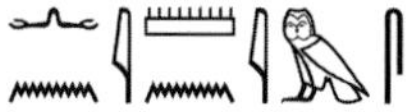	*nn Jmn jm=s*	*Amun is (was) not there* (literally *at it*).

6 Rearrange the words in transliteration, into their correct order, to match the hieroglyphs. Then translate these circumstantial statements with whichever tense you think fits best.

a  *=j =j ḥꜣ.t ẖr ḫʿ.w*

b  *ʿnḫ.w tꜣ ḥr nb.w*

c  *njswt =j nb m*

d 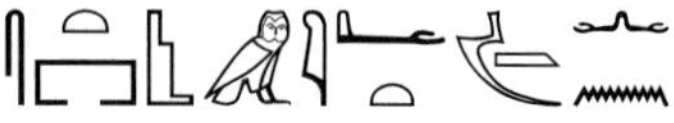 *s.t mꜣʿ.t m =s nn*

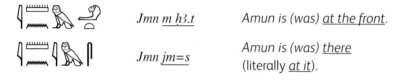

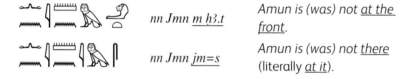

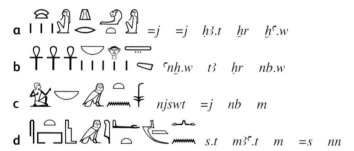

REVIEW OF SENTENCE TYPES

In English, you can usually speak without having to think much about which word comes where. As you have seen in previous units and in this unit, the position is different in Egyptian. The Egyptians had four basic types of sentence, each following specific rules for the order of words. If you are able to recognize them, you will find it easier to spot how a string of words comes together to form a coherent statement, for example where you have to insert a form of *to be* in English, when there is none in Egyptian, or where a new sentence begins.

The following review of sentence types you have already looked at does not offer any new grammar but is intended as a guide to help you to understand how Middle Egyptian differs from English. Each example shows a word-for-word translation into English and then a more coherent translation that demonstrates how you can switch the word order or where you need to add a word to make it read better.

Verbal sentences (see Unit 6) begin with a verb followed by the subject, which is either a full noun or an attached pronoun. Verb forms with *.n* express past tense and those without *.n* present tense, past tense or intended future. The following examples are translated with intended future because this is what the sentences were most likely to mean.

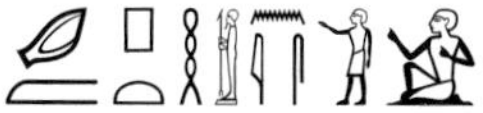

sḏm Ptḥ njs=j

listen Ptah prayer my → May Ptah listen to my prayer.

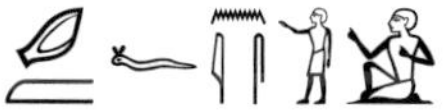

sḏm=f njs=j

listen he prayer my → May he listen to my prayer.

The other three sentence types do not begin with a verb and require the insertion of a form of *to be*. All can refer to statements in the past or present. Only present tense is used in the examples below, to keep it simple.

Nominal sentences make statements using a noun (see Unit 7). Either two nouns are set side by side or there is one noun only followed by *pw* meaning *he, she* or *it*.

Ywyꜣ rn=f

Yuya name his → His name is Yuya.

Ywyꜣ pw

Yuya he (she, it) → It is Yuya.

Adjectival sentences make a descriptive statement (see Unit 8). They begin with an adjective in Egyptian followed by a noun.

nfr wꜣj.t=f

perfect road his → His road is perfect.

Adverbial sentences make a circumstantial statement (see above). They begin with a noun followed by an adverbial phrase. Adverbial sentences are negated with *nn*.

grg m ḥꜣtj=j

falsehood in heart my → *Falsehood is in my heart.*

nn grg m ḥꜣtj=j

not falsehood in heart my → *Falsehood is not in my heart.* Or: *There is no falsehood in my heart.*

7 Study the following sentences and identify which sentence type they belong to. Then choose their correct translation from the two options offered.

a  *Jmn-Rꜥ pw sḏm snmḥ*

It is Amun-Ra who listens to the prayer.
This Amun-Ra will listen to the prayer.

b  *nfrw=k m ḥr=j*

You are as beautiful as my face.
Your beauty is in my face.

c  *sn-tꜣ=ṯn n Ptḥ*

May Ptah pray for you.
May you pray to Ptah.

d  *jyj.n=j r ḥw.t-nṯr=k sḏm=k njs=j*

I have come to your 'listening temple' in order to pray.
I have come to your temple. May you listen to my prayer.

e  *nn twt m jz=f ḥrj jmj-wrt Wꜣs.t*

There is no statue in his tomb, which is on the west bank of Thebes.
There is no statue in his upper tomb on the west bank of Thebes.

f  *Jmn-ḥtp rn=f wḥm tꜣ.w nb.w rn pn*

Amenhotep, his name is repeated by all these lands in his name (= on his behalf).
His name is Amenhotep. May all lands repeat (= say repeatedly) this name.

Explore

We know many prayers from the time of the New Kingdom because they are inscribed on tomb walls and stelae found at Thebes. Most of them are restricted to simple phrases. Others outline in quite some detail the individual circumstances of the worshipper. In 1911, the Egyptologist Adolf Erman called this phenomenon 'personal piety'. Despite the Christian undertones it had at the time, the term is still used to express the intimacy with which the gods are approached.

The following passages are taken from three prayers that belong in this context. First, go through the hieroglyphs and find signs and words that you already know. Next, try to transliterate and translate the prayers, keeping an eye on which sentence types are being used. The guidance below should help you to identify the key parts of the text and make the best translation you can.

1 Study this prayer of a scribe called Menna.

(1) 

(2) 

(3) 

- **a** Which deity is Menna praying to, according to the first line?
- **b** Complete the whole of line 1. *Wnn-nfr Wenennefer* is an epithet of Osiris and could be translated as *the good one exists* or *who exists well*, but it is usually not translated.
- **c** Have a go at line 2. The line begins with *jyj.n=j*. A second sentence starts at *jb=j*.
- **d** Now go to line 3 and transliterate it word for word.
- **e** For your translation of this line, switch the order of the words and add a form of *to be* where necessary.
- **f** Why do you think *ḥꜣtj* is placed at the front of this sentence?

2 Study this prayer of a painter called Pay.

(1) 

(2) 

- **a** In the first line, Pay explains the reason for his prayer. What does he wish to *mꜣꜣ see*?
- **b** Now go through line 1 again and try to transliterate and translate it.
- **c** For line 2, begin with the first few words and stop after *=f*, where a sentence ends.
- **d** The word  is written twice in the remainder of the line. It is a verbal adjective referring to *Rꜥ*. How do you translate it in both cases in this line?
- **e** Now complete the transliteration and translation of line 2.

3 **The prayer of Pa-en-nebu, who was a** *ḥrj jmnt.t Wꜣs.t* ***overseer of Western Thebes*****, is more complex. The transliteration is done for you, so you can concentrate on the grammar and the translation.**

> **WEB TIP**
> If you would like to see an image of this inscription, visit www.thebritishmuseum.org. Click 'Research' in the menu at the top of the page, then 'Collection online'. Type '8497' into the search field and select 'stela; 19th Dynasty; Deir el-Medina'. The text below is written on the back of the stela of which you can see a photo.

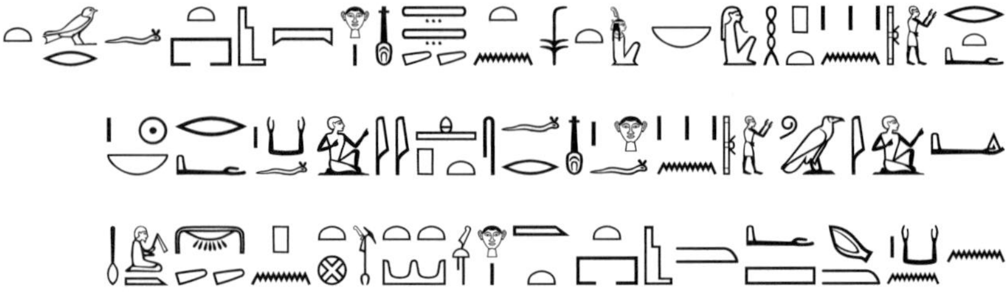

(1)

(2)

(3)

(1) *rdj.t jꜣw n Ptḥ nb Mꜣꜥ.t njswt tꜣ.wj nfr ḥr ḥrj s.t=f wr.t*

(2) *dj=j jꜣw n ḥr=f nfr s:ḥtpj=j kꜣ=f rꜥ nb*

(3) *n kꜣ n sḏm-ꜥš m s.t Mꜣꜥ.t ḥrj jmnt.t Wꜣs.t Pꜣ-n-nbw mꜣꜥ-ḫrw*

- **a** Which line contains the name and title of Pa-en-nebu?
- **b** Translate the final line, which is similar to the final line of Meri-Waset's prayer.
- **c** Compare the transliteration of lines 1 and 2 with the hieroglyphs and look up the meaning of words in the vocabulary list in this unit if you need to.
- **d** Now go to line 1 and translate it. It begins with a label followed by a series of epithets of the god Ptah, one including an adjective ending in *–j*.
- **e** In line 2, which words are verbs?
- **f** Split line 2 at the two verbs and then translate the two verbal sentences, adding *as* between them.
- **g** Read out the transliteration.

Drawing hieroglyphs

1 **Have a go at writing these hieroglyphs typically used in Egyptian prayers.**

a 

b 

c 

d 

Test yourself

1 Try to find a good translation for these adjectives ending in *–j* by looking at the meaning of the noun and preposition.

a noun:  *tp head* adjective:  *tpj* ___________

b preposition:  *ḫft opposite* adjective:  *ḫftj* ___________

2 Transliterate and translate these circumstantial statements.

a 

b 

3 Match the sentences with their correct sentence type.

a 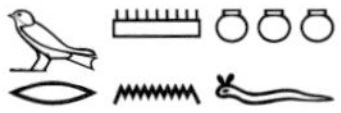

wr mnw=f His monument is great.

b 

rdj.n=j n=s jꜣw I gave praise to her.

c 

ḥw.t-nṯr jm=s A temple is in it.

d 

Jmn jt=j Amun is my father.

verbal sentence
nominal sentence
adjectival sentence
adverbial sentence

SELF-CHECK

	I CAN
●	read simple prayers
●	create adjectives from nouns and prepositions
●	make a statement that expresses circumstances
●	recognize different types of sentence

10 One god or many?

In this unit you will learn how to:

- **read Egyptian hymns**
- **translate the infinitive in a sentence**
- **express a state of being**
- **connect sentences fluently.**

THE THEOLOGY OF LIGHT

Many hymns of the 18th Dynasty praised the sun god Ra. The *wbn* (*rising*) of the sun in the east and its setting in the west were interpreted as a daily journey across the sky by Ra and other deities surrounding him. Towards the end of the 18th Dynasty, the 'heretic' king Akhenaten founded a new capital, which he called *ꜣḫ.t-Jtn* (Akhetaten, literally *Horizon-of-Aten*) to celebrate a new theology of light. Whereas previous kings saw the course of the sun as an interaction of Ra with other deities, Akhenaten believed that the sun disc *pꜣ Jtn* (*the Aten*) was alone. He thought that the *st.wt* (*rays*) of Aten would *s:ḥḏ* (*illuminate*) all the people and offer life to him, his wife Nefertiti and their children. This is depicted above in the drawing.

Owing to his new ideas, Akhenaten changed his birth name Amenhotep (*Amun-is-satisfied*) into Akhenaten (*Efficient-for-Aten*). His theology of light is often called 'monotheism', the belief in one god. However, outside the royal court, most people continued to worship the traditional gods. Akhetaten, located in Middle Egypt, is called Amarna today and the period of Akhenaten's reign is referred to as the Amarna period. This period ended shortly after the death of Akhenaten, when the kings of Egypt returned to worshipping many gods.

Why would you say that the *ꜣḫ.t* *horizon* is important to the new theology of light and sun?

Vocabulary builder

THE LIGHT OF THE ATEN

1 Read these new words aloud.

	*st.t*	*ray*
	*wbn*	*rise*
	*wꜣj*	*to be distant*
	*mꜣ*	*to see*
	*wꜥj*	*to be alone*
	*ḫprw*	*manifestation*
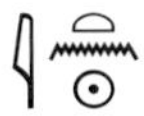	*jtn*	*sun disc*
	*ꜣḫ.t*	*horizon*
	*jꜣb.t*	*east*
	*ꜥn*	*to be beautiful* (i.e. beautiful to look at)
	*tjt*	*image*
	*ꜣḫ*	*efficient*
	*s:ḥḏ*	*to illuminate* (literally *to make bright*)

2 Investigate how words that you know already can be written differently by completing this table and answering the question in 2c.

	known	new	transliteration	translation
a			___________	*sky*
b			___________	___________

c The verb *to see* has three stems in Egyptian: *mꜣꜣ*, *mꜣ* and *mꜣn*. The stem *mꜣn* is typically used for the intended future (*mꜣn=f He may see*) and the stem *mꜣ* in the past tense (*mꜣ.n=j I saw*). Why do you think *mꜣꜣ* is called a geminating form of *mꜣ*?

ATEN KEEPS NATURE ALIVE

3 Read these words aloud.

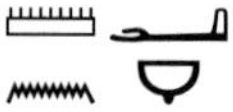	*mnꜥ*	*to nurse*
	*šꜣ*	*field*
	*rwḏ*	*to grow*
	*tr*	*season*
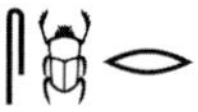	*s:ḫpr*	*to make exist*
	*s:qb*	*to make cool*
	*mḥ*	*to fill*

4 **Look at the list of new words again and focus on these new sound signs. Match them with their correct transliteration.**

a	 (lasso)	*st*
b	 (pool with lilies)	*tr*
c	 (scarab)	*šꜣ*
d	 (harpoon)	*tjt*
e	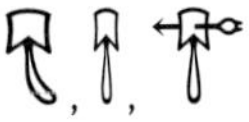 (cow hide, with and without arrow)	*ḫpr*
f	 (whip)	*wꜥ*
g	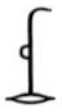 (palm rib over mouth)	*jꜣb*
h	 (part of eye make-up)	*ꜣḫ*
i	 (sun between eastern and western desert mountain)	*tj*
j	 (standard)	*mḥ*
k	 (pestle)	*wꜣ*
l	 (crested ibis)	*ꜣḫt*

5 **Find these new classifiers within the vocabulary and look closely at what they depict. Try to match them with their correct meaning.**

a		LIGHT
b		FEEDING
c		STATUE
d		ROAD
e		COOL WATER
f		LOOKING

THE GREAT HYMN TO THE ATEN

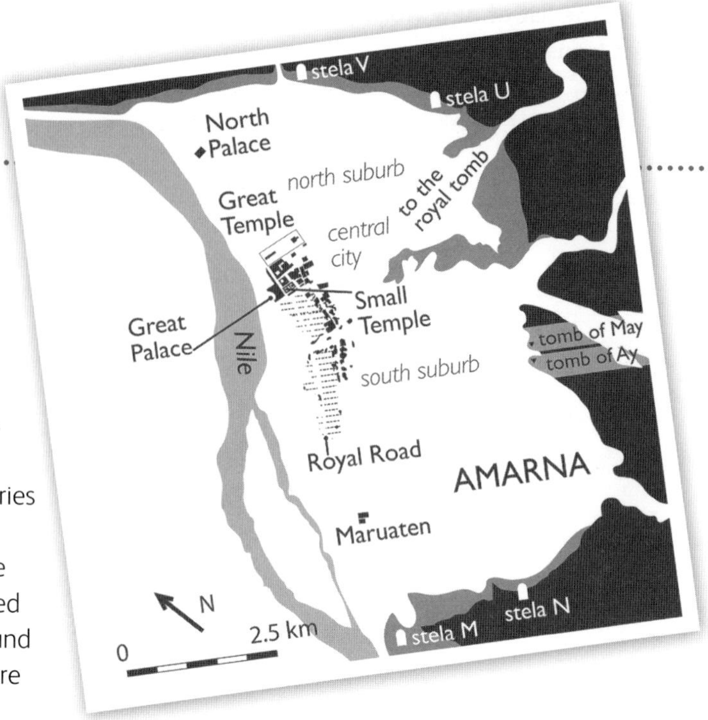

Akhetaten was laid out as a gigantic cult stage for the theology of light. It was located in a natural bay formed by the rock cliffs of the Eastern Desert. Several stelae were carved into the cliffs and across the river into the Western Desert plateau to delineate the boundaries of Akhetaten. The inscriptions on the stelae describe the major temples of the city, many of which have been discovered by archaeologists. The temples were found to have open courts, where offerings were presented to the light of the sun.

The most elaborate manifesto of the new theology is what we call the Great Hymn to the Aten. Originally perhaps sung for the Aten, it was found inscribed on the entrance walls of the rock tomb of Ay, one of the highest-ranking officials during the Amarna period. Ay later became king himself, but then abandoned the new capital. He left his tomb there unfinished and returned to the old gods. Akhetaten is today one of the best-preserved cities of ancient Egypt. Apart from the palaces and temples, it has extensive living quarters, which are not mentioned in the inscriptions on the boundary stelae nor in the hymn.

Read through the passage of the Great Aten Hymn below and try to answer these questions.

1 Do you think that the text speaks about the daily journey of the sun god from *east* to *west*?

2 In which line does the text speak of the Aten being *alone*?

(1) 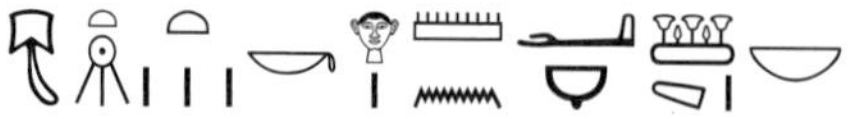

(2) 

(3) 

(4) 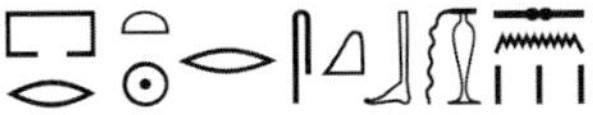

(5) 

(6) 

(7) 

(8) 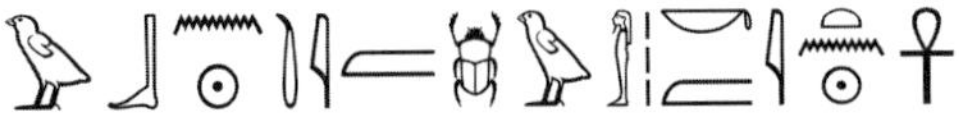

LANGUAGE INSIGHT

The phrase  *jry=k nb* means *everything you have made.*

3 Focus on lines 2 to 6 and try to work out the overall subject by looking at the words used.

Language discovery

1 Try to find the best translation of the infinitive used in the sentence in line 1 of the hymn. Follow these steps to help you.

a Transliterate the line. You will find any new words in the vocabulary section.

b Now translate the line word for word.

c Finally, work out how you would say this sentence in fluent English.

2 Go through lines 7 and 8 of the hymn and focus on the verb patterns.

a Look at the two hieroglyphs after the verbs *wꜥj* and *wbn*. How would you transliterate them?

b Judging from the context of the preceding lines, do you think that this ending means *I*, *you* or *they*?

3 Line 2 begins with two sentences that are literally translated as *You rise. They live.* How could you possibly connect the statements in the English translation to express the intention of the scribe better?

STATEMENTS USING THE INFINITIVE

Middle Egyptian has several options for expressing action. The one you have learned so far is in a verbal sentence that begins with the verb. Another option is to place the subject first and then add a preposition and an infinitive. The prepositions 𓅓 *m* and 𓁷 *ḥr* indicate that the action happens at the same time as the action in the previous sentence, whereas 𓂋 *r* refers to future action. Before verbs of motion, *m* implies action in the near future, as in English *I am coming down*. A good way of translating these types of sentences is to start with a word-for-word translation first and then to try to transform it into a fluent statement, as shown below. Use the present or past progressive in English for sentences with *m* and *ḥr* and the future tense for those with *r*.

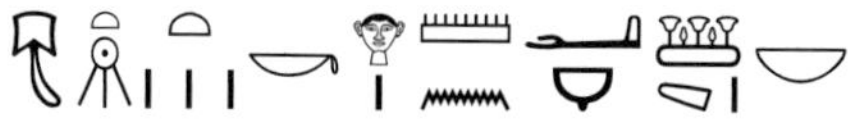

st.wt=k ḥr mnꜥ šꜣ nb

Word for word: *rays your upon nursing field every*

Fluently: *Your rays are nursing every field* or *Your rays were nursing every field.* The choice of tense in the translation depends on which tense has been used in the sentence before this one.

st.wt=f r s:ḥḏ tꜣ.wj

Word for word: *rays his towards illuminating the two lands.*

Fluently: *His rays will illuminate the two lands.*

Statements using the infinitive in the way described here are called 'pseudoverbal construction' in Egyptology. This is because, on the level of meaning, they describe action just as verbal sentences do. However, in terms of sentence structure in the Egyptian text, they follow the word order of adverbial sentences, in which the subject is followed by a preposition and a noun. In fact, grammatically speaking, the infinitive is a noun with verbal meaning and is therefore translated literally as *nursing*.

4 Try to find a fluent translation for these sentences, which all contain examples of the infinitive. You can follow the steps for translation described previously, to help you.

a  *st.wt=k r s:qb=n*

b  *Ptḥ ḥr sḏm=sn*

c  *ḥm=f m ḫntj*

Sentences using an infinitive are often introduced by  *jw* (éeoo). This word might mean something like *truly* or *definitely*, but most Egyptologists do not translate it.

jw st.wt=f r s:ḥḏ tꜣ.wj

His rays will illuminate the two lands.

jw=sn r s:ḥḏ tꜣ.wj

They will illuminate the two lands.

5 To get used to how *jw* works and which prepositions express which tense, try to fill the gaps in the following sentences in the transliteration.

a *The Aten is rising in the eastern horizon (= the horizon of the east).*

_____ *pꜣ Jtn* _____ *wbn m ꜣḫ.t* _____

b *He will rise in it.*

jw= _____ _____ _____ *jm=* _____

c *They are filling the two lands with his rays.*

_____ = _____ _____ *mḥ* _____ *m* _____ = _____

d *I am coming to see his image.*

_____ = _____ _____ _____ *r* _____ *tj.t=* _____

6 Now look at these sentences. Find the infinitive after the prepositions *m*, *ḥr* and *r*.

a 

b 

c 

d 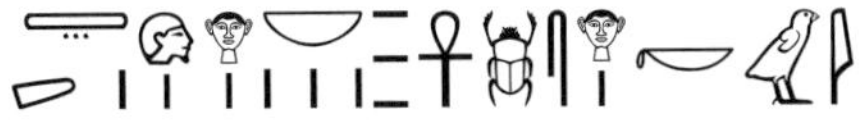

7 Go back to exercise 6 and try a transliteration and translation.

EXPRESSING STATE OF BEING

Egyptian verbs have a specific set of endings that express a state of being in the past or present, rarely also in the future. Grammarians refer to these verb forms as the 'stative'. It is particularly popular with verbs which describe a state of being, such as *w3j to be distant*, *ꜥn to be beautiful* or *wꜥj to be alone*. The endings are separated with a full stop in transliteration. Their form depends on the preceding word, which functions as their subject. For example, when the subject is the first person singular, *I*, then the ending of the stative is also first person singular. The stative is preceded by *jw*, when the subject is an attached pronoun.

Have a look at how the stative works in transliteration, to understand how the endings change depending on the subject. The following table shows the endings, using the verb *w3j* as an example. The subject and the endings are marked in bold to show how they agree in person, gender and number.

singular (sg)		plural (pl)	
*jw=**j** w3j.**kw***	*I am distant.*	*jw=**n** w3j.**wjn***	*We are distant.*
*jw=**k** w3j.**tj***	*You are distant.* (masc.)	*jw=**ṯn** w3j.**tjwnj***	*You are distant.*
*jw=**ṯ** w3j.**tj***	*You are distant.* (fem.)		
*jw=**f** w3j.**w***	*He is distant.*	*jw=**sn** w3j.**w***	*They are distant.*
*jw=**s** w3j.**tj***	*She is distant.*		
*(jw) **Jtn** w3j.**w***	*Aten is distant.*		

Many adjectives can be used as a verb and then appear in the stative, for example *ḏsr sacred* and *jw=s ḏsr.tj It is (was) sacred*. When the stative is used with verbs that express action, such as *wbn to rise*, it implies the result of this action. For example, *jw=k wbn.tj* literally means *you are risen*, i.e. *you are up (in the sky)*. Since the stative refers to a result of an action that has happened before, it is usually translated with the present perfect (*you have risen*) or, in narrative contexts, the past perfect (*you had risen*). The stative is the standard way of expressing the past tense of verbs of movement, such as *jyj to come*, for example *jw=j jyj.kw I have come*.

8 Complete the sentences in transliteration by deciding which pronouns and stative endings need to be added.

a *jw=______ ꜥn.______ You* (masculine singular) *are beautiful.*

b *jw ḥm.t-njswt wr.t ꜥn.______ The great queen was beautiful.*

c *p3 Jtn wꜥj.______ The Aten is alone.*

d *jw p.t w3j.______ The sky is distant.*

e *ḫꜥ.w=f ḏsr.______ nṯrj.______ His crowns are sacred and divine.*

f *jw=______ ḫꜥj.______ m s.t-Ḥrw I have appeared on the throne of Horus.*

In hieroglyphs, the semi-consonants *j* and *w* can be omitted in the endings of the stative. In the first person singular, a seated man is often added to the ending as a classifier, when a man is speaking. The list below shows a range of possible options for how the endings are written in hieroglyphs.

I	*.kw*	 or  or 
you (sing.), *she*	*.tj*	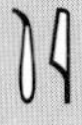 or  or 
he, they	*.w*	, often omitted in hieroglyphs

The forms of the first and second person plural are rare, but are listed here for the sake of completeness.

we	*.wjn*	
you (pl.)	*.tjwnj*	

9 Now bring all you have learned about the stative together and try to transliterate and translate the following sentences. Supply the correct endings in transliteration, when they are not spelled out in full in hieroglyphs.

a 

b 

c 

d 

e 

f 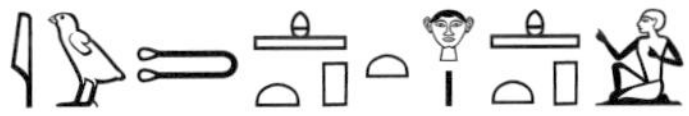

CONNECTING SENTENCES

English uses a variety of connectors between sentences to make a text fluent and coherent. Examples of connectors are *however, so, as, while, because*, and *and*. Egyptian has some of these words, too, but more often, connectors are not employed.

You can translate a text word for word and sentence by sentence and leave it there. However, your translation might lack the flow that you would expect from a text in English. To achieve greater fluency, you can add connectors to your translation. For example, connect two statements that you think are of equal importance with *and*. If you believe that one of them offers background information, you can translate it as a subordinate clause introduced with *as* or *when*. The form *sḏm=f*, for instance, is translated with *He listens* or *He listened* in a main clause as opposed to ... *as he listens* or ... *when he listened*, when interpreted as being part of a subordinate clause. When the same form expresses intended future, you translate it with *May he listen* in a main clause, whereas in a subordinate clause a translation with ... *so that he will listen*, which expresses purpose, often makes good sense. The form *sḏm.n=f*, which you have learned as meaning *He listened*, can also be translated with... *when he listened* or ... *after he had listened*. When a verb appears in the stative and is not introduced with *jw*, for example *wꜥj.tj* instead of *jw=k wꜥj.tj*, it has the meaning … *while you are alone* or … *being alone*. Similarly, adverbial sentences such as *jw=f m p.t* can be interpreted as main clause (*He is in the sky*) or subordinate clause (, … *while he is in the sky*).

Here is an example of different translations for line (2) of the Great Hymn to the Aten. The connectors are underlined in the translation. Many Egyptologists prefer the first option because the hymn praises the Aten by describing his activities, but the other translations are correct, too.

wbn=k ꜥnḫ=sn rwd=sn n=k

<u>When</u> you rise, they live <u>and</u> grow for you.

May you rise <u>so that</u> they will live <u>and</u> grow for you.

You rise <u>as</u> they live. May they grow for you.

10 Now go back to the Great Hymn to the Aten and transliterate and translate the entire text. Try to improve your translation by using connectors between the sentences as you think they suit the meaning of the text best.

Explore

There are more prayers and hymns to the Aten inscribed on the tomb walls of high officials at Amarna. The first of the two following texts is an excerpt from the tomb of an official called *May*. The second is the beginning of the Great Aten Hymn. You have translated another part of this text in the previous section.

Read through the hieroglyphs and try to answer the questions.

(1) 

(2) 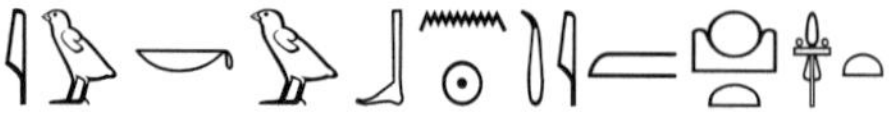

(3) 

(4) 

(5) 

(6) 

...

(7) 

(8) 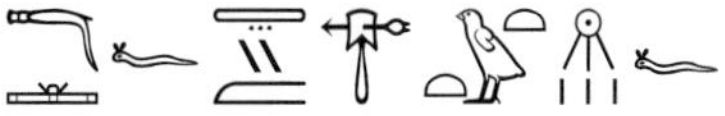

1 Judging from the pronouns and endings used, in which lines is the Aten addressed in the second person (*you*) and in which ones in the third person (*he*)?

2 Line 6 tells you who benefits from the light of Aten. Who could it be?

3 Transliterate and translate the entire text sentence by sentence. In line 1, translate *nfr* as *perfectly*. The phrase *jm=s* in line 7 refers back to the feminine noun *3ḫ.t-Jtn* *Akhetaten* mentioned in a section of the text before this one.

4 Now revise your translation to make it a fluent text.

The second text, the beginning of the Great Aten Hymn, is reproduced on the next page from its original publication. Concentrate on the column in the middle and try to answer these questions.

5 What do you note about the way the sign ⊙ is written in the text?

6 The column explicitly says for whom the Aten is shining. Can you find who it is?

7 Work your way through the second column word for word and transliterate and translate it up to *zꜣ=k*. This is where a new phrase, which is not further considered here, begins.

LANGUAGE INSIGHT

The modern copyist of the text wrote *sic* next to . In a correct spelling, this sign should be  because it is part of . *Sic* means *like this* and Egyptologists use this word to show that there is a mistake or anomaly in the ancient text.

8 Now try to turn your translation into a more fluent form.

Drawing hieroglyphs

1 Have a go at drawing the following hieroglyphs from the Great Hymn to the Aten.

a 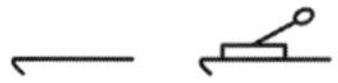

b 

2 Now try to reproduce lines (5) to (7) of the hymn in hieroglyphs.

Test yourself

1 What does the following sentence mean? Select the correct answer.

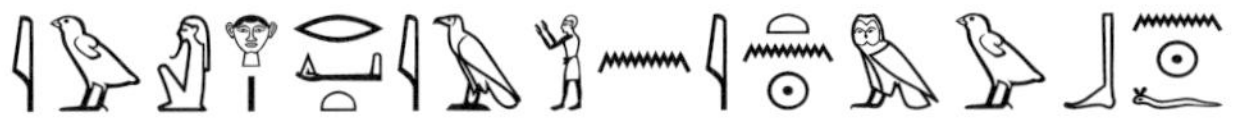

jw=j ḥr rdj.t j3w n Jtn m wbn=f

a *His Majesty is giving praise to the Aten. May he rise!*

b *I am giving praise to the Aten, while he rises.*

c *I will give praise to the Aten at his rising.*

d *I am on my face giving praise to the Aten, when he rises.*

2 Complete the transliterations and then translate.

a 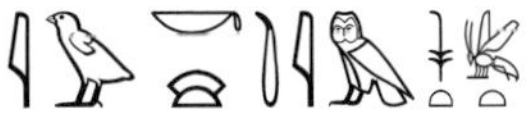 *jw=_____ ḫꜥj._____ m njswt-bjt*

b 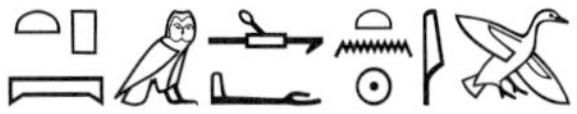 _____ _____ *wꜥj._____ m p.t*

c  *jw=_____ nfr._____*

SELF-CHECK

	I CAN
●	read Egyptian hymns
●	translate the infinitive in a sentence
●	express a state of being
●	connect sentences fluently

11 The negative confession

In this unit you will learn how to:

- **read the 'negative confession'**
- **express the passive voice**
- **negate action**
- **emphasize circumstances.**

JUDGEMENT IN THE AFTERLIFE

The Egyptians believed that they were judged in the afterlife for what they had done during their lifetime. According to the depiction above, they thought that their heart was weighed against justice in the hall of *mꜣꜥ.tj* (*double justice*). Justice was depicted by a feather or with a seated figure wearing a feather. Both symbolized the goddess of justice, Ma'at. The deceased were guided to a pair of scales by Anubis, the jackal-headed god of mummification, and then interrogated by a panel of deities, shown seated above the scales. They confessed that they *n* (*did not*) do anything *ḏw* (*evil*) or committed an *jsf.t* (*injustice*) against other people. Thoth, the Ibis-headed god of writing, recorded the confession on a papyrus scroll. After the judgement, the deceased were brought before Osiris, the lord of the netherworld who confirmed their righteousness.

The negative confession was part of a rich body of spells written on papyri, coffins and other objects placed in the burials of the rich. The spells include the names of deities, doors and gates that the deceased had to *rḫ* (*know*) if he or she wanted to be protected from demons. For this reason, these funerary texts have been described as a 'literature of knowledge', which the deceased could consult in their afterlife, distinct from tales and poems written for the entertainment of the living.

1 What might *mꜣꜥ.tj double justice* mean?

2 Why do you think the hieroglyph means *did not*?

Vocabulary builder

THE NEGATIVE CONFESSION

1 Read these new words aloud.

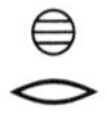	*ḫr*	*to* (e.g. come *to* somebody)
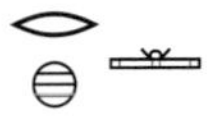	*rḫ*	*to learn, to know*
	*wn, wnn*	*to exist*
	*wsḫ.t*	*hall*
	*tn*	*this* (feminine form of *pn*)
	*m=k wj*	*Look, I ...* (at the beginning of a sentence)
	*dr*	*to repel*
	*jnj*	*to bring, to fetch*
	*jsf.t*	*injustice*
	*rmṯ*	*people*
	*n*	*do not, did not*
	*sm3r*	*to eat*
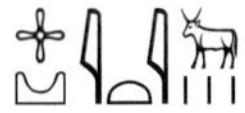	*wnḏw.t*	*offering bread*
	*jwy.t*	*bad*
	*bw*	*thing*
	*ḏw*	*evil*

LANGUAGE INSIGHT

The geminating verb *wn/wnn* has two stems, a simple one and one with duplicated, or 'geminating', final letter. The duplicating stem *wnn* is usually used in the infinitive and for the verbal adjective, whenever it expresses intense, repeated or continued action.

2 **What do you notice about the spelling of *m=k* in hieroglyphs?**

3 **The texts in this unit contain new spellings of vocabulary that you already know. Complete the table to make sure that you know how to transliterate and translate the words in their new spelling.**

	known	new	transliteration	translation
a			__________	*to grow, to be strong*
b			*m-ẖnw*	__________
c		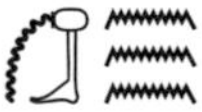	__________	__________
d			*grg*	__________

4 **Look at the shapes of these new signs and have a go at working out what they depict. If you find it hard to recognize what is depicted, describe what you see.**

a  *wn* __________

b  *jw* __________

c  *jn* __________

5 **Study the new words in section 1 above again and concentrate on the classifiers used.**

a What do you think  stands for?

b The sign  is sometimes used as a classifier replacing . Which word is written using it?

c The swallow with a forked tail  and the sparrow with a round tail  look similar, but have different meanings. Which of the two is a classifier meaning *small, bad*?

d Can you speculate why  is used as a classifier in the word *wsḫ.t hall*?

THE NEGATIVE CONFESSION IN THE BOOK OF THE DEAD

The Book of the Dead is a collection of funerary spells known from copies from the New Kingdom and later, with forerunners in the Middle Kingdom. Sometimes called the 'bible of the Egyptians', it was a guide for the deceased on how to live on in the netherworld. The spells contain a diverse range of texts, including protective spells against demons, hymns to the sun god and the negative confession. The Book of the Dead is not a book in the modern sense because it was written on papyrus scrolls. The number and order of spells vary greatly in the preserved copies, depending on the preference for specific spells by the owner. Papyrus was expensive and beyond the means of most Egyptians. Whether the Book of the Dead reflected common belief or only the ideas of the wealthy is difficult to say. The Egyptians certainly attached great value to it, which is why it was written in hieroglyphs, the typical script of monumental inscriptions, rather than in hieratic, the everyday script of accounts and letters.

As you can see in the example that follows, the hieroglyphs appear in a slightly abbreviated form called 'cursive hieroglyphs'. Different from the other texts you have studied so far, the individual signs in the Book of the Dead are arranged to be read from right to left, whereas the columns are read in the opposite direction, from left to right. This is called 'retrograde writing', which is otherwise typical of texts used for healing and witchcraft. It suggests that the Egyptians saw funerary literature as part of 'magical' practice.

The text reproduced here in standard hieroglyphs is taken from a spell numbered 125 by Egyptologists, which contains the negative confession.

1 Try to follow how cursive hieroglyphs and retrograde writing work. Find lines 4 to 8 of the text below in the three columns of the original text. Line 4 begins in the lower part of column 1, where the arrow is.

2 How does the phrase 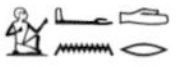 in line (6) differ from the original in cursive hieroglyphs?

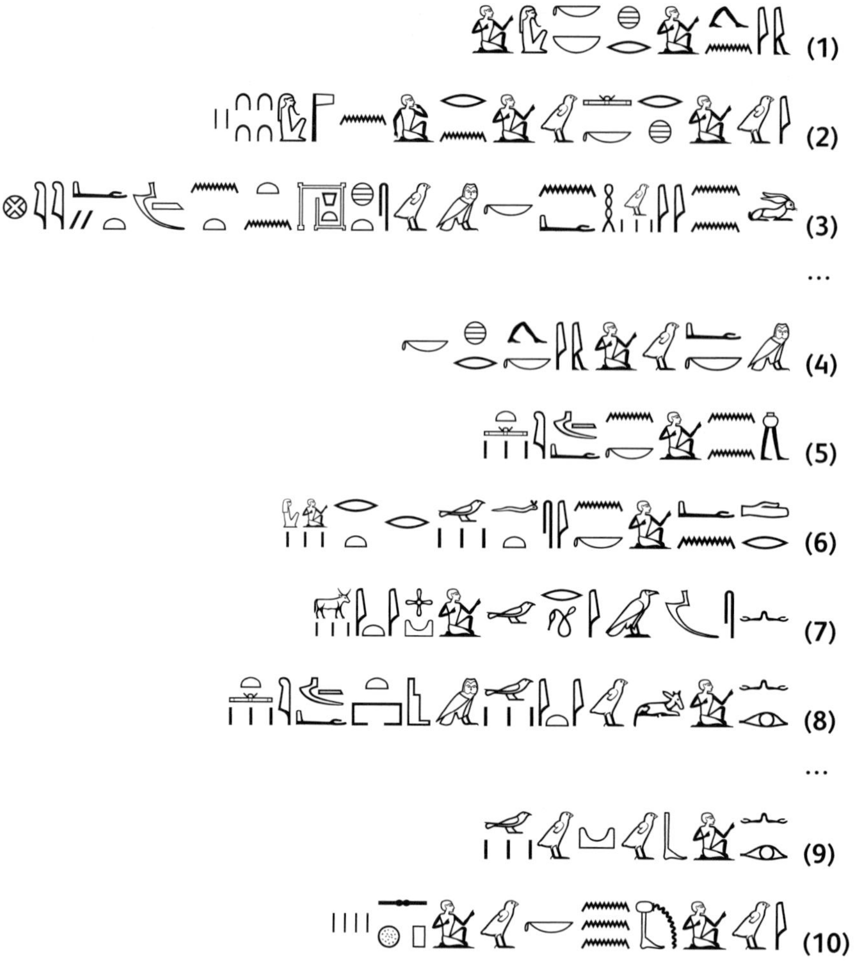

3 Line 1 says *I have come to you, my lord*. Who is speaking, and who do you think *my lord* is?

4 Can you see how many deities were on the judgement panel?

5 What does the deceased claim to know, according to line 2?

6 Which lines contain the negative confession, beginning with the negation *n*?

Language discovery

1 Compare the meaning of two verb forms in Middle Egyptian.

a How would you translate line 4, where [hieroglyph] after [hieroglyphs] stands for the ending *.kw*?

b Which form of the verb is used in line 1 and which one in line 4?

2 Does the negative confession, recorded in lines 7 to 9, refer to activities that the deceased has not done in the past or will not do in the future?

PASSIVE VOICE

The stative expresses a result or state of being, as you learned in the previous unit. However, it has another important function. It expresses the passive voice, whenever the meaning of a verb allows it. For example, when used in the stative, the verb *dr to repel* means *to be repelled* and the verb *jnj to bring* means *to be brought*. In contrast, the verb *jyj to come* has no passive voice in English, so you translate the stative of this verb with active voice.

jsf.t dr.tj *Injustice has been repelled.* (Not: *Injustice has repelled.)*

When the subject is an attached pronoun, it is preceded by *jw*.

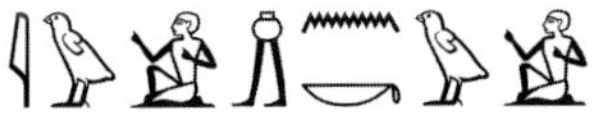

jw=j jnj.kw *I have been brought.* (Not: *I have brought.*)

You can replace *jw=j I* with *m=k wj Look, I …*

m=k wj wḏ3.kw *Look, I have travelled.*

Verbs that can be used in both the active and the passive voice, such as *to repel* and *to bring*, are called 'transitive verbs', whereas those that cannot are called 'intransitive verbs'. The stative of transitive verbs is always translated with the passive voice in English and the stative of intransitive verbs with the active voice.

3 Choose the correct translation of the sentences in transliteration, depending on whether the stative expresses active or passive voice in English.

a	*jw=k m3.tj*	You have been seen.	You see.
b	*jw=j gmj.kw*	I have found.	I have been found.
c	*jw=sn rwd.w*	They are strong.	They strengthen.
d	*jw=s s:ʿḥʿ.tj*	She has erected.	It has been erected.
e	*m=k wj rdj.kw*	Look, I have been given.	Look, I was giving.
f	*jw=f wbn.w*	He has risen.	He has been raised.

The verb *to know* can be used in both the active and passive voice in English, for example *you know* and *you are known*. However, in Egyptian, the stative of *rḫ* expresses active voice only. This is because *rḫ* literally means *to find out*, the result of which is rendered with the stative in Egyptian and is best translated with *to know*.

jw=j rḫ.kw rn n nṯr 42 I know the name of the 42 gods.

4 Transliterate and then translate these sentences which all use a form of the stative. Decide whether you need to use the active or passive voice in English.

a 

b 

c  *r more than*

d 

EMPHASIS

Emphasis lends meaning, rhythm and direction to an otherwise monotonous statement. In speech, you can raise your voice, pause artificially or underline your words with gestures. These oral techniques will have existed in ancient times, too, but were not recorded in writing.

However, in a few instances, it is clear from word order and the use of specific forms that certain elements of a sentence were emphasized. In Unit 9, you saw that a scribe could emphasize a word by placing it before the sentence and resuming it later, for example *jb=j nn grg jm=f My heart, no falsehood is in it*, where the emphasized word *jb=j* is later resumed with *=f*.

Another option is to employ specific forms of the verb. For example, the stative of verbs of motion (*coming, going, travelling*, etc.) expresses simple movement and its result. In contrast, the past tense with *.n* of the same verbs emphasizes the direction, purpose or circumstances of the movement typically expressed with an adverbial phrase, i.e. a preposition plus noun or pronoun or an adverb. You can translate the emphatic past, for example *jyj.n=j*, with *That I have/had gone is …* When used in this emphatic function, the *sḏm.n=f* form is never introduced with *jw*.

m=k wj jyj.kw ḫr=k Look, I have come to you. (Simple movement: stative of *jyj*)

jyj.n=j ḫr=k nb=j That I have come is to you, my lord. (Emphasis on direction: past tense of *jyj*)

In a string of sentences, the emphasis might not be placed on the adverbial phrase immediately following the verb, but on the following sentence. Here is an example from lines (1) and (2) of the negative confession. The emphasized sentence is underlined in translation.

jyj.n=j ḫr=k nb=j jw=j rḫ.kw rn n nṯr 42

I have come to you, my lord, <u>because I know the name of the 42 gods</u>.

If you wish to express the emphasis explicitly in the wording of your translation, you could rephrase the sentence:

That I have come to you, my <u>lord</u>, is only because I know the name of the 42 gods.

5 Go through these sentences and decide which translation is better, depending on whether stative or past tense with *.n* is used.

a 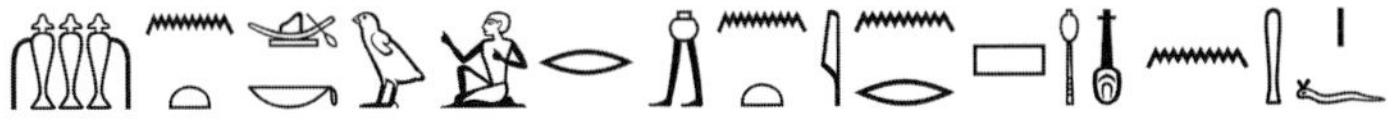

ḫntj.kw r jnj.t jnr ḥḏ nfr n ḥm=f

I have travelled south to fetch bright beautiful stone for His Majesty.

That I have travelled south is in order to fetch bright beautiful stone for His Majesty.

b 

jw m3ꜥ.t jyj.t r s.t=s

Ma'at has come (in)to its place.

That Ma'at has come is (in)to its place.

c 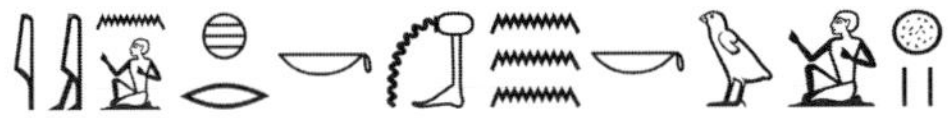

jyj.n=j ḫr=k wꜥb.kw zp 2

I have come to you, while I am pure, pure. (literally *pure two times*)

That I have come to you is only as I am pure, pure.

d 

wḏ3.n=f r jrj.t r3-pr pn

He travelled in order to build this temple.

That he travelled is to build this temple.

NEGATION OF ACTION

Action is negated with the word *n do not, did not*. This negation is placed at the beginning of a sentence. The major trick with *n* is what you might call 'tense swapping'. Whenever *n* precedes a verb in the past tense, for example *n sḏm.n=f*, it expresses present tense (*he does not hear*), whereas it expresses past tense (*he did not hear*) when it precedes a verb without *.n*, such as *n sḏm=f.*

n jrj=j bw ḏw *I* ***did not*** *do anything evil.*

n jrj.n=j bw ḏw *I* ***do not*** *do anything evil.*

6 Familiarize yourself with the concept of 'tense swapping' in both transliteration and translation. Negate the following sentences, making sure you use the correct tense in Egyptian.

a *sm3r.n=k wnḏw.t You have eaten offering bread.*

b *jnj=f n=k m3ˁ.t He brings you Ma'at.*

c *sḏm Ptḥ njs=j Ptah hears my prayer.*

d *s:ˁnḫ.n=j rn.w=sn I kept their names alive.*

7 Now try a transliteration and translation of these negated sentences.

a 

b 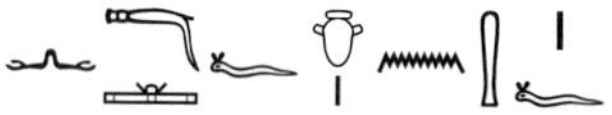

c  *sm3 to kill*

8 Now go back to the negative confession. Bring everything you have learned together and transliterate and translate the entire text.

Explore

A life of righteous behaviour was essential for a favourable judgement in the afterlife, but it was also important when Egyptians prayed to a deity in their daily life. The following passage is taken from the prayer of the scribe Amenhotep who lived during the later New Kingdom, around 1200 BCE. The stela depicts Amenhotep and his son both praying to Ptah. Try to find the hieroglyphs reproduced below in the upper right part of the stela, and then answer the questions.

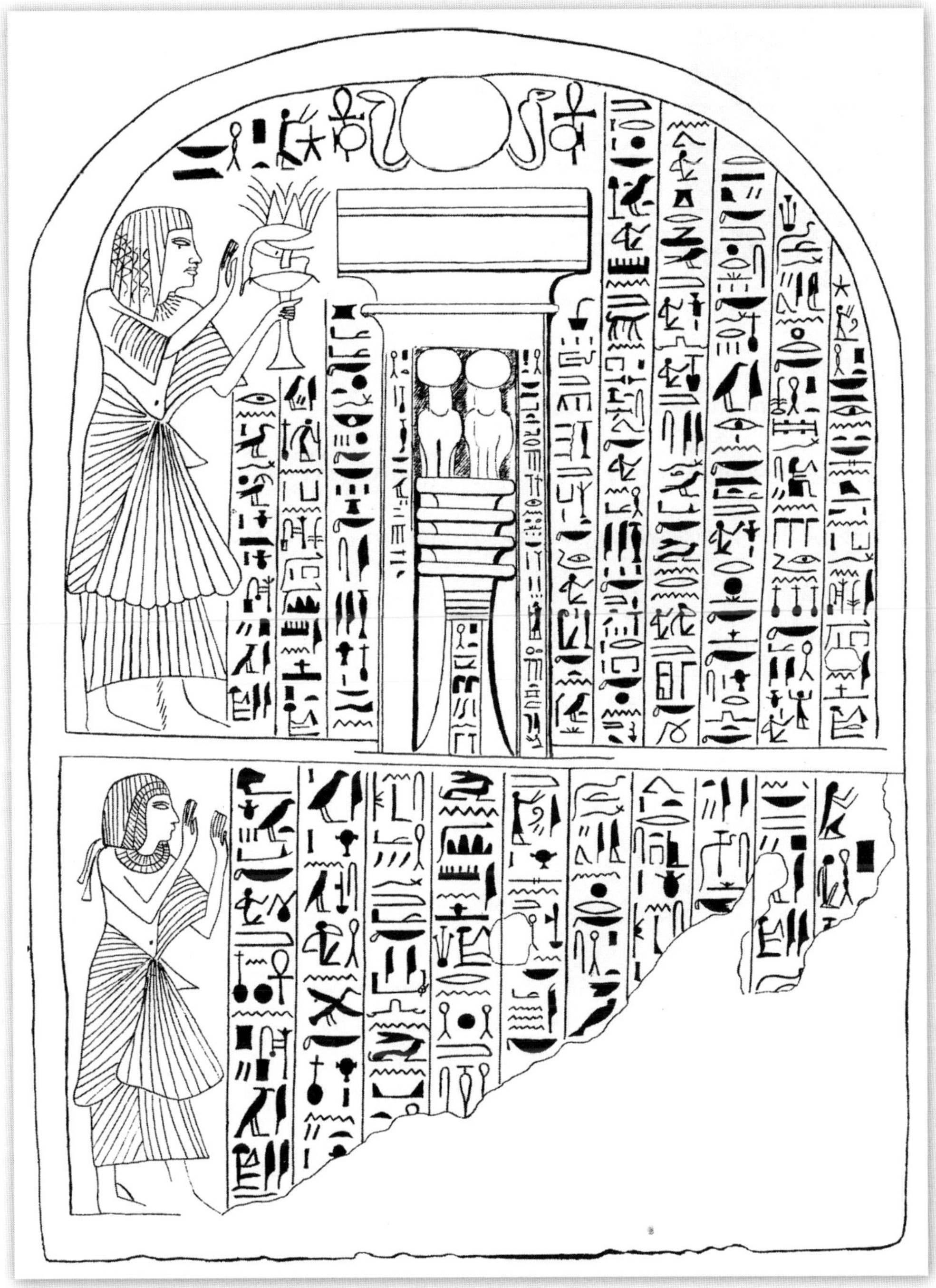

1 **What might the building depicted in the centre of the upper part of the stela represent?**

 (1)

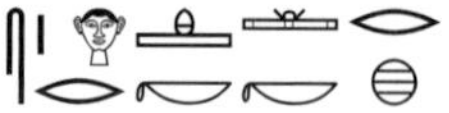 (2)

 (3)

 (4)

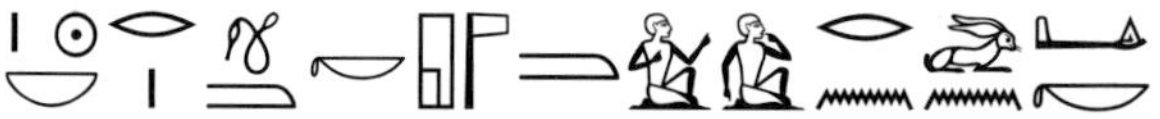 (5)

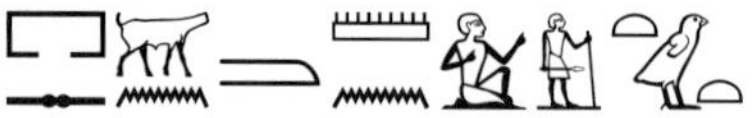 (6)

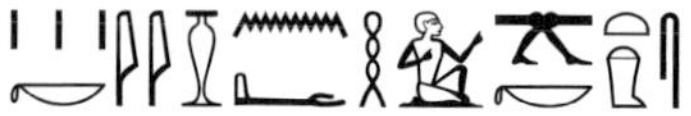 (7)

2 **Which lines contain negative sentences?**

3 **What do you notice about the way the word** *jsf.t* **is written in hieroglyphs?**

4 **Read aloud these new words, which you will need for the prayer of Amenhotep.**

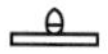	*ḥtp*	*to be happy* (*ḥr* about)
	*zmꜣ*	*to unite* (*m* with)
	*rꜣ*	*mouth*
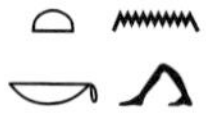	*tkn*	*to approach*
	*sṯꜣ*	*to drag*
	*ḥzj*	*to praise*
	*ḥr*	*because of* (form of the preposition  before an attached pronoun)

5 Note these new signs used in the prayer of Amenhotep.

 (vessel) *ḥz*

 (lung and windpipe) *zmꜣ*

 (rosette) *wn*

 (door bolt with coil of robe) *zṯꜣ*

6 Transliterate and translate the prayer line by line. The following guidance will help you through the text.

- **a** Begin with the first line. *jw* can also introduce verbal sentences. The single stroke below  means *=j I*.
- **b** The beginning of line 2 can be transliterated *rḫ=k* or *rḫ=kw*, each having a distinct meaning. Decide which option makes better sense and complete the line. *ḥtp* expresses intended future.
- **c** In lines 3 and 4, watch out for the 'tense swapping'.
- **d** Line 5 contains two parts. The second begins with a stative of *rwd to be firm* that refers to *rn* in the first part. *rꜣ* has the meaning *mouth (of everybody)*.
- **e** Line 6 is a sentence in the stative. The final *=s* refers to *ḥw.t-nṯr* in the previous line.
- **f** Decide whether the first word of line 7 is stative, past tense or intended future and translate it accordingly. *ḥzy=k* means *those you praise*.
- **g** How would you interpret the final line?

7 Now bring the entire prayer into a fluent translation.

Drawing hieroglyphs

1 Follow the step-by-step guide and draw the hieroglyphs used in the words *mꜣꜥ.t* and *jsf.t*.

a 

b 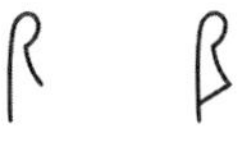

2 Now have a go at drawing this line from the negative confession. It will also help you to consolidate your knowledge of many of the signs you have already learned.

Test yourself

1 Do these sentences express the active or passive voice? Translate.

a 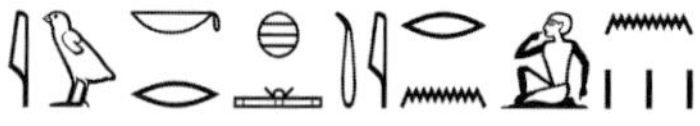 *jw=k rḫ.tj rn=n*

b  *jw jsf.t dr.tj*

2 For which sentence would the Egyptians use *jyj.n=j*: the one that emphasizes circumstances **(a)** or the one that does not **(b)**.

a *It is in order to unite with the gods who are with you that I have come to you.*

b *I have come to you in order to (r) unite with the gods who are with you.*

3 Select the correct translation of these negated sentences.

a  *n tkn=j Wsjr grg ẖr ḥꜣ.tj=j*

I do not approach Osiris, when falsehood is in my heart.

I did not approach Osiris, when falsehood was in my heart.

b  *n jnj.n=j n=k Mꜣꜥ.t*

I do not bring Ma'at to you.

I did not bring Ma'at to you.

SELF-CHECK

	I CAN
●	express passive voice
●	emphasize circumstances
●	negate action

12 The temple cult

In this unit you will learn how to:

- **read temple inscriptions**
- **use strong pronouns**
- **translate weak pronouns.**

MYTH AND RITUAL IN EGYPTIAN TEMPLES

Egyptian temple walls are decorated over and over again with scenes that show the king performing rituals before a deity. These ceremonies include the opening of the door to a shrine in which the statue of a deity was housed, as the image shows, as well as offering food to the statue, clothing it and purifying it with *snṯr* (*incense*). The inscriptions accompanying the scenes link the rituals to the Osiris myth, the most important Egyptian myth centring on the legitimate transmission of power from one king to the next. The Egyptians believed that Horus and Osiris were the divine equivalents of the reigning and the deceased king. When Osiris died, his brother Seth stole the *jr.t Ḥrw* (*eye of Horus*) and claimed royal power, even though Horus was the legitimate successor. Symbolically, the king returned the eye during the temple ritual, since his offerings to the gods were interpreted as the *eye of Horus*. In return for the offerings, he received *njswy.t* (*kingship*) and other royal prerogatives from the gods. In other words, temple cult justified kingship as a divine institution on earth that maintained the cosmic and social order. However, there is a line to draw between ideology and practice. Whereas the scenes suggest that only the kings interacted with the gods, we know from administrative documents that in reality it was temple priests who performed the rituals. The public was excluded from temple cult. To what extent ordinary Egyptians knew what happened in a temple, and how to interpret it, is unclear.

1 How is the association of *incense* with the gods expressed in the hieroglyphs for this word?

2 What do you notice about the order of signs in the hieroglyphic writing of *snṯr*?

Vocabulary builder

THE TEMPLE CULT

1 Read these new words aloud.

	*ḏd mdw*	*speaking words*
	*jn*	*by*, also written 
	*qn.t*	*valour*
	*Tm*	*Atum* (the primeval sun god)
	*Wnn-nfr*	*Wenennefer* (*Who-exists-perfectly*, epithet of Osiris)
	*jr.t*	*eye*
	*Ḫntj-jmn.tjw*	*Khentamentiu (Foremost-of-the-Westerners*, epithet of Osiris*)*
	*3s.t*	*Isis* (wife of Osiris and mother of Horus)
	*w3s*	*dominion*
	*snb*	*health*
	*3w.t-jb*	*joy* (literally *length of heart*)
	*snṯr*	*incense*, also written 
	*sṯj*	*perfume*, also written  and 
	*jʿj*	*to wash*
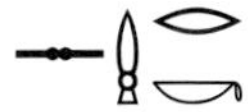	*s:ẖkr*	*to adorn*
	*ʿ*	*arm*

CULTURE INSIGHT

The west is where the sun goes down and where, according to Egyptian belief, the realm of the dead is located. The epithet *Foremost-of-the-Westerners* means that Osiris is the king of the dead, just as his successor Horus is the king of the living.

2 Study the new words again and concentrate on how the hieroglyphs representing the human eye and the forearm are used: as sound sign, picture sign or classifier. Then select the correct usage in the words below. In 2f, select both usages of the forearm.

a		*jr.t*	*eye*	sound – picture – classifier
b		*jrj*	*to do*	sound – picture – classifier
c		*mꜣ*	*to see*	sound – picture – classifier
d		*dr*	*to repel*	sound – picture – classifier
e		*ꜥ*	*arm*	sound – picture – classifier
f		*jꜥj*	*to wash*	sound – picture – classifier

3 These words are not new, but are written with different hieroglyphs in this unit or have an additional meaning. Familiarize yourself with them by adding their transliteration.

a		__________	*strong; strength*
b		__________	*spell*
c		__________	*year*
d		__________	*the evil*
e		__________	*face*

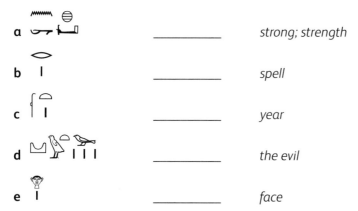

4 Study also these words that are more particular for individual temple spells.

	*ḏfꜣ*	*to clean*
	*pr-wr*	*per-wer* (literally *great house*, the shrine of the statue)
	*ḥjḥj*	*to search for*

CULTURE INSIGHT

According to myth, the *pr-wr* is a sanctuary located in Upper Egypt. To identify the statue shrine in the temple of Abydos with the *pr-wr* was another means of 'mythologizing' temple cult.

5 Go through the new vocabulary and find these new hieroglyphs used to write them. Then select the correct reading of the new signs.

a		(staff):	*md* or *mwd*?
b		(spine and spinal cord):	*ꜣw* or *wꜣ*?
c		(sled):	*jtm* or *tm*?
d		(face in profile):	*ẖnt* or *sn*?
e		(flame coming out of vessel):	*sṯj* or *snṯr*?
f		(bundle?):	*sṯj* or *ṯs*?
g		(decorative element):	*hkr* or *ẖkr*?
h		(red crown):	*n* or *j*
i	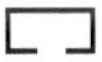	(plan of a house):	*pr* or *wr*?

THE TEMPLE OF SETI I AT ABYDOS

The Egyptians believed that Osiris was buried at Abydos in a tomb that we know today belonged to king Djer, a pharaoh of the First Dynasty. The blending of Osiris with an early king made temple cult at Abydos a centre for the worship of both Osiris and royal ancestors. The best-preserved temple at this site was erected by Rameses II and dedicated to his predecessor Seti I, Osiris, Isis and other deities. The wall reliefs, which we will study in this unit, give detailed insight into the rituals performed in the temple.

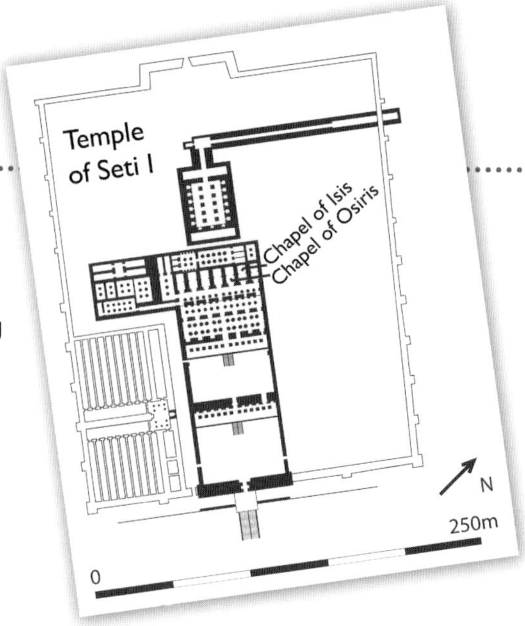

Have a look at the first example below, taken from the ritual for opening the door of the shrine. Study the image at the beginning of this unit to see where the hieroglyphs of questions 1–3 were placed in the scene.

1 Lines 1 and 2 begin with the phrase *speaking words*. From the position of the inscription, who do you think is speaking here?

2 Look at the words behind the groups  and  in lines 1, 2 and 4. What does Osiris give (*dj*) to the king?

Above Osiris

 (1)

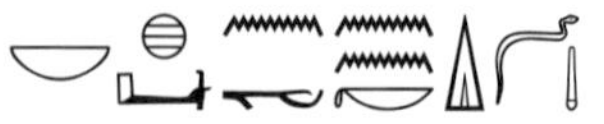 (2)

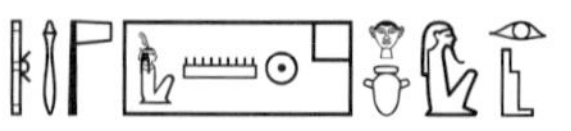 (3)

In front of Osiris

 (4)

3 Try a transliteration and translation of the epithets of Osiris in line 3. The group  stands for  *Rˁ* Ra.

The next example below depicts the king kneeling before Osiris. Study the depiction and inscriptions from the scene and answer these questions.

4 What do you think the king is offering?

5 Which columns above the scene are written from right to left and which ones from left to right?

6 Which epithets of Osiris do you recognize in the two columns written above him? You can also refer to your answer to exercise 3 to help you.

7 Where else in the inscriptions above the king do these epithets appear?

8 What is the label below the incense burner saying? Have a go at a transliteration and translation.

LANGUAGE INSIGHT

Notice that the scribe made two mistakes here: ⊂ is written where it should say ⊂; and the word *s.t* *seat* is written *js.t* in hieroglyphs.

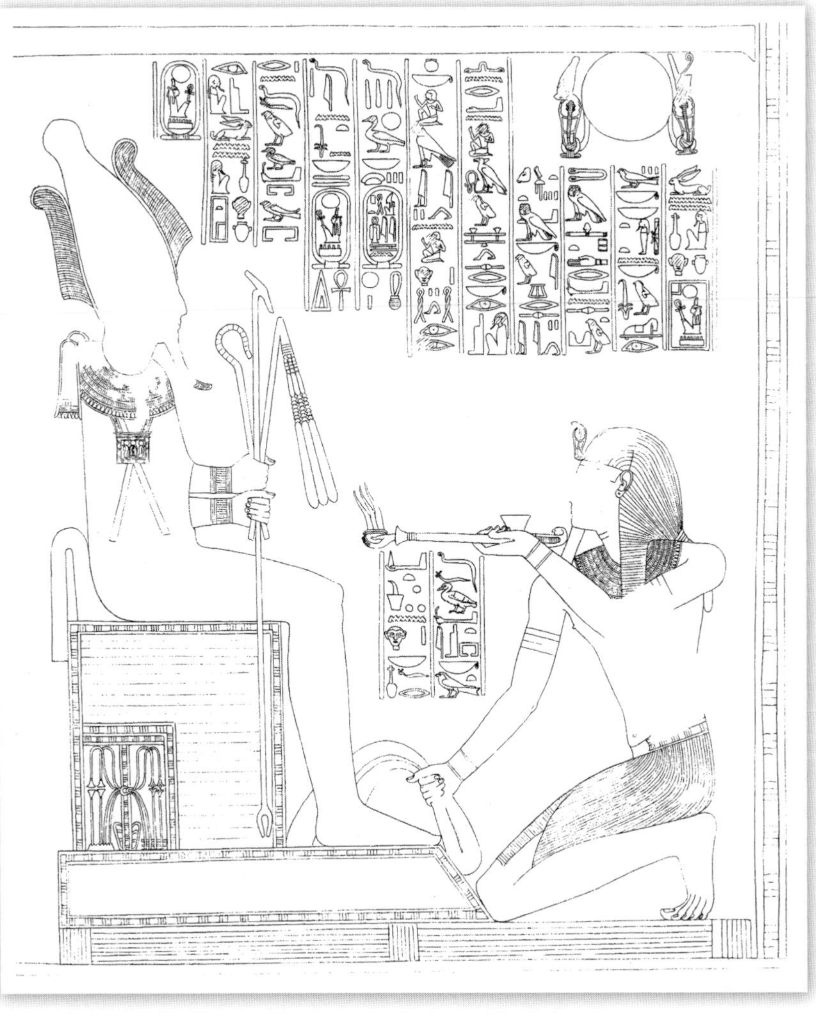

Language discovery

1 Investigate the conventions of Egyptian temple inscriptions.

a Return to the first example above and select what you think is the correct transliteration and translation of the following phrase:

dj.n=j n=k qn.t	*I have given you valour.*
dj.n n=k qn.t	*Valour has been given to you.*
dj.n=k n=j qn.t	*You have given me valour.*

b Each ritual is accompanied by a  *rꜣ spell for doing so-and-so* to be spoken by the king. Study the inscriptions above the kneeling king. What does it say this ritual is for?

c What might be the function of the group  *ḏd mdw jn* written at the beginning of the fourth column from the left in the same scene?

2 In the spell for this scene, the king identifies himself with Horus by stating . Try a translation of this phrase.

3 Can you work out the meaning of the sentence ?

4 Now return to the scene with the kneeling king and its associated hieroglyphs. Complete the gaps in this translation and transliteration. The text begins in the fifth column from the left.

ḏd mdw ______ njswt nb tꜣ.wj Mn-Mꜣꜥ.t-Rꜥ dj ꜥnḫ

Speaking words ______ the lord of the two lands Men-Ma'at-Ra, given life

ḏd mdw zꜣ-Rꜥ nb ḫꜥ.w Sty mrj.n-Ptḥ ______ ______

Speaking words (by) the son of Ra, lord of the ______, Seti Whom-Ptah-loves, like Ra.

jnk Ḥrw ______=j ḥr ḥjḥj ______=j

I am ______. That I have come (to you) is while searching for my two eyes.

n rdj.n=j ______=s r=k Wsjr Ḫntj-jmn.tjw

I ______ not ______ that they will be distant from you, Osiris, Foremost of the Westerners.

m=k wj ẖr=s ______ m ḥtp dr.n=s ḏw.t=k nb.t

Look, I am carrying them, while they ______ safe, after they have repelled all your ______.

twt n=k sw Wsjr Wnn-nfr ______ Ḥw.t-Mn-Mꜣꜥ.t-Rꜥ

It is fitting for you, Osiris Wenennefer who resides in the Enclosure-of-Men-Ma'at-Ra.

> **LANGUAGE INSIGHT**
>
> The text presents a few issues. For example, the negation *n* is written instead of simply , perhaps because the scribe interpreted as a phonetic complement of . Another difficulty is the use of the dual *jr.tj two eyes*. It is later repeated with the attached pronoun feminine singular *s it* (= *the eye*) in the singular, but in the translation needs to be rendered with *they, them*, i.e. *the two eyes*. The expression *twt n=k sw It is fitting for you* is an adjectival sentence, which exhibits features that we have not looked at yet, but which are introduced later in Unit 14. For the time being, you can simply take it for granted.

5 Summarize the meaning of the spell in your own words.

TEMPLE INSCRIPTIONS

Temple inscriptions and their position in a scene follow a fairly consistent template. The standard elements explained in greater detail below include:

- the name and epithets of the deity, written above or behind the deity
- the speech of the deity granting the king kingship and other prerogatives
- the names and titles of the king, written above or behind the king
- the title of the spell that the king spoke while he performed the ritual
- the spell that links the offering to myth
- the label for the activity in which the king is shown, introduced with an infinitive and often written next to the activity performed.

The speeches, of the deity and of the king, are each introduced by *ḏd mdw Speaking words* or *ḏd mdw jn Speaking words by*. The full writing of this group is , but it usually appears in an abbreviated form, for example or .

 *ḏd mdw jn Wsjr Speaking words by Osiris*

The speech of the deity begins with the phrase *dj.n=j n=k*. Many Egyptologists translate the form *dj.n=j* as *Herewith I give* in the particular context of temple inscriptions, although it looks like the past tense *I gave*. The attached pronoun *=j* is regularly omitted in hieroglyphs, but added to the transliteration to clarify how the grammar works.

dj.n=j n=k snb nb Herewith I give you all health.

The title of the spell typically begins with *r3 spell*. It tells the priest which activity the spell is to be used for, for example *spell for opening the door*.

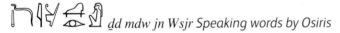

r3 n ḏf3 pr-wr Spell for cleaning the per-wer.

6 Transliterate these phrases from other temple inscriptions by putting the jumbled-up words on the right-hand side into their correct order.

a ʿnḫ   dj.n   nb   =k   wꜣs   n   =j

b wn   ꜥꜣ.wj   rꜣ   n

c jn   mdw   ꜣs.t   ḏd   wr.t

7 Translate the phrases in the previous exercise. *wn* means *to open* and ꜥꜣ means *door wing*.

STRONG PRONOUNS

Unlike in English, there are different ways of saying *I* (and *you, he, she, it, we, they*) in Egyptian. So far, you have learned that the attached pronouns ![glyph] =*j*, ![glyph] =*k* and so on are used for this purpose in verbal sentences. In other sentence types, the Egyptians used a different set of pronouns called strong pronouns. These are strong enough to stand on their own and do not require a word going before them. This is why grammarians also call them independent pronouns. Strong pronouns also carry the emphasis in a statement. In *jnk Ḥrw I am Horus*, for example, the purpose is to say that *I*, rather than somebody else, *is Horus*. First, have a look at the forms of the strong pronouns.

singular			plural		
	jnk	*I*		*jnn*	*we*
	ntk	*you (masc.)*	or	*ntṯn*	*you*
or	*ntṯ*	*you (fem.)*			
	ntf	*he, it*	or	*ntsn*	*they*
or	*nts*	*she, it*			

The first person singular can be written in different ways depending on who is speaking, for example ![glyph] for a king speaking and ![glyph] and ![glyph] when the identity of the speaker was not expressed. There is no clear reason why ○ was used instead of — in *jnk*. The initial *j* in *jnk* is often omitted in hieroglyphs.

The initial *j* of *jnn* is usually written with the group ![glyph], which is more typical of later phases of the Egyptian language. As with attached pronouns, the sounds *s* and *t* can be written with ![glyph] or — and ○ or ⟳ respectively, in strong pronouns.

8 Match the hieroglyphs with the correct translation and transliteration of each strong pronoun.

a  *jnk* *he*

b 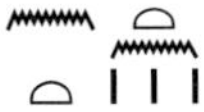 *ntk* *she*

c  *ntf* *you* (masc. sing.)

d  *nttn* *I*

e  *nts* *you* (plural)

Strong pronouns are typically placed at the beginning of a sentence in Egyptian and are followed by a noun. In translation, you add a form of *to be* in the past or present tense between strong pronoun and noun, as in a simple nominal sentence.

jnk Ḥrw I am (was) Horus.

9 Complete the transliteration and translation of these sentences with strong pronouns.

a  *jnk z3=k* _____ *was your* _____.

b 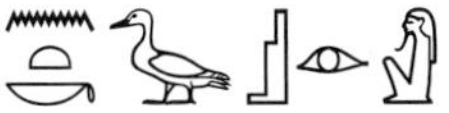 _____ *z3 Wsjr* *You are the son* _____ _____.

c  _____ *rmṯ* _____ *They are the people of Egypt.*

d  _____ *mw.t-* _____ _____ _____ *the mother of* _____ _____.

10 Now have a go yourself at both a transliteration and translation of similar sentences.

a 

b 

c 

d 

e 

WEAK PRONOUNS

Weak pronouns are the third series of pronouns in Egyptian. They always follow a preceding word but are not directly attached to it. Grammarians also call them, therefore, dependent pronouns. In the singular, they have their own specific forms, whereas the plural forms are identical to those of attached pronouns.

singular			plural		
	*wj*	*I, me*	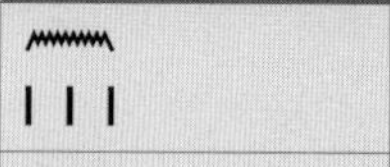	*n*	*we, us*
	*ṯw*	*you* (masc.)	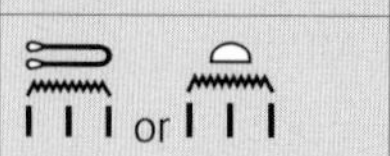	*ṯn*	*you*
	*ṯn*	*you* (fem.)			
	*sw*	*he, him, it*	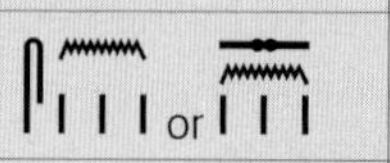	*sn*	*they, them*
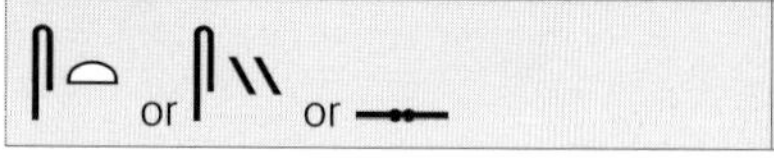	*st, sj*	*she, her, it*			

The hieroglyphic spelling of the weak pronoun, for the first person singular, depends again on who is speaking – a man, a woman or a king, etc. The final *j* can be omitted in hieroglyphs both in the first person singular and the third person singular feminine. The third person singular feminine has two forms, *st* and *sj*.

11 Notice the overlap and differences between the different types of pronouns by matching the attached pronouns with their correct equivalents. For example, the third person singular of the attached pronoun (a) can be matched with the third person singular of the strong pronouns (3) and of the weak pronouns (B). Do the same for the other attached pronouns.

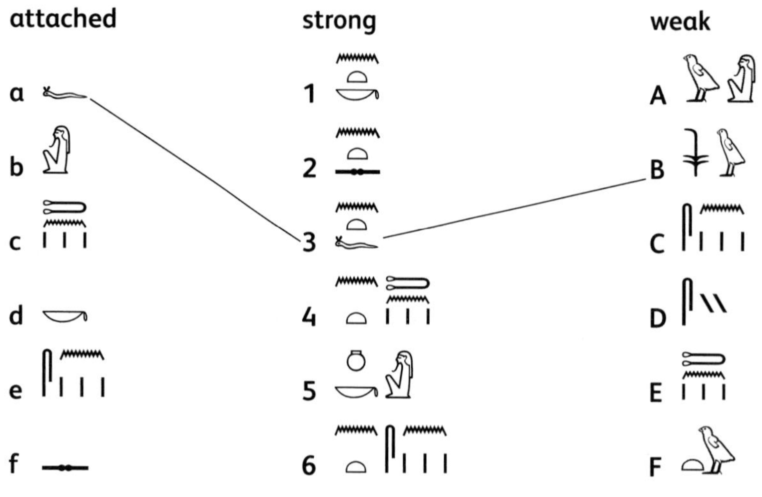

The correct translation of weak pronouns depends on the type of sentence in which they are used. When they function as the subject in an adverbial sentence or before the stative, they are translated *I, you, he, she, it, we, you, they* and can be preceded by *m=k*. This introductory phrase means something like *Look, …* or *Behold, …*

m=k wj ẖr=s Look, I am under it.

m=k wj jyj.kw Behold, I have come.

The introductory phrase *m=k* is written , when the sentence that follows is addressed to a male person. It changes its form to  *m=ṯ* and  *m=ṯn* in a conversation with a woman or a group of people respectively. The sentence in the example above, spoken to a woman, would be *m=ṯ wj jyj.kw*. The difference in Egyptian is not expressed in translation: *Look* (you woman), *I have come.*

12 What do the following sentences with weak pronouns mean in English?

a  *m=ṯ wj ẖr jr.tj=j*

b  *m=k ṯw s:ẖkr.tj*

c  *m=ṯn sn ḥr ḏd mdw n=ṯn*

d To whom are the sentences in a, b and c spoken: a man, a woman or a group of people?

In verbal sentences, weak pronouns mean *me, you, him, her, it, us, you, them*. They function as the 'direct objects'. The direct object expresses the person or thing that the subject is acting upon. In the following example, *me* is the person upon whom *he* is acting.

dr=f wj He repels me.

The Egyptians moved weak pronouns as close to the predicate of a verbal sentence as possible. Weak pronouns can follow the predicate directly, unless the subject is an attached pronoun, as in the example above. The same sentence would have the following word order, when the noun *Ḥrw* replaces *=f*:

dr wj Ḥrw Horus repels me.

If both direct and indirect objects (see Unit 6) are pronouns, the indirect pronoun comes first.

dr n=k wj Ḥrw Horus repels me for you.

You may not necessarily notice that the words have changed their position in the Egyptian sentence and yet still produce a correct translation. However, sometimes it is important to remember that pronouns travel in verbal sentences. In the example above, you could make *n=k* the subject of the sentence in the past tense, i.e. *dr.n=k wj Ḥrw You have repelled me, Horus*. The two translations are both correct, but have entirely different meanings. Which translation fits better is, as is often the case, a question of context and interpretation.

13 Study these verbal sentences and choose their correct transliteration and translation from the options presented. Keep an eye on the form and position of the weak pronouns.

a 

s:ḫkr sw Ḥrw m ḫʿ.w=f May Horus adorn him with his crowns.

s:ḫkr wj Ḥrw m ḫʿ.w=f May Horus adorn me with his crowns.

s:ḫkr=k sw Ḥrw m ḫʿ.w=f May you adorn him and Horus with his crowns.

b 

jʿj mw ṯw snṯr Water washes you and incense.

jʿj=ṯ wj m snṯr You wash me with incense.

jʿj ṯw snṯr May incense wash you.

14 Consolidate your knowledge of pronouns in Egyptian by completing these sentences, using a strong, weak or attached pronoun as appropriate.

a	*m=k* ______ *r jrj.t ḫ.t*	*Look, he will do the thing.* (= *perform the ritual*)
b	*jw=* ______ *r jrj.t ḫ.t*	*He will do the thing.*
c	*ȝs.t* ______ *mw.t* ______	*Isis, you are his mother.*
d	*m=ṯ* ______ *jyj.tj ḫr=* ______	*Look, she has come to you.* (masc. sing.)
e	*dj.n=* ______ *n=* ______ ______	*Herewith I give them to you.* (fem. sing.)
f	*pr-wr dfȝ* ______ ______ *m snṯr*	*The per-wer, I clean it with incense.*

Explore

Whenever a ritual text was copied from a papyrus scroll on to a temple wall, it was adapted to fit its context. Work through the following scene from the temple at Abydos to learn about what changes a new context can bring. It is once again the ritual for offering incense, but this time performed for Isis. Use what you have learned in this unit to understand the scene.

1 What is the king doing?

2 Find the spell for this ritual in the scene and transliterate and translate it.

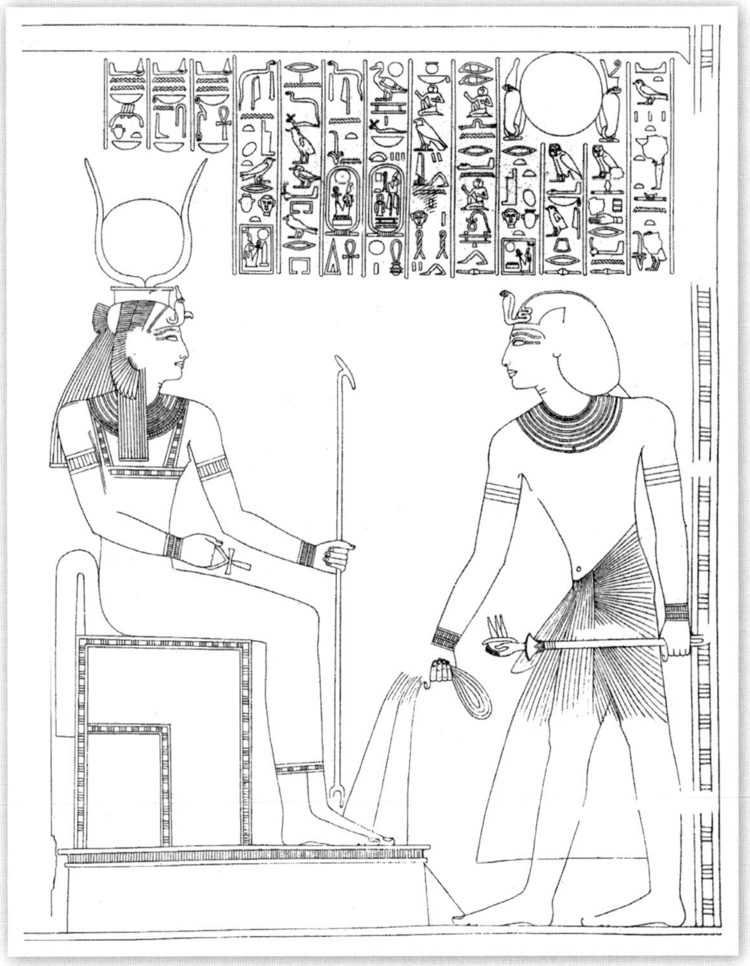

3 What does Isis give the king, according to the inscriptions written above her?

4 Return to the scene with the kneeling king in the previous section. Compare its spell with the spell in the scene with Isis, beginning in the sixth column from the right, and make a note of all the differences.

5 What would you say were the reasons for the differences in the spell for Isis?

The following spell for offering incense shows another interesting feature of temple cult, namely the play with the sound of words and its relevance for interpreting ritual action. The entire spell is based on associating key words with other words that sounded similar. Try to understand how playing with sound works in the spell.

6 Go through the hieroglyphs in the spell and look up the two new words in the text in the vocabulary builder.

(1) 

(2) 

(3) 

(4) 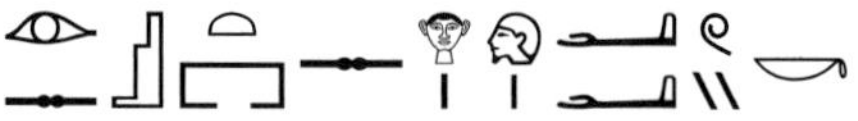

7 Now have a closer look at the sound and meaning of the words in the text.

a Transliterate and translate the first two lines, formed from three verbal sentences each beginning with *jyj*.

b Which words are associated with each other in the first line by their sound?

c The second line weaves the key word into the spell. Which one do you think it is?

d Which consonants are used more than once in lines 1 and 2 and would thus have dominated the sound of the spell?

e How is the key word of line 2 associated with the sound of lines 1 and 2?

f Try to work out the transliteration and translation of lines 3 and 4.

g How would you say the spell links the ritual to Egyptian myth?

h Now try to read out the transliteration of the entire spell.

Drawing hieroglyphs

1 Have a go at drawing these signs used for writing typical epithets of Osiris.

a 

b 

2 Now, try drawing the name and epithets of Osiris  *Wsjr Wnn-nfr Ḫntj-jmn.tjw* ***Osiris Wenennefer, Foremost-of-the-Westerners.***

Test yourself

1 What do these typical phrases from temple inscriptions mean?

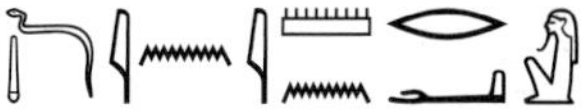 *ḏd mdw jn Jmn-Rꜥ*

 *dj.n=j n=k njswy.t Tm*

2 Complete each transliteration with the correct form of strong pronouns and then translate.

a  __________ *mw.t=f*

b  __________ *zꜣ=j*

c  __________ *Wnn-nfr*

d  __________ *nṯr.w Wꜣs.t*

3 Correct the translations of the following sentences, using the correct pronoun in English.

a  *m=k wj ḥr Mꜣꜥ.t* — *Look, you were under Ma'at.*

b  *jꜥj=j ṯw* — *He may wash us.*

c  *m=k sn ḥr rdj.t snṯr* — *Look, you are giving incense.*

SELF-CHECK

	I CAN
●	read temple inscriptions
●	use strong pronouns
●	translate weak pronouns

13 Storytelling

In this unit you will learn how to:

- **recognize major particles**
- **translate relative clauses**
- **analyse longer passages of text**
- **apply grammar from previous units to translate new texts.**

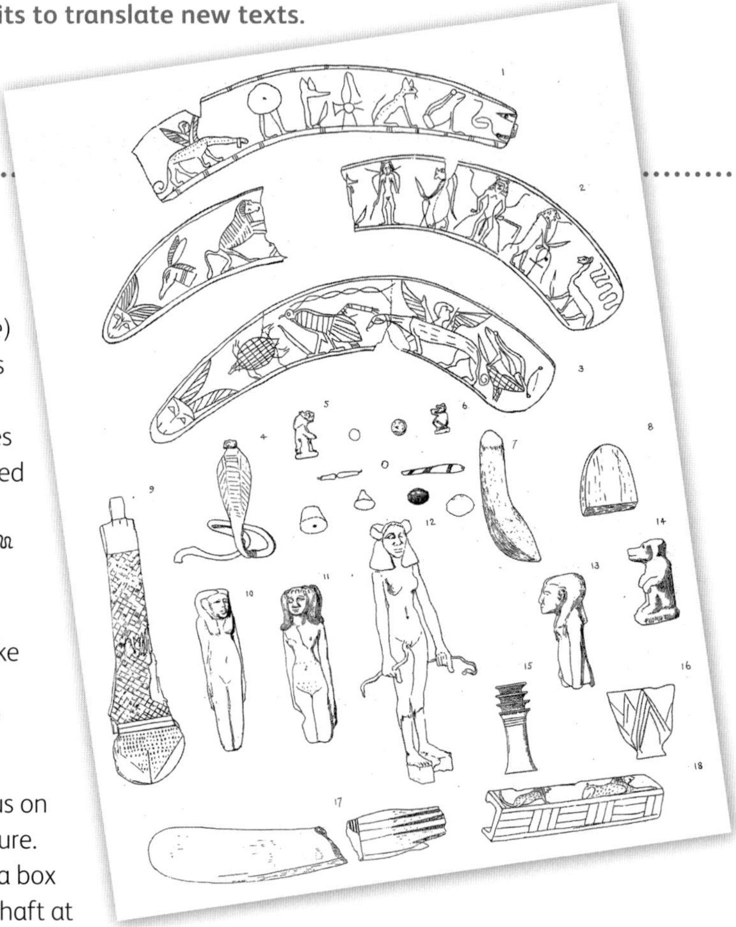

COURTIERS, SNAKES AND HEALING PRACTICE

Stories about kings, princes and life at the *ẖnw* (*royal residence*) were popular in ancient Egypt, just as they are today. One famous ancient Egyptian tale recounts the adventures of a court official who was shipwrecked on an island in the *wꜣḏ-wr* (*sea*). There he met a gigantic *ḥfꜣw* (*snake*) whose family had been killed by a star that had fallen from the sky. Both the official and the snake struggle with the loss of their regular social ties, as the text in the 'Explore' section of this unit illustrates.

The find circumstances of the papyrus on which this story was written are obscure. However, similar texts were found in a box that had been deposited in a burial shaft at Thebes. The box also contained papyri with medical instructions and ritual texts. The objects depicted above were found scattered around it. These include wands, amulets and figurines of women and snakes, typically used in healing practices. There are no inscriptions telling us who the owner of the box was and it is not entirely clear whether the objects were originally placed inside the box. However, we can try to bring the different lines of evidence together and speculate whether the papyri and the objects belonged to a lector priest. Lector priests assisted at temple rituals and, we believe, helped with healing people, so they had some access to written knowledge. An 'intellectual' of his time, our lector priest might have held a snake figurine over the belly of a pregnant woman to protect her from demons, reciting magic spells and telling the story of the courtier and the snake.

AUTHOR'S NOTE

In this unit, you will learn how to read a long passage of text by combining a range of different aspects of grammar, which you have encountered in previous units. A few new points will be introduced, but the emphasis is on consolidating and applying your knowledge. Since the texts are a little longer now, there are more words for you to look at, grouped below according to their meaning and word type. Read through all of them and identify all the new signs. Some of the words are rarely used and are typical only of the texts discussed in this unit. Those marked with an asterisk (*) appear frequently outside literary texts and are worth memorizing. A few more new words are listed in the 'Explore' section rather than in the 'Vocabulary builder', to make it easier for you to find them for the translation of the text in that section.

Vocabulary builder

'THE SHIPWRECKED SAILOR'

1 Read these new words aloud.

Nouns describing the environment

	*w3w*	*wave*
	*w3ḏ-wr* (*)	*sea* (literally the 'great green')
	*jw* (*)	*island*
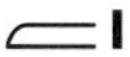	*gs* (*)	*side* (here *side of the island*, i.e. shore)
	*nwy*	*water*
	*ḫrw*	*voice* (here *noise*)
	*qrj*	*thunder*
	*ḫt* (*)	*wood*

Nouns describing the snake

	*ḥfꜣw*	*snake*
	*ḥꜥw* (*)	*body*
	*ẖ.t* (*)	*belly*
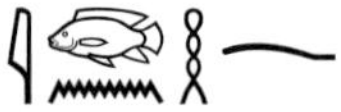	*jnḥ*	*eyebrow*
	*nbw* (*)	*gold*
	*ḫsbd*	*lapis lazuli*
	*mꜣꜥ*	*true*

Verbs

	*jb*	*to think*
	*gmgm*	*to tremble*
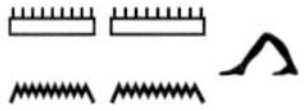	*mnmn*	*to shake*
	*kfj*	*to uncover*
	*gmj* (*)	*to find*
	*zẖr*	*to cover*
	*jṯj* (*)	*to seize*
	*s:nḏm*	*to dwell*
	*wꜣḥ*	*to put*
	*dmj*	*to touch*
	*wpj* (*)	*to open*

Small words

	*ʿḥʿ.n* (*)	*then*
	*m-bꜣḥ* (*)	*in front of*
	*nm*	*who?*
	*ntj* (*)	*which, who*

2 Go back to the new vocabulary and match these new signs with their correct transliteration or use as a CLASSIFIER.

a  (papyrus + cobra)	*nbw*
b  (black ibis)	BREAK, CROSS, NUMBER
c  (piece of meat)	*bꜣ*
d  (bead collar)	*gm*
e  (robe + walking legs)	*wꜣḏ*
f  (crossed sticks)	BODY
g  (jabiru)	*gs*
h  (penis with fluid)	*jw*
i 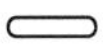 (strip of land)	BEFORE
j  (plinth)	*jṯ*

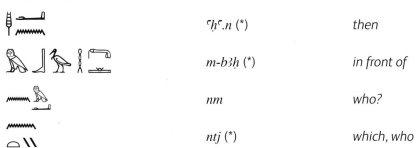

'THE SHIPWRECKED SAILOR' (1): ENCOUNTER WITH THE SNAKE

The tale of the courtier and the snake is known in Egyptology as 'The Shipwrecked Sailor'. In the framing narration, the courtier announces his story. He then begins to tell the audience about his misfortune: the storm that hit his boat, the loss of his comrades, his arrival on the island, his loneliness and, eventually, his conversation with the snake. The tale makes many references to myth and theology. It is perhaps not a folk tale but a highly sophisticated and deliberately composed piece of literature.

The passage below tells of the first encounter between the courtier and the snake. The original text was written in hieratic. Following standard practice in Egyptology, it is transcribed below in hieroglyphs to make it simpler to read.

Study the hieroglyphs and the transliteration and try to grasp the gist of the passage. Then answer the questions.

1 The snake is a fictitious creature. Find the lines in which it is described. Which materials are his *ḥꜥw* ***(body)*** **and** *jnḥ.wj* ***(two eyebrows)*** **made of?**

ꜥḥꜥ.n sḏm.n=j ḫrw qrj

jb.kw wꜣw pw n wꜣḏ-wr

ḫt.w ḥr gmgm tꜣ ḥr mnmn

kfj.n=j ḥr=j

gmj.n=j ḥfꜣw pw jw=f m jyj.t

ḥꜥw=f zḫr.w m nbw

jnḥ.wj=fj m ḫsbd mꜣꜥ

ꜥḥꜥ.n rdj=f wj m rꜣ=f

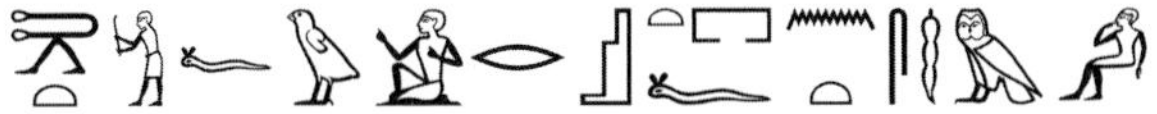

jtj=f wj r s.t=f n.t s:nḏm

w3ḥ=f wj nn dmj.t=j

jw wpj.n=f r3=f r=j

jw=j ḥr ḫ.t=j m-b3ḥ=f

ʿḥʿ.n ḏd.n=f n=j

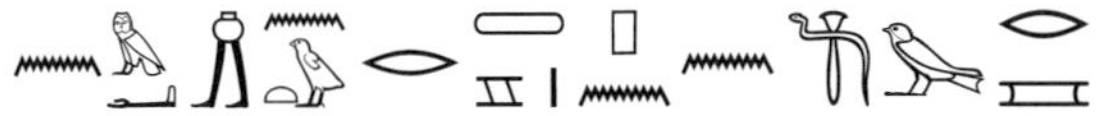

nm jnj ṯw r jw pn n w3ḏ-wr

ntj gs.wj=fj m nwy

LANGUAGE INSIGHT

The pronoun *=f his* changes to *=fj his* when it is attached to a noun in the dual, for example *jnḥ.wj=fj his two eyebrows*. In the final line of the passage from 'The Shipwrecked Sailor', the noun *gs* is written without dual strokes, but it must be the dual *gs.wj* because of the attached pronoun.

2 According to the first two lines, the courtier hears a loud noise. What does he initially think has caused the noise?

3 How do you understand the miracle expressed with the words *w3ḥ=f wj nn dmj.t=j*?

4 The second-to-last line contains a question. What do you think the snake is asking the official?

LANGUAGE INSIGHT

The negation *nn*, when followed by the infinitive, is translated as *without* followed by the –ing form, for example *without doing*.

Language discovery

1 Try to explain the grammar in the following phrases from the text, to consolidate what you learned in previous units.

a Are *wꜣw pw n wꜣḏ-wr* and *ḥfꜣw pw* verbal sentences (Unit 6) or nominal sentences (Unit 7) translated with a form of *to be*?

b *ḫt.w ḥr gmgm, tꜣ ḥr mnmn* and *jw=f m jyj.t* are statements using an infinitive after a preposition (see Unit 10). Would you translate them with the past progressive, present progressive or future tense?

c *ḥꜥw=f zẖr.w m nbw* is translated with *His body was covered with gold* instead of with *His body covers with gold*. Why (see Unit 11)?

d In the translation of *jnḥ.wj m ḫsbd mꜣꜥ* and *jw=j ḥr ẖ.t=j m-bꜣḥ=f*, you need to add a form of *to be* before the preposition. Which type of sentence do these belong to (see Unit 9)?

e Which tense do the phrases *sḏm.n=j, kfj.n=j, gmj.n=j, wpj.n=f* and *ḏd.n=f* express?

f Can the phrases *rdj=f, jṯj=f* and *wꜣḥ=f* express past tense?

2 Some Egyptian words help you recognize the beginning of a new sentence. Can you find the two words in 'The Shipwrecked Sailor' that fulfil this function?

3 The final line of the text adds a comment to *this island of the sea* introduced with . Try to translate the line word for word first and then find a more fluent wording in English.

PARTICLES

Long passages of text look at first glance like an uninterrupted flow of signs and words. It is therefore useful to find signals that help you to split up the text into more manageable sections. There are a few words in Egyptian that do this. Grammarians call them particles. These are words or short phrases that can nuance the meaning of a statement, but more often simply have grammatical functions, such as indicating that a new sentence begins. Frequently used Egyptian particles are *jw* and *m=k*, which you learned in Units 10 and 11, as well as *ꜥḥꜥ.n*.

jw can introduce all sentence types, but it is most typical of verbal and adverbial sentences and before the stative. It is followed by verbs, nouns or attached pronouns and is not usually translated. *jw* is not used before emphatic forms and the intended future. It indicates that the following sentence is a main clause but, when a pronoun is attached to it, it can also introduce a subordinate clause and is then translated with *while*.

m=k can also introduce all sentence types and is particularly popular before adverbial sentences and the stative. It is followed by verbs, nouns or weak pronouns. It calls for the attention of the audience and is usually translated as *Look, …* or *Behold, …* This particle changes its form to *m=ṯ* when a woman is addressed and to *m=ṯn* in a conversation with a group of people (see Unit 12). Sentences beginning with *m=k* are main clauses.

ꜥḥꜥ.n introduces verbal and adverbial sentences and is popular before the stative. It is followed by verbs, nouns or attached pronouns. It is typical of narrative texts and is translated as *Then …*. Sentences beginning with *ꜥḥꜥ.n* are main clauses in the past tense in English. In Egyptian, you find verbs with and without the past infix *.n* being used after *ꜥḥꜥ.n*, for example *ꜥḥꜥ.n rdj=f wj He put* (literally: *gave*) *me* and *ꜥḥꜥ.n rdj.n=f wj He put me.*

The three particles offer useful information for the translation. They tell you:

- that the following sentence is a main clause, with some exceptions for *jw*
- that a *sḏm=f* form following them expresses past or present tense, but not the intended future
- that a *sḏm.n=f* form following them is not an emphatic form.

As a rule of thumb, a *sḏm.n=f* form that is not preceded by a particle is either emphatic (*That he has listened is …*) or subordinate (*When he listened, …*). This rule applies to verbs of motion as well as to other verbs.

4 Return to the text of 'The Shipwrecked Sailor' and investigate how particles are used in it.

a Find the three sentences introduced by *jw* and translate them.

b Replace *jw* with *m=k* in the sentences in question a and change the following pronoun if necessary.

c Now translate the sentences you created in question b.

d Finally, translate the three sentences beginning with *ꜥḥꜥ.n* in the text.

RELATIVE CLAUSES

You have learned that verbal adjectives (see Unit 7) and adjectives ending in *–j* (see Unit 9) are often best translated with a relative clause in English beginning with *who* or *which*. Egyptian also has a separate word,  *ntj*, that introduces relative clauses. *ntj* is placed after a noun and can be translated with *who*, when the noun refers to a person, or *which* after a thing.

jw pn ntj m nwy

this island which is in the water

In the example above, *ntj which* is the subject of the relative clause. In the following example from 'The Shipwrecked Sailor', the subject of the relative clause is not *ntj* but a different word, namely *gs.wj=fj*. You can still translate *ntj* provisionally as *which*. Then rephrase the sentence to something more appropriate in English, as shown here in the underlined phrases.

jw pn ntj gs.wj=fj m nwy

Provisional: *this island which its two sides are in the water*

Rephrased: *this island whose two sides are in the water*

5 The following phrases contain a noun with a relative clause. Rephrase their word-for-word rendering to produce a better translation in English.

a  *Rʿ ntj m p.t* Ra who/which in sky

b  *jb=j ntj ḥr grg* heart my who/which under falsehood

c 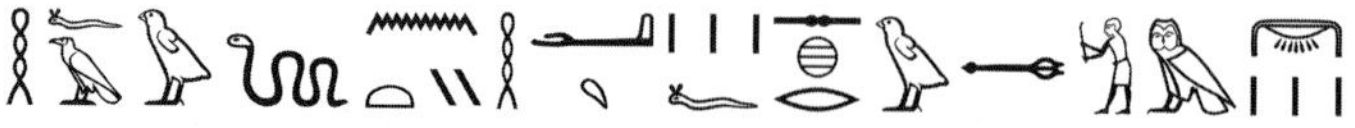 *ḥfꜣw ntj ḥʿw=f zḫr.w m nbw* snake who/which body his covered with gold

d  *rꜣ rdj=f wj jm=f* mouth who/which put he me in it

ntj changes its form depending on the number and gender of the preceding noun. When the noun is feminine singular, it becomes *ntt*, and in the plural the form is *ntjw* after masculine nouns and *ntt* after feminine nouns.

> **LANGUAGE INSIGHT**
>
> The hieroglyph stands for *tjw*, but is sometimes used interchangeably in ancient texts with the simple vulture, which you know as *ꜣ*.

 *dp.t ntt m nwy* the boat which is in the water

 *rmṯ ntjw ḥnʿ=f* the people who were with him

6 Match the nouns in the left-hand column with the correct form of *ntj*, as shown.

a  *nṯr* the god

b  *mry.t* the shore

c  *ḫrd.w* the children

d  *ḫsbd mꜣʿ* true lapis lazuli

e  *qrs.t=k* your burial

f 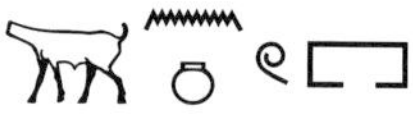 *ḫnw* the residence

 *ntj* who/which

 *ntt* who/which

 *ntjw* who/which

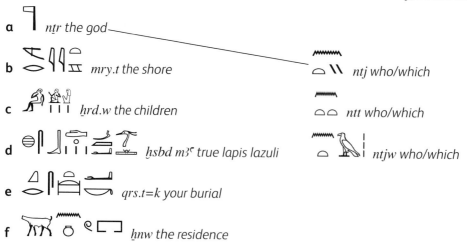

ntj does not have to be preceded by a noun. In these cases, you can still translate it with *who* and *which*, but it is sometimes clearer to translate it with *the person who*, *the thing which*, *the one who* or similar. As you can see in the following example, there is a difference in English between simply *who*, which implies the meaning *whoever*, and *the one who*, which refers to a definite person or deity. Technically, the meaning of *ntj* is closer to the second option, but a simple *who* is also fine in translation.

 *rḫ.kw ntj m p.t I know who is in heaven.* Or: *I know the one who is in heaven.*

7 Fill in the gaps in the transliteration and translation, using the correct form of *ntj* and an appropriate wording in the English.

a 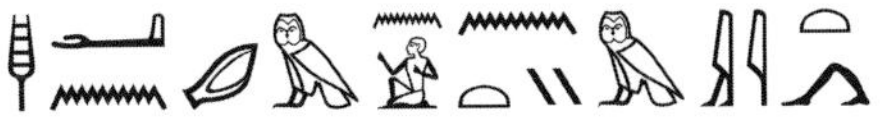 *ꜥḥꜥ.n sḏm.n=j _____ m jyj.t*

Then I heard __________

b  *jw wpj.n=f rꜣ=f r _____ m bꜣḥ=f*

He opened his mouth __________

c 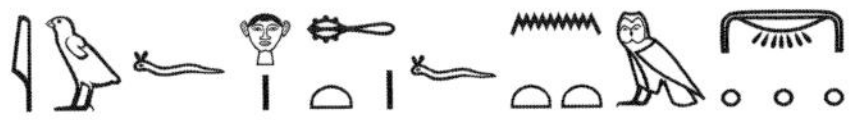 *jw=f ḥr ḫ.t=f _____ m nbw*

He was on his belly __________

d  *m=k wj ḥr gmj.t _____ m dp.t tn*

Look, I am finding __________ (*dp.t* boat)

8 Now go back to 'The Shipwrecked Sailor' and attempt a translation of the entire text, using what you have practised in this unit to help you.

a Begin with a word-for-word translation.

b 'The Shipwrecked Sailor' is a piece of literature. Try to improve your translation by inserting *and*, *while*, *that* and other connecting words to make the story sound like a literary text in English, too.

Explore

At the end of the story of 'The Shipwrecked Sailor', the snake foretells a happy end for the courtier who will return to his previous life. The following passage records the snake's promise and the farewell of the official. It is almost a summary of what the Egyptians believed an ideal life would be like. Study the new words and, most importantly, the new signs used in this text, and then answer the questions.

'THE SHIPWRECKED SAILOR' (2): PROMISE AND FAREWELL

1 Read these new words aloud and go through the new signs of this unit.

	*spr* (*)	*to get* (*r to*)
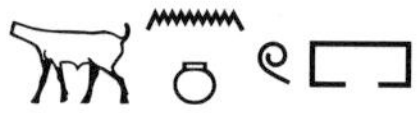	*ẖnw* (*)	*royal residence*
	*qnj*	*embrace*
	*ẖrd.w* (*)	*children*
	*rnpj*	*to rejuvenate*
	*m-ẖnw* (*)	*within*
	*qrs.t* (*)	*coffin*
	*hꜣj* (*)	*to go down*
	*mry.t*	*shore*
	*m hꜣw*	*near* (literally *in the nearness of*)
	*dp.t* (*)	*ship*
	*jꜣš*	*to shout* (*n to*)
	*mšꜥ* (*)	*crew, troop*
	*ḥknw*	*praise*
	*nb*	*lord*
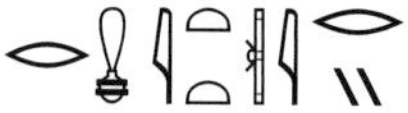	*r mjt.t jry*	*likewise* (literally *to the likeness of it*)

 (rib) *spr*

 (goatskin) *ẖn*

 (child) *ẖrd*

 (coffin) BURIAL

 (soldier) *mšꜥ*

2 Now read through the following text. Which particle tells you that it is taken from a narrative tale?

3 Does the snake promise in line 3 that the official will see his family or the king when he returns home?

4 According to the promise in line 4, what else apparently mattered to the Egyptians?

5 Who is waiting for the courtier in the boat that will bring him back, according to line 6?

(1) 

(2) 

(3) 

(4) 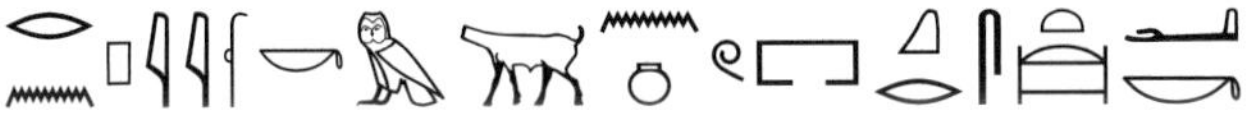

(5) 

(6) 

(7) 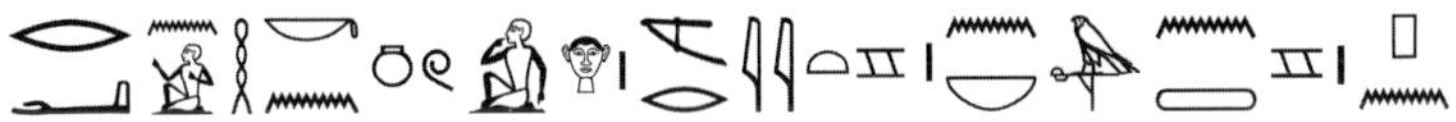

(8) 

6 Use what you have learned in this and previous units and try to produce a coherent translation of the text. Remember to transliterate it first. Resist the temptation to look up the answer in the key after you have worked on each line. Instead, have a go at the entire text first. The following guidance will help you.

- **a** Begin with line 1, which introduces the speech of the snake to the official.
- **b** In line 2, note the use of the weak pronoun (see Unit 12) after *m=k*.
- **c** The Egyptian wording in line 3 is a little unusual for English speakers, but it does make sense when you translate it literally.
- **d** In line 4, note that *ẖnw* means *royal residence*, whereas *m-ẖnw* means *inside* or simply *in*.
- **e** The narration continues in line 5 with a stative. Most words in this line are new, so look them up in the vocabulary builder.
- **f** In line 6, the word *mšꜥ* is written with the plural strokes but grammatically is treated as a singular, as you can see from the form of *ntj*.
- **g** The phrase *nb n jw pn* in line 7 refers to the snake.
- **h** Line 8 begins with a form of *ntj* that refers to the crew of the boat.

Drawing hieroglyphs

1 Here are the sound signs *gm* and *ẖn* for you to practise drawing.

a 

b 

2 'The Shipwrecked Sailor' was written in hieratic from right to left with parts of the text arranged into columns. Turn the two signs from exercise 1 around and find them in the following hieratic phrases: a *gmj.n=j* and b *ẖnw*.

a

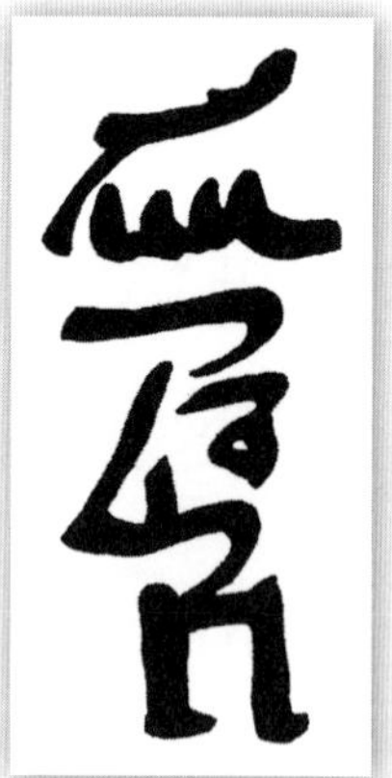

b

3 Try to work out which hieroglyph the other hieratic signs stand for. Then write the phrases in hieroglyphs, arranging the signs in the same way in which they are written in hieratic.

Test yourself

1 Match the particles with their correct translation and grammatical use.

		translation	followed by
a 	*ʿḥʿ.n*	*Look, …*	main clause
b 	*jw*	*Then …*	main or subordinate clause
c 	*m=k*	not translated or *while*	main clause

2 Select the correct transliteration and then the correct translation of the following relative clauses.

a 

dp.t ntj ḥrjt mry.t — *the boat which is on the shore*
dp.t ntt ḥr mry.t — *the boat which is on the upper shore*

b 

ntjw jm=s — *those who are in it*
ntj=j jm=s — *the one in which I was*

c 

nṯr ntj rḫ=k wj rn=f — *the god whose name I know*
nṯr ntj rḫ.kw rn=f — *the god whose name you know*

SELF-CHECK

	I CAN
●	recognize major particles
●	translate relative clauses
●	analyse longer passages of text
●	apply grammar from previous units to translate new texts

14 Foreign encounters

In this unit you will learn how to:

- **interpret longer passages of text**
- **use weak pronouns in adjectival sentences**
- **identify and translate questions.**

IMAGINING DIFFERENT WORLDS

The Egyptians had diverse relationships with their neighbours, ranging from military conflict to diplomacy and from migration to trade. Egyptian sources describe other societies in some great detail. They record the names of foreign people and depict their dress and body features. The illustration here, for example, from a tomb at Beni Hassan, shows a bearded Bedouin from the Levant. His name is *Ibsha* and he wears a fringed decorated robe.

Foreigners usually appear in a stereotyped way in Egyptian art. This means that those aspects that differ from Egyptian customs are emphasized and diversity within the foreign society is downplayed. Texts and the depictions of foreigners thus feature only a limited range of aspects. However, they are an attempt by Egyptians at translating a foreign culture into Egyptian language and modes of display. This is where they overlap with fiction. Both required imagination and engagement with a world different from their own daily experience.

The label in the illustration says that *Ibsha* is a 𓈉𓋾 *Hyksos*. The Hyksos are the Bedouin that ruled over Northern Egypt during the Second Intermediate Period (*c.*1600 BCE). Can you transliterate and translate this Egyptian title, which is the basis for the Greek term *Hyksos*?

Vocabulary builder

1 Read these new words aloud.

Names

	*Kpnj*	*Byblos* (a town in modern Lebanon)
	*Qdm*	*Qedem* (a place located perhaps in Syria)
	*ꜥmwnnšj*	*Amunenshi*
	*Rṯnw*	*Syria*
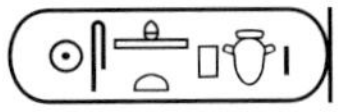	*S:ḥtp-jb-Rꜥ*	*Sehetepibra* (name of Amenemhet I)

Nouns

	*rnp.t*	*year*
	*gs*	*a half*
	*ḥqꜣ*	*ruler*
	*rꜣ*	*language*
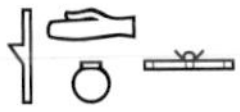	*qd*	*character*
	*šsꜣ*	*skills*
	*ḫpr.t*	*occurrence, event*

Verbs

	*fḫ*	*to leave (r for)*
	*ḥzj*	*to travel*
	*jrj*	*to spend*
	*pḥ*	*to reach, to come to*
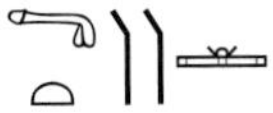	*mtj*	*to witness, to give witness for*

Question words

m	*who?, what?*
jšst	*who?, what?*
jn-jw	*do?, did?*

Other types of words

jm	there
ḥrj	upper
nn	this
ḥr	because of

2 Find these new signs in the vocabulary list above. Study how they are used in the words and then match them with their correct transliteration.

a (censer for fumigation) *pḥ*

b (lid of chest) *mt*

c (hindquarters of feline) *s3*

d (penis) *kpn*

> **LANGUAGE INSIGHT**
>
> Note these hieroglyphs that often go together as a group to represent a string of sounds. Make sure you distinguish from .
>
> *qd*
>
> *nn*

3 What do you think the new classifier in *fḫ* *to leave* depicts?

4 **The vocabulary list for this unit includes a range of words that you already encountered, but that now, in this context, have a second meaning. Consolidate your knowledge and complete the table by adding the meanings of the words you already know.**

		new translation	known translation
a		*jrj* *to spend*	___________
b		*gs* *a half*	___________
c		*jm* *there*	___________

5 **Similarly, the list includes known words with a different spelling. Add the transliteration to familiarize yourself with the different ways in which the words appear in hieroglyphs.**

	known spelling	new spelling	transliteration	translation
a			___________	*ruler*
b			___________	*upper*
c			___________	*to travel*

6 **The following word is transliterated like a word you have learned before. How can you distinguish the meaning of the known from the new word?**

	known word		new word	
ḥzj	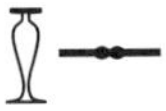	*to praise*		*to travel*

SINUHE THE EGYPTIAN

One of the finest pieces of ancient Egyptian literature tells of the adventures of Sinuhe, a high court official under Amenemhat I (1991–1962 BCE). According to the story, Amenemhat I died and Sinuhe fled abroad. The text does not say why Sinuhe left the country. Perhaps Amenemhat I was assassinated and Sinuhe, who had served this king, feared for his life, too. The ambiguous portrayal of Sinuhe as almost a coward is in contrast to his success abroad. Sinuhe spent several years in Syria, where he became co-leader of the *wḥy.t tribe* of a man called Amunenshi. At the end of his life, Sinuhe was summoned back to Egypt by the successor to Amenemhat I. He returned to Egypt, was welcomed at court and was promised a proper Egyptian burial.

The text offers a panorama of the close interaction between Egypt and the Eastern Mediterranean world during the Middle Bronze Age (*c.*2000–1500 BCE). It centres on values embodied by the Egyptian court, such as loyalty to the king and living according to Ma'at. The ancient Egyptian story inspired the 1941 novel *Awdat Sinuhi* (*The return of Sinuhe*) by Egyptian Nobel prize winner Naguib Mahfouz and, most famously, Mika Waltari's *Sinuhe the Egyptian*, published in 1945, with a Hollywood movie released in 1954. No doubt, modern readers find the story of Sinuhe as breathtaking as the ancient Egyptians did.

The following extract describes the moment when Sinuhe meets Amunenshi. First, go through the hieroglyphs and transliteration and answer these questions to get a sense of the passage.

1 Find the place names mentioned in the text and look up their location on the map on page xiv.

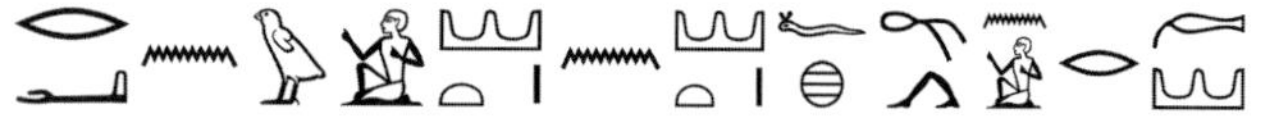

rdj.n wj ḫꜣs.t n ḫꜣs.t fḫ.n=j r Kpnj

ḥzj.n=j r Qdm jrj.n=j rnp.t gs jm

jnj.n wj ʿmwnnšj

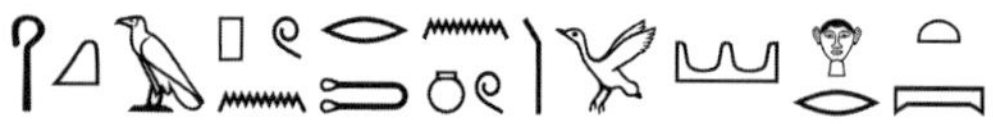

ḥqꜣ pw n Rṯnw ḥrj.t

ḏd=f n=j nfr ṯw ḥnʿ=j sḏm=k rꜣ n Km.t

ḏd.n=f nn rḫ.n=f qd=j sḏm.n=f šsꜣ=j

mtj.n wj rmṯ Km.t ntjw jm ḥnʿ=f

ʿḥʿ.n ḏd.n=f n=j pḥ.n=k nn ḥr m jšst pw

jn-jw wn ḫpr.t m ḫnw

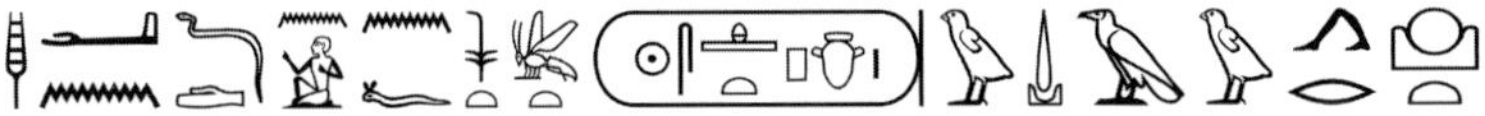

ʿḥʿ.n ḏd.n=j n=f njswt-bjt Sḥtp-jb-Rʿ wḏꜣ.w r ꜣḫ.t

2 Who is Amunenshi, according to the fourth line?

> **LANGUAGE INSIGHT**
>
> The name  *ʿmwnnšj* is not Egyptian, and the scribe struggled with rendering it in hieroglyphs. He might have added the sign  *zꜣ son* (see Unit 15) after *ʿmw*, because he understood the name as *Amu's son Nenshi*, a perfectly Egyptian naming pattern of that time.

3 Find the phrase  in the text. How would you translate it?

4 Following on from question 3, who then are the  mentioned in the seventh line?

5 Which expression does Sinuhe use in the final line to say that Amenemhet I has died?

Language discovery

1 Amunenshi promises Sinuhe that . How would you translate this sentence?

2 What does Amunenshi ask Sinuhe? Look out for the question words and try to find a good translation of these sentences.

a 

b 

c 

WEAK PRONOUNS IN ADJECTIVAL SENTENCES

The adjectival sentences that we have come across so far have a noun as their subject (see Unit 8). The passage about Sinuhe shows that whenever the subject is a pronoun, weak pronouns are used. In the English translation, you switch the word order of adjective and subject and add a form of *to be* between them.

nfr ṯw ḥnʿ=j

word for word: *good you with me*

fluent: *You (are, were, will be) good with me.* Or in context: *You will be fine with me.*

3 Select the correct pronoun from the options listed and transliterate these sentences.

a  (i)  (ii) 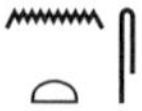 (iii) 

It is beautiful more than every thing. Or: *It is more beautiful than anything else.*

b  (i)  (ii)  (iii) 

He was strong.

c  (i)  (ii)  (iii) 

You are great, my lady.

QUESTIONS

The Egyptians had no equivalent of the question mark in English, but there are other indicators that help you to recognize that a sentence is meant as a question. To start with, there are two different types of question. The first type expects an answer *yes* or *no*. In Egyptian, it is typically introduced by  *jn-jw* or simply  *jn*. You can translate the sentence first without *jn-jw* and then transform it into a question. In English, these types of question would normally begin with *Do…?* or *Did…?* or with a form of to be, for example *Is…?* or *Were…?*

jn-jw wn ḫpr.t m ẖnw

Translation without *jn-jw*: *An occurrence existed at the residence.*

Translation as a question: *Did an occurrence exist at the residence?* More fluently: *Did something happen at the residence?*

4 Imagine that, upon his return, people were curious to know what happened to Sinuhe. What does the audience ask him? Translate the following:

a 

b 

c 

The second type of question asks for individual words, explanations or circumstances. In English, these questions begin with question words such as *What…?*, *Who…?*, *Which…?*, *How…?*, *Where…?*, *When…?* or *Why…?* Egyptian has words for *what?*, *who?* and *which?*, and expresses the other question words by combining these with a preposition.

 *m who?, what?*  *ḥr m because of what? = why?*

 *nm who?* (see Unit 13), probably derived from *jn m by whom?*

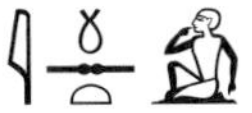 *jšst what?*  *mj jšst like what? = how?*

 *zj which?*  *ḥr zj jšst because of which, what? = why?*

zj precedes the word it belongs to, for example *zj jt which father?* In English, the other question words are placed at the beginning of a sentence, whereas in Egyptian they usually occupy the position of the word that they are asking for. You can leave it in this position in a word-for-word translation and then transform the sentence into a fluent English sentence afterwards.

jšst pw

Word for word: *what it is?*

Fluent: *What is it?*

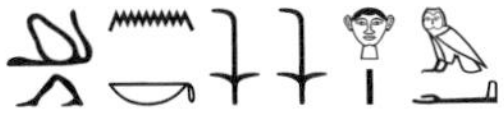

pḥ.n=k nn ḥr m

Word for word: *Reached you this because of what?*

Fluent: *Why did you reach this?* Or, in the context of Sinuhe's story: *Why did you come here?*

The emphasis in this sentence is placed on the preposition plus question word: *Why did you come here?* For this reason, this construction is common with the *.n*-past (see Unit 11).

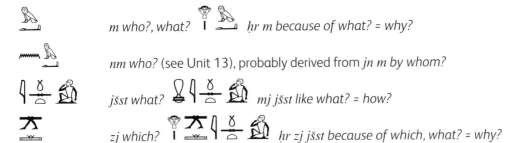

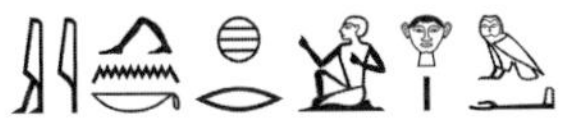

jyj.n=k ḫr=j ḥr m

Word for word: *Came you to me because of what?*

Fluent: *Why did you come to me?*

5 Again, imagine that the people cannot stop asking Sinuhe about his adventures. Transliterate and translate what they want to know.

a 

b 

c 

d 

e 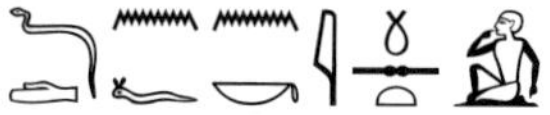

6 Here are a few questions that will help you to consolidate your understanding of the grammar.

a In verbal sentences, the subject usually follows the verb directly. Why is this different in these sentences from the story about Sinuhe?

rdj.n wj ḫꜣs.t n ḫꜣs.t

jnj.n wj ꜥmwnnšj

mtj.n wj rmṯ.w Km.t?

b Why does the text say *Rṯnw ḥrj.t* rather than *Rṯnw ḥrj*?

c What is the function of  in the sentence *mtj.n wj rmṯ Km.t ntjw jm ḥnꜥ=f*?

d Which form of the verb is  in the final line?

7 Translate the entire Sinuhe text. You can render it word for word first and then rephrase it to make it sound more fluent.

Explore

Throughout Pharaonic history, the Egyptians traded goods with the people of a land they called Punt. The wall reliefs in the funerary temple of queen Hatshepsut, shown above, depict the Puntites and their environment as the Egyptians saw them. According to the reliefs, Punt was ruled by several chiefs, together with their wives – depicted as obese women. The people of Punt lived in elevated houses resting on posts, which were reached with a ladder. Trade with them revolved predominantly around luxurious products, which the Puntites themselves had received through long-distance trade with other societies. For the Egyptians, the most important product from Punt was incense used in Egyptian temple rituals.

There is a longstanding debate about where Punt was located – whether near modern Ethiopia or, more likely perhaps, on the southern tip of the Arabian Peninsula. Certainly, the Egyptians saw it not only as a trading partner but also as a fascinating land,  *tꜣ-nṯr god's land* as they called it. For this reason, Hatshepsut imitated the incense tree terraces of Punt when she built her funerary temple on the Theban west bank, today a popular tourist destination opposite Luxor. The temple has various platforms and tree gardens and its wall reliefs convey the spirit of the Egyptians' fascination with Punt. The following labels and text are taken from the scene in the wall relief depicted. It shows the key players on the Egyptian and the Puntite side exchanging goods, not surprisingly with a focus on what the Egyptians received from the people of Punt.

1 Have a look at the people in the scene.

a On which side are the Puntites depicted and where are the Egyptians?

b What do you notice about the body shape of the girl depicted in the lower row?

2 Now read through the hieroglyphs from the scene. They are reproduced here at a larger scale to help you read them.

a Label in front of and above the chief of Punt in the upper row.

b Label in front of the Egyptian official in the upper row.

c Label in front of the Egyptian official and his troop in the lower row.

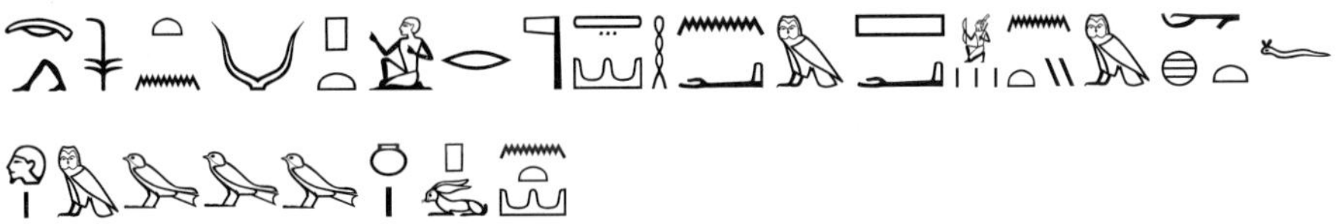

d Label of Puntite chief in the lower row called *Pꜣ-rꜣ-ḥw Parahu*:

e the woman behind him called *Jty Ity*: 

f the two male adults: , probably a misspelling of 

g the girl: 

h the ass: 

i The speech of the chief of Punt.

> **LANGUAGE INSIGHT**
>
> *ḫm.t rmṯ* in the first line of 2i means *which the people* (= *the Egyptians*) *do not know.*

3 Read these words aloud.

	*wr*	*chief*
	*jn.w*	*goods, luxurious products*
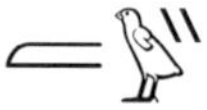	*gs.wj*	*shore*
	*šzp*	*to receive*
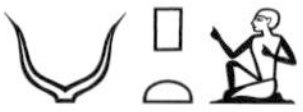	*wpw.tj*	*deputy*
	*mšꜥ*	*crew, troop* (alternative writing for )
	*m-ḫt*	*behind*
	*tp-m*	*before*
	*ꜥꜣ*	*ass*
	*fꜣj*	*to carry*
	*hꜣj*	*to come down*
	*sqd*	*to travel* (The seated man is not usually included in this word, but it appears in the text examples in this unit.)

4 Now try to transliterate and translate the inscriptions. The labels begin with either a noun or an infinitive.

5 Have a closer look at the Egyptian perspective on their encounter with the Puntites.

a Why do you think the ass had its own label?

b Why do you think the Egyptians put the questions into the mouth of the chief of Punt?

As you might have sensed from the exercises in this section, the scene with the Puntites is not an objective representation of reality, but the Egyptian interpretation thereof. Images and texts focus on those aspects that were relevant to the Egyptians, such as their interaction with the chiefs, the goods being traded and the otherness of the exotic landscape.

Drawing hieroglyphs

Have a go at drawing these hieroglyphs taken from the tale of *Sinuhe*.

a 

b 

Test yourself

1 Choose the correct translation of the adjectival sentences.

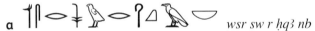

a  *wsr sw r ḥqꜣ nb*

Any (other) ruler is stronger than him.

He is stronger than any (other) ruler.

b  *mꜣꜥ st*

It is correct.

You are right.

c  *mnw=j nfr sn*

My monuments, they are beautiful!

I have made them beautiful monuments!

2 Choose the phrase the Egyptians would have employed to ask the following questions.

a *Did Sinuhe go to Upper Syria?* (i)  (ii)  (iii) 

b *Who were the people there?* (i)  (ii) 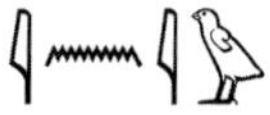 (iii) 

c *Why did he return to Egypt?* (i)  (ii) 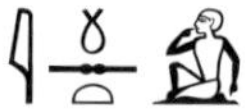 (iii) 

SELF-CHECK

	I CAN
●	interpret longer passages of text
●	use weak pronouns in adjectival sentences
●	identify and translate questions

15 Household records

In this unit you will learn how to:

- **read documents and letters**
- **recognize and translate commands**
- **use relative forms**
- **recognize forms of colloquial language.**

SCRIBES, LITERACY AND BUREAUCRACY

The Egyptians were among the first societies in history that used writing to communicate over long distances and create records for central administration and, later, for private households. Letters, decrees, legal documents and accounts were written with ink on papyrus, as the image of a scribe above shows, or on discarded pottery shards and stone flakes called 'ostraca'. Most scribes were trained only to perform simple administrative and accountancy tasks. They learned the hand-written script – hieratic, and in later periods demotic – whereas hieroglyphs were mastered by only a few specialists.

Whether kings were able to read and write is doubtful. Although they exerted power through the written word, they left the practicalities of writing, which must have been difficult to learn, to their scribes. For most Egyptians, writing skills were not necessary to their daily lives. They would ask a village scribe to write letters and other documents for them if needed. The wealth of preserved written documents might suggest to us today that life in ancient Egypt was strictly regulated by bureaucracy. However, at a local level, kinship ties and community life are likely to have played a much more important role in the organization of society than administration did.

Vocabulary builder

1 Read these new words aloud.

Titles and administration

	*mtj-n-z3.w*	*controller of the phyles*
	*jmj-z3 n qnb.tj n w.w*	*guard of the district counsellor*
	*b3k*	*servant* (*b3k jm* *humble servant*, literally *servant there*)
	*jmj-r3*	*overseer* (literally either *who/what is in the mouth* (= the tongue that gives commands) or *in whom is a mouth* (to give commands))
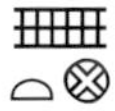	*sp3.t*	*district*
	*Ḥw.t-M3ˁ.t*	*Hut-Ma'at* (literally *Enclosure-of-justice*; the location of this place is unknown)

CULTURE INSIGHT

A *phyle* is a group of ritual assistants who were employed by each temple and on duty for a month at a time. The set of phyles rotated throughout the year.

Letters and documents

	*jr*	*As for …,*
	*s:wḏ3 jb*	*to inform; message* (*r* or *ḥr about*; literally *to make (somebody's) heart safe*)

Property

	*pr*	*house*
	*jmj.t-pr*	*transfer of deed* (literally *(document) in which the house is* or *what is in the house*)
	*h3w*	*matters, belongings*

Phases in the life of an official

	*msj*	*to give birth (msy n born to)*
	*dhn*	*to appoint*
	*tnj*	*to be old*
	*mdw j3w*	*staff of old age*

Expressions of time and space

	*3.t*	*moment (m t3 3.t immediately)*
	*ḥ3.t*	*front (ẖr ḥ3.t previously*, literally *under the front)*
	*s3*	*back*

Other words

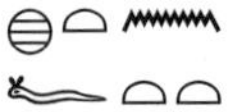	*ḫft ntt*	*because*
	*jmj*	*give!, cause that …!, let …!*

2 Judging from their translation, what would you say the meanings of the titles **,**  **and**  **have in common?**

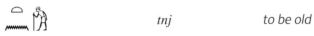

3 Study how these new signs are used in the words in the vocabulary. Then match them with their correct description and transliteration.

a		jabiru (a stork)	*b3*
b		rolled-up shelter for papyrus	*ms*
c		corner	*jmj*
d		two wooden planks	*qnb.t*
e		three animal skins	*z3*
f		lid of a chest	*s3*

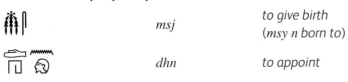

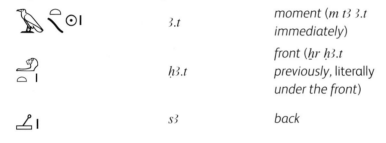

PAPYRI FROM LAHUN

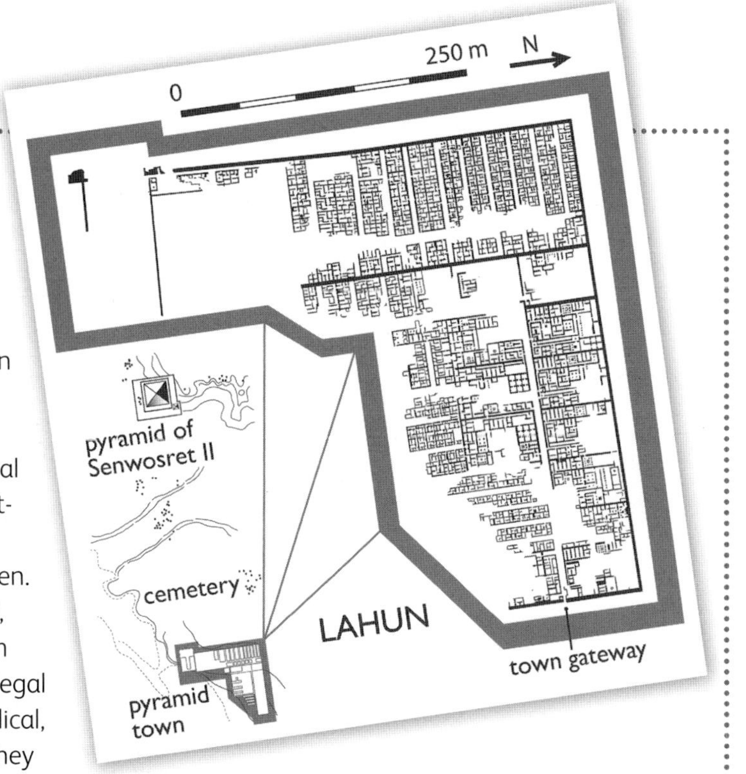

Lahun, also known as Illahun or Kahun, is the modern name of a village located near the pyramid of Senwosret II (1877–1870 BCE). The pyramid was built together with a town that accommodated priests, workmen and officials alongside their families. The town was laid out on an orthogonal grid with ten large villas for the highest-ranking officials and several mid-sized and many small houses for the workmen. After the excavation of Lahun in 1890, papyri from the same site appeared on the antiquities market. They included legal documents, letters, accounts, and medical, mathematical and literary texts, and they shed light on the complexity of life in the town. One of them records the transfer of a deed belonging to an official called *Mery*. Mery was an overseer of the temple phyles and might have lived in one of the mid-sized houses. The text reveals that he married a second wife, presumably after his first wife had died, although it does not say this. Since he had children by both women, he set up a written document stating who should receive what from his property.

The editor of Mery's text, Stephen Quirke, has transcribed the hieratic document into hieroglyphs to make it simpler for other Egyptologists to read it. We will concentrate on the arrangement Mery has made. The final three lines, not considered here, contain a list of witnesses for the arrangement.

Go through the hieroglyphs below and compare them with their transliteration and translation and see whether you can work out the arrangements that Mery made. Then try to answer the questions.

1 Who benefits from Mery's transfer of deed?

2 Does the text say when the property should be transferred: is it before or after Mery's death?

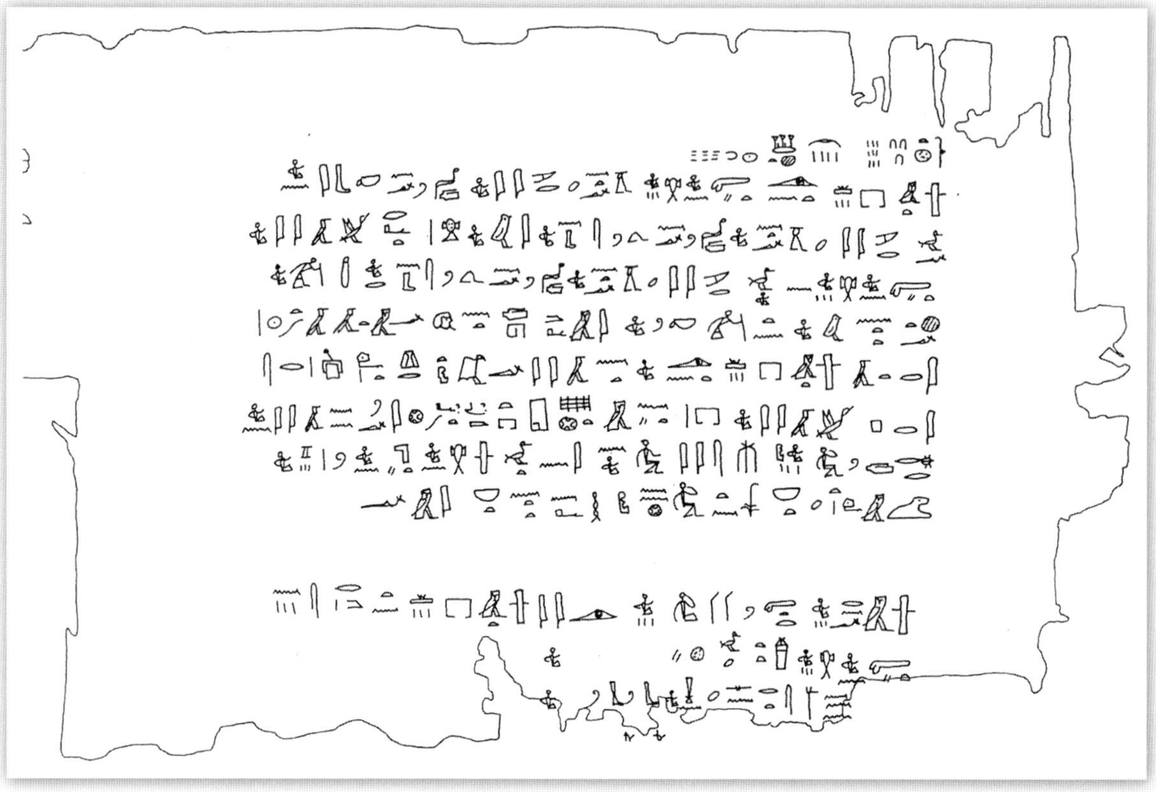

rnp.t-zp 39 3bd 4 3ḫ.t 19

jmj.t-pr jrj.t.n mtj-n-z3 Jnj-jt=f z3 Mry ḏdw n=f Kbj

n z3=f Mry z3 Jnj-jt=f ḏdw n=f Jwj-snb jw=j ḥr rdj.t p3y=j

mtj-n-z3 n z3=j Mry z3 Jnj-jt=f ḏdw n=f Jwj-snb r mdw j3w=j

ḫft ntt wj tnj.kw jmj dhn.tw=f m t3 3.t

jr t3 jmj.t-pr jrj.t.n=j n t3y=f mw.t ḥr ḥ3.t z3 r=s

jr p3y=j pr ntj m sp3.t Ḥw.t-M3ʿ.t jw=f n n3y=j n

ḫrd.w msy n=j jn z3.t jmj-z3 n qnb.tj n w.w

Sbk-m-ḥ3.t z3.t Nb.t-Nn-njswt ḥnʿ nt.t nb.t jm=f

Regnal year 39, fourth month of winter, day 19.

Transfer of deed, which the controller of the phyles Antef's son Mery, called Kebi, has made for his son Mery's son Antef, called Iuiseneb.

I am giving my (office of a) controller of the phyles to my son Mery's son Antef, called Iuiseneb, for (being) my staff of old age because I have grown old. Let him be appointed immediately.

As for the transfer of deed which I have previously made for his mother: (turn your) back to it.

As for my house that is in the district of Hut-Ma'at: it will be for my children, born to me by the daughter of the guard of the district counsellor Sobekemhat's daughter Nebetnennisut, together with everything that is in it.

3 Who are these people in relation to Mery? Answer the question by looking carefully at the kinship terms used in the document.

a Antef, called Iuiseneb

b Antef

c Nebetnennisut

d Sobekemhat

4 Look at the text again. What might the technical term  **in line 4 mean, given that Mery is handing over his office, i.e. his source of income, to his son?**

5 Why does Mery transfer his office to his son?

6 What does Mery say about the transfer of the deed he had previously made for his first wife?

Language discovery

1 How would you describe the function of  **in lines 6 and 7 in the document?**

2 Investigate the naming conventions of people in Mery's transfer of deed.

a What do you notice about the word order in the names of these individuals?

Jnj-jt=f zꜣ Mry Antef's son Mery

Mry zꜣ Jnj-jt=f Mery's son Antef

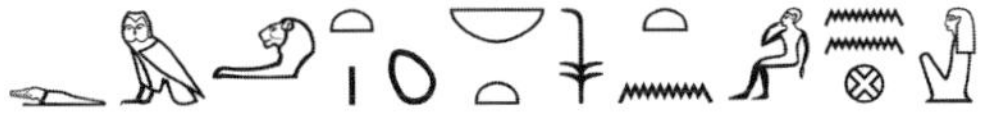

Sbk-m-ḥꜣ.t zꜣ.t Nb.t-Nn-njswt Sobekemhat's daughter Nebetnennisut

b Which phrase in the name of Mery, whose second name is Kebi, is translated with *called* in the text?

CONVENTIONS IN DOCUMENTS AND LETTERS

The phrase  *jr* is translated as *As for …* or *Concerning …* You can think of it as a bullet point that introduces a matter, which is then addressed. In Mery's transfer of deed, *jr pꜣy=j pr jw=f n nꜣy=j n ẖrd.w As for my house: it will be for my children, pꜣy=j pr my house* is the matter that is picked up with *=f it* in the next sentence.

Middle Kingdom administrative texts have a particular way of dealing with names. Where you would expect in Egyptian *Mry zꜣ Jnj-jt=f Mery, son of Antef*, they switch the two names, saying:  *Jnj-jt=f zꜣ Mry* the equivalent of which in English is *Antef's son Mery*. One explanation might be that the name of the father  *Jnj-jt=f* was placed in front to honour him, which is similar to what you learned about the honorific transposition of royal and divine names. The words *zꜣ son* and *zꜣ.t daughter* are then both often written with this sign .

Egyptians were given a name at birth but many later acquired a second name, perhaps a nickname used by friends. The second name could be used in a document to distinguish an individual from another with the same birth name. Thus, Mery called Kebi was different from another individual called Mery who had a different second name. The Egyptian phrase that introduces the second name is  *ḏdw n=f to whom is (also) said*. The form *ḏdw* is a verbal adjective and the phrase *ḏdw n=f* literally means *who is said to him*. Since the literal translation does not make good sense in English, the standard translation is *called*.

There are a few more conventions, which you will go on to look at later in the 'Explore' section. The verbal adjective of *ḏd* is also used to express who is sending and receiving a letter. This 'address line' begins with the name of the sender followed by *ḏd n who speaks to* and the name of the receiver. For example,  *Mry ḏd n Jnj-jt=f* means *Mery who speaks to Antef*, where Mery is the sender and Antef the receiver.

CULTURE INSIGHT

The use of the verb *to speak* in the 'address line' suggests that a letter was the literal transcript of an oral dictation. In practice, however, scribes might have changed the wording of the sender to make it comply with the conventions of the written expression. Perhaps the Egyptians trusted in direct face-to-face conversation more than in a piece of writing and for this reason maintained the illusion that a letter was an oral communication not mediated by a third party.

When a sender writes to his superior, he often speaks of himself humbly in the third person as  *bꜣk jm*, literally *servant there*, instead of saying *I*. The phrase is conventionally translated in Egyptology as *humble servant*.

The name of the superior is regularly followed by the signs , an abbreviated spelling for *ꜥnḫ (w)ḏꜣ s(nb) life, prosperity, health*. This group expresses good wishes for the superior who shall live, be prosperous and be healthy. It is often transliterated in an abbreviated fashion as *ꜥ.w.s.* and rendered in the written translation as *l.p.h.*

3 **See how these conventions work by having a go at the transliteration and translation of these phrases typically found in legal documents and letters.**

a 

b 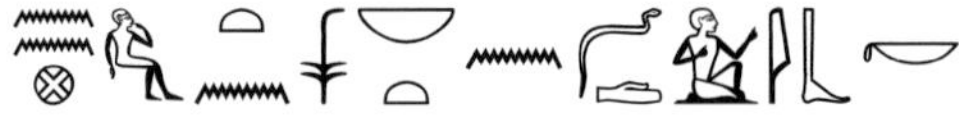

c 

d 

e 

f 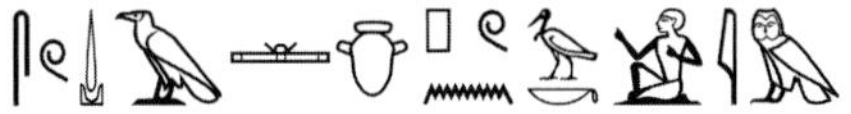

COMMANDS

4 **Go back to Mery's document and find this command  in the hieroglyphs, transliteration and translation. How might you translate it literally?**

The Egyptians expressed commands by using the base of a verb without any endings. This form is called the imperative. You can only tell from the context whether the command is given to a male or a female individual or to one person or a group of people, although plural strokes can be added in the latter case without making a difference to the transliteration and translation.

 *sḏm Listen!*

 *jnj n=j sw Bring him to me!*

The person acting is implied in the verb. It means that it is not written with a separate word. This is why the lack of a subject in a sentence tells you that the verb very likely expresses a command. The same is true for commands in English, for example *Listen!* instead of *Listen you!*, where the subject *you* is implied in the command *Listen!* You will typically find commands in texts that record direct speech, such as in a letter.

Some verbs have irregular forms in the imperative. The most common example is  *jmj give!, cause that …!, let …!* derived from the verb *rdj/dj*.

 *jmj dhn.tw=f Cause that he may be appointed!*

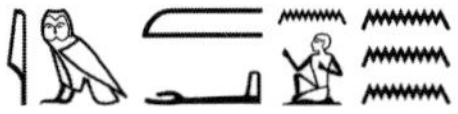 *jmj n=j mw Give me water!*

Note:  *mw* means *water*.

5 Change the predicate of these sentences from the intended future into the imperative in order to understand better what is meant by 'implied subject' in commands. The first example is done for you.

a 

sḏm=k rmṯ *May you listen to the people.* → *sḏm rmṯ* *Listen to the people!*

b 

__________ *May you appoint him.* → __________ __________

c 

ʿpr=k p3y=k bw nfr *May you furnish your goodness.* → __________ __________

d 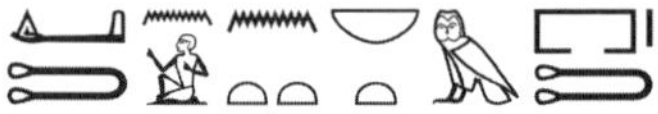

__________ *May you give me everything that is in your house.* → __________ __________

RELATIVE FORMS

6 Mery's document includes these two relative phrases. Which word is added in the English translation compared with the Egyptian original?

a  *jmj.t-pr jrj.t.n Mry*

transfer of deed which Mery had made

b  *jmj.t-pr jrj.t.n=j*

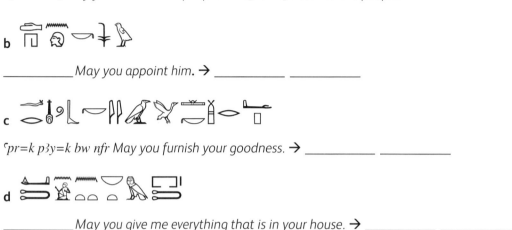

transfer of deed which I had made

Relative forms have much in common with the verbal adjectives discussed in Unit 7: they add information about the noun that precedes them; their form changes according to the gender and number of the preceding noun; weak verbs can duplicate their second letter; and they are translated with a relative clause in English. However, unlike verbal adjectives, they have only active voice meaning and take an additional *.n* in the past tense. More importantly, relative forms are always followed by a new subject, which is either a noun or an attached pronoun.

The following examples show how the relative forms work and how you translate them.

jmj.t-pr jrj.t.n=j

Word for word: *transfer of deed – made – I*

In context: *the transfer of deed which I have made*

The relative form *jrj.t.n=j* in the phrase above shows a *.t* ending because *jmj.t-pr* is feminine. It is past tense, as the *.n* is indicating. The subject of the relative form is *=j* I. In translation, you switch the word order of the relative form and the new subject. You can insert *which*, or *whom* if it is a person, before the relative clause, although this is usually dropped in English for the sake of brevity, and you would simply say *the transfer of deed I have made* instead of *the transfer of deed which I have made.*

The following example shows the duplication of the second letter in weak verbs. The duplication is typical of statements that refer to habitual, repeated or intense action in the past or present, which you can try to express in your translation.

jrj.n=j ḫ.t mrr.t rmṯ

I have done (the thing) which the people love very much.

7 Complete the transliteration of the following phrases formed from a noun and a relative form.

a  *jmj.t-pr* _____ _____

b  _____ *=f* _____ = _____

c  *Jnj-jt=f* _____ _____

d  _____ _____ *Nb.t-nn-njswt*

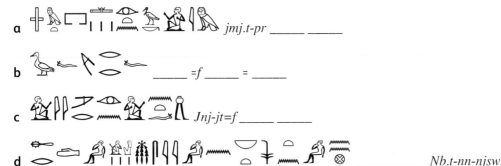

8 Now translate the phrases in exercise 7. You can begin with a word-for-word translation and then find a more fluent expression, as shown previously.

In some cases, the noun that precedes the relative form is repeated with an attached pronoun that follows a preposition. You can translate these phrases word for word first, as usual, and then bring the words into a more natural-sounding order in English, by replacing the attached pronoun with *which* or *whom*. The preposition and the attached pronoun that repeats the noun are underlined in the examples below in order to help you understand the grammar.

h3w h3b.n=j sw n=k ḥr=sn

Word for word: *matters – sent – I – to – you – him – about – them*

In context: *the matters about which I sent him to you*

nb=j h3b.n=j n=f s:wḏ3-jb

Word for word: *lord – my – sent – I – to – him – communication*

In context: *my lord to whom I sent communication*

9 Try a translation of the following phrases, which include a relative form, following the steps described above.

a 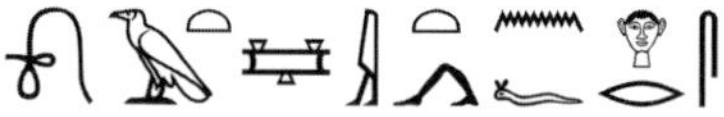 *w3j.t jyj.t.n=f ḥr=s*

b  *s.t nb.t jrj.t.n=j mnw jm=s*

c  *dj=f ḫ.t nb.t nfr.t wꜥb.t ꜥnḫ.t nṯr jm=s*

The noun that precedes the relative form can be dropped in Egyptian. In English, you can add provisionally (*the thing which*) or (*the person who*), before you find a more fluent expression. The omission of the noun is especially popular with expressions followed by *nb* translated as *everything (which)* or *anybody (who).*

 *mj mrr=f like (the thing that) he loves or simply as he likes*

 *jrj.t=j nb.t everything (which) I have made*

10 Here are a few phrases, where the noun is omitted before the relative form. Try a translation and transliteration, adding provisional phrases as explained above.

a 

b 

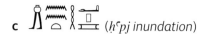

c 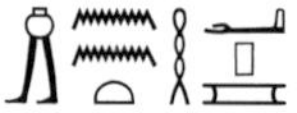 (*ḥꜥpj inundation*)

d 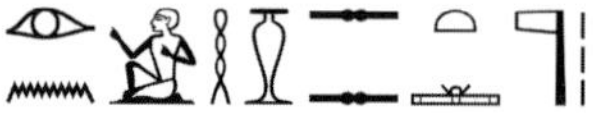

COLLOQUIAL LANGUAGE

11 The scribe of Mery's document used some colloquial forms. Look up the following phrases in the text and find their transliteration and translation.

a 

b 

c 

d 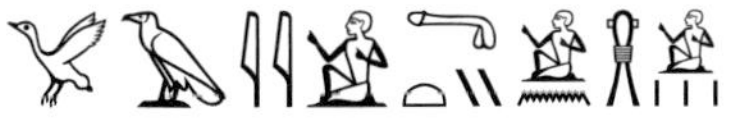

e 

f 

Unlike formal inscriptions on temple walls and stelae, letters and private documents tend to be written in a language closer to how people were speaking on the streets. The documents from Lahun show a range of such grammatical features. One of them is the use of the definite article *p3 the*, which standard Middle Egyptian avoids. High-ranking officials prided themselves in their inscriptions on not using this word, apparently because *p3* was considered a too ordinary expression. Another colloquial phrase, derived from the definite article, is the expression of possession with *p3y=* followed by the attached pronoun and preceding the noun which is possessed. Standard Middle Egyptian would prefer to attach the pronoun directly to the noun. The following table shows the differences.

	standard Middle Egyptian	colloquial Middle Egyptian
the house	*pr*	*p3 pr*
my house	*pr=j*	*p3y=j pr*

Both the definite article *p3* and the possessive article *p3y=* agree in gender with the noun they precede. Their feminine forms are *t3* and *t3y=*.

before a masculine noun	before a feminine noun
p3 pr the house	*t3 mw.t* the mother
p3y=j pr my house	*t3y=j mw.t* my mother
p3y=f pr his house	*t3y=f mw.t* his mother

The forms of the plural, both masculine and feminine, are *nꜣ* and *nꜣy=*. Unlike the singular, an additional — *n* is inserted before the noun it precedes. The noun can, but does not have to be set in the plural because the plural is sufficiently marked by the plural forms of the article.

plural nouns

nꜣ n ẖrd the children

nꜣy=j n ẖrd.w my children

nꜣy=f n ẖrd.w his children

12 What do these phrases in colloquial Middle Egyptian mean? Translate them.

a   *pꜣy=s pr*

b   *tꜣ sn.t*

c   *nꜣ n hꜣw*

d   *tꜣy=sn jmj.t-pr*

e   *pꜣ s:wḏꜣ-jb*

f   *nꜣy=j n nṯr.w*

13 Go back to the colloquial phrases in the previous exercise. Transform them into standard Middle Egyptian, using the tables above for comparison, and transliterate.

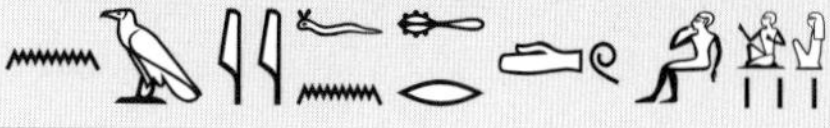

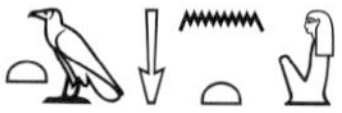

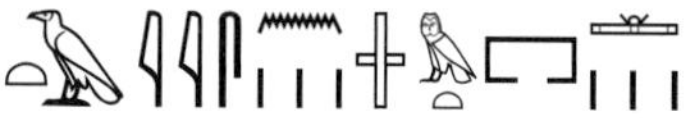

Explore

The following is a communication between *Nnj Neni* and *Jyj-jb Iyiib*. Like Mery's transfer of deed, it was originally written in hieratic on a papyrus from Lahun. The provenance suggests that Iyiib resided at Lahun and exchanged messages with people working elsewhere. The letter includes a series of standard wishes and formulas in the first part and then reports a conflict which involved two other men called *W3ḥ Wah* and *Ttj Teti*. The letter refers to people and issues mentioned in a previous message, which the sender and receiver were familiar with but which are lost to us.

To help you with the understanding of the letter, the transliteration is already done for you, so you can concentrate on the translation and interpretation of the content. Try to answer these questions first, to get a sense of the document, before you look at the details.

1 Work out the relationship between Neni and Iyiib by applying your knowledge of administrative conventions in Egyptian.

- **a** Where are the sender and receiver written in the hieroglyphs?
- **b** Is Neni sending or receiving the letter?
- **c** Find the group *ʿ.w.s. l.p.h.* in the hieroglyphs. Which words are written before it?
- **d** Following on from your answer to the previous question, would you say that Neni is Iyiib's superior or that, on the contrary, Iyiib is Neni's superior?
- **e** Who then is the *b3k jm humble servant*, mentioned in the fifth line of the main body of the letter?

2 Now read through the hieroglyphs of the text. Compare them with their transliteration and note all new words.

3 Read aloud the new words in the letter, arranged below in order of their appearance in the text.

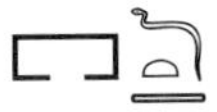	*pr-ḏ.t*	*funerary domain* (property from which the offerings to a deceased were paid)
	*r ntt*	*(to the effect) that* (introduces the content of a message)
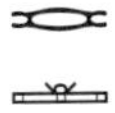	*ʿḏ*	*to be fine*
	*wḏ3*	*to be safe*
	*ḥzw.t*	*praise*
	*Spdw*	*Soped* (a deity)
	*j3bt.t*	*east*
	*psḏ.t*	*ennead*

CULTURE INSIGHT

Each Egyptian temple was dedicated to one main deity. However, this deity had an entourage of subordinate gods called *psḏ.t*. The term literally means *ennead*, a word derived from the Greek word for *nine*. In theory a *psḏ.t* was formed of nine deities, but in reality the number varied from temple to temple. The term was used nevertheless in all cases out of convention.

	*ḥr*	*about*
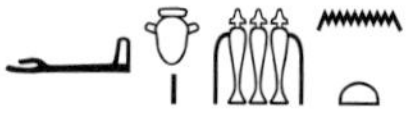	*dj jb ḫnt*	*to pay attention to*
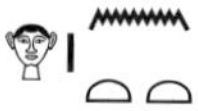	*ḥr ntt*	*for, because* (introduces a reason)
	*kꜣ*	*So, …* (introduces a new thought)
	*ꜥpr*	*to furnish*
	*bw nfr*	*goodness*
	*gr*	*also*
	*ḫrw fj*	*…, he said*
	*ḫft jrj*	*accordingly*

LANGUAGE INSIGHT

The word *bw*, literally meaning *place*, is used with adjectives to form abstract terms. Thus, *bw nfr* can mean *good place*, but also *goodness*. Other examples are *bw mnḫ excellence* from *mnḫ excellent* and *bw ḏw the evil* derived from *ḏw evil*.

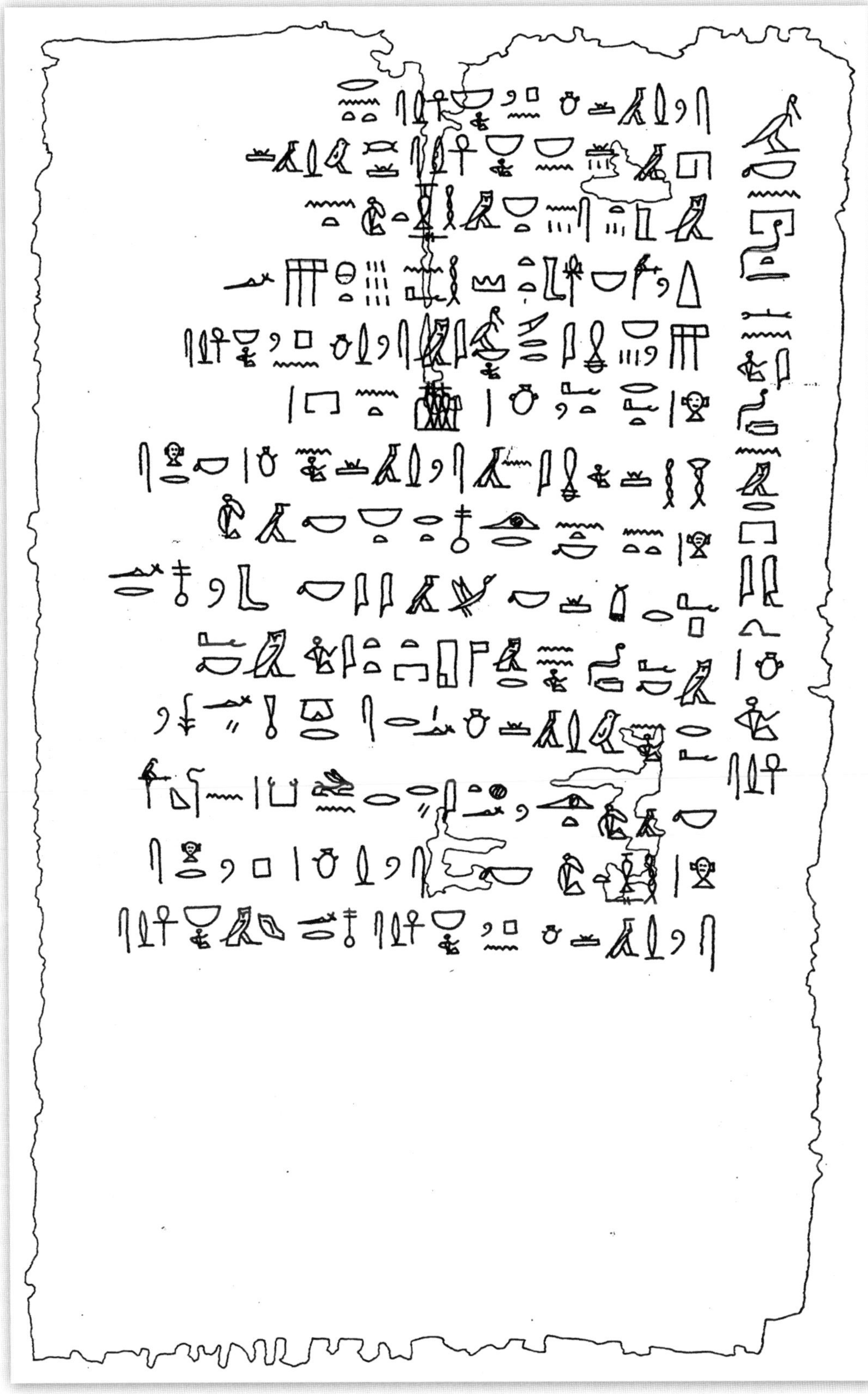

Sender and receiver:

bꜣk n pr-ḏ.t Nnj ḏd n jmj-rꜣ pr Jyj-jb ꜥ.w.s.

Greetings:

s:wḏꜣ-jb pw n nb=j ꜥ.w.s r ntt

hꜣw nb n nb=j ꜥ.w.s. ꜥḏ.w wḏꜣ.w

m s.wt=sn nb.wt m ḥzw.t n.t Spdw nb jꜣbt.t

ḥnꜥ psḏ.t=f nṯr.w nb.w mj mrr bꜣk jm

Setting the scene for the issue of the letter:

s:wḏꜣ-jb pw n nb=j ꜥ.w.s. ḥr rdj.t dj.tw jb ḫnt pr

Wꜣḥ mj nꜣ s:wḏꜣ.n=j jb=k ḥr=s

ḥr ntt ntk jrr nfr.t nb.t

kꜣ ꜥpr=k pꜣy=k bw nfr

The problem:

m=k ḏd.n n=j jmj-rꜣ ḥw.t-nṯr Ttj

m=k rdj.n=j wḏꜣ jb=f r=s gr ḫrw=fj sw

kꜣ jr.tw ḫft jrj r wn kꜣ n ḥqꜣ ḥr ḥzw.t=k

Greetings and subservience:

s:wḏꜣ-jb pw ḥr=s

s:wḏꜣ-jb pw n nb=j ꜥ.w.s.

nfr sḏm nb=j ꜥ.w.s

4 Now try a translation of the entire text. This is a challenging exercise, but one that allows you to put into practice much of what you have learned throughout the course.

Drawing hieroglyphs

1 Try to draw the following hieroglyphs. This will help you distinguish the various hieroglyphs representing birds.

a 

b 

2 Have a go at writing the phrases *pꜣy=k bw nfr* ***your goodness*** **and** *bꜣk jm* ***humble servant*** **from the letter of Neni, which use these two hieroglyphs.**

Test yourself

1 What does the group  placed after the name or title of a superior mean?

2 Choose which of the two phrases is a command.

a 

b 

3 Translate these phrases, which include a relative form.

a  *ḥm.t=f mrj.t=f*

b 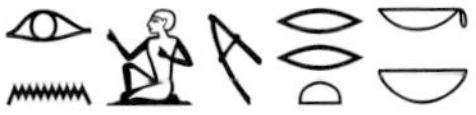 *jrj.n=j mrr.t=k nb.t*

4 Select the phrases that are written in colloquial language.

a 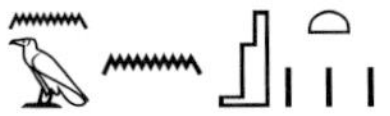 *the places*

b  *my father*

c  *their gods*

d  *everything that is in it*

SELF-CHECK

	I CAN
●	read documents and letters
●	recognize and translate commands
●	use relative forms
●	recognize forms of colloquial language

16 Border traffic

In this unit you will learn how to:

- **read royal decrees**
- **translate negations**
- **use verbal adjectives in the future tense.**

EGYPTIAN FORTS IN LOWER NUBIA

When the Aswan High Dam was opened in 1971, many archaeological sites in Lower Nubia – the area between the First Cataract south of Aswan and the Second Cataract near the modern Egyptian-Sudanese border – were flooded and the people living there were resettled. During the construction process, an unprecedented worldwide effort was made to relocate the major monuments of this area, such as the temples at Abu Simbel and Philae. In addition, archaeologists recorded the remains at several sites that today are covered with water. These included a series of forts originally built during the Middle Kingdom. They were erected by Egyptian kings primarily to control the exploitation of the Nubian gold mines in the Eastern desert. Later, in the New Kingdom, they provided an infrastructure for Egyptians to settle there permanently and mix with the local population.

The image above shows a drawing of the fort at Semna, which is the site we are going to concentrate on in this unit. The drawing was made during a scientific expedition to Egypt and Nubia in the mid-19th century led by Egyptologist Karl Richard Lepsius on behalf of the Prussian king. The peaceful scenery depicted can easily make us forget the aggressive expansion of the Middle Kingdom state into Nubia.

Vocabulary builder

THE SMALL SEMNA STELA OF YEAR 8

1 Read these new words aloud.

	*rsj*	*southern*
	*znj*	*to pass*
	*nḥsj*	*Nubian*
	*ẖdj*	*to sail downstream (= to sail north)*
	*ḥrj*	*to travel on land*
	*k3j*	*boat*
	*mnmn.t*	*flock*
	*wpw-ḥr*	*except*
	*jwj*	*to come* (same meaning as *jyj*)
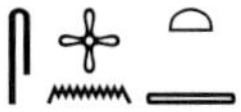	*swn.t*	*trade* (*jrj swn.t to trade*)
	*Jqn*	*Mirgissa*
	*wpw.tj*	*messenger; deputy* (see Unit 14)
	*r3-pw*	*or* (follows the two terms it is connecting)
	*swt*	*however*
	*s:w3j*	*to pass* (*ḥr by*)
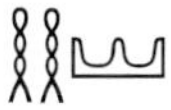	*Ḥḥ*	*Semna*

2 Go through the vocabulary and match these new signs with their correct transliteration.

a  (combination of the sounds  *r* and  *sw*) *nḥ*

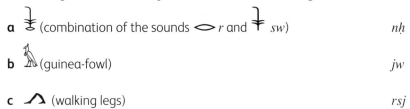

b  (guinea-fowl) *jw*

c  (walking legs) *rsj*

3 Here are two words you know already but that are spelled differently in this unit. Complete the table to work out how they are transliterated and translated.

	known spelling	new spelling	transliteration	translation
a		,	*s:rwd*	__________
b			__________	*border*

LANGUAGE INSIGHT

The large Semna stela shows yet another spelling of *s:rwd* as  with the hieroglyph depicting a frog.

THE SMALL SEMNA STELA OF YEAR 8

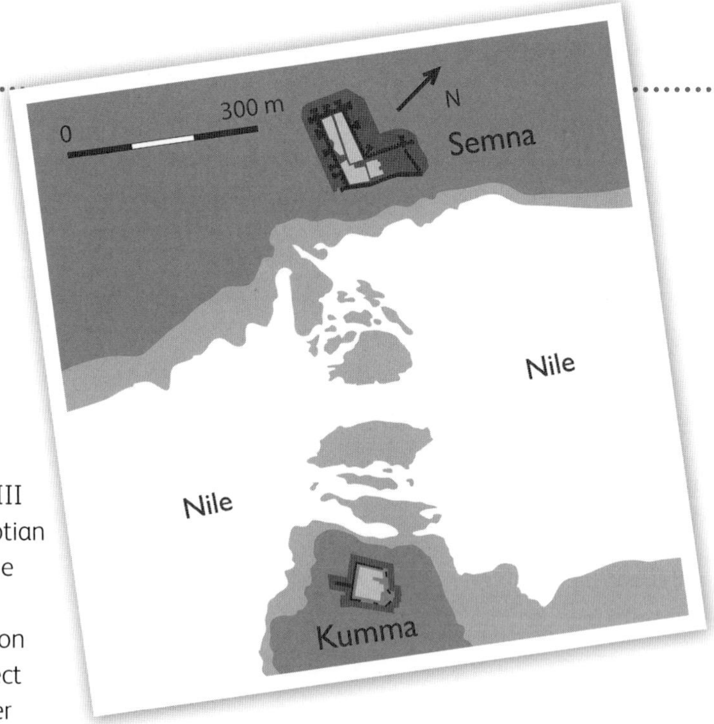

The fort of Semna lies opposite the fort of Kumma, a few kilometres to the south of the Second Cataract, where the fort of Mirgissa is located. Together, Semna and Kumma formed a powerful stronghold towering over the traffic on the river and over the land routes that ran along the Nile. Both forts were erected by Senwosret III (1872–1853 BCE) who extended Egyptian control into this area. In addition to the archaeological remains, two inscribed stelae were uncovered that shed light on the history of Semna. These texts reflect the official Egyptian view on the border traffic which the Egyptians controlled. However, reading between the lines, it appears that both Egyptians and Nubians depended on each other and profited from the exchange of goods, services, and information. Senwosret III erected the smaller of the two stelae in his regnal year 8 and the larger one in year 16.

Read through the hieroglyphs, the transliteration and translation of the smaller Semna stela, shown below, and then try to interpret it by answering the questions.

Sign above inscription: *jmn.t*

(1) *t3š rsj jry m rnp.t 8 ẖr ḥm n njswt-bjt H̱ꜥj-k3.w-Rꜥ dj ꜥnẖ ḏ.t*

(2) *r nḥḥ r tm rdj.w znj sw nḥsj nb m ẖdj*

(3) *m ḥrj.t m k3j mnmn.t nb.t n.t*

(4) *nḥsj.w wpw-ḥr nḥsj jw.tj=fj r jrj.t swn.t m Jkn*

(5) *m wpw.tj r3-pw jrj.t=tw nb.t nfr.w ḥnꜥ=sn nn swt rdj.t*

(6) *s:w3j k3j n nḥsj.w m ẖdj ḥr ḥḥ r nḥḥ*

Sign above inscription: *West*

(1) *Southern border made in year 8 under the Majesty of the king of Upper and Lower Egypt May-the-ka-souls-of-Ra-appear, given life for ever*

(2) *and ever in order to prevent any Nubian from passing it while sailing north,*

(3) *travelling on land (or) in a boat, (nor) any flock of*

(4) *the Nubians except for a Nubian who will come to trade at Mirgissa*

(5) *or as a messenger. Everything that one does shall be good with them without, however, letting*

(6) *a boat of the Nubians pass sailing north to Semna, forever.*

1 What could you deduce from the sign above the inscription?

2 How would you interpret the figures carved below the inscription?

3 Under what circumstances was a Nubian allowed to travel north of Semna, according to the inscription on the stela?

Language discovery

1 Find these verbal adjectives and the relative form within the hieroglyphs of the text. How are they transliterated and translated?

a 

b 

c 

LANGUAGE INSIGHT

The word  *=tw* is an impersonal attached pronoun meaning *one*. Different from other forms of the attached pronouns, *=tw* is used only after verbs and particles to express the subject in a sentence.

2 Go back to the text and find the two negations in hieroglyphs and the transliteration.

a How are they translated in English?

b How would you translate literally the negated phrases *r tm rdj.w znj sw nḥsj nb* and *nn swt rdj.t s:w3j k3j n nḥsj.w*?

AUTHOR'S NOTE

The inscription on the small Semna stela is an example of how difficult it can be to translate Egyptian texts. Here are some of the different ways that the phrase in line 5, rendered here as *Everything that one does shall be good with them* has been translated over the years by different Egyptologists. Alan Gardiner translated it as *Every good thing shall be done with them*, whereas José Galán thinks that the sentence means *One shall trade with them all goods*. This is in contrast to Aylward Blackman's translation of *... any business that one may transact lawfully with them*. Each translation rests on its own analysis of the grammar and historical interpretation.
The translation used here assumes that *nfr.w* is the stative of the verb *nfr to be good* in the third person singular with future meaning, although the feminine form *nft.tj* would be expected because its subject *jrj.t=tw nb.t* is feminine, and that the text calls for a peaceful treatment of the Nubians unless they travel north without having asked the Egyptians for permission. Although not all texts are as controversial as this, the small Semna stela shows that our understanding of grammar can influence our view of historical reality.

VERBAL ADJECTIVES EXPRESSING FUTURE TENSE

You learned in Unit 7 that verbal adjectives in Egyptian are tenseless. They can refer to an action in the past, present or future. Middle Egyptian has a second series of verbal adjectives expressing future tense only, almost always in the active voice. You translate them with *who will* or *which will*. Like normal adjectives, verbal adjectives expressing future tense agree in gender and number with the preceding word. They show distinct endings that are derived from the forms of the attached pronouns in the third person. Have a look at the forms of the endings first and then work your way through the examples. The verbal adjectives and their translation are underlined.

	singular	plural
masculine	*.tj=fj* 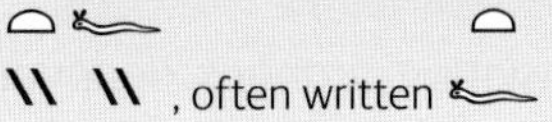, often written	*.tj=sn* 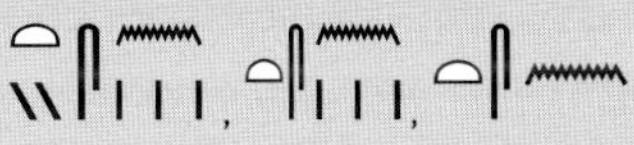
feminine	*.tj=sj* 	

 *nḥsj* *jwj.tj=fj* a Nubian who will come

 *ḫ3s.t* *wnn.tj=sj* *ḥr mw=f* a foreign land which will exist on his water (= which will be loyal to the king)

 *m33.tj=sn* (people) who will see

3 Familiarize yourself with the various forms and translations of verbal adjectives that express the future tense by completing the table.

a  

sḏm=f he listens — ___________ *who will listen*

b  

___________ *he makes* — ___________ ___________

c  

jwj=sn ___________ — ___________ ___________

d  

___________ ___________ — *s:rwd.tj=fj* ___________

Verbal adjectives expressing future tense appear regularly in the offering formula, more specifically in the so-called 'appeal to the living'. The appeal was addressed to the visitors to a tomb and asked them to make an offering to the deceased.

4 Translate the first part of the following example, after you have made a transliteration.

, *may you offer bread and beer …*

These are the new words you need for this exercise:  *j O!, …* and  *ꜥbꜣ stela.*

NEGATIONS

Middle Egyptian has a series of different negations. Their translation changes, depending on the grammatical context in which they are employed. Have a look at how the three most frequent negations work in context. Some forms and uses have been introduced already in previous units and are reviewed here for completeness. Others are new.

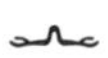 *n*

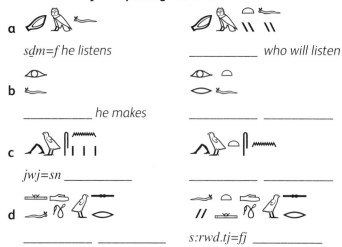

This negation is placed at the beginning of verbal sentences in the past and present tense and then means *do not* or *did not*, when the Egyptian verb is in the active voice (see Unit 11), and *is not* or *was not* when the Egyptian verb is in the passive voice formed with *.tw*.

n sḏm=f he did not hear (not *he does not hear*)

n sḏm.n=f he does not hear (not *he did not hear*)

n sḏm.tw=f he was not heard (not *he is not heard*)

n sḏm.n.tw=f he is not heard (not *he was not heard*)

n can also be combined with *js*, often in a way so that *n … js* encloses the first part of a sentence. In the sentence below, for example, the noun *Ḥrw* is preceded by *n* and followed by *js*. When *n … js* negates a nominal sentence, it is translated with *not*.

n Ḥrw js pw It is not Horus.

5 Select the correct translation of these sentences negated with *n*.

a *n sḏm.n=k st*

You do not listen to it.

You did not listen to her.

She does not hear you.

b *n ntk js zj* (*zj* man)

You did not summon a man.

You are not a man.

The man did not pray.

c *n jnj.tw n=j Ḏdj pn* (*Ḏdj* Djedi is a name)

I have not brought this Djedi.

I do not bring this Djedi.

This Djedi was not brought to me.

6 Try a translation of this negated sentence that uses a verb in the passive voice.

n msj.tw=f js n=k

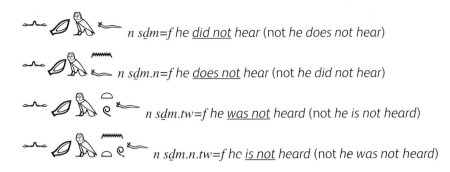

 *nn*

This negation has a wider use, and its translation depends on what follows it: an adverbial sentence, a noun, an infinitive or a verb. When *nn* negates adverbial sentences, it is translated with *not* (see Unit 9). *nn* can also precede a noun whose existence it negates, literally meaning *not existent is*. Before an infinitive, you translate it with *without* (see Unit 13). It can also negate a verb in the intended future and then it means *will not*.

 *nn grg m jb=j Falsehood is <u>not</u> in my heart.*

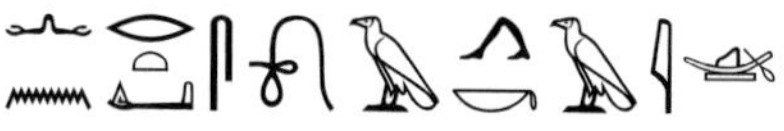 *nn rdj.t s:w3j k3j <u>without</u> permitting that a boat passes*

 *nn msj.w=f <u>Not existent are</u> his children. (= He has no children.)*

 *nn sḏm=f He <u>will not</u> listen.*

7 Look at which types of words and phrases follow *nn* in the following sentences and then translate them.

a  *nn mw.t=k ḥnᶜ=k*

b  *m=k ṯw m njw.t nn ḥq3 ḥw.t=s* (*ḥq3 ḥw.t mayor*)

c  *nn dj=j jṯj=ṯ sw*

d 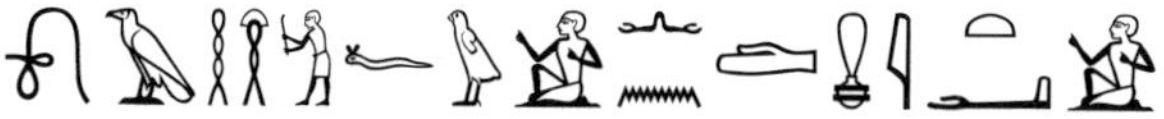 *w3ḥ=f wj nn dmj.t=j* (from Unit 13)

 *tm*

 *tm*, which can also be written  and , is used with verbal adjectives and the infinitive. When it negates a verbal adjective, it is translated with *who/which does not*, *who/which did not* or *who/which will not*. When it negates an infinitive, you translate it with *not*. This is different from *nn* before an infinitive, which means *without*. The negated verb that follows *tm* takes the ending *.w*. These examples show a phrase in the affirmative first and then in its negated form.

 *sḏm who listens* or *who listened* or *who will listen*

 *tm sḏm.w* <u>*who does not*</u> *listen* or <u>*who did not*</u> *listen* or <u>*who will not*</u> *listen*

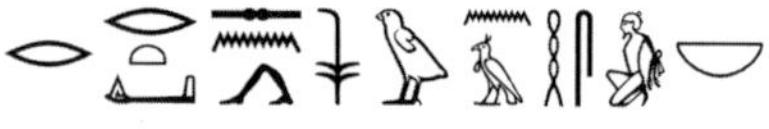 *r rdj.t znj sw nḥsj nb in order to permit that any Nubian passes it*

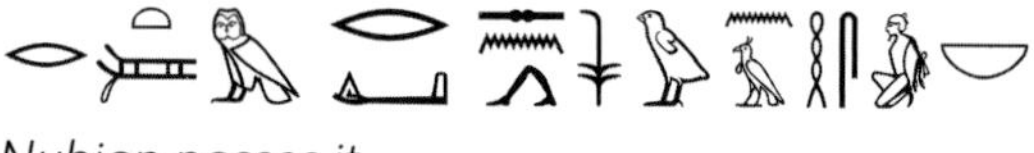 *r tm rdj.w znj sw nḥsj nb in order <u>not to permit</u> that any Nubian passes it*

The ending *.w* of the negated verb is usually not written in hieroglyphs, but should be added to the transliteration because it was pronounced. This form is called a 'negatival complement'. The rule is that *tm* takes on the grammatical functions of the word that it negates, while the negatival complement adds the content, i.e. the activity that is negated. In the example *r rdj.t sw nḥsj nb*, *rdj* has the ending *.t* because it is an infinitive. In the negative version, *tm* is the infinitive, while *rdj.w* becomes the negatival complement saying which action is negated and it therefore loses the *.t* ending.

You can see the same rule in the next example, where *tm* takes on the ending of the verbal adjective in the future tense  *tj=fj*, while the verb *sḏm* becomes a negatival complement in the negated version.

 *zꜣ sḏm.tj=fj* a son who will listen

 *zꜣ tm.tj=fj sḏm.w* a son <u>who will not</u> listen

You can compare the function of *tm* with the English negation *doesn't*. The phrase *she goes* is negated with *she doesn't go* instead of with *she goes not*. The word *doesn't* tells you that a verb in the third person singular of the present tense is negated, but you do not know which action it refers to. The content of what is being negated is the verb *go*, which has transferred its original ending *–es* to *doesn't*.

8 Have a look at how *tm* changes the form of the verb it negates. Compare the hieroglyphs in the following pairs and then add the missing transliteration and translation of the negated phrase to the right-hand column. Follow the examples that have been explained above.

a  

zꜣ.t sḏm.tj=sj a daughter who will listen ____________ ____________

b  

r jnj.t jnw in order to bring luxurious goods ____________ ____________

c  

rꜣ n mwt ky zp spell for dying another time ____________ ____________

9 Now transliterate and translate these phrases using *tm*.

a 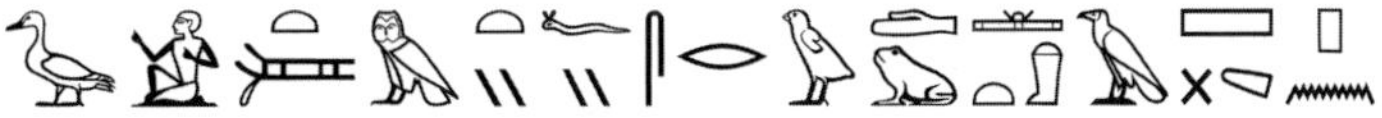

b  (*ḏꜣj* to travel) a funerary spell

c 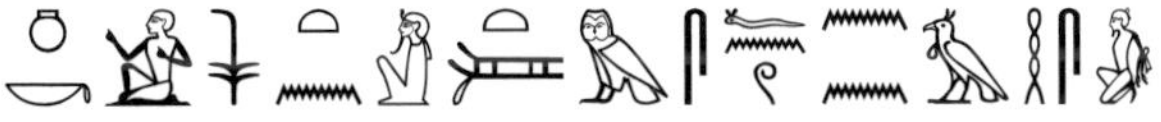 (*sfn n* to be mild with), from the large Semna stela

Explore

The new grammar presented in this unit is also essential for understanding the inscription on the large Semna stela that Senwosret III erected in his regnal year 16. This text begins with a long royal hymn, written in the first person singular. Senwosret III describes himself as a strong-willed and clever warlord who knows how to deal with the 'wretched' Nubians. He also prides himself on having pushed the border of Egypt farther south than any of his predecessors. The final part of the stela picks up on this point. Here, Senwosret speaks about what will happen to his successors depending on whether or not they maintain his border. This is the section of the stela that we will focus on.

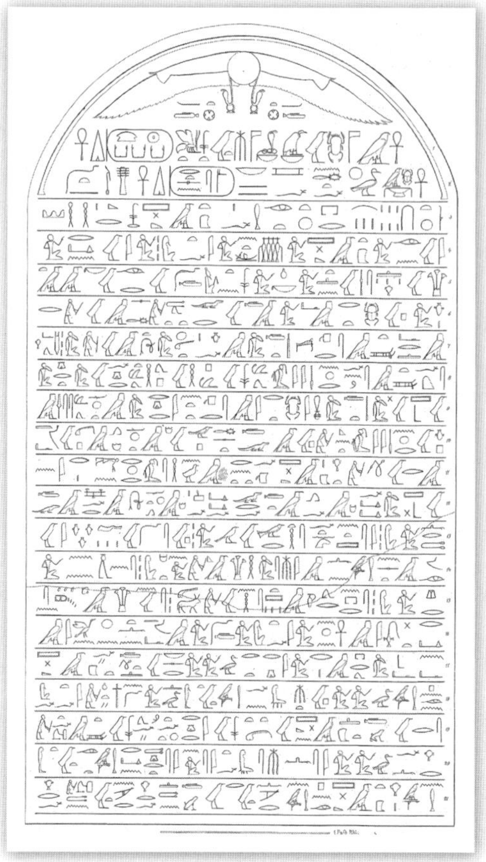

Study the new words you will need for this text and then read through the text passage, enlarged below. Have a go at the transliteration and translation of this text. Since it is the final text in the course, we are asking you to work through the text on your own – just as an Egyptologist would do! See how far you can get without looking up the transliteration and translation. You have the skills now to be able to make a word-for-word translation and then to revise your translation until you are happy with the result. It is entirely normal if you need several attempts and a bit of time before the text starts to make good sense and reveal its meaning.

Here are a few more new words you will need for your translation. Read them aloud.

 *grt* *however*

 *=j* *I, me, my* (used for kings and gods)

 *twt* *suitable, fitting*

LANGUAGE INSIGHT

The basic meaning of *twt* comes close to *model* or *ideal* in English. When used as a noun it is translated as *statue*, which is the ideal physical image of somebody. As an adjective it means *suitable, fitting*, expressing the ideal fit between mental model and reality.

nḏtj	*to protect*
wtṯ	*to beget*
fḫ	*to loosen*, here: *to give up*
ꜥḥꜣ	*to fight* (*ḥr for*)
jsṯ grt	*For, …* (introduces a new topic)
n mrw.t	*in order that* (also written)
rwd	*to be firm*
=tn	*you* (alternative way of writing)

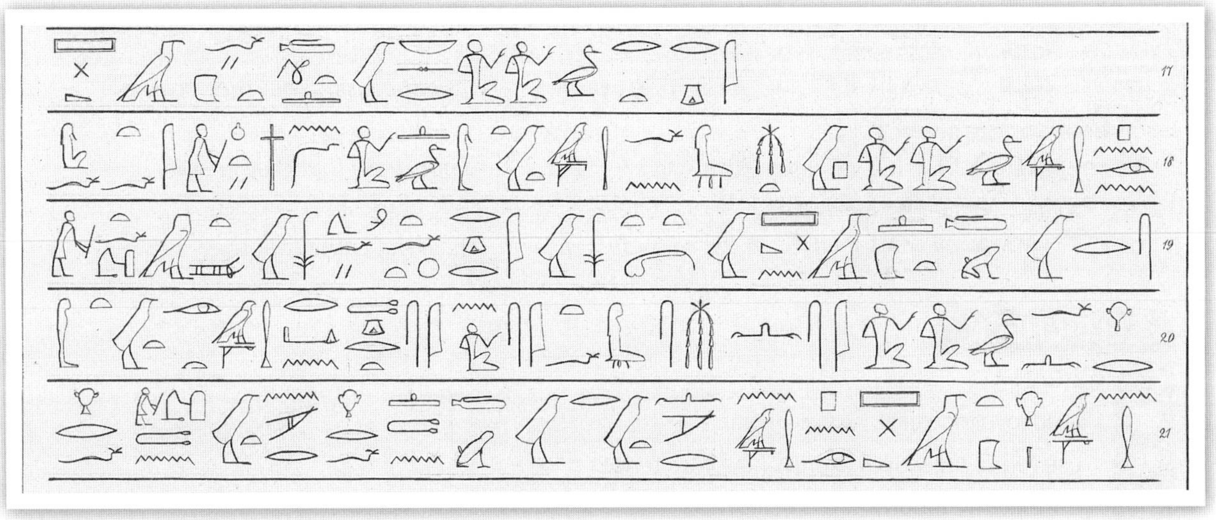

LANGUAGE INSIGHT

The composer of the inscription used some special effects to bring the text to life. In the fourth line of the enlarged passage, for example, *pw He is* is not written after . See what happens if you drop this phrase in the translation, too, to get a sense of the lively character of the text!

Drawing hieroglyphs

1 Here are two final hieroglyphs which you can practise drawing.

a 

b 

2 Now try to write a whole phrase in hieroglyphs. How would you write *a son who will not fight for this border*? The phrase combines several signs you have learned to draw on this course.

Test yourself

1 Which of the two forms is a verbal adjective meaning *(somebody) who will fight*?

a 

b 

2 Match the negative expressions in hieroglyphs and transliteration with their correct translation. If you wish to improve the literal translation given below, replace *causing* and *cause* with *permitting* and *permit*.

a  *n rdj=f znj=sn sw* — *without causing that they pass it*

b  *nn rdj.t znj=sn sw* — *to not cause that they pass it*

c  *tm rdj.w znj=sn sw* — *he did not cause that they pass it*

SELF-CHECK

	I CAN
●	read royal decrees
●	use verbal adjectives expressing future tense
●	translate negations

Grammar reference

Transliteration and pronunciation

Egyptian hieroglyphs can be written from right to left, from left to right and from top down. You establish the direction of an inscription by studying the hieroglyphs that depict animated beings. You will always look into their faces when you read them. For example,  is written from left to right, whereas an inscription with this group  is to be read from right to left.

SOUNDS

We can reconstruct the sound of consonants in Middle Egyptian fairly well. Each consonant is rendered with a Roman letter in transliteration. Most of them are familiar in English. These include *b, p, f, m, n, r, h, z, s, k, g, t* and *d*. Three sounds are familiar in English, but take additional strokes and dots in transliteration: *š* (sh), *ṯ* (tj) and *ḏ* (dj). The sounds *q* and *ḥ* are produced deep in the throat, but Egyptologists pronounce them simply k and h. The sounds *ḫ* and *ẖ* are both pronounced kh by Egyptologists, although *ẖ* is softer and must not be conflated with *ḫ* in transliteration. The letter *ꜣ* stands for the glottal stop, i.e. the interruption in the flow of the voice in the'atre instead of theatre. Egyptologists pronounce it aa for convenience. The glottal stop is different from *ꜥ*, a sound produced deep in the throat and pronounced by Egyptologists also as aa. Although Egyptologists pronounce *ꜣ* and *ꜥ* as a vowel, these two sounds are consonants. Egyptian had two semi-consonants: *j*, which can be pronounced y and ee, and *w*, pronounced w or oo. When they are the final sound of a word or used in a grammatical ending, they are often not expressed with a separate hieroglyph, but were inferred in speech and are therefore transliterated.

ꜣ	aa	*p*	p	*h*	h	*z*	z	*t*	t
j, y	y, ee	*b*	b	*ḥ*	h	*s*	s	*ṯ*	tj
w	w, oo	*f*	f	*ḫ*	kh	*š*	sh	*d*	d
ꜥ	aa	*m*	m	*ẖ*	kh	*q*	k	*ḏ*	dj
		n	n			*g*	g		
		r	r			*k*	k		

We know little about which vowels were used between these consonants. Egyptologists add a short e between them in order to be able to pronounce a word, but the pronunciation in ancient times might have been significantly different.

Out of convention, names of individuals, deities, kings and places are capitalized in transliteration, just as in English, for example *Km.t Egypt* rather than *km.t*.

SOUND SIGNS

A hieroglyph used as a sound sign represents one sound or a string of sounds. As such, it can be used in any word that includes these sounds or strings of sounds, irrespective of what the hieroglyph depicts and what the word means. In this function, a hieroglyph comes closest to how individual letters work in English.

Single-sound signs, also called uniliteral or uniconsonantal signs, are transliterated with one letter. Multi-sound signs are transliterated with two or three letters. Single-sound signs can be added to a multi-sound sign to complement one of their letters. In this case they are not transliterated because they only repeat a letter of the multi-sound sign to help with the correct reading. For example, in  *sḏm*, the single-sound sign  *m* only complements the multi-sound sign  *sḏm* and is not transliterated. If a scribe wanted to write *sḏmm*, he would usually have to put an additional *m*: .

PICTURE SIGNS

Picture signs, also called ideograms, mean what they represent and are transliterated with the Egyptian word that designates this thing. In many cases, a single stroke is added to the hieroglyph. For example, the sign  depicts the plan of a house and the group  tells you that it means *house*. It is simple to translate the word as *house* once you know what the sign represents, but you need to know the Egyptian word for *house*, which is *pr*, in order to transliterate it. When the Egyptian word is feminine, the *.t*-ending is usually expressed in hieroglyphs with . For example,  represents the crossroad of a town. If a scribe wanted to make sure that it should be pronounced *njw.t town*, he would not simply write , but , where functions as a complement. Although the single stroke appears regularly after a picture sign, it can be omitted, for example when the word is part of an official title, as in  *ꜥnḫ n njw.t soldier of the town*.

CLASSIFIERS

Classifiers, also called determinatives, are added to the end of the word to indicate its general meaning. Different from picture signs, they remained mute in speech and are not transliterated. In  *ḥw.t enclosure*, the sign  functions as a classifier BUILDING rather than as a picture sign and is therefore not transliterated.

COMBINATIONS AND ABBREVIATIONS

Although it is often clear how a sign is used, there are some hybrids and special spellings. This is because Egyptians played with sounds and signs. Here are a few examples.

The walking legs can be combined with a single sound sign, which represents the core sound of a word. For example, the core sound of *jṯj to seize* is *ṯ*, which is written in hieroglyphs. Since *to seize* involves movement, it is written as a combination of and the classifier as  *jṯj*. This use of hieroglyphs is known for a restricted number of common words.

Some signs are used as abbreviations. An important case is . Usually, this is the sound sign *sw*. However, it is also an abbreviated spelling for 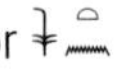 *njswt king*, but only in the context of specific titles and standard phrases, such as  *z3-njswt son of the king (prince)* or  *ḥtp dj njswt an offering which the king gives*.

Word types

ARTICLES

Formal Middle Egyptian does not have an article equivalent to English *the* and *a*. In colloquial Middle Egyptian texts, such as letters, the definite article *the* is expressed with  *p3* (masc. sing.),  *t3* (fem. sing.),  *n3 n* (pl.). For defined versus undefined nouns, see also under Relative clauses below.

NOUNS

Middle Egyptian nouns (things, persons, abstract ideas) have a gender and number. Gender and number are expressed in the transliteration with a specific set of endings added to the stem of the word after a full stop. There are several ways in which the endings appear in hieroglyphs. The most popular forms are written below next to the transliteration.

	masculine	feminine
singular	no particular ending	*.t*
dual	*.wj* , , doubling the classifier or the core sign of a word	*.tj* , , doubling the classifier or the core sign of a word
plural	*.w* , , tripling the classifier or the core sign of a word	*.wt* , , tripling the classifier or the core sign of a word

Adjectives, including verbal adjectives (participles) and relative forms, can be used as a noun in Egyptian. In these cases, you add *person* or *thing* in the translation, for example *nfr.t (a) beautiful (thing), something beautiful* derived from the adjective *nfr beautiful*, or *jrj.t.n=k nb.t every (thing) you have made* derived from the relative form *jrj.t.n=k which you have made.*

The infinitive is a noun whose meaning derives from a verb, for example *jyj.t the coming*, usually translated without the article as *coming*.

The word *nn not existent is* negates the existence of a thing or person, for example in *nn ẖrd.w=f His children are not existent* (= *He has no children*). Before the infinitive, it means *without*, as in *nn dmj.t=j without touching me* (literally *without my touching*).

Two nouns set side by side can express possession. They are connected with *of* in the English translation, for example *nb Wꜣs.t lord of Thebes*. The word order is switched in hieroglyphs, when the possessing person is a deity or a king (honorific transposition). However, in transliteration you place the words in the order in which they were pronounced and you add a hyphen to indicate the switching in the hieroglyphic writing, for example *ḥw.t-nṯr enclosure of the god*, i.e. *temple*.

To express possession, two nouns can also be connected with *n of*. This connector, also called genitival adjective, agrees in gender and number with the first noun, i.e. *n.t* (fem. sing.) in *s.t n.t s:nḏm the place of dwelling* and *nw* (pl.) in *rm.w nw jtrw fish of the river.*

When two nouns appear side by side, they can also be a pair and are connected in translation with *and* or *or*: *Ptḥ Jmn Ptah and Amun* or *Ptah or Amun*. Another interpretation of two nouns set side by side is that the second noun comments on or adds information to the first. In the combination of title and name, you simply translate word for word as in *zš Jmn-ḥtp the scribe Amenhotep*. In other cases you add a comma, for example *Nw.t mw.t=k Nut, your mother*. The second noun (*mw.t=k*) that comments on the first (*Nw.t*) is called an apposition.

NB: You can understand *Nw.t mw.t=k* also as a nominal sentence *Nut is your mother*; see below under Sentence types.

PRONOUNS

Pronouns replace nouns in a sentence. For example, instead of *The king has appeared*, you can also say *He has appeared*; or *This (one) has appeared* if you want to point to a particular king; or *Who has appeared* if you wish to turn the statement into a question; or *Somebody has appeared* if it is not clear who exactly has appeared. *He* is a personal pronoun, *this* a demonstrative pronoun, *who* an interrogative pronoun and *somebody* an indefinite pronoun.

Personal pronouns. Personal pronouns refer to individuals and things in the first, second or third person singular and plural. Middle Egyptian has attached, weak and strong personal pronouns. Their translation varies according to how they are used in a sentence. The following review uses the third person singular masculine as an example for the translation. The hieroglyph used to write the first person singular expresses who is speaking, for example the sign of a seated woman is written when a woman speaks.

Personal pronouns: attached pronouns. Attached pronouns, also called suffix pronouns, are used after nouns to express possession (*his*), after verbal predicates to express who is acting (*he*), after infinitives to express either who is acting (*he*) or who is acted upon (*him*), after *jw* and *ꜥḥꜥ.n* to express the subject (*he*) and after prepositions to express the object of the preposition (*for him*). In transliteration, they are attached with an equals sign to the preceding word.

	singular	plural
1st sing.	*=j I, me, my*	*=n we, us, our*
2nd sing. masc.	*=k you, your*	*=ṯn you, your*
2nd sing. fem.	*=ṯ you, your*	
3rd sing. masc.	*=f he, him, his*	*=sn they, them, their*
3rd sing. fem.	*=s she, her*	

The impersonal attached pronoun *=tw one* is only used in subject position.

After nouns in the dual, the attached pronouns of the 2nd person sing. masc. and the 3rd person sing. masc. and fem. can also take dual strokes: *kj your*, *fj his* and *sj her*, for example *ꜥ.wj=fj his two arms.*

The attached pronouns are used after *ḏs self*, for example *ḏs=f himself.*

In colloquial Middle Egyptian, the attached pronouns follow *pꜣy=* (before masc. sing. nouns), *tꜣy=* (before fem. sing. nouns) and *nꜣy= n* (before nouns in the sing. or pl.) to express possession (*his*), for example *pꜣy=f pr his house* or *nꜣy=j n nṯr my gods.*

Personal pronouns: weak pronouns. Weak pronouns, also called dependent pronouns, are used after *m=k* to express the subject in the adverbial sentence pattern (*he*), after adjectives to express the subject in an adjectival sentence (*he*), and after verbal predicates to express the direct object in verbal sentences (*him*).

	singular	plural
1st sing.	*wj I, me*	*n we, us*
2nd sing. masc.	*ṯw you*	*ṯn you*
2nd sing. fem.	*ṯn you*	
3rd sing. masc.	*sw he, him*	*sn they, them*
3rd sing. fem.	*sj, st she, her*	

Personal pronouns: strong pronouns. Strong pronouns, also called independent pronouns, do not require a word preceding them. They are followed by a noun, sometimes also by *pw*, to express the predicate in a nominal sentence (*he*).

	singular	plural
1st sing.	*jnk I*	*jnn we*
2nd sing. masc.	*ntk you*	*ntṯn you*
2nd sing. fem.	*ntṯ you*	
3rd sing. masc.	*ntf he*	*ntsn they*
3rd sing. fem.	*nts she*	

Demonstrative pronouns. The demonstrative pronoun *pn this* follows the noun it is emphasizing, for example *sn pn this brother*. After feminine nouns, its form changes to *tn this*, as in *sn.t tn this sister*. In the plural, it precedes the noun, which can be set in the plural or singular, and takes an additional *n*: *nn n these*, for example *nn n nṯr these gods* or *nn n nṯr.w these gods* (literally *these of god* and *these of gods*).

Interrogative pronouns (question words). Middle Egyptian uses *m* or *nm* in questions for English *who?* and *what?* and *jšst* for *what?* These words can be combined with a preposition and are then translated with other interrogative pronouns in English, for example *because of what? = why?* and *mj jšst like what = how?* To ask *which?* the Egyptians used *zj* before a noun.

Indefinite pronoun. The most important indefinite pronoun in Middle Egyptian is *nb any, every*. It does not refer to a specific person or thing and is therefore called indefinite. This word is used in the same way adjectives are used: it follows a noun and agrees with it in gender and number. However, the feminine and the plural endings are often not written in hieroglyphs, but are transliterated to help the reader understand the grammar better. Note that *nb*, *nb.t* means *any, every* when it follows a noun, and *lord of, lady of* when it precedes a noun.

ADJECTIVES

Adjectives are used after nouns to modify their meaning or add a detail. They agree in gender and number with the noun, for example *ḫ.t nb.t nfr.t every good thing*, where *every* and *good* say which *thing* is meant. The feminine and plural endings are often not expressed in the hieroglyphs, but in this course are transliterated to explain the grammar to the reader, for example  *ḫ.t nb.t nfr.t*, where no *.t* ending is written after *nb* and *nfr* in the hieroglyphs.

Adjectives derived from prepositions and nouns end in *–j*. This ending is often written with the dual strokes , but these can also be omitted. You transliterate *–j* in any case. You can translate adjectives ending in *–j* provisionally with *who is*, for example  *ḥrj who is upon* derived from the preposition *ḥr upon*, and those derived from a noun with *who belongs to*, for example  or  *njw.tj who belongs to the town*, before you find a more fluent translation, for example *ḥrj upper* and *njw.tj local.*

Adjectives formed from verbs, i.e. participles and relative forms, are discussed below under Verbs.

Egyptian adjectives can be followed by a noun that modifies or specifies their meaning. For example, in *Ptḥ nfr ḥr Ptah beautiful of face* or *Ptah beautiful in view of (his) face*, the noun *ḥr face* says in which respect Ptah is *nfr* beautiful. A translation with *of* or *in view of* is fine. You may wish to try to find a more fluent wording, for example *Ptah with a beautiful face*. The construction is known as the '*nfr ḥr* construction' in Egyptology.

Adjectives are also used in adjectival sentences to express the predicate. In this function, they are placed at the beginning of the sentence and their form is invariably masculine singular. See also below under Adjectival sentences.

PREPOSITIONS

Prepositions are used before a noun or an attached pronoun to describe the circumstances of an action or a state of being. Before an infinitive, they either describe an action relative in tense to the action of the main clause (relative tenses) or are used in the pseudoverbal construction; see below under Adverbial sentences. Some prepositions add a phonetic complement in hieroglyphs, or even a sound when followed by an attached pronoun; see the examples below. The meaning of an Egyptian preposition often corresponds to several different prepositions in English. The most common prepositions are *m*, *n* and *r*. Their use and meaning are explained here in greater detail. They can form compound prepositions in conjunction with other words. Other common prepositions are *mj like*, *ḥnꜥ with*, *ḥr upon*, *while* (before infinitive), *ḫnt before*, *ḫr to*, *ḫr under*, *tp on* and *ḏr since*.

-  *m* + noun,  *jm=* + attached pronoun: *in* (place, time, state of being); *at* (time, place) *from* (place); *as* (expressing identity); *out of* (material), *while* (before infinitive). Nisbe:  *jmj*: *being in, being at, being from, being as, being out of*. Compound prepositions:  *m-ꜥ with, by, from, because of*;  *m-m among*;  *m-ḥꜣ.t in front of*;  *m-ḥrj-jb in the midst of*;  *m-ḫt after; behind*; , also written  *m-ḫnw in*;  *m-bꜣḥ in the presence of, before*;  *tp-m before*
- *r* + noun,  *jr=* + attached pronoun: *to(wards)* (place, aim); *at* (place, time); *more than* (expressing comparison); *against* (person, place); *concerning* (an issue); *in order to* (before infinitive). Nisbe:  *jrj*: *being towards, concerning, belonging to*. Compound prepositions:  *r-gs beside; next to*;  *r-gs.wj next to*

- *n* + noun or attached pronoun: *to* (introduces indirect object); *for* (person, thing), *because of*. The hieroglyph *n* is also used to express possession and means *of*; see above under Nouns. Compound prepositions with initial *n*: *n mrw.t for, in order that* (before verbs), rarely written

ADVERBS

Adverbs take the position of a preposition plus noun or a preposition plus attached pronoun in an Egyptian sentence. Examples are *jm there* (for *at this place* or *at it*); *thereof* (for *out of this material* or *out of it*) derived from the preposition *m* and *nfr perfectly* derived from the adjective *nfr perfect*.

VERBS

(See also the overview of verb forms at the end of this grammar reference.)

Verbal classes. Verbs express an action (*jṯj to seize*) or a state of being (*ꜥḥꜥ to stand*). Egyptian verbs are classified according to the number of their radicals, i.e. their letters or 'literals', and by the quality of these radicals: whether they are weak, have the causative prefix *s:* or geminate. Below are examples of the most common classes. Some of these verb classes have particular endings or features in specific verb forms.

- Strong 3-literal verbs: *sḏm to hear* has the three strong radicals *s*, *ḏ* and *m*
- Weak 3-literal verbs: *gmj to find* has the three radicals *g*, *m* and *j* of which the final *j* is weak and usually not written in hieroglyphs
- Causative 3-literal verbs: *s:rwd to cause to be firm, to make firm, to erect* (derived from *rwd to be firm*) has the three radicals *r*, *w* and *d* with a causative prefix *s:*.
- Causative 2-literal verbs: *s:mn to make enduring, to establish* (derived from *mn to endure*) has the two radicals *m* and *n* with a causative prefix *s:*.
- Geminating 2-literal verbs: *wn to exist*, which also appears as *wnn to exist*, has the two radicals *w* and *n* of which the second, *n*, geminates, i.e. is duplicated, in some forms.

sḏm=f: **past tense, present tense, intended future.** When *sḏm=f* is used as the predicate of a verbal sentence (see below under Sentence types), its subject is either a noun or an attached pronoun, for example *sḏm Ptḥ Ptah listens* and *sḏm=f he listens*. You should decide from the context whether *sḏm=f* is best translated with past tense (*he listened*), present tense (*he listens*) or the intended future (*he may listen*). When there is a particle introducing the sentence, *sḏm=f* never expresses the intended future. When a *sḏm=f* form is used in a subordinate clause (see below under Sentences in context), it is translated with *when he listened* (past), *as he listens* (present) or *(so) that he will listen* (intended future). Subordinate clauses in the intended future express either the purpose of the action described in the main clause (*so that*), or they follow words that imply future action, for example *to cause*, *to decree* or *to say*, and are then translated with *that*.

The infix *.tw* is used to express passive voice, for example *sḏm.tw=f he is (was, may be) heard.*

Geminating and weak 3-literal verbs show the duplication of their final radical, whenever habitual or repeated action is expressed, for example *jrr=f he does repeatedly* or *mꜣꜣ=f he sees (habitually)* or *he supervises*. The intended future of this verb is *mꜣn=f he may see.*

sḏm.n=f: **past tense.** The form *sḏm.n=f*, with the infix *.n*, always expresses past tense. It is translated with *he listened* in a main clause or with *when he (had) listened* in a subordinate clause. When there is no particle preceding *sḏm.n=f*, it means that the sentence is a subordinate clause or that the form is emphatic and translated with *That he listened is …* (see paragraph after the next paragraph).

The infix .*tw* is used to express passive voice, for example *sḏm.n.tw=f he was heard.*

Geminating verbs usually show the duplication of their final radical, with the exception of *m3.n=f he saw,* which is more common than *m33.n=f.*

sḏm=f **and** *sḏm.n=f*: **emphatic forms.** Both *sḏm=f* and *sḏm.n=f* can be used at the beginning of a sentence to emphasize an adverbial phrase or an entire sentence that follows them. When interpreted as emphatic forms, *sḏm=f* is provisionally translated with *That he listens is …* and *sḏm.n=f* with *That he listened is …* For examples with improved translation, see below under Sentences in context: emphasis. Only emphatic *sḏm.n=f* features in the units of this course.

The forms of the emphatic series look almost identical to those of the *sḏm=f* and *sḏm.n=f* forms reviewed above. However, weak 3-literal verbs and geminating verbs duplicate their final radical in the *sḏm=f* form, for example *jrr=f That he makes is …* and *wnn=f That he exists is …* When a verb of motion appears in the *sḏm.n=f* form it always is the emphatic form, whereas the stative is used to express simple past tense of these verbs. Particles, including *jw*, *ʿḥʿ.n* or *jsṯ*, are never used before emphatic forms. There is no emphatic form for the intended future.

sḏm.w: **stative.** The stative expresses a state of being as the result of an action. It is best translated with the present perfect or the past perfect in English. Whenever a verb can be translated with the passive voice (so-called transitive verbs), the stative expresses the passive. For example, *ḥzj.kw* means *I have been praised* because *to praise* can be used in the passive. In contrast, *jyj.kw* is a form of the intransitive verb *jyj to come* and is translated with *I have come*, rather than *I have been come*, which does not make sense in English. The stative of *rḫ to learn* means *to know* and is not translated with the passive voice, e.g. *rḫ.kw* means *I know* rather than *I am known*. Verbs of motion use the stative to express past tense, e.g. *jyj.kw I have come*, whereas *jyj.n=j* is an emphatic form and means *That I have come is …* See the previous paragraph.

In the hieroglyphs, the endings of the stative are usually, but not always, placed after the classifier of the verb. In the transliteration, they are added after a full stop. The endings refer back either to the subject of the sentence or to another noun or pronoun. In the latter two cases they are translated with a subordinate clause in English, as *while he has been heard* or *while he had been heard.* The endings are:

	singular	plural
1st person	.*kw* , , ,	.*wjn*
2nd person	.*tj* , ,	.*tjwnj*
3rd person masc.	.*w* or not written in hieroglyphs	.*w* or not written in hieroglyphs
3rd person fem.	.*tj* , ,	

The geminating verbs usually use the simple stem in the stative. The elision of the semi-consonantal ending .*w* with the week radical –*j* of weak verbs has sometimes prompted the writing of –*y* in the third person singular masculine.

sḏm, *sḏm.w*, *sḏm.tj=fj*: **verbal adjectives (participles).** Verbal adjectives are adjectives with verbal meaning, equivalent to the English participles ending in –ing (active voice) and –ed (passive voice), for example *loving* and *(be)loved*, both derived from the verb *to love*. Middle Egyptian has two series of verbal adjectives, one that expresses future tense and active voice and another expressing either active or passive voice in no specific time setting. Like other adjectives, verbal adjectives follow a noun and agree in gender and number with it. They can also replace a noun and you then translate with *somebody who* or *something which*.

The verbal adjective that expresses future tense has a distinct series of endings:

	singular	plural
masculine	*.tj=fj*	*.tj=sn*
feminine	*.tj=sj*	

An example of a future verbal adjective following a noun is *z3 sḏm.tj=fj a son who will listen.* When the verbal adjective is used without a noun preceding it, *sḏm.tj=fj* is translated with *somebody who will listen.*

The future verbal adjectives are negated with *tm.tj=fj, tm.tj=sj, tm.tj=sn* followed by the negatival complement of the verb ending in *.w* (usually not written in hieroglyphs): *z3 tm.tj=fj ꜥḥ3.w ḥr=f a son who will not fight for it.*

The second series of verbal adjectives often shows no ending in the hieroglyphs, although they had a vowel ending that was spoken, as the cases with written ending in *-y* and *-w* demonstrate. Since we only have the hieroglyphs, we can recognize these verbal adjectives often only by how they are used in the context of a sentence. For example, they are never followed by an attached pronoun. The following review shows examples with and without ending in the masculine singular and how they are translated. For the feminine singular and the plural, see below.

- *s:mn* no indication of tense; active and passive voice possible
  establishing or *who/which established, who/which establishes, who/which will establish*
  established or *who/which was established, who/which is established, who/which will be established*
- *s:mnw* no indication of tense; passive voice more likely than active voice
  establishing or *who/which established, who/which establishes, who/which will establish*
  established or *who/which was established, who/which is established, who/which will be established*

Weak verbs with three radicals can show a greater variety of endings:

- *ḥzz* no indication of tense, active and passive voice possible. The duplication of the second radical express repeated or habitual action, although this nuance is usually not rendered in the translation.
  praising or *who praised, who praises, who will praise*
  praised or *who was praised, who is praised, who will be praised*
- *mry* no indication of tense, passive voice only. Final *-y* is a good indicator of the passive voice.
  (be)loved or *who was beloved, who is beloved, who will be beloved*

The feminine ending of verbal adjectives is *.t*. The plural forms can have the ending *.w* and *.yw* in the masculine and simple *.t*, *.wt* or *.yt* in the feminine. However, these endings are regularly omitted in hieroglyphs. In order to help the reader understand the grammar better, you can add them in the transliteration, just as you do with normal adjectives.

Here are a few examples of verbal adjectives in context:

- 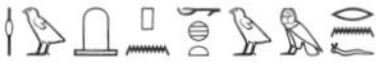 *wḏ pn ḫtj.w m rn=f this stela inscribed with his name* (You could interpret *ḫtj.w* here also as a stative. Since *to inscribe* is a transitive verb, you would translate it with passive voice, just as in the translation above.)
-  *nṯr.w wnn.yw jm the gods who are there*
- 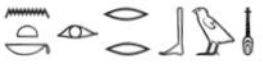 *ntk jrr bw nfr You are somebody who is doing good.*

sḏm=f **and** *sḏm.n=f*: **relative forms.** Like verbal adjectives, relative forms follow a noun, agree in gender and number with this noun, have forms similar to those of the verbal adjectives and are often best translated with a relative clause in English beginning with *whom* or *which*. The major difference is that they have a new subject, either a noun or an attached pronoun. Moreover, when relative forms refer to an action in the past, they are written with the infix *n*.

The weak verbs with three radicals show most variation, including the duplication of the second radical and the writing with . The forms of the masculine singular are:

-  *jrj=f whom or which he makes*
-  *jry=f whom or which he makes*
-  *jrr=f whom or which he makes* (repeatedly)
-  is written for both *jrj=f* or *jrr=f*.
-  *jrj.n=f whom or which he made*

If the preceding noun is feminine, this is how the forms look:

-  *jrj.t=f which he makes*
-  *jrr.t=f which he makes*
- 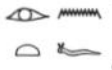 *jrj.t.n=f which he made*

You recognize a relative form usually by looking at entire sentences or longer passages of text. A typical example of the use of the relative form is when individuals say who their parents are, for example:

-  *Sbk-ḥtp jrj.n Snb Sobekhotep whom Seneb has made* (= *fathered*)

The word that precedes a relative form is resumed with an attached pronoun, when it follows a preposition in the phrase after the relative form. In the next example, the preceding noun *w3j.t* is resumed with *=s* after *ḥr*.

-  *w3j.t jyj.t.n=f ḥr=s the road on which it came*

When the preceding noun is dropped, you add *somebody* or *something* in the translation.

- 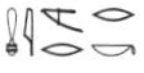 *mj mrr=k like something which you like* or simply *as you like*

The omission of the noun is particularly popular in Egyptian with *nb everybody* or *everything*.

▶ *jrr.t=k nb.t everything you did*

sḏm: **infinitive.** The infinitive expresses action as such, without saying whether it happens in the past, present or future. You translate it in English either with *to* or with an *–ing* form. All examples of infinitives in this course are in the active voice, but Egyptian infinitives sometimes express passive voice, for example *dr to repel, repelling* or *to be repelled, being repelled*. Egyptian verbs have no particular endings apart from the weak verbs with three radicals and the causative verbs with two radicals, which both show the ending *.t*, for example *gmj.t to find, finding* and *s:rḫ.t to let know, letting know*.

The infinitive is a noun with verbal meaning and it is therefore used in the same way nouns are used: in labels that accompany a scene, for example *dj.t sntr giving incense* written next to a king who offers incense to a god; after a preposition to express relative tense, for example *m ḫntj while sailing south*; and after a preposition to express the predicate of an adverbial sentence, for example *jw=f ḥr s:ḥḏ tꜣ.wj he is illuminating* (literally *he upon illuminating*) *the two lands*. The preposition *ḥr* expresses action contemporaneous to the action of a previous sentence, the preposition *m* before verbs of motion the near future, and the preposition *r* the future. *ḥr* and *m* before infinitives are translated with present or past progressive in English (*is coming, was seeing*) and *r* with future tense (*will shine*).

When an attached pronoun follows the infinitive, this expresses either the direct object of the infinitive (*ḥr s:ḥḏ=sn while illuminating them*, literally *upon their illuminating*) or indicates who is acting (*m-ḫt wḏꜣ=f after he had travelled*, literally *after his travelling*).

The infinitive is negated with *tm* followed by the negatival complement ending in *.w* (usually not written in hieroglyphs): *r tm rdj.w in order not to cause*. The negation negates the existence of the action and is translated with *without*: *nn rdj.t without causing* or *without permitting*.

sḏm: **imperative.** The imperative expresses command. The forms are identical with the forms used for *sḏm=f* without the attached pronoun. The major exception to this rule is *jmj give!, cause that …!* written (and similar), which is the imperative of *rdj/dj*. As in English, the subject in Egyptian is implied in the imperative, which is why a suffix pronoun cannot follow the imperative.

Geminating verbs use both the simple and the geminating stem in the imperative.

sḏm.w: **negatival complement**. The negatival complement has the ending *.w*, but this is usually not written in hieroglyphs. It is used after the negation *tm*. The purpose of *tm* is to make a negative statement (*not*) and take over the grammatical role of the word that is negated, while the negatival complement adds the content of the action that is negated. An English example of a similar construction is the negation of *she goes* with *she doesn't go*. In the negated statement, *doesn't* functions as the negation and has taken over the grammatical role of *goes* in the affirmative sentence (predicate in the third person singular of the present tense). This is the equivalent of *tm*, whereas *go* is similar to the negatival complement, saying which particular action is negated.

NUMERALS

The Egyptians counted in tens. They use 𓏤 to count from 1 to 9, 𓎆 for 10, 𓍢 for 100, 𓆼 for 1,000, 𓂭 for 10,000, 𓆐 for 100,000 and 𓁨 for 1,000,000. Numerals are set out from highest to lowest. The numbers usually follow the counted entity.

- 𓊹𓎆𓎆𓎆𓎆𓏤𓏤 *nṯr 42 42 gods*

A typical phrase in the offering formula is *ḫ3 m one thousand (of)*:

- 𓆼𓅓𓄀𓅿 *ḫ3 m k3 3pd one thousand ox and fowl*

PARTICLES

Particles can add a nuance to a sentence or have a purely grammatical function and are then not translated. The intended future, the imperative and the emphatic verb forms are not used after the following particles. With the exception of *jw*, these particles introduce main clauses.

- 𓇋𓅱 *jw* is not translated. It can introduce all sentence types, but is particularly popular with verbal and adverbial sentences. *jw* is used before verbs, nouns and attached pronouns. When *jw* precedes a sentence whose subject is a noun, it usually indicates that the sentence is a main clause, whereas with pronominal subject the sentence can be either a subordinate clause introduced with *as* or *while* in the translation.
- 𓅓𓎡 *m=k* means *Look, ...* or *Behold, ...* and can introduce all sentence types. It is used before verbs, nouns and weak pronouns. When a woman is addressed, it changes its form to 𓅓𓍿 *m=ṯ*. Speaking to a group, the Egyptians used 𓅓𓍿𓈖𓏥 *m=ṯn*.
- 𓊢𓂝𓈖 *ꜥḥꜥ.n* means *Then ...* and introduces verbal and adverbial sentences. It is typical of narrative texts. Sentences that begin with this particle are translated with past tense.
- 𓇋𓋴𓍿 *jsṯ* means *Meanwhile ...* and can be used with all sentence types. The combination 𓇋𓋴𓍿𓎼𓂋𓏏 *jsṯ grt* *Now, however, ...* introduces a new thought.

Sentence types

Middle Egyptian has four different sentence types, distinguished by the word type that functions as the predicate, by the use of pronouns that express the subject, and by word order. Sentence types tell you how individual words relate to each other, e.g. which word says who is acting and which word says who is acted upon. Since Middle Egyptian does not have full stops to indicate the end of a sentence, sentence types help to divide a continuous string of words into meaningful statements.

ELEMENTS OF THE SENTENCE

Egyptian sentences have the same elements as English sentences. The predicate expresses the action or state of being; the subject says who is acting; the direct object is the thing or person whom the subject acts upon; the indirect object tells you to whom or for whom something is done; and adverbial phrases add the circumstances of an action, usually formed of a preposition and a noun, a preposition and a pronoun or an adverb. An attribute is a phrase that depends on a noun, for example an adjective, a noun or a relative clause.

VERBAL SENTENCES

The predicate of a verbal sentence is an Egyptian verb (*sḏm=f* past, present, intended future; *sḏm.n=f* past; imperative). It is the first word of the sentence, unless the sentence is introduced by a particle. The subject of a verbal sentence is expressed with a noun or an attached pronoun, the direct object with a noun or a weak pronoun and the indirect object with the preposition *n* followed by noun or attached pronoun. Adverbial phrases follow these elements. Attributes can be added to any noun in the sentence. The first line of the following table shows the order of the different elements in a verbal sentence, whenever nouns are used for the subject, the direct and the indirect objects.

-	predicate	subject	direct object	indirect object	adverbial phrase
particle	verb	noun	noun	*n* noun	preposition plus noun or attached pronoun; adverb
particle	verb	attached pronoun	weak pronoun	*n=* attached pronoun	

The order of words has to be changed in translation to make it fit English grammar.

- *dj Ptḥ kꜣ ꜣpd n kꜣ n Mry m ḥb nb n rnp.t*

may give Ptah ox fowl to ka-soul of Mery on feast every of year (word for word)

May Ptah give ox and fowl to the ka-soul of Mery on every feast of the year. (fluent)

In this example, *dj* is the predicate, *Ptḥ* the subject, *kꜣ ꜣpd* the direct object, *n kꜣ n Mry* the indirect object – in which *n Mry* is an attribute to *kꜣ* – and *m ḥb nb n rnp.t* an adverbial phrase – in which *nb* and *n rnp.t* are attributes to *ḥb*. Since the subject comes before the direct object, you can tell that *Ptah gives ox and fowl* and not that *ox and fowl give Ptah*.

The second line of the table above indicates which pronouns are used for which element. However, word order can change according to the 'strength' of subject, direct object and indirect object: the weaker an element, the closer it moves to the predicate. The weakest element is the attached pronoun, second-weakest is the preposition *n* plus attached pronoun, second-strongest is the weak pronoun and the strongest is a noun. The position of the adverbial phrase in the sentence does not change. The type of pronoun used usually tells you how to translate a sentence, but you may find the review below useful to understand how the 'rule of strength' affects word order.

When the subject is an attached pronoun, the word order does not change or changes only marginally. The pronominal elements are underlined in the following examples.

- *dj=f kꜣ ꜣpd n kꜣ n Mry* (no change)

  May he give ox and fowl to the ka-soul of Mery.
- *dj=f sn n kꜣ n Mry* (no change)

  May he give them to the ka-soul of Mery.
- *dj=f n=f kꜣ ꜣpd* (indirect object *n=f* precedes direct object *kꜣ ꜣpd*)

  May he give him ox and fowl.
- *dj=f n=f sn* (indirect object *n=f* precedes direct object *sn*)

  May he give them to him.

When the subject is a noun, there is more change.

- *dj <u>sn</u> Ptḥ n kꜣ n Mry* (direct object *sn* precedes subject *Ptḥ*)

  May Ptah give <u>them</u> to the ka-soul of Mery.
- *dj <u>n=f</u> Ptḥ kꜣ ꜣpd* (indirect object *n=f* precedes subject *Ptḥ*)

  May Ptah give <u>them</u> to the ka-soul of Sobekhotep.
- *dj <u>n=f sn</u> Ptḥ* (indirect object *n=f* precedes direct object *sn* and subject *Ptḥ*)

  May Ptah give <u>them to him</u>.

Verbal sentences are negated with 𓂜 *n* or 𓂜𓈖 *nn*, which precede the predicate. 𓂜 *n* expresses past tense, when used with *sḏm=f* (*n sḏm=f he did not listen*), and present tense with *sḏm.n=f* (*n sḏm.n=f he does not listen*). 𓂜𓈖 *nn* negates the intended future (*nn sḏm=f may he not listen*).

The stative is used in the adverbial sentence pattern; see below.

ADVERBIAL SENTENCES

These include pseudoverbal construction and stative sentences.

Standard adverbial sentences. In adverbial sentences, the predicate is an adverbial phrase. Unlike in verbal sentences, the subject precedes the predicate. Depending on which particle is used, it is replaced either with attached or weak pronouns. The examples are restricted to *jw* and *m=k* to show the difference.

	subject	predicate	adverbial phrase
particle	noun	preposition plus noun or attached pronoun; adverb	preposition plus noun or attached pronoun; adverb
jw=	attached pronoun		
m=k	weak pronoun		

In the English translation, you will have to add a form of *to be* between the subject and the predicate. Since adverbial phrases can refer to events in the past or present, you decide from the context which tense you think fits best.

- *jb=j ẖr mꜣʿ.t My heart (is, was) under truth (= is or was truthful).*

The subject can be replaced by *jw=* plus attached pronoun or by *m=k* plus weak pronoun.

- *jw=f ẖr mꜣʿ.t* or *m=k sw ẖr mꜣʿ.t It (is, was) truthful.*

The adverbial sentence is negated with 𓂜𓈖 *nn not*, which precedes the subject. No particle is used before or after it. When the subject is a pronoun, a weak pronoun is used:

- *nn sw ẖr mꜣʿ.t It is not truthful.*

Statements using the infinitive (pseudoverbal construction). The pseudoverbal construction follows the adverbial sentence pattern. The only difference is that the predicate is formed from a preposition and the infinitive of a verb. The infinitive can take a direct object and an indirect object, which follow the infinitive.

	subject	predicate	adverbial phrase
particle	noun	preposition plus infinitive of a verb (followed by nouns and pronouns to express direct and indirect objects)	preposition plus noun or attached pronoun; adverb
jw=	attached pronoun		
m=k	weak pronoun		

The preposition *ḥr* expresss that the action happens at the same time as the event of the previous sentence. The preposition *m* has a similar meaning, but it can also express the immediate future when used before verbs of motion. Sentences with *ḥr* or *m* plus infinitive are translated in English with present or past progressive. The preposition *r* expresses future action and is translated with future tense (*will*).

- *jw=f ḥr s:ḥḏ tꜣ.wj He (is, was) upon illuminating the two lands.* More fluently: *He is illuminating (or was illuminating) the two lands.*
- *jw=f r s:ḥḏ tꜣ.wj He (is) towards illuminating the two lands.* More fluently: *He will illuminate the two lands.*
- *jw=f m jyj.t It (is, was) coming.*

In these examples, *ḥr s:ḥḏ*, *r s:ḥḏ* and *mjyj.t* are predicates and *tꜣ.wj* a direct object depending on the infinitive *s:ḥḏ*.

Since these sentences follow the adverbial sentence pattern but have verbal meaning, they are called 'pseudoverbal construction'.

Stative. Sentences with a stative as the predicate also follow the adverbial sentence pattern. Here, the predicate is the stative of a verb.

	subject	predicate	adverbial phrase
particle	noun	stative	preposition plus noun or attached pronoun; adverb
jw=	attached pronoun		
m=k	weak pronoun		

The endings of the stative refer to the subject that precedes the stative. The subject is a noun, an attached pronoun after *jw* or a weak pronoun after *m=k*.

- *jw=k ḥzj.tj m ẖnw You were praised in the residence.*
- *Jtn wꜥj.w Aten is alone.*

Only in the first person singular does a subject not have to precede the stative.

- *ḥzj.kw ḥr=s I was praised for it.*

When the stative follows a noun that is not the subject of the sentence, it often comes close to a relative clause in English and is translated with *which* or a participle. In the following example, the stative *zš.w* *inscribed* does not belong to the subject *=j*, but to *wḫꜣ a column* and is therefore translated thus.

- *jw s:ꜥḥꜥ.n=j wḫꜣ zš.w m rn jt.w=j I erected a stela which had been inscribed with the name of my fathers.* Or simply: *I erected a stela inscribed with the name of my fathers.*

ADJECTIVAL SENTENCES

The predicate of an adjectival sentence is an adjective. It is placed at the beginning of a sentence and is always in the masculine singular, irrespective of the gender and number of the subject. The subject follows the predicate and is either a noun or a weak pronoun.

	predicate	subject	adverbial phrase
particle	adjective	noun	preposition plus noun or attached pronoun; adverb
particle	adjective	weak pronoun	

You switch the position of the subject and predicate in the English translation and add a form of *to be* in the past or present tense, whichever you think fits best the context.

- *nfr wꜣj.wt=f His roads (are, were) perfect.*
- *mꜣꜥ st It (is, was) true.*

When the sentence has an indirect object formed of *n* and an attached pronoun, it precedes the subject, according to the 'rule of strength' in verbal sentences; see above.

- *twt n=k sw It (is, was) fitting for you.*

NOMINAL SENTENCES

Nominal sentences have a noun or strong pronoun as the predicate. In translation, you need to add a form of *to be* in the past or present tense after the predicate, whichever tense you think is most appropriate in a given context. The subject is either a noun or a demonstrative pronoun, often *pw* or *nn* meaning *he, she, it is* or *was*. In this position, the demonstrative pronoun is called a copula. When the subject is a noun, the two nouns (subject and predicate) are set side by side:

	predicate	subject	adverbial phrase
particle	noun	noun	preposition plus noun or attached pronoun; adverb
particle	strong pronoun	noun	
particle	noun	copula *pw* or *nn*	
particle	strong pronoun	copula *pw* or *nn*	

In the following two examples, *mw.t=k* is the subject and *Nw.t* and *nts* are the predicates:

- *Nw.t mw.t=k Nut (is, was) your mother.*
- *nts mw.t=k She (is, was) your mother.*

Here are the same sentences with the copula *pw* replacing *mw.t=k*:

- *Nw.t pw It (is, was) Nut.*
- *nts pw It (is, was) her (literally It is/was she.)*

Nominal sentences are negated with 𓂜 *n not*. The negation is placed at the beginning of a sentence. It usually has a second element 𓇋𓋴 *js*, which is not translated. Together, *n … js* embrace the first element of the nominal sentence:

- *n ntk js zj You are not a man.*

Sentences in context

QUESTIONS

A question that requires an answer *yes* or *no* is introduced by *jn-jw* in Middle Egyptian:

- *jn-jw wn ḫpr.t m ḫnw Does something that happened exist in the royal residence?* More fluently: *Did something happen in the royal residence?*

jw can be dropped, and sometimes both *jn* and *jw* are dropped. This is as if in English you would simply raise your voice at the end of a sentence, e.g. *Something happened in the royal residence?* Since the Egyptians did not have a question mark, these questions are difficult to recognize as such and it is only in the wider context of a text that you notice that they should be translated as one.

Other questions are formed with interrogative pronouns, for example 𓅓 *m* used after the preposition *ḥr*:

- *pḥ.n=ṯn nn ḥr m That you have reached this is because of what?* More fluently: *Why did you come here?*

EMPHASIS

In order to emphasize a word in a sentence, the Egyptians put it at the front, i.e. they anticipated it. The anticipated noun is repeated with a pronoun in the sentence. In the example below, *=f it* repeats *ḥ3tj=j my heart.*

- *ḥ3tj=j nn grg jm=f My heart, there is no falsehood in it.*

The word *jr As for…* can be used to introduce the anticipated word:

- *jr p3y=j pr jw=f n n3y=j n ẖrd.w As for my house: it shall be for my children.*

There are several ways of saying *He is a king* in Egyptian, each emphasizing different aspects. In the sentence *njswt pw*, the word *njswt* yields the most interesting information, saying that he is the *king*, not something else. In contrast, *ntf njswt* places the focus on *ntf*, which means that *he*, and not somebody else, is the king. Another option is *jw=f m njswt*, literally meaning *He is (as) the king*, foregrounding the identity of the person referred to.

The emphatic forms *sḏm=f* and *sḏm.n=f* emphasize an adverbial phrase or an entire sentence that follows these forms. You can try to express this emphasis in the translation by changing the word order or adding words:

- *jyj.n=j ḫr=k nb=j That I have come is <u>to you</u>, my lord.* Or: *To you, my lord, I have come.*
- *jyj.n=j ḫr=k wꜥb.kw zp 2 That I have come to you is <u>while I am pure, pure</u>.* Or: *It is only because I am pure, pure, that I have come to you, my lord.*

MAIN AND SUBORDINATE CLAUSES

Many Egyptian sentences can be interpreted as either main clauses or subordinate clauses. If you interpret two sentences as main clauses, you can consider connecting them with *and* in the translation, even if this word is not written in the Egyptian text. Subordinate clauses are introduced with connecting words (conjunctions) in English, such as *while, when* or *as*, but less often so in Egyptian. Depending on context, you can use these three words in your translation of a sentence or sometimes also *because, although, so that* or an –ing form. For example, *jw=f m p.t* means *He is in the sky* as a main clause and *while he is in the sky* or *because he is in the sky* or *being in the sky* when interpreted as a subordinate clause. The translations of *sḏm=f, sḏm.n=f* and the stative in a main versus a subordinate clause are given above in the review of verb forms; see also the overview of verb forms at the end of the grammar reference.

There is often no clear indication in the hieroglyphic text for the correct interpretation of a sentence as a main or subordinate clause. However, the particles *m=k* and *ꜥḥꜥ.n* indicate that a sentence is a main clause. The particle *jw* can introduce both main and subordinate clauses.

In the following examples, the sentences that are interpreted as subordinate clauses are underlined in the transliteration and the English translation, and an explanation for the interpretation is added.

- *wḏ ḥm=f jrj.tw mr pn His Majesty decreed that a canal (may) be made*. Intended future after *wḏ to decree.*
- *hꜣj.n=j m spꜣ.t=j mꜣn=j nfrw=k I have come down from my nome so that I (may) see your perfection.* Intended future expressing the purpose of coming down; note that *hꜣj* is an emphatic form emphasizing what is said in the subordinate clause, i.e. the purpose.
- *jw wpj.n=f rꜣ=f r=j jw=j ḥr ḫ.t=j He opened his mouth to me, while I was on my belly*. An adverbial sentence interpreted as describing the background situation for the action described in the main clause.
- *m=k wj ḫr=s jyj.t m ḥtp Look, I am under it, which has come in peace*. Perhaps better: *Look, I have it safe with me*. A stative interpreted as subordinate clause to *=s*, which is not the subject of the main clause, expressing the state of being in which it (= the two eyes of Horus) is.
- *ḏd.n=f nn sḏm.n=f šsꜣ=j He said this because he had heard (of) my skills*. From context, the sentence *sḏm.n=f šsꜣ=j* introduces the reason for the speech. The past *sḏm.n=f* form, instead of *sḏm=f*, is used because he must have heard of my skills prior to making his speech.
- *jw jrj=j n=k mꜣꜥ.t m jb=j rḫ.kw ḥtp=k ḥr=s I did justice in my heart because I know that you are happy about it*. The stative *rḫ.kw I know* most likely introduces the reason for doing justice, and the phrase *ḥtp=k ḥr=s* depends on I know and is therefore translated with that.

RELATIVE CLAUSES

Relative clauses depend on a preceding noun. In English, they are usually introduced by the relative pronouns *who, whom, whose* or a preposition plus *whom* (*for whom* and similar), when the preceding noun is a person, and by *which* or a preposition plus *which* in the case of a thing. In English the relative pronoun can be dropped for the sake of brevity, which makes it sometimes difficult to recognize a relative clause as such in English, for example *the woman you saw* instead of *the woman whom you saw.*

Several types of words and phrases are best translated with a relative clause in English, including adjectives ending in *–y*, verbal adjectives (participles) and relative forms. However, Middle Egyptian also has 'true' relative clauses. They are introduced by the relative converter *ntj who, which*, which changes its form depending on the gender and number of the preceding noun.

	singular	plural
masculine	 *ntj who, which*	 *ntjw who, which*
feminine	 *ntt who, which*	

The relative clause is often an adverbial sentence in which the relative converter functions as the subject.

rmṯ Km.t ntjw jm the people of Egypt who were there

When the relative converter is not the subject, the preceding noun is often resumed with an attached pronoun in the relative clause. You can translate the relative converter provisionally with *who* or *which* and then find a more adequate wording.

jw ntj gs.wj=fj m nwy the island which its two sides are in the flood. More fluent: *the island whose two sides are in the flood*

The noun preceding *ntj* is sometimes dropped. You can add *somebody* or *something* or simply translate *ntj* as usual with *who* and *which*.

mtj.n wj ntj jm ḥnᶜ=f (Somebody) who was there with him witnessed me.

Nouns followed by a relative clause with *ntj* are 'defined'. It means that they take the definite article *the* in the English translation, as you can see in the translations above. When the Egyptians wanted to say ***an*** *island whose sides are in the flood*, they used a subordinate clause: *jw jw gs.wj=fj m nwy*, literally *an island while its two sides are in the flood* (note that the first *jw* here means *island* and the second *jw* is the particle.)

Overview of verb forms I: strong 3-literal verbs

sḏm=f, *sḏm.n=f* AND STATIVE

(main = main clause, subordinate = subordinate clause)

 *sḏm=f*

present	*He hears* (main)	*as he hears* (subordinate)
past	*He hears* (main)	*as he hears* (subordinate)
intended future	*He may hear* (main)	*(so) that he hears* (subordinate)
emphatic form	*That he hears is*	
relative form	*whom he hears*	

 *sḏm.n=f*

past	*He heard* (main)	*when he (had) heard* (subordinate)
emphatic form	*That he heard is*	
relative form	*whom he heard*	

 or  *sḏm.w*

stative	*He has been heard* (main) *He had been heard* (main)	*while he has been heard* (subordinate) *while he had been heard* (subordinate)

VERBAL ADJECTIVES (PARTICIPLES)

 *sḏm* or  *sḏmw*

past	*who/which heard*	*who/which was heard*
present	*who/which hears*	*who/which is heard*
future	*who/which will hear*	*who/which will be heard*

 or  *sḏm.tj=fj*

future	*who/which will hear*

IMPERATIVE, INFINITIVE AND NEGATIVAL COMPLEMENT

 *sḏm*

imperative	*Hear!*
infinitive	*hearing* (NB: *sḏm=f his hearing* means *hearing him*)

 or  *sḏm.w*

neg. complement	*hear*

Overview of verb forms II: weak 3-literal verbs

sḏm=f, *sḏm.n=f* AND STATIVE

(main = main clause, subordinate = subordinate clause)

 or 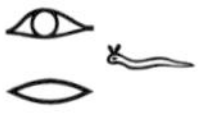 *jrj=f* (simple action)

present	*He makes* (main)	*as he makes* (subordinate)
past	*He has made* (main)	*as he has made* (subordinate)
intended future	*He may make* (main)	*(so) that he makes* (subordinate)
relative form	*whom he makes* also written  *jry=f*	

 or 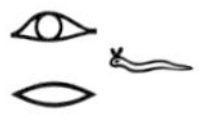 *jrr=f* (habitual or intense action)

present	*He makes* (main)	*as he makes* (subordinate)
past	*He made* (main)	*as he made* (subordinate)
emphatic	*That he makes is*	

𓁹𓈖𓆑 *jrj.n=f*

past	*He made* (main)	*when he (had) made* (subordinate)
emphatic form	*That he made is*	
relative form	*whom he made*	

𓁹 or 𓁹𓅱 *jrj.w* also 𓁹𓇌 *jry*

stative	*He has been made* (main)	*while he has been made* (subordinate)
	He had been made (main)	*while he had been made* (subordinate)

VERBAL ADJECTIVES (PARTICIPLES)

𓁹 or 𓁹𓂋 *jrj* (simple action)

past	*who/which made*	*who/which was made*
present	*who/which makes*	*who/which is made*
future	*who/which will make*	*who/which will be made*

𓁹𓂋𓂋𓅱 *jrrw* or 𓁹𓂋𓂋 or 𓁹𓂋 *jrr* (habitual or intense action)

past	*who/which made*	*who/which was made*
present	*who/which makes*	*who/which is made*
future	*who/which will make*	*who/which will be made*

𓁹𓇌 *jry*

past		*who/which was made*

𓁹𓏏𓆑𓏭𓏭 or 𓁹𓏏𓆑 *jrj.tj=fj*

future	*who/which will make*

IMPERATIVE, INFINITIVE AND NEGATIVAL COMPLEMENT

𓁹 *jrj*

imperative	*Make!*

𓁹𓏏 *jrj.t*

infinitive	*making* (NB: *jrj.t=f his making* usually means *making him*)

𓁹 or 𓁹𓅱 *jrj.w*

neg. complement	*make*

Key to exercises

Unit 1

2 **a** shes; **b** djet; **c** kébeb; **d** khet; **e** tjez; **f** khet; **g** heh; **h** zesh; **i** peh; **j** ménekh; **k** medj

3 **a** wében; **b** wer; **c** wéser; **d** khéroo; **e** fédoo; **f** réwed; **g** rédee; **h** yénee; **i** hézee

4 **a** zaa; **b** taa; **c** áaped; **d** aak; **e** aadj; **f** méshaa; **g** aa-aa

5 **a** *m* m; **b** *r* r; **c** *ḏ* dj; **d** *b* b; **e** *f* f; **f** ʿ aa

6 **a** *ḏf*; **b** *mr*; **c** *rʿ*; **d** *ʿb*; **e** *ḏr*

7 **a** top down; **b** left to right; **c** top down; **d** top down; **e** left to right; **f** left to right and the second group top down

8 **a** *pn*; **b** *ḏs*; **c** *ntk*; **d** *kt*; **e** *rʿ*

TEST YOURSELF

1 b, t, sh, dj, r, aa, aa, kh

2 nétes, péter, tjen, boo, maa-aa, hézee, khézee, óodjaa

3 **a** *t*; **b** *k*; **c** *p*; **d** *z*; **e** ʿ

4 **a** *ntf*; **b** *rn*; **c** *ḥnʿ*; **d** *sḏm*

5 **b** ; **c** 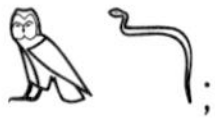; **d** ; **e** 

Unit 2

REQUESTING AN OFFERING

1 The phrase is usually translated *justified*, which means that the deceased has spoken the truth during the judgement of the afterlife.

2 The order of signs is reversed.

VOCABULARY BUILDER

1 hétep, néesoot, dee, hétepet, djéfaa, péteh, zéker, óoseer, en kaa en, maa-aa khéroo

2 *r* in *Zkr*, ʿ in *mꜣʿ-ḫrw*, *ḏ* in *ḏfꜣ*, *f* in *ḏfꜣ*, *n* in *n kꜣ n*, *z* in *Zkr*, *t* in *ḥtp*, *ḥtpt*, *njswt*, *Ptḥ*, *k* in *Zkr*, *ḥ* in *Ptḥ*

3 **a** loaf on a mat; **b** triangular loaf of bread; **c** pair of arms; **d** pedestal; **e** oar

4 sébek, em, heb, aankh (the e between n and kh is usually omitted because the pronunciation also works without adding an e), en neeoot

STELA OF SOBEKEMHAB

1 The upper two lines

2 **a** Ptah-Sokar-Osiris; **b** second line from top and inscription 2; **c** upper man and woman; **d** *dj=f*

3 Inscription 1: hétep dee néesoot, péteh zéker óoseer, dee ef hétepet djéfaa, en kaa en, aankh en néeoot, Sébek em heb, maa-aa khéroo. Inscription 2: aankh en néeoot, Sébek em heb. Inscription 3: eet ef, Bébee, maa-aa khéroo. Inscription 4: nébet per, Sénoot, máa-aa khéroo. Inscription 5: hémet ef. Inscription 6: nébet per, Néboo em résee

LANGUAGE DISCOVERY

1 **a** inscription a; **b** inscription e; **c** inscriptions b and c; **d** inscriptions d and f

2 **a** top down and left to right; **b** top down and right to left; **c** top down and left to right; **d** top down and right to left

3 **a** inscription a, line 2; **b** inscription a, line 1; **c** inscription a, line 1;
d inscription a, line 1; **e** inscription a, line 1; **f** inscription a, line 2, and inscription 2;
g inscription a, line 2; **h** inscription a, line 2, and inscription c

4 They repeat the sounds of the multi-sound signs.

5 **a** top down and left to right; **b** right to left and top down

6 **a** and ; **b** ; **c** ; **d** and 

EXPLORE

1 left to right

2 

3 *ḥtp dj njswt Sbk dj=f ḏfꜣ n kꜣ n Ptḥ-m-ḥꜣb mꜣꜥ-ḫrw*

4 *An offering which the king gives to Sobek. May he give food to the ka-soul of Ptahemhab, justified*

5 **b** *pḥ*; **c** *ḥz*; **d** *nb*

TEST YOURSELF

1 **a** right to left; **b** left to right; **c** left to right; **d** right to left

2 **a** *mꜣꜥ*; **b** *ḥb*; **c** *ḥtpt*; **d** *ꜥnḫ*

3 **a** *for the ka-soul of the officer of the town regiment*; **b** *may he give food*; **c** *Sobekemhab, justified*; **d** *an offering which the king gives*

Unit 3

KINSHIP

Female kinship terms end in *.t*.

VOCABULARY BUILDER

1 zaa, zaat, sen, sénet, hem, hémet, eet, moot

2 **a** *zꜣ*; **b** *ḥm*; **c** *j*

3 They function as phonetic complements.

4 **b** *jt=f*; **c** *sn.t=f*; **d** *sn=f*; **e** *ḥm.t=f*; **f** *zꜣ=f*; **g** *zꜣ.t=f*

5 **a** *ꜥꜣ*; **b** *nṯr*; **c** *ẖ*; **d** *nfr*; **e** *nb*; **f** *wꜥb*; **g** *ḏd*; **h** *ꜣb*; **i** *w*; **j** *ḏw*; **k** *jmꜣḫ*

NAMES AND FAMILY

1 A table with offerings

2 Right to left

3 The hieroglyphs in the lower part were added in the space left free, after the figures had been cut.

4 *m3ʿ-ḫrw justified*

5 Twice

6 *Khnumu*: above man in the centre of the lower part; *Zat-Khnumu*: behind seated woman; *Zat-Hathor*: in front of seated woman; *Kherty*: behind man at left hand side of lower part; *Zat-Kherty*: in front of woman at right hand side of lower part; *Za-Kherty*: between man and woman in lower part; *Zat-Kherty*: in front of woman at right hand side of lower part

LANGUAGE DISCOVERY

1 Male: *sn, jt*; female: *sn.t, z3.t, ḥm.t, mw.t*

2 𓏏

3 Inverted

4 *m3ʿ-ḫrw* after male family member: *sn=f, Zj-n-Wsr.t, jt=f, m3ʿ.t-ḫrw*

m3ʿ.t-ḫrw after female family members: *mw.t=f, ḥm.t=f*

Note, however, that the first standing woman *sn.t=f* is also called *m3ʿ-ḫrw*. See later in this unit for an explanation.

5 **a** m; **b** f; **c** m; **d** f; **e** f; **f** m; **g** m; **h** m

6 𓊹 *nṯr a god*; 𓊹𓏏 *nṯr.t a goddess*; 𓎟 *nb the lord*; 𓎟𓏏 *nb.t the lady*; 𓋴𓈖 *sn brother*; 𓋴𓈖𓏏 *sn.t sister*

7 **a** *nṯr ʿ3*; **b** *nb.t ʿ3.t*; **c** *mw.t nb.t*; **d** *ḥtp.t wʿb.t*; **e** *jt=f jm3ḫy*; **f** *ḥb nfr*

8 **a** *nṯr nfr*; **b** *z3.t nb.t*; **c** *ḫ.t nb.t wʿb.t*; **d** *ḥm.t nfr.t*; **e** *jt m3ʿ-ḫrw*; **f** *sn nb*

9 **a** *a good god*; **b** *every daughter*; **c** *every pure thing*; **d** *the beautiful wife*; **e** *a justified father*; **f** *every brother*

EXPLORE

1 **a** *ḥtp dj njswt*; **b** the name of a deity; **d** *ḥtp dj njswt dj Wsjr nb Ḏdw nṯr ʿ3 nb 3bḏw*; **e** *an offering which the king gives to Osiris, lord of Busiris, great god, lord of Abydos*

2 **a** 𓂞𓆑 *dj=f* and the end *m3ʿ-ḫrw*; **b** *n k3 n Zj-n-Wsr.t m3ʿ-ḫrw*; **c** *for the ka-soul of Senwosret, justified*; **d** a list of offerings

3 **a** péret khéroo taa hénket (you can also say 'héneket', but the e between n and k is usually omitted because it is not needed for the pronunciation) kaa áaped shes ménkhet (you can also say 'ménekhet', but again the e is usually omitted for the same reasons as above); péret khéroo taa hénket khet nébet néfret (the e between f and r is usually omitted, as above) wáabet péreet em bah nétjer aa-aa; péret khéroo taa hénket kaa áaped khet nébet néfret wáabet áankhet nétjer eem; **b** *pr.t-ḫrw t3 ḥnq.t a voice offering, bread and beer*; **c** a prayer for the deceased; **d** *šs mnḫ.t linen and alabaster*, *prj.t m-b3ḥ nṯr ʿ3 that come before the great god*, *ʿnḫ.t nṯr jm on which a great god lives*; **e** *pr.t-ḫrw t3 ḥnq.t k3 3pd šs mnḫ.t ḫ.t nb.t nfr.t wʿb.t ʿnḫ.t nṯr jm*; **f** *a voice offering, bread and beer, ox and fowl, linen and alabaster, everything good and pure of which a god lives*

DRAWING HIEROGLYPHS

2 **a** ; **b** ; **c** 

TEST YOURSELF

1 **a** *mw.t=f*; **b** *sn=f*; **c** *zꜣ.t*; **d** *jt*; **e** *ḥm.t=f*; **f** *ḥm*; **g** *sn.t=f*

2 **a** f; **b** m; **c** m; **d** f

3 **a** *every son*; **b** *good offering*; **c** *great lord*; **d** *every great mother*

4 *May he give a voice offering, bread and beer, ox and fowl, linen and alabaster and everything good and pure on which a god lives.*

Unit 4

SACRED KINGSHIP

1 Because Egypt was believed to consist of two parts, Upper and Lower Egypt.

2 Falcon, goose, vulture

VOCABULARY BUILDER

1 héroo, raa, nébtee, néesoot beet, wáadjet, taa, aankh, djet, méree, dee

2 *Wꜣḏ.t*, *ḏ.t*, also *nb.tj* explained later in this unit

3 **a** *Wꜣḏ.t*; **b** *tꜣ*; **c** *ꜥnḫ*; **d** *mry*; **e** *mry*

4 kháoo, séker, méntjoo (or 'ménetjoo', as you prefer), kháset, daar, set

5 **a** *ḫꜥ*; **b** *d*; **c** *ꜣ*; **d** *sqr*; **e** *ḫꜣs*; **f** *mn*; **g** *ṯ*; **h** *st*

6 It is not written in hieroglyphs.

EGYPT AND THE SINAI

1 Probably the imagery

2 Reading skills might have been very limited in the general population.

3 In the hands of Sahure and the two figures of the king behind him and in the inscription above Sahure

4 (1) héroo neb kháoo néesoot beet sáahoo raa dee aankh djet, (2) nétjer aa-aa, (3) séker méntjoo khásoot néboot, (4) daar khásoot néboot

5 Top line

6 *lord of the crowns; given life for ever*

7 *great god*

8 From the top down and from right to left.

9 Striking down the Mentu-Bedouin

LANGUAGE DISCOVERY

1 The Horus title and the title king of Upper and Lower Egypt

2 It illustrates the meaning of the word striking down (with a mace).

3 **a** Horus; **b** Ra; **c** foreign land; **d** life

4 In the second and third columns the signs mean the same as what they depict in a–c, whereas they differ in d.

5 Foreign land, because the hieroglyph is written three times

6 They describe the action shown, i.e. striking down the Bedouin.

7 **a** the first column; **b** King of Upper and Lower Egypt and Son of Ra; **c** the same, i.e. *ʿnḫ-mswt who-lives-of-births*; **d** *Zj-n-Wsr.t*

8 **a** male individual; **b** male individual; **c** female individual; **d** cultivated land; **e** cobra

9 **a** pic; **b** class; **c** class; **d** pic; **e** pic; **f** class

10 **a** two sons; **b** gods; **c** mothers; **d** two lands

11 **a** a land; **b** the lands; **c** two gods; **d** gods; **e** foreign lands; **f** two mothers; **g** the sister; **h** daughters; **i** the two daughters

12 **a** taa; **b** táaoo; **c** nétjerooee; **d** nétjeroo; **e** khásoot; **f** móotee; **g** sénet; **h** záaoot; **i** záatee

13 **a** *t3 land – t3.wj two lands*; **b** *ḫ3s.t foreign land – ḫ3s.wt foreign lands*; **c** *z3 a son – z3.wj two sons*; **d** *nb.t lady – nb.tj two ladies*

14 **a** smiting; **b** striking down; **c** speaking; **d** inspecting

EXPLORE

1 In the column on the right-hand side

2 *given life for ever*

3 In the rectangle of the Horus name

4 **a** in the centre of the upper line of the inscription; **b** above the king to the left; **c** in the centre of the upper line, behind the title *King of Upper and Lower Egypt*; **d** towards the end of the upper line

5 **a** 4 x; **b** 2 x; **c** 2 x; **d** 2 x

6 **a** *lord of the two lands*; **b** *great god*; **c** *good god* or *perfect god*; **d** *foreign lands*

7 *sqr mnṯw ḫ3s.wt nb.wt smiting the Mentu-Bedouin and all foreign lands*

8 another scene of the king smiting an enemy

9 *W3ḏ.t Wadjet*

TEST YOURSELF

1 Red crown of Lower Egypt, white crown of Upper Egypt, smiting an enemy, name, titles

2 Horus, Two Ladies, Golden Horus, King of Upper and Lower Egypt, Son of Ra

3 **a** class; **b** pic; **c** class; **d** pic

4 **a** *nṯr.wj two gods*; **b** *ḫʿ.w crowns*; **c** *s.tj two seats*; **d** *mw.wt the mothers*

5 *striking down*

Unit 5

THEBES AND AMUN

1 The crossroads of a town

2 Enclosure of the god

VOCABULARY BUILDER

1 hoot, éeree-en-ef, néheh, ménoo, éener, hedj, róodet, wáaset, éemen, néset

2 **a** *jnr stone*; **b** *nḥḥ eternity*; **c** *Wꜣs.t Thebes* ; **d** *rwd.t strength*; **e** *ḥw.t enclosure*; **f** *Jmn Amun*

3 **a** pic; **b** sound; **c** sound; **d** sound; **e** sound; **f** sound; **g** sound; **h** sound

THE FUNERARY TEMPLE OF AMENHOTEP III

1 The king. The name in the cartouche written in the central column belongs to Seti I. In the restored version of the stela, it looks as if he was making the offerings. Originally, the figure of the king depicted Amenhotep III.

2 Amun-Ra

3 Lines 2 and 3 of the stela

4 First line

5 End of the second line

6 éeree-en-ef em ménoo-ef en eet-ef éemen neb nésoot táaooee, éeret én-ef hoot-nétjer shépset her éemee-wéret en wáaset, ménoo en néheh er djet em éener hedj néfer en róodet

LANGUAGE DISCOVERY

1 **a** *m mnw=f*; **b** *n jt=f*; **c** *n=f*; **d** *ḥr jmj-wrt*; **e** *r ḏ.t*; **f** *m jnr*

2 **a** *n*; **b** —; **c** the two words are set side by side; **d** the words have switched their position

3 **b**

4 **a** It is not written in hieroglyphs; **b** It has the ending *.t*; **c** *making*

5 **a** *n Ptḥ*; **b** *m jnr*; **c** *r Wꜣs.t*; **d** *m ꜣbḏw*; **e** *m ḥw.t-nṯr*; **f** *ḥr=f*

6 **a** *n kꜣ for the ka-soul*; **b** *m jnr out of stone*; **c** *ḥr s.t on the throne*; **d** *m Ḏdw in Busiris*; **e** *m njswt as a king*

7 **a** *lady of Thebes*; **b** *son of Ra*; **c** *the father of the mother*; **d** *a monument of eternity*; **e** *wife of the king*

8 **7a** i e; **7b** c-f; **7c** h j; **7d** a d; **7e** g-k

9 **a** *mnw=f his monument*; **b** *nb n njw.t lord of the town*; **c** *s.t-Ḥrw throne of Horus*; **d** *sn=f his brother*; **e** *jt n njswt the father of the king*; **f** *ḥw.t-nṯr=f his temple*

10 **a** *Jmn nb Wꜣs.t*; **b** *Wsjr nb ꜣbḏw*; **c** *Jmn-Rꜥ njswt-nṯr.w*; **d** *Ḏdw ꜣbḏw*

11 **a** Amun, lord of Thebes; **b** Osiris, lord of Abydos; **c** Amun-Ra, king of the gods; **d** Busiris and Abydos

12 **a** strong; **b** weak; **c** strong; **d** strong; **e** strong; **f** weak

13 **a** incorrect; **b** correct; **c** incorrect; **d** incorrect; **e** incorrect; **f** correct

EXPLORE

1 Almost all parts, but *Rꜥ* is added after *Jmn* and the classifier of *Jmn* is missing.

2 *jrj.n=f m mnw=f n jt=f Jmn-Rꜥ nb ns.wt tꜣ.wj He made it as his monument for his father Amun-Ra, the lord of the thrones of the two lands*

3 *ḥrj.t-jb* and *m mꜣw.t*

4 *making for him a noble sanctuary as something new*

5 *of bright good stone of Anu*

6 the phrase *nb ns.wt t3.wj*

7 *sꜥḥꜥ n=f ḥw.t ꜥ3.t m m3w.t*

8 *erecting for him a great enclosure as something new*

9 It says that the building is *made of stone of strength.*

TEST YOURSELF

1 Osiris, lord of Busiris

2 **a** *food for his ka-soul*; **b** *temple out of stone*; **c** *monument of eternity to eternity* (= *eternal monument*); **d** *Amun in the town*

3 **a** *jt=f his father*; **b** *nb W3s.t lord of Thebes*; **c** *k3 n Ptḥ the ka-soul of Ptah*; **d** *z3.t-njswt daughter of the king* (= *princess*)

4 **b**

5 *jnj.t*

Unit 6

REMEMBRANCE IN LOCAL COMMUNITIES

1 Because it affected the way the living were organized.

2 It begins with *s:*

VOCABULARY BUILDER

1 se-rood, se-ménekh, se-máa-aa, ked, se-áahaa, wéhem, ren, hoot-kaa, toot, paat, shépes, zesh

2 **a** An *s:* is added. **b** The *s:* changes the meaning from *being something* to *making somebody be something*, often better translated with a new verb in English. **c** *to make somebody live* or *to keep somebody alive*

3 **a** man building a wall; **b** noble person on chair; **c** writing equipment (palette, bag for ink, reed holder); **d** pintail duck flying; **e** leg (and hoof) of an ox; **f** chisel; **g** mast; **h** crook with package; **i** pot above waterlines (the water is inside the pot; hence this group has the meaning *inside*); **j** circle with lines (possibly representing a stylised placenta)

4 **a** *s:rwd, s:mnḫ, s:rwd, s:m3ꜥ, zš, m3.t*; **b** *p3.t*; **c** *twt*; **d** *wḫ3*

KHNUMHOTEP AT BENI HASSAN

1 Procession of statues (*twt.w*).

2 His *ka-chapels*

3 No. The plural strokes at the beginning of column (5) must belong to a preceding word.

4 The sign for *nṯr* is placed within the sign for *ḥw.t* rather than before it.

5 The plural strokes are used twice, and the classifier has erranously taken an additional stroke as if it was a picture sign.

6 se-róod-en-ee ren en eet-ee se-ménekh-en-ee hoo-oot kaa éereeoo shémes-en-ee tóotoo-ee er hoot nétjer se-máa-aa-en-ee en-sen paat-sen

LANGUAGE DISCOVERY

1 **a** *=j*; **b** *=sn*; **c** verbs with *=j*: *s:rwd, s:mnḫ, šms, s:mꜣꜥ*; nouns with *=j*: *jt, twt*; noun with *=sn*: *pꜣ.t*; preposition with *=sn*: *n*; **d** *šms.n=j I followed, jt=j my father, ḥw.t-kꜣ=sn their ka-chapel; n=sn for them*

2 **a** *s:rwd, s:mnḫ, šms.n=j, s:mꜣꜥ* **b** *.n*; **c** the water line

3 verb

4 **a** *his father, he made, for him*; **b** *my father, I erected, for me*; **c** *her name, she followed, to her*; **d** *their god, they built, on them*; **e** *your statue, you kept alive, for you*

5 **a** *s:mꜣꜥ.n=f he put in order;* **b** *ḥw.t-kꜣ=sn their ka-chapel*; **c** *n=ṯn for you*; **d** *njw.t=n our town*; **e** *wḥm.n=k you repeated*; **f** *rn=ṯ your name*; **g** *n=n for us*

6 **a** man; **b** king; **c** not indicated; **d** woman; **e** not indicated

7 **6a** *ḏs=j myself;* **6b** *mnw=j my monument*; **6c** *jrj.n=j I made*; **6d** *zꜣ=j my son*; **6e** *ḥw.t-kꜣ=j my ka-chapel*

8 **a** *s:ꜥḥꜥ.n=sn*; **b** *qd.n=f;* **c** *s:mnḫ.n=ṯn;* **d** *jrj.n=ṯ;* **e** *wḥm.n=j*

9 **a** *I established the name of my father.* **b** *I embellished his ka-chapels.* **c** *I followed my statues to the temple.* **d** *I put their offering bread in order for them.*

10 **a** *s:mnḫ.n=j mnw=j m njw.t=j*; **b** *s:ꜥnḫ.n zꜣ rn n jt=f*; **c** *qd.n=sn n=k ḥw.t-nṯr*

11 **10a** *I embellished my monuments in my town.* **10b** *The son keeps the name of his father alive.* (You could interpret *n jt=f* also as an indirect object and translate *The son keeps the name <u>for</u> his father alive.*) **10c** *They built a temple for you.*

EXPLORE

1 *Granite*

2 **a** line (1); **b** the name of Khnumhotep; **c** he kept it alive; **d** Khnumhotep recorded his biography on his buildings.

3 **a** (2) *qd.n=j*, (3) *s:ꜥḥꜥ.n=j*, (4) *s:ꜥnḫ.n=j*, (5) *wḥm.n=j*; **b** *=j*; **c** (1) *jrj.n=j mnw=j m-ẖnw njw.t=j* (2) *qd.n=j wḫꜣ* (3) *s:ꜥḥꜥ.n=j sw m wḫꜣ.w n mꜣṯ zš m rn=j ḏs=j* (4) *s:ꜥnḫ.n=j rn n jt=j ḥr=sn* (5) *wḥm.n=j jrj.t=j ḥr mnw=j nb* (1) *I made my monument inside my town.* (2) *I built a hall.* (3) *I erected it with granite columns inscribed with my own name.* (4) *I kept the name of my father alive on them.* (5) *I repeated what I did on all of my monuments.* (literally *on every (my) monument*).

4 **a** *s:ꜥnḫ* se-ankh; **b** *n=ṯn* en-tjen; **c** *mꜣṯ* maatj

TEST YOURSELF

1 **a** *twt=j my statue*; **b** *jrj.n=sn they made*; **c** *n=ṯn for you*; **d** *ḏs=f himself*; **e** *ḥw.t-kꜣ=j my ka-chapel*; **f** *r=s towards it*; **g** *nṯr=n our god*; **h** *šms.n=ṯ you followed*

2 **a** and **d**

3 **a** *wḥm.n=j rn nfr n jt.w=j*; **b** *jrj.n=f mnw n njswt r ḏ.t*

Unit 7

ROYAL NAMES

1 In order to honour the sun god.

2 𓉻 and 𓀜

VOCABULARY BUILDER

1 nékhet, kháaee, Máa-aat, se-mén, hep, khépesh, hóoee, éemen-hétep, hékaa, wer, poo, néesoot, wéser, nétjeree, waah, khérep, péhtee, djéser, men-khéper-raa sétep-en-raa

2 **a** *Rꜥ, Mꜣꜥ.t, Jmn*; **b** *nṯrj, ḏsr*; **c** *nḫt, ḫpš, wsr, pḥtj*; **d** *ḥqꜣ, njswt*

3 **a** *ḏsr*; **b** *nḫt*, also classifier FORCE; **c** *wsr*; **d** *pḥ*; **e** *ḫrp*; **f** *wꜣḥ*; **g** *stp*; **h** *wr*; **i** *ḥqꜣ*; **j** *ḫpš*; **k** *ḫt*

4 **a** Each represents a part of the sign in the first column. **b** (i) with double reed, (ii) and (iii) omitted, (iv) writing imitates dual ending in *–j*; **c** The words are written in an abbreviated form, reduced to their core sign.

MARRIAGE AND EMPIRE

2 The first part is about Amenhotep III, the second about Tiy.

3 Re und Ma'at in *Nb-Mꜣꜥ.t-Rꜥ*, Amun in *Jmn-ḥtp ḥqꜣ-Wꜣs.t*

4 *ḥm.t-njswt wr.t great royal wife*

5 Line 6

6 *tj*

LANGUAGE DISCOVERY

1 **a** Golden Horus name; **b** the adjective; **c** *great of strength, with great strength*

2 **a** (1) *ꜥnḫ Ḥrw Kꜣ-nḫt Ḫꜥj-m-Mꜣꜥ.t* (2) *nb.tj S:mn-hp.w S:grḥ-tꜣ.wj* (3) *Ḥrw-nbw ꜥꜣ-ḫpš Ḥwj-Sṯtjw*
b (1) *May live the Horus Strong-Bull Who-appears-with-Ma'at* (2) *Two Ladies Who-establishes-the-laws Who-pacifies-the-two-lands* (3) *Golden Horus With-great-strength Who-smites-the-Asiatics*

3 **a** (7) *rn n jt=s Ywjꜣ* (8) *rn n mw.t Ṯwjꜣ*; **b** *is*; **c** *ḥm.t pw n.t njswt nḫt*; **d** *She is the wife of a strong king*

4 **a** *njswt ꜥꜣ pḥtj*; **b** *njswt nḫt ꜥ*; **c** *Zꜣ.t-Ḥw.t-Ḥrw mꜣꜥ.t-ḫrw*; **d** *Ptḥ nfr ḥr*

5 **a** *the very strong king*; **b** *a king with a strong arm*; **c** *Zat-Hathor justified*; **d** *Ptah with a beautiful face*

6 **a** *Ḥrw Wsr.t-kꜣ.w Horus With-strong-ka-souls*; **b** *Ḥrw-nbw Nṯrj.t-ḫꜥw Golden Horus With-divine-crowns*

7 **a** *s:mn establishing, established*; **b** *ḫrpw guiding, guided*; **c** *sqr striking down, stroke down*; **d** *wḥmw repeating, repeated*; **e** *s:ꜥḥꜥ erecting, erected*; **f** *ḥwj smiting, smitten*

8 **a** *who/which established/establishes/will establish; who/which was/is/will be established*; **b** *who guided/guides/will guide; who was/is/will be guided*; **c** *who/which struck/strikes/will strike down; who was/is/will be struck down*; **d** *who/which repeated/repeats/will repeat; who/which was/is/will be repeated*; **e** *who/which erected/erects/will erect; who/which was/is/will be erected*; **f** *who/which smote/smites/will smite; who/which was/is/will be smitten*

9 **a** *dy* *given*; **b** *ḫꜥꜥ* *appearing*; **c** *ḥww* *smiting* or *smitten*

10 **a** *ḫrp*; **b** *ḫꜥꜥ*; **c** *mn.t*; **d** *jry.t*; **e** *s:ꜥnḫ.t*; **f** *s:mn.w*

11 **a** *a king who guides the living*; **b** *the king who appears on the throne of Horus*; **c** *ka-chapels that endure in their town*; **d** *a temple which is made out of stone*; **e** *a daughter who keeps the name of her father alive*; **f** *laws which were established in the two lands*

12 **a** *Your name is Tjuya.* **b** *Your father is Ptah.* **c** *Amenhotep is our lord.* **d** *Amun-Ra is the king of the gods.*

13 **a** *ḥqꜣ pw n Sṯtjw*; **b** *zꜣ=f pw wsr*; **c** *ḥm.t pw n njswt rn=s Ty*; **d** *Jmn nṯr=j*

14 **a** *Jmn-ḥtp Ḥqꜣ-Wꜣs.t pw wr pḥtj It is Amenhotep Ruler-of-Thebes with great strength*; **b** *rn n sn=f Ptḥ-m-ḥꜣb The name of his brother is Ptahemhab*; **c** *mw.t=k pw Nw.t rn=s She is your mother, her name is Nut*; **d** *ḥqꜣ pw ḥwj mnṯ.w He is a ruler who smites the Mentu-Bedouin.*

EXPLORE

1 *Son of Ra* title

2 **a** *Kꜣ-nḫt Ḫꜥj-m-Wꜣs.t Strong-bull Who-appears-in-Thebes*; **b** *Mn-ḫpr-Rꜥ Stp-n-Rꜥ Enduring-is-the-manifestation-of-Ra Whom-Ra-has-chosen*; **c** *Ḏsr-ḫꜥ.w Ḫrp-pḥtj With-sacred-crowns Who-guides-the-strength* (perhaps better *Who-leads-with-strength*); **d** *Wꜣḥ-njswy.t-Rꜥ-m-p.t Whose-kingship-endures-like-Ra's-in-the-sky* (literally *Enduring-of-kingship-like-Ra-in-the-sky*)

3 Perhaps for a visit of Senwosret III to Lahun or for a statue of the king in the temple.

4 They are verses. Line 1 is a refrain repeated before each verse.

5 **a** ; **b** 

6 (2) éesoo néhet poo néhmet séndjoo em-aa khéroo-ef (3) éesoo djoo poo médjer djaa er ter en néshnen pet

8 **a** *pw*; **b** (2) *Indeed, he is a shelter*; (3) *Indeed, he is a mountain*

9 **a** verbal adjective; **b** because it refers to the feminine word *nh.t*; **c** *which protects*
d *which protects the fearful one from his foe*

10 *Indeed, he is a mountain which resists the storm at the time of the raging of the sky.*

TEST YOURSELF

1 **a** *Strong-bull With-great-strength*; **b** *Who-has-divine-crowns*; **c** *Long-living*

2 **a** *Horus Who-keeps-the-two-lands-alive*; **b** *Strong-bull Who-smites-every-land*

3 **a** *Ma'at-is-the-ka-soul-of-Ra*; **b** *He is the ruler of the Mentu-bedouin.*

Unit 8

THE FIRST CATARACT

1 Egypt is characterized as being urban, Nubia as being rocky.

2 CROSSING

VOCABULARY BUILDER

1 hem, wedj, mer, pen, em máaoot, wáaeet, óodjaa, khéntee, em-khet, se-kher, kaash, khézee, se-wésekh, taash, kémet

2 a *ḥm, wḏ, mr, wꜣj.t, ḥm, Kꜣš, tꜣš, Km.t*; **b** *ẖzj*; **c** *ḫntj, rdj, jyj*; **d** *s:ḫr, s:wsḫ*; **e** *wḏ, wḏꜣ*

3 a *s:mn to establish*; **b** *rn name*; **c** *rdj to give, to cause*

4 a *mr*; **b** *wꜣj*; **c** *ḏꜣ*; **d** *ḫnt*; **e** *wsḫ*; **f** *tꜣ*; **g** *km*; **h** *ḥm*; **i** *jy*

5 a SAILING; **b** BAD; **c** STELA; **d** ENEMY

THE CANAL INSCRIPTION OF SENWOSRET III

1 the crowns both of Upper and of Lower Egypt

2 *good god, lord of the two lands*

3 in line 2

LANGUAGE DISCOVERY

1 a 8; **b** at the end of the line; **c** 140 cubits = 70m long, 20 cubits = 10m wide, 15 cubits = 7.50m deep

2 a i *ḫꜥj*, ii *wḏ*, iii *jrj.tw*, iv *wḏꜣ*, v *ḫntj*, vi *s:ḫr.t*; **b** *ḫꜥj* and *jrj.tw* future tense, *wḏ* past tense; **c** *ḫꜥj* the king has travelled, *ḫntj* he is sailing South, *ḫꜥj* he will smite

3 a *good roads appear the ka-souls Ra eternity*; **b** *Good are the roads of May-the-ka-souls-of-Ra-appear-eternally.* Or: *The roads of May-the-ka-souls-of-Ra-appear-eternally are perfect.*

4 a *nṯr 42 42 gods*; **b** *zp 2 two times = twice*; **c** *tꜣ 215 215 loaves of bread*; **d** *ḫꜣ m ḫ.t nb.t nfr.t wꜥb.t one thousand of all things good and pure*

5 a *rnp.t-zp 16 ꜣbd 3 pr.t* regnal year 16, third month of growing, **b** *rnp.t-zp 30 ꜣbd 2 šmw 27 ḫr ḥm n Ḥrw Kꜣ-nḫt Ḫꜥj-m-Mꜣꜥ.t dj ꜥnḫ* regnal year 30, second month of harvest, day 27, under the Majesty of Horus Strong-bull Who-appears-with-Ma'at given life; **c** *rnp.t-zp 2 ꜣbd 3 ꜣḫ.t 1 ḫr ḥm n njswt-bjt Nj-Mꜣꜥ.t-Rꜥ* regnal year 2, third month of inundation, day 3, under the Majesty of the king of Upper and Lower Egypt Ni-Ma'at-Ra

6 a *jrj ḥm=f mr pn*; **b** *s:ḫr=j Kꜣš ẖzj.t*; **c** *wḥm=ṯn rn=f*; **d** *jyj=sn m ḥtp*

7 a *His Majesty may make this canal.* **b** *I smite wretched Kush.* **c** *You repeated his name.* **d** *May they come in safety.*

8 a *wḏ=f s:ꜥḥꜥ wḏ pn m ḥw.t-nṯr* He decreed that this stela be set up in the temple. **b** *rdj nb=j ḫntj=j r Wꜣs.t* My lord has caused that I may sail upstream to Thebes. Or: My lord let me sail south to Thebes.

9 a *ḫꜥj=f m s.t-Ḥrw r s:ḫr.t ḫꜣs.t nb.t* May he appear on the throne of Horus in order to smite every foreign land. **b** *s:wsḫ ḥm=f tꜣš Km.t m wḏꜣ r Kꜣš* His Majesty extended the border of Egypt while travelling (while he travelled) to Kush. **c** *qd=j jz=j ḥr s:mnḫ ḥw.t-kꜣ=j* I built my tomb while establishing my ka-chapel.

10 a *wretched Kush*; **b** *Kush is wretched.* **c** *The rulers of the foreign countries were strong.* **d** *the strong rulers of the foreign countries*; **e** *The bright monument is great and the stone is beautiful.* **f** *The monument of bright beautiful stone is great.*

11 a *wsr ḥm=f r ḥqꜣ nb* His Majesty is strong more than every ruler. Or: His Majesty is stronger than any (other) ruler. **b** *ꜥꜣ wꜣj.t n.t Ḫꜥj-kꜣ.w-Rꜥ* The road of May-the-ka-souls-of-Ra-appear is great.

EXPLORE

1 Third year

2 Line 2

3 Line 6

4 **a** *rnp.t-zp 3 3bd 3 šmw 15 ḫr ḥm n nb n ḫ3s.t nb.t Jmn-m-ḥtp nṯr-ḥq3-Jwnw* *Regnal year 3, third month of Harvest, day 15, under the Majesty of the lord of every foreign land Amenhotep God-and-ruler-of-Heliopolis;* **b** *ꜥḥꜥ.n rdj.n ḥm=f jrj.tw wḏ* *Then His Majesty caused that this stela may be made. Or: Then His Majesty had this stela made.* **c** *s:mn.w m r3-pr pn* **d** *passive voice erected;* **e** *which was erected in this temple;* **f** *ḥtj.w m rn wr n nb t3.wj z3-Rꜥ Jmn-m-ḥtp nṯr-ḥq3-Jwnw m pr jt.w nṯr.w* **g** *which was inscribed with the great name of the lord of the two lands, the son of Ra Amenhotep God-and-ruler-of-Heliopolis in the temple of his fathers, the gods* **h** *m-ḫt jyj.t m Rtnw ḥrj.t* *after he had come from Upper Syria.* **i** *s:ḫr.n=f rqy.w=f nb.w ḥr s:wsḫ t3š.w Km.t* *He smote all his enemies while extending the borders of Egypt.*

TEST YOURSELF

1 *rnp.t-zp 36 3bd 2 pr.t 9 ḫr ḥm n njswt-bjt Nb-M3ꜥ.t-Rꜥ* *Regnal year 36, second month of inundation, day 9, under the Majesty of the king of Upper and Lower Egypt Neb-Ma'at-Ra*

2 **a** *Amenhotep caused that a canal be made as something new.* **b** *He decreed that they sail upstream to wretched Kush in order to smite the rulers.* **c** *His Majesty made for him this monument, while he extended the borders of Egypt.*

3 **a** *The great name of His Majesty is beautiful.* **b** *He is my lord with sacred crowns.*

Unit 9

ENCOUNTERING THE GODS

1 They raised both arms for worshipping and prayed with one arm raised.

2 *ḫntj*

VOCABULARY BUILDER

1 khénet, éepet-soot, yáaoo, sen-taa, sédjem, nees, máa-aa, tep, eeb, kher, háatee, nen, géreg, eem, sédjem-aash, haat, néfroo, dóoaa, hétep, néhee, senémeh, her, se-hétepee, raa neb

2 **a** *offering, to go down;* **b** *on, face*

3 **a** *m;* **b** *jb;* **c** *ḥ3t;* **d** *n;* **e** *grg;* **f** *sḏm;* **g** *nm;* **h** *jpt;* **i** *j3w;* **j** *j;* **k** *tp;* **l** *dw3*

4 **a** *m3ꜥ.t Ma'at;* **b** *jyj to come*

THE PRAYER OF MERI-WASET

1 *n k3 n sḏm-ꜥš m s.t M3ꜥ.t Mry-W3s.t m3ꜥ-ḫrw* *for the ka-soul of the servant in the Place of Truth Meri-Waset, justified*

2 Amun-Ra

3 (2) *rdj.t j3w n Jmn-Rꜥ njswt nṯr.w* (3) *sn-t3 n k3=k nb nṯr.w* (2) *Giving praise to Amun-Ra, the king of the gods;* (3) *praying to your ka-soul, lord of the gods*

LANGUAGE DISCOVERY

1 **b** *-j*; **c** with the dual strokes in *ḫntj* and not expressed in the hieroglyphs of *ḫrj*; **d** *who is related to the front, who is on*; **e** *foremost of Luxor, living on earth*

2 *is* both in lines (8) and (9)

3 (4) *dj=k jry=j j3w*, (5) *sḏm=k njs=j*, (7) *jyj.n=j n=k* (4) *Let me give praise* (literally *may you cause that I make praise*), (5) *may you listen to my prayer* (*=j my* is not written in hieroglyphs, but inferred in the translation and transliteration because this is likely to be what Meri-Waset intended to say), (7) *I have come to you*

4 **a** *nṯr*; *who/which is related to god → divine*; **b** *town*; *njw.tj*; *who/which is related to the town → local*; **c** *under*; *ḫrj*

5 **a** *nṯr=ṯn njw.tj your local god*; **b** *nṯr nb ḥrj jb ḥw.t-nṯr Jmn every god who resides in* (literally *who is in the heart of*) *the temple of Amun*; **c** *s.t nṯr.jt a divine throne*; **d** *Wsjr ḫntj jmn.tjw Osiris foremost of the Westerners*

6 **a** *ḫꜥ.w=j ḫr ḥ3.t=j My crowns are in front of me* (literally *under my front*); **b** *ꜥnḫ.w nb.w ḥr t3 All living are on the earth*; **c** *njswt m nb=j The king is (as) my lord*; **d** *nn m3ꜥ.t m s.t=s Ma'at is not at its place*, or: *Ma'at is not where it should be.*

7 **a** *It is Amun-Ra who listens to the prayer* (nominal sentence); **b** *Your beauty is in my face* (adverbial); **c** *May you pray to Ptah* (verbal); **d** *I have come to your temple. May you listen to my prayer* (verbal, twice); **e** *There is no statue in his tomb which is on the west bank of Thebes.* (adverbial negated); **f** *His name is Amenhotep. May all lands repeat this name.* (nominal; verbal)

EXPLORE

1 **a** Osiris; **b** *rdj.t j3w n Wsjr sn-t3 n Wnn-nfr giving praise to Osiris, praying to Wenennefer*; **c** *jnj.n=j n=k jb=j m3ꜥ.t ḫr ḥ3.t=f I have come to you. My heart, Ma'at is in front of it* (literally: *under its front*). → *I have come to you, Ma'at being at the front of my heart.* **d** *ḥ3tj=j nn grg jm=f*; **e** *heart – my – not – falsehood – in – it → My heart, there is no falsehood in it.* **f** in order to emphasize it

2 **a** *nfrw=k your beauty* **b** *dj=j n=k j3w m33=j nfr.w=k May I give praise to you. I see your beauty → Let me praise you as I see your beauty*; **c** *dw3=j Rꜥ m ḥtp=f I praise Ra at his going down → I praise Ra, while he is going down*; **d** *who listens*; **e** *sḏm nḥy sḏm snmḥ who listens to a request, who listens to a prayer.*

3 **a** line 3; **b** *for the ka-soul of the Servant in the place of Truth, the overseer of Western Thebes Pa-en-nebu, justified*; **d** *giving praise to Ptah, lord of Ma'at, king of the two lands, with a beautiful face, who is on his great seat* (*s.t wr.t great seat* means the sanctuary of a temple); **e** *dj, s:ḥtpj*; **f** *May I give praise to his beautiful face (as) I satisfy his ka-soul every day.* **g** rédeet yáaoo en Peteh neb Maa-aat néesoot taa-óoee néfer her héreet set-ef wéret, dee-ee yáaoo en her-ef néfer se-hétepee-ee kaa-ef raa neb, en kaa en sédjem-aash em set Maa-aat héree eeménet wáaset paa-en-néboo maa-aa-khéroo

TEST YOURSELF

1 **a** *who/which is related to the head → first*; **b** *who/which is opposite → hostile* (usually used as a noun meaning *enemy*)

2 **a** *Rꜥ m p.t Ra is in heaven.* **b** *nn grg m jb=k No falsehood is in your heart.*

3 **a** adjectival sentence; **b** verbal sentence; **c** adverbial sentence; **d** nominal sentence

Unit 10

THE THEOLOGY OF LIGHT

The horizon is where the sun seems to touch the earth to start and end shining every day.

VOCABULARY BUILDER

1 sétet, wében, wáaee, máa-aa, wáaee, khéproo, éeten, áakhet, yáabet, aan, teet, aakh, se-hedj

2 **a** *p.t sky*; **b** *M3ˁ.t Ma'at*; **c** Because the final letter of *m3* is duplicated ('geminates') in *m33*.

3 ménaa, shaa, rood, ter, se-khéper, se-keb, meh

4 **a** *w3*; **b** *š3*; **c** *ḫpr*; **d** *wˁ*; **e** *st*; **f** *mḥ*; **g** *tr*; **h** *tjt*; **i** *3ḫt*; **j** *j3b*; **k** *tj*; **l** *3ḫ*

5 **a** ROAD; **b** LOOKING; **c** COOL WATER; **d** STATUE; **e** LIGHT; **f** FEEDING

THE GREAT HYMN TO THE ATEN

1 No.

2 Line 7

3 The lines speak about rising, living and growing and about what *you made*, i.e. what Aten created, which includes the seasons and the sky.

LANGUAGE DISCOVERY

1 **a** *st.wt=k ḥr mnˁ š3 nb*; **b** *Your rays on nursing every field*; **c** *Your rays are nursing every field.*

2 **a** *tj*; **b** *you*

3 *When you rise, they live.*

4 **a** *Your rays will make us cool.* **b** *Ptah is listening to them.* **c** *His Majesty is sailing upstream.*

5 **a** *jw p3 Jtn ḥr wbn m 3ḫ.t j3b.t*; **b** *jw=f r wbn jm=s*; **c** *jw=sn ḥr mḥ t3.wj m st.wt=f*; **d** *jw=j m jyj.t r m33 tj.t=f*

6 **a** *wbn*; **b** *jyj.t*; **c** *ḫˁj.t*; **d** *s:ḫpr*

7 **6a** *p3 jtn ḥr wbn m 3ḫ.t j3b.t rˁ nb The Aten is rising in the Eastern horizon every day*; **6b** *jw ḥm=f m jyj.t m ḥw.t-nṯr n.t p3 Jtn His Majesty was coming from the temple of the Aten*; **6c** *ḫpr.w Jtn r ḫˁj.t m p.t The manifestations of Aten will appear in the sky*; **6d** *jw=k ḥr s:ḫpr ˁnḫ.w nb.w ḥrj.w-tp t3 You are making exist all living ones who are on earth.*

8 **a** *jw=k ˁn.tj*; **b** *jw ḥm.t-njswt wr.t ˁn.tj*; **c** *p3 Jtn wˁj.w*; **d** *jw p.t w3j.tj*; **e** *ḫˁ.w=f ḏsr.w nṯrj.w*; **f** *jw=j ḫˁj.kw m s.t-Ḥrw*

9 **a** *jw 3ḫ-n-Jtn wsr.w r njswt nb Akhenaten is stronger than any other king*; **b** *jw p3 Jtn w3j.w m p.t The Aten is distant in the sky*; **c** *jw=k nfr.tj wr.tj wsr.tj You are perfect, great and strong*; **d** *jw=sn ḫˁj.w m W3s.t They have appeared in Thebes*; **e** *jw=j ḫntj.kw r K3š I have sailed upstream to Kush*; **f** *jw=ṯ ḥtp.tj ḥr ḥtp=j You are happy about my offering.*

10 (1) *st.wt=k ḥr mnˁ š3 nb* (2) *wbn=k ˁnḫ=sn rwd=sn n=k* (3) *jrj=k tr.w r s:ḫpr jry=k nb* (4) *p.t r s:qb=sn* (5) *jrj.n=k p.t* (6) *w3j.tj r wbn jm=s r m3 jry=k nb* (7) *jw=k wˁj.tj* (8) *wbn.tj m ḫpr.w=k m jtn ˁnḫ*

Your rays nurse every field. When you rise, they live and grow for you. You have made the seasons in order to bring everything you have made to life and the winter to make them cool. You made the sky, while it is distant, in order to rise in it and to see everything you have made. You are alone, rising in your manifestations as living Aten.

EXPLORE

1 *You* in lines 1 to 5, *he* in lines 7 and 8.

2 *your efficient image, the ruler of Ma'at* presumably means the king.

3 *(1) ḫꜥj=k nfr m 3ḫ.t n.t p.t (2) jw=k wbn.tj m 3ḫ.t j3b.t (3) mḥ.n=k t3.wj m nfr.w=k (4) jw=k ꜥn.tj wr.tj (5) jw=k m Rꜥ (6) st.wt=k ḥr tj.t=k 3ḫ.t ḥq3 M3ꜥ.t* **...** *(7) jw p3 Jtn ḥr wbn jm=s (8) mḥ=f t3.wj m st.wt=f*
(1) You appear perfectly in the horizon of the sky. (2) You have risen in the Eastern horizon, (3) you filled the two lands with your beauty, (4) you are beautiful, you are great, (5) you are Ra (literally you are as Ra), (6) your rays are on your efficient image, the ruler of Ma'at. (7) The Aten rises in it (= in Akhetaton) (8) he fills the two lands with his rays.

4 *You appear perfectly in the horizon of the sky, when you rise in the Eastern horizon. When you have filled the two lands with your beauty, you are beautiful and great, being Ra, while your rays are on your efficient image, the ruler of Ma'at. ... The Aten rises in it, as he fills the two lands with his rays.*

5 The sign *ꜥnḫ life* is added in one case. The rays of the sun end in hands.

6 *your son*, that is the king

7 *j3w n=k wbn=k m 3ḫ.t p3 Jtn ꜥnḫ nb nḥḥ sn-t3 n wbn=k m p.t r s:ḥḏ t3 nb m nfr.w=k st.wt=k ḥr z3=k*
Praise to you, you rise in the horizon, the living Aten, lord of eternity. Praying to your rising in the sky in order to illuminate every land with your beauty, your rays are on your son.

8 *Hail to you, when you rise in the horizon, living Aten, lord of eternity! Praying to you, as you rise in the sky to illuminate every land with your beauty, while your rays are on your son.*

TEST YOURSELF

1 b *I am giving praise to the Aten, while he rises.*

2 a *jw=k ḫꜥj.tj m njswt-bjt You have appeared as the king of Upper and Lower Egypt.* **b** *p3 Jtn wꜥj.w m p.t The Aten is alone in the sky.* **c** *jw=s nfr.tj She is beautiful.*

Unit 11

JUDGEMENT IN THE AFTERLIFE

1 Perhaps *absolute justice*, just as the dual *t3.wj the two lands* means the entirety of Egypt.

2 Because it is the gesture of negation.

VOCABULARY BUILDER

1 kher, rekh, wen, wénen, wéskhet, ten, mek óoee, der, éenee, éesfet, rémetj, en, sémaar, wéndjoot, yóoeet, boo, djoo

2 Initial *m* is written with an additional 𓂝. NB: You will also find the combination of 𓅓 and 𓂝 for simple *m* at the beginning of words.

3 a *rwd*; **b** *inside*; **c** *wꜥb to be pure*; **d** *falsehood*

4 a hare; **b** deer lying down (it depicts, in fact, a newborn hartebeest); **c** *nw*-pot on legs

5 a people; **b** *dr*; **c** 𓅪 **d** The sign depicts the plan of a house, and the hieroglyphs written in it repeat the word *wsḫ.t hall*.

SPELL 125 OF THE BOOK OF THE DEAD

2 One 𓈖 has been removed from the original text. This is because the original text contains a mistake here. Two 𓈖 do not make sense.

3 The deceased is speaking to Osiris whom he calls *my lord*.

4 42

5 He claims that he knows the name of the 42 deities.

6 Lines 7 to 9.

LANGUAGE DISCOVERY

1 **a** *I have come to you.* **b** past tense in line (1), stative in line (4)

2 Activities of the past

3 **a** *You have been seen.* **b** *I have been found.* **c** *They are strong.* **d** *It has been erected.* **e** *I have been given.* **f** *He has risen.*

4 **a** *m=k wj ḥzj.kw ḫr=s I have been praised because of it.* **b** *jw=j rḫ.kw nṯr pn I know this god.* **c** *jb nfr.w r ḫ.t nb.t The heart is better than anything else.* **d** *wḫꜣ.w zš.w m rn=sn ḏs=sn The columns have been inscribed with their own names.*

5 **a** *I have travelled south to fetch bright beautiful stone for His Majesty.* **b** *Ma'at has come (in)to its place.* **c** *That I have come to you is only as I am pure, pure.* **d** *That he travelled is to build this temple.*

6 **a** *n smꜣr=k wnḏw.t You have not eaten offering bread.* **b** *n jnj.n=f n=k mꜣꜥ.t He does not bring you Ma'at.* **c** *n sḏm.n Ptḥ njs=j Ptah does not hear my prayer.* **d** *n s:ꜥnḫ=j rn.w=sn I did not keep their names alive.*

7 **a** *n jrj=f mꜣꜥ.t He did not do justice.* **b** *n mḥ=f jb n ḥm=f He did not fill the heart of His Majesty* (= *He was not trusted by His Majesty*). **c** *n smꜣ=j rmṯ.w I did not kill people.*

8 (1) *jyj.n=j rḫ.kw nb=j* (2) *jw=j rḫ.kw rn n nṯr 42* (3) *wnn.yw ḥnꜥ=k n wsḫ.t tn n.t mꜣꜥ.tj* (4) *m=k wj jyj.kw ḫr=k* (5) *jnj.n=j n=k mꜣꜥ.t* (6) *dr.n=j n=k jsf.t r rmṯ.w* (7) *n smꜣr=j wnḏw.t* (8) *n jrj=j jwy.t m s.t mꜣꜥ.t* (9) *n jrj=j bw ḏw* (10) *jw=j wꜥb.wk zp 4*

That I have come to you, my lord, is because I know the name of the 42 deities who are (literally *who exist: wnn.yw* is a verbal adjective) *with you in this hall of double justice. … Behold, I have come to you after I had brought Ma'at to you and repelled injustice from people for you. I did not eat offering bread. I did not do anything bad instead of* (literally *at the place of*) *justice. … I did not do an evil thing. I am pure, pure, pure, pure* (literally *I am pure, (to be repeated) four times*).

EXPLORE

1 The entrance gate of the temple of Ptah, where the god would listen to the prayer. The inscription of the door jambs starts with *Ptḥ*.

2 Lines 3 and 4.

3 It is written with two 𓇋 instead of the usual one.

4 *hétep, zémaa, raa, téken, sétjaa, hézee, her*

6 **a** *jw jrj=j n=k mꜣꜥ.t m jb=j I did justice for you in my heart.* **b** *rḫ.kw ḥtp=k ḥr=s I know that you are happy about it.* **c** *n tkn=j grg m jb=j n zmꜣ=j m jsf.t I did not approach falsehood in my heart, I did not unite with injustice.* **d** *dj=k wn rn=j m ḥw.t-nṯr=k rwd.w m rꜣ rꜥ nb May you let my name be in your temple, while it is firm in the mouth of everybody every day.* **e** *twt=j mn.w m-ẖnw=s My statue endures inside it.* **f** *sṯꜣ.kw ḥnꜥ ḥzy=k I am dragged with those you praise;* **g** Amenhotep wishes that the statue representing him is carried around in a temple procession with the statue of other nobles.

7 *I have done justice for you because I know that you are happy about it. I did not approach falsehood in my heart and I did not unite with injustice. Let my name be in your temple, firm in the mouth of everybody every day, while my statue remains in it and I am dragged together with those you praise.*

TEST YOURSELF

1 **a** *You know our name.* **b** *Injustice has been repelled.*

2 **a**

3 **a** *I did not approach Osiris, when falsehood was in my heart;* **b** *I do not bring Ma'at to you.*

Unit 12

MYTH AND RITUAL IN EGYPTIAN TEMPLES

1 By using the hieroglyph 𓊹 meaning *god* (*snṯr* might be derived from *s:nṯrj to make divine* and literally mean *(the substance) that makes divine*; or it comes from *sn-nṯr smell of god*)

2 Honorific transposition: The hieroglyph 𓊹 *nṯr* is put at the front, although it was pronounced after *s*.

VOCABULARY BUILDER

1 djed médoo, yen, kénet, tem, wénen néfer, éeret, khéntee-eeménteeoo, áaset, waas, séneb, áaoot eeb, senétjer, sétjee, yáaee, se-khéker, aa

2 **a** picture; **b** sound; **c** classifier; **d** classifier; **e** picture; **f** sound, classifier

3 **a** *nḫt;* **b** *rꜣ;* **c** *rnp.t;* **d** *ḏw.t;* **e** *ḥr*

5 **a** *md;* **b** *ꜣw;* **c** *tm;* **d** *ẖnt;* **e** *snṯr;* **f** *sṯj;* **g** *ẖkr;* **h** *n;* **i** *pr*

THE TEMPLE OF SETI I AT ABYDOS

1 Osiris

2 (1) *qn.t nb.t all valour,* (2) *nḫt nb all strength,* (4) *njswy.t Rꜥ rnp.wt Tm the kingship of Ra and the years of Atum*

3 *ḥrj-jb Ḥw.t-Mn-Mꜣꜥ.t-Rꜥ nṯr ꜥꜣ who is in the heart of (= who resides in) the Enclosure-of-Men-Ma'at-Ra, great god*

4 He burns incense and offers a piece of cloth.

5 First two columns on the left: from right to left; other columns: from left to right

6 *Wnn-nfr ḥrj-jb Ḥw.t-Mn-Mꜣꜥ.t-Rꜥ*

7 In the final column on the right-hand side.

8 *dj.t snṯr n ḥr=k nfr ḏfꜣ js.t=k wr.t Giving incense to your beautiful face, cleaning your great seat*

LANGUAGE DISCOVERY

1 **a** *dj.n=j n=k qn.t I have given you valour;* **b** *r3 n ḏf3 pr-wr spell for cleaning the per-wer;* **c** *It introduces the speech of the king.*

2 *I am Horus.*

3 *m=k wj ẖr=s I am under them.* It means *I carry them* or *I am having them.*

4 *ḏd mdw jn njswt nb t3.wj Mn-M3ꜥ.t-Rꜥ dj ꜥnḫ*

Speaking words by the lord of the two lands Men-Ma'at-Ra, given life

ḏd mdw z3-Rꜥ nb ḫꜥ.w Sty Mrj.n-Ptḥ mj Rꜥ

Speaking words (by) the son of Ra, lord of the crowns, Seti Whom-Ptah-loved, like Ra.

jnk Ḥrw jyj.n=j ḥr ḥjḥj jr.tj=j

I am Horus. That I have come (to you) is as I was searching for my two eyes.

n rdj.n=j w3j=s r=k Wsjr Ḫntj-jmn.tjw

I do not cause that they will be distant from you, Osiris, Foremost-of-the-Westerners.

m=k wj ẖr=s jyj.tj m ḥtp dr.n=s ḏw.t=k nb.t

I am carrying them, while they have come safe, after they have repelled all your evil.

twt n=k sw Wsjr Wnn-nfr ḥrj-jb Ḥw.t-Mn-M3ꜥ.t-Rꜥ

It is fitting for you, Osiris Wenennefer who resides in the Enclosure-of-Men-Ma'at-Ra.

5 The king identifies himself with Horus and confirms that he is returning his two eyes to his father Osiris. He says that he will prevent them from being removed from Osiris, that they are safe with him and that, with their power, they have repelled everything evil from Osiris. The repelling is done by the incense whose perfume cleans the sanctuary.

6 **a** *dj.n=j n=k ꜥnḫ w3s nb;* **b** *r3 n wn ꜥ3.wj;* **c** *ḏd mdw jn 3s.t wr.t*

7 **6a** *Herewith I give you all life and dominion;* **6b** *spell for opening the two doors;* **6c** *speaking words by Isis*

8 **a** *ntf* he; **b** *nttn you* (pl.); **c** *jnk* I; **d** *nts* she; **e** *ntk you* (masc. sing.)

9 **a** *jnk z3=k I was your son.* **b** *ntk z3 Wsjr You are the son of Osiris.* **c** *ntsn rmṯ Km.t They are the people of Egypt.* **d** *nts mw.t n.t njswt She is the mother of the king.*

10 **a** *ntk Tm You are Atum.* **b** *jnk Wnn-nfr I am Wenennefer.* **c** *ntf Ḥrw dr ḏw.t n jt=f He is Horus who repels the evil for his father.* **d** *nts 3s.t mw.t Ḥrw* She is Isis, the mother of Horus. **e** *jnk Ptḥ nfr ḥr I am Ptah with a beautiful face.*

11 **a** 3B; **b** 5A; **c** 4E; **d** 1F; **e** 6C; **f** 2D

12 **a** *Behold, I am carrying my two eyes.* **b** *Look, you are adorned.* **c** *Behold, they are speaking words to you.* **d** 12a to a woman, 12b to a man, 12c to a group of people

13 **a** *s:ḫkr sw Ḥrw m ḫꜥ.w=f May Horus adorn him with his crowns.* **b** *jꜥj ṯw snṯr May incense wash you.*

14 **a** *m=k sw r jrj.t ḫ.t;* **b** *jw=f r jrj.t ḫ.t;* **c** *3s.t ntṯ mw.t=f;* **d** *m=ṯ sj jyj.tj ẖr=k;* **e** *dj.n=j n=ṯ sn* **f** *pr-wr ḏf3=j sw m snṯr*

EXPLORE

1 He burns incense and holds a piece of cloth.

2 *r3 n ḏf3 pr-wr spell for cleaning the per-wer*

3 *ꜥnḫ w3s nb all life and dominion snb nb all health 3w.t-jb nb.t all joy*

4 In order of appearance: 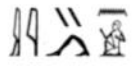 versus ,  versus , *r=k* versus *r=ṯ*, *Wsjr Ḫntj-jmntj.w* versus *ꜣs.t*,  lacking in spell for Isis, *ḏw.t=k nb.t* versus *ḏw.t=k* or *ḏw.t nb.t* (sign not fully preserved), *twt n=k sw* versus *twt n=ṯ sw*, name of Isis lacking at the end of the spell

5 use of feminine instead of masculine pronouns, some omissions due to space constraints, changes in spelling perhaps also due to space constraints or personal preference

6 *sṯj perfume*, *ꜥ arm*

7 **a** (1) *jyj snṯr jyj sṯj nṯr* (2) *jyj sṯj=s r=k sṯj jr.t-Ḥrw* (1) *May the incense come, may the perfume of the god come*, (2) *may its perfume come to you, the perfume of the eye of Horus.* **b** *snṯr* and *sṯj nṯr*; **c** *jr.t-Ḥrw*; **d** *j/y, s, n, ṯ, r*; **e** The phrase *jr.t-Ḥrw* repeats two of the major consonants in lines 1 and 2. **f** *jꜥj=s ṯw s:ḫkr=s ṯw jrj=s s.t=s ḥr-tp ꜥ.wj=k May it wash you, may it adorn you, may it take* (literally *make*) *its seat on your two arms.* **g** It links the coming of the incense (*jyj snṯr*) to the eye of Horus (*jr.t-Ḥrw*) through playing with sound, as you have seen in the previous question. The fumes of the incense settle on the arms of the temple statue, a process perhaps to be interpreted as the eye of Horus, i.e. the incense, returning to the statue. **h** éeyee senétjer éeyee sétjee nétjer, éeyee sétjee-es er-ek sétjee éeret-héroo, yáaee-es tjoo se-khéker-es tjoo éeree-es set-es her-tep áaooee-ek

TEST YOURSELF

1 **a** *Speaking words by Amun-Ra*; **b** *Herewith I give you the kingship of Atum.*

2 **a** *nts mw.t=k you are my mother*; **b** *ntf zꜣ=j he is my son*; **c** *jnk Wnn-nfr I am Wenennefer*; **d** *ntsn nṯr.w Wꜣs.t they are the gods of Thebes*

3 **a** *Look, I was under Ma'at.* **b** *I may wash you.* **c** *Look, they are giving incense.*

Unit 13

VOCABULARY BUILDER

1 wáaoo, waadj wer, éeoo, ges, nóoee, khéroo, kéree, khet, héfaaoo, háaoo, khet, éeneh, néboo, khésbed, máa-aa, eeb, gémgem, ménmen, kéfee, gémee, zékher, éetjee, se-nédjem, waah, démee, wépee, áahaa-en, em baah, nem, nétee

2 **a** *wꜣḏ*; **b** *gm*; **c** BODY; **d** *nbw*; **e** *jṯ*; **f** BREAK, CROSS, NUMBER; **g** *bꜣ*; **h** BEFORE; **i** *jw*; **j** *gs*

'THE SHIPWRECKED SAILOR' (1): ENCOUNTER WITH THE SNAKE

1 *his body was covered with gold* and *his two eyebrows are out of true lapis lazuli* (lines 6 and 7)

2 *a wave of the sea*

3 *he put me without touching me*

4 *Who brought you to this island of the sea?* Literally: *Who (is) (the one) who has brought you to this island of the sea? nm* is used like a strong pronoun, meaning *who is*. Its use is similar in this case to *jnk I am* (see Unit 12). *jnj* is the verbal adjective of *jnj to bring*, meaning *who brings* or *who has brought* (literally *bringing*).

LANGUAGE DISCOVERY

1 **a** Nominal sentences translated with a form of *to be* (see Unit 7); **b** The preposition *ḥr* indicates that the action expressed in the infinitive happens contemporaneously with the action of the

previous sentence. The preposition *m* before a verb of motion tells you that the action expressed in the infinitive is about to happen. Since the text is a narrative in the past tense, you would translate all three infinitives with the past progressive (*was doing*). **c** *zḫr.w* is third person singular stative, and the stative expresses passive voice, whenever the verb allows, which is the case for *to cover* – *to be covered*; **d** adverbial sentence; **e** Forms with *.n* express past tense; **f** yes

2 *ꜥḥꜥ.n, jw*

3 Word for word: *which his two sides in the water*. Fluently: *whose two sides are in the water*

4 **a** *He opened his mouth to me; I was on my belly before him; he was coming;* **b** *m=k wpj.n=f r3=f r=j, m=k wj ḥr ẖ.t=j m-b3ḥ=f, m=k sw m jyj.t;* **c** *Look, he opened his mouth to me. Look I am on my belly before him. Look, he was coming.* **d** *ꜥḥꜥ.n sḏm.n=j ḫrw qrj Then I heard the noise of a storm. ꜥḥꜥ.n rdj=f wj m r3=f Then he put me into his mouth. ꜥḥꜥ.n ḏd.n=f n=j Then he said to me.*

5 **a** *Ra who is in the sky;* **b** *my heart which is under* (= *carrying* or *loaded with*) *falsehood;* **c** *the snake whose body is covered with gold;* **d** *the mouth in which he put me*

6 **a** *ntj which;* **b** *ntt which;* **c** *ntjw who;* **d** *ntj which;* **e** *ntt which;* **f** *ntj which*

7 **a** *ꜥḥꜥ.n sḏm.n=j ntj m jyj.t Then I heard the one who was coming.* **b** *jw wpj.n=f r3=f r ntjw m-b3ḥ=f He opened his mouth to those who were before him.* **c** *jw=f ḥr ẖ.t=f ntt m nbw He was on his belly which was out of gold.* **d** *m=k wj ḥr gmj.t ntt m dp.t tn Look, I am finding the one (woman) who is in this boat.* Or if *ntt* refers to a thing rather than a woman: *Look, I am finding what is in this boat.*

8 **a** *Then heard I voice thunder, I thought wave it is of sea, wood on trembling, earth on shaking, uncovered I face my, found I snake it is – it in coming, body his covered with gold, two eyebrows his out of lapis lazuli true, then give he me in mouth his, seize he me to place his of dwelling, put he me without touching my, – opened he mouth his to me, – I on belly my, then said he to me, who bring you to island this of sea which two sides his in water;* **b** *Then I heard the noise of a thunderstorm, and I thought that it was the wave of the sea as the trees were trembling and the earth shaking. When I uncovered my face* (*kfj.n=j ḥr=j* is not introduced by a particle and therefore interpreted here as a subordinate clause), *I realized that it was a snake coming* (literally *it was a snake, while it was coming*), *its body being covered with gold and its two eyebrows being made out of true lapis lazuli. Then it put me into its mouth and brought me to its home. It seized me without even touching me! It opened its mouth to me, while I was on my belly* (*jw* is followed by the attached pronoun *=j* and interpreted here as introducing a subordinate clause). *Then it said to me: 'Who brought you to this island of the sea whose two sides are in the water?'*

EXPLORE

1 séper, khénoo, kénee, khéredoo, rénpee, em khénoo, kéreset, háaee, méreet, em háaoo, dépet, yaash, méshaa, hékenoo, neb, er méetet éeree

2 *ꜥḥꜥ.n*

3 His family, more specifically *ẖrd.w=f his children.*

4 *qrs.t a burial*

5 *mšꜥ a crew*

6 **a** *ꜥḥꜥ.n ḏd.n=f n=j Then he said to me.* **b** *m=k ṯw r spr r ẖnw Look, you will reach the residence* **c** *mḥ=k qnj=k m ẖrd.w=k so that you will fill your embrace with your children* (*mḥ=k* is interpreted as intended future in a subordinate clause). **d** *rnpj=k m-ẖnw qrs.t=k and (so that you will) rejuvenate in your burial.* **e** *ꜥḥꜥ.n=j hꜣj.kw r mry.t m hꜣw dp.t tn Then I went down to the shore near this boat.* **f** *ꜥḥꜥ.n=j ḥr jꜣš n mšꜥ ntj m dp.t tn Then I was shouting to the crew which was in this boat* **g** *rdj.n=j ḥknw ḥr mry.t n nb n jw pn after I had given praise on the shore to the lord of this island* (*rdj.n=j* is not introduced by a particle and understood here as a subordinate clause), **h** *ntjw jm=sn r mjt.t jry and those who were in it likewise.*

DRAWING HIEROGLYPHS

2 Sign **1a**  is the top sign of **2a** . Sign **1b**  is the top sign of **2b** .

3  and 

TEST YOURSELF

1 **a** *Then…,* main clause; **b** not translated or *while*, main or subordinate clause; **c** *Look, …,* main clause

2 **a** *dp.t ntt ḥr mry.t the boat which is on the shore;* **b** *ntjw jm=s those who are in it;* **c** *nṯr ntj rḫ.kw rn=f the god whose name I know*

Unit 14

IMAGINING DIFFERENT WORLDS

ḥqꜣ ḫꜣs.t ruler of the foreign land

VOCABULARY BUILDER

1 képenee, kédem, rétjenoo, se-hétep-eeb-raa, rénpet, ges, hékaa, raa, ked, shésaa, khépret, fekh, hézee, éeree, peh, métee, em, eeshéset, yen éeoo, eem, héree, nen, her

2 **a** *kpn;* **b** *sꜣ;* **c** *pḥ;* **d** *mt*

3 **a** loose string meaning OPEN, LOOSEN

4 **a** *to make;* **b** *side;* **c** *in* (form of *m* before attached pronouns)

5 **a** *ḥqꜣ;* **b** *ḥrj* **c** *wḏꜣ*

6 **a** from the classifier WALKING

SINUHE THE EGYPTIAN

1 *Byblos* (modern Lebanon), *Qedem* (exact location unknown), *Upper Syria, Egypt*

2 the ruler of Upper Syria

3 *Egyptian* (literally *the language of Egypt*)

4 *the Egyptians* (literally *the people of Egypt*)

5 *wḏꜣ.w r ꜣḫ.t travelled to the horizon*

LANGUAGE DISCOVERY

1 *You will be fine with me.*

2 **a** *Because of what have you reached this?* **b** *What is it?* **c** *Did something happen at the residence?*

3 (iii) *nfr st r ḫ.t nb.t;* **b** (i) *nḫt sw;* **c** (ii) *wr ṯw nb.t=j*

4 **a** *Did you leave Byblos?* **b** *Was he the ruler of Upper Syria?* **c** *Did the Egyptians give witness for you?*

5 **a** *nm ꜥmwnnšj Who is Amunenshi?* **b** *ḥzj.n=k r jšst Where did you travel?* **c** *zj rmṯ jm ḥnꜥ=f Which people were there with him?* **d** *sḏm=k r3 n m Whose language did you hear?* **e** *ḏd.n=f n=k jšst What did he say to you?*

6 **a** The direct object is a weak pronoun and the subject a noun. For this reason, the direct object moves closer to the verb and is placed before the subject. **b** Because place names are feminine nouns even if they do not have a feminine ending. **c** It introduces a relative clause. It is plural because it refers to the plural word *rmṯ.w*. The relative clause is an adverbial sentence and *ntjw* is its subject. **d** stative

7 *Foreign country gave me to foreign country, after I had left Byblos* (literally *That foreign country gave me to foreign country was after I had left Byblos; rdj.n* is not introduced by a particle and interpreted here as an emphatic form. The emphasis in the sentence is on the departure from Byblos, historically a town with strong Egyptian links and thus the last 'civilized' point on Sinuhe's travels, before his vagrancy in an unknown world began). *After I had left for Qedem and had spent a year and a half there* (two subordinate *sḏm.n=f* forms), *Amunenshi who was the ruler of Upper Syria fetched me. He said to me: 'You will be fine with me and you will (even) hear (some) Egyptian.' That he said this* (emphatic *sḏm.n=f* form) *was because he knew my character, had heard of my skills and because the Egyptians who were there with him had given witness for me. Then he said to me: 'Why did you come here? What is it? Did something happen at the residence?' Then I said to him: 'The king of Upper and Lower Egypt Sehetepibra* (the name means *Who-causes-that-the-heart-of-Ra-is-happy*) *has travelled to the horizon.'*

EXPLORE

1 **a** Puntites on the left, Egyptians on the right; **b** She shows first signs of obesity, thus is growing to be like her mother.

3 wer, éenoo, gésooee, shézep, wépootee, méshaa, em khet, tep em, aa-aa, fáaee, háaee, séked

4 **a** *jyj.t jn wr n Pwn.t ḥr jn.w=f r-gs.wj w3ḏ-wr Coming by the chief of Punt carrying* (literally *under*) *his goods to the sea shore.* **b** *šzp jn.w n wr n Pwn.t jn wpw.tj-njswt Receiving the goods of the chief of Punt by the royal deputy.* **c** *spr wpw.tj-njswt r t3-nṯr ḥnꜥ mšꜥ ntj m-ḫt=f tp m wr.w n.w Pwn.t Reaching of the royal deputy (to) the god's land with a troop which was behind him before the chiefs of Punt.* **d** *wr n Pwn.t P3-r3-hw the chief of Punt Pa-ra-hu;* **e** *ḥm.t=f Jty his wife Ity* **f** *z3.wj=fj his two sons;* **g** *z3.t=f his daughter;* **h** *ꜥ3 f3j ḥm.t=f the ass that carries his wife;* **i** *pḥ.n=ṯn nn ḥr zj jšst r ḫ3s.t tn ḫmt.n rmṯ Why have you come here to this land which people* (= the Egyptians) *do not know? jn-jw h3j.n=ṯn ḥr w3j.wt ḥrj.wt Did you come down on the upper roads? jn-jw sqd.n=tn ḥr mw ḥr t3 Did you travel here on the water or on the land?*

5 **a** This was probably unusual for Egyptian 'first ladies' who travelled more comfortably. **b** Perhaps because they found it difficult to reach Punt. The questions underline the achievements of the Egyptian expedition.

TEST YOURSELF

1 **a** *He is stronger than any (other) ruler.* **b** *It is correct.* **c** *My monuments, they are beautiful!*

2 **a** (i); **b** (iii); **c** (iii)

Unit 15

VOCABULARY BUILDER

1 métee en záaoo, éemee zaa en kénbetee en noo-oo, baak, éemee raa, sépaat, hoot maa-aat, eer, se-óodjaa eeb, per, éemeet per, háaoo, mésee, déhen, ténee, médoo yáaoo, aat, haat, saa, khéfet netet, éemee

2 Controller, guard and overseer describe supervisory responsibilities.

3 **a** two wooden planks *jmj*; **b** jabiru (a stork) *b3*; **c** three animal skins *ms*; **d** two wooden planks *jmj*; **e** corner *qnb.t* **f** lid of a chest *s3*

PAPYRI FROM LAHUN

1 Mery's son Antef is given the title and the children of his second wife receive his property.

2 It is not clear. His son was handed over the title while Mery was still alive, whereas the transfer of the house might be planned to happen either before or after his death.

3 **a** Mery's son: **b** Mery's father; **c** Mery's second wife; **d** Mery's father-in-law of his second wife

4 *r mdw j3w=j for (being) my staff of old age* could mean that Antef has to pay for Mery's subsistence

5 Because he has grown old.

6 The first transfer of deed shall be destroyed.

LANGUAGE DISCOVERY

1 It introduces the matter that is up for discussion.

2 **a** The word *z3* is placed after instead of before the first name; **b** *ḏdw n=f*

3 **a** *Sbk-m-ḥ3.t ʿ.w.s. Sobekemhab l.p.h.*; **b** *Kbj ḏd n Nb.t-nn-njswt Kebi who speaks to Nebetnennisut;* **c** *jmj-r3 ḥw.t-nṯr overseer of the temple;* **d** *Jnj-jt=f ḏdw n=f Snb Antef called Seneb;* **e** *Mry z3 Jnj-jt=f Mery called Antef;* **f** *s:wḏ3 jb pw n b3k jm It is a message of the humble servant.*

4 *Cause that he may be promoted!*

5 **a** *sḏm=k rmṯ May you listen to the people.* → *sḏm rmṯ.w Listen to the people!* **b** *ḏhn=k sw* → *dhn sw Appoint him.* **c** *ʿpr p3y=k bw nfr Furnish your goodness.* **d** *dj=ṯ n=j ntt nb.t m pr=ṯ* → *jmj n=j ntt nb.t m pr=ṯ Give me everything that is in your house.*

6 *which*

7 **a** *jmj.t-pr jrj.t.n b3k jm*; **b** *z3=f mrr=f*; **c** *Jnj-jt=f jrj.n Mry*; **d** *ẖrd.w msjw.n Nb.t-nn-njswt*

8 **7a** *Transfer of deed which the humble servant made;* **7b** *his son whom he loves;* **7c** *Antef whom Mery made (= begot);* **7d** *the children to whom Nebetnennisut gave birth*

9 **a** *road – came – he – on – her (= it) → the road on which he came* (said about a statue, so *the road on which it came* makes betters sense in English); **b** *place – every – made – I – monument – at – her (= it) → every place at which I made a monument;* **c** *give – he – thing – every – good – pure – live – god – (out) of – her (= it) → May he give everything good and pure from which a god lives*

10 **a** *jrj.t.n=j nb.t everything I did;* **b** *sḏm.t.n=s nb.t everything she has heard;* **c** *jnn.t ḥꜥpj what the inundation brings;* **d** *jrj.n=j ḥzz.t nṯr.w I have done what the gods praise.*

11 **a** *the transfer of deed;* **b** *in the moment;* **c** *my house;* **d** *my (office of) controller of the phyles;* **e** *his mother;* **f** *my children*

12 **a** *her house;* **b** *the sister;* **c** *matters;* **d** *their transfer of deed;* **e** *the message;* **f** *my gods*

13 **a** *pr=s;* **b** *sn.t;* **c** *h3w;* **d** *jmj.t-pr=sn;* e *s:wḏ3-jb;* **f** *nṯr.w=j*

EXPLORE

1 **a** in the column to the right of the main text; **b** Neni is sending the letter; **c** *Jyj-jb* and *nb=j;* **d** Jyj-jb is Neni's superior; **e** The *humble servant* is Neni.

3 per djet, er nétet, aad, óodjaa, hézoot, sépedoo, yáabtet, pésdjet, her, dee eeb khénet, her nétet, kaa, áaper, boo néfer, ger, khéroo fee, khéfet éeree

4 Sender and receiver:

The servant of the funerary domain Neni who speaks to the steward Iyiib l. p. h.:

Greetings:

It is a message to my lord l. p. h. that all matters of my lord l. p. h. are fine (stative) *and safe* (stative) *at all their (correct) places in the praise of Sopdu, the lord of the East, his ennead and all deities as the humble servant likes.*

Setting the scene for the issue of the letter:

It is a message to my lord l. p. h. about causing that attention may be paid (*dj.tw* is intended future after the infinitive of *rdj* and has the passive element *.tw*) *to the house of Wah like what I have informed you about* (a relative form, literally *like the (things) that I have made your heart safe about it*), *for you are (somebody) who does* (verbal adjective) *everything good. So, may you furnish your goodness.*

The problem:

Look, the overseer of the temple Teti told me: 'Look, I have informed him about it', he said.

One shall do accordingly so that the ka-soul of the ruler exists under your praise (literally for the existing of the ka-soul of the ruler under your praise)

Greetings and subservience:

It is a message about it.

It is a message to my lord l. p. h.

It is good to listen to my lord l. p. h. or *It is good that my lord l. p. h. listens* (literally *Good is the listening of my lord.* This is an adjectival sentence in which the infinitive *sḏm listening* functions as the subject. *Lord* in the phrase *listening of my lord* can either be a direct object to *listening* (listening to my lord) or the agent of *listening* (my lord listens).)

TEST YOURSELF

1 The group *ꜥnḫ wḏꜣ snb* (*ꜥ.w.s*) means *life, prosperity, health (l. p. h.)* and expresses the wishes of the writer to his superior.

2 **b**

3 **a** *his wife whom he loves*; **b** *I have made everything you like.*

4 **a**; **b**

Unit 16

VOCABULARY BUILDER

1 résee, zénee, néhesee, khédee, héree, káaee, ménmenet, wépoo her, éeooee, sóonet, éeken, wépootee, raa poo, soot, se-wáaee, heh

2 **a** *rsj*; **b** *nḥ*; **c** *jw*

3 **a** *s:rwd* to establish; **b** *tꜣš* border

THE SMALL SEMNA STELA OF YEAR 8

1 It might have been erected in the western part of the fort.

2 The figures of captives look like the classifier of the word *nḥsj Nubian* used in the inscription and reinforce the Egyptian claim of control over the local population.

3 To trade at the fort of Mirgissa and to bring news to Egypt.

LANGUAGE DISCOVERY

1 **a** *jry* made; **b** *jrj.t=tw nb.t everything that one does*; **c** *jwj.tj=fj who will come*

2 **a** *tm* not, *nn* without; **b** *in order not to cause* (or: *permit*) *that any Nubian will pass it and without, however, causing* (or: *permitting*) *that a boat of the Nubians will pass*

3 **a** *sḏm=f* he listens, *sḏm.tj=fj* who will listen; **b** *jrj=f* he makes, *jrj.tj=fj* who will make; **c** *jwj=sn* they come, *jwj.tj=sn* who will come; **d** *s:rwd=f* he establishes, *s:rwd.tj=fj* who will establish

4 *j ꜥnḫ.w tpj.w-tꜣ s:wꜣj.tj=sn ḥr ꜥbꜣ pn O!, those who live on earth and who will pass by this stela, …*

5 **a** *You do not listen to it.* **b** *You are not a man.* **c** *Djedi was not brought to me.*

6 *He was not born to you.*

7 **a** *Your mother is not with you.* **b** *Look, you are (as) a town, not existent is his mayor.* → *Look, you are a town that has no mayor.* **c** *I will not cause that you take him.* → *I will not let you take him.*
d *He seized me without touching me.*

8 **a** *zꜣ.t sḏm.tj=sj a daughter who will listen, zꜣ.t tm.tj=sj sḏm.w a daughter who will not listen*; **b** *r jnj.t jnw in order to bring luxurious goods, r tm jnj.w jnw in order not to bring luxurious goods*; **c** *rꜣ n mwt ky zp spell for dying another time, rꜣ n tm mwt.w ky zp spell for not dying another time*

9 **a** *zꜣ tm.tj=fj s:rwd.w tꜣš pn a son who will not strengthen this border*; **b** *rꜣ n tm ḏꜣj.w r jꜣb.t spell of not travelling to the East*; **c** *jnk njswt tm sfn.w n nḥsj I am a king who is not mild with a Nubian.*

EXPLORE

géret, ee, toot, nédjtee, wétetj, fekh, áahaa, éesetj géret, en méroot, rood, tjen

jr grt zꜣ=j nb s:rwd.tj=fj tꜣš pn jrj.n ḥm=j

zꜣ=j pw msj.tw=f n ḥm=j

twt zꜣ nḏtj jt=f

s:rwd tꜣš n wtṯ sw

jr grt fḫ.tj=fj sw tm.tj=fj ꜥḥꜣ.w ḥr=f

n zꜣ=j js n msj.tw=f js n=j

jsṯ grt rdj.n ḥm=j jrj.tw twt n ḥm=j

ḥr tꜣš pn jrj.n ḥm=j

n mrw.t rwd=ṯn ḥr=f n mrw.t ꜥḥꜣ=ṯn ḥr=f

However, as for any (of) my son(s) who shall keep this border save which My Majesty has made (relative form):

He is my son, he is born to My Majesty.

Suitable is a son [perhaps more fluently: *An ideal son is] who protects his father and who will keep the border of the one who begat him* [verbal adjective] *safe* [adjectival sentence].

However, as for one who shall give it up and who will not fight for it [2 x future verbal adjective]*:*

Not my son (for *He is not my son*)*! He was not born to me!*

Now, however, My Majesty had a statue of My Majesty made (literally *caused that a statue of My Majesty was made*) *on this border, which My Majesty has made* [relative form], *in order that you shall be firm on it and in order that you shall fight for it.*

DRAWING HIEROGLYPHS

2 

TEST YOURSELF

1 a

2 a *he did not cause that they pass;* **b** *without causing that they pass it;* **c** *to not cause that they pass it*

Egyptian–English word list

The words are arranged in the order of the alphabet shown at the bottom of the pages in this section. The feminine ending *.t* is ignored for this purpose because the list follows the bases of the words. This means, for example, that *ꜣ.t moment* precedes *ꜣw length* because the base of the feminine word *ꜣ.t* is *ꜣ*, which goes before the base *ꜣw* in the alphabet. Words derived from the same base are listed under one entry, for example *sn.t sister* is a sub-entry to *sn brother.*

ꜣ

ꜣ.t moment; m tꜣ ꜣ.t immediately

ꜣw length; ꜣw.t-jb joy

ꜣbḏw Abydos

ꜣpd fowl

ꜣḫ efficient

ꜣḫ.t horizon; also written and

ꜣḫ.t inundation (a season)

ꜣs.t Isis (name of a goddess, wife of Osiris and mother of Horus)

j

j O!, …

=j I , me, my; also written , , , , or not written in hieroglyphs

jꜣw praise; also written and and and

jꜣb.t east; jꜣbt.t east

jꜣš to shout (*n to*)

jyj to come (*m from*); also written and

Jyj-jb Iyiib (name of a male individual)

jw island

jw while (particle, often not translated)

jwj to come (same meaning as *jyj*)

jwy.t bad

Jwnw Heliopolis (location of the most important temple of the sun god)

jꜥj to wash

jb heart (the basic meaning is perhaps *guts*)

jb to think

Jp.t-s.wt Luxor

jm= in; form of the preposition *m* before an attached pronoun; *jm there; jmj-wrt west bank; jmj.t-pr transfer of deed; jmj-zꜣ n qnb.tj w.w guard of the district counsellor; jmj-rꜣ overseer*

jmj give!, cause that …!, let …!

jmꜣḫy the revered

Jmn Amun; Jmn-ḥtp Amenhotep (royal name)

jn by; also written

jn-jw Do?, Did? (changes a statement into a question)

jnj to bring, to fetch; jn.w goods, luxurious products

jnn we

jnr stone

jnḥ eyebrow

jnk I

jr As for …,

jr.t eye

jrj to do; to spend (time)

js.t place (old spelling for *s.t*)

jsw indeed

jsf.t injustice; also written

jst grt Now, however, (used at the beginning of a sentence)

jšst who?, what?

Jqn Mirgissa (name of a site located near the Second Cataract)

jt father; also written and and and

jtn sun disc

jṯj to seize

jdb riverbank

w

wꜣj to be distant

wꜣj.t road, passage

wꜣw wave

wꜣḥ to put

wꜣḥ to endure; Wꜣḥ Wah (name of a male individual)

wꜣs dominion; Wꜣs.t Thebes (abbreviated)

wꜣḏ fresh, green; Wꜣḏ.t Wajdet (cobra goddess representing Lower Egypt); *wꜣḏ-wr sea* (literally *the Great Green*)

wꜣḏw.t depth

wj I, me, also written and and

wʿj to be alone

wʿb pure; also written

wbn to rise

wpj to open

wpw.tj deputy, messenger; also written

wpw-ḥr except

wn to exist; duplicating stem used for some verb forms *wnn; Wnn-nfr Wenennefer* (literally *Who-exists-perfectly*, epithet of Osiris)

wnḏw.t offering bread

wr great; chief; also written

wḥm to repeat

Wsjr Osiris; also written (divine equivalent of deceased king)

wsr strong; see also *Zj-n-Wsr.t*

wsḫw broad; wsḫw breadth; wsḫ.t hall

wtṯ to beget

wḏ to decree; stela (inscribed with a decree); also written

wḏꜣ to travel; also written

wḏꜣ to be safe

ʿ

ʿ arm

ʿꜣ great; also written

ʿꜣ ass

ʿbꜣ stela

ʿpr to furnish

ʿn to be beautiful (i.e. beautiful to look at)

ʿnw Tura (name of a limestone quarry near Cairo)

ʿnḫ to live; life; *ʿnḫ wḏꜣ snb life, prosperity, health*, abbreviated *ʿ.w.s. l.p.h.*; *ʿnḫ n njw.t officer of the town regiment*

ʿḥꜣ to fight

ʿḥʿ.n Then (particle with narrative meaning used at the beginning of a main clause)

ʿḏ to be fine

b

 *b3k servant; b3k jm humble servant* (literally *servant there*)

 *bw thing; place*;  *bw nfr goodness*

p

 *p.t sky*; abbreviated writing

 *p3 the*;  *p3y=* used to express possession, see unit 15

 *p3.t offering bread*

 *pw this*; in nominal sentence *he, she, it* (*is, was*)

Ptḥ Ptah (main deity in Memphis)

pn this

 *pr house*;  *pr-ḏ.t funerary domain* (property originally reserved for funding the offering cult of a deceased individual);  *pr-wr per-wer* ('great-house', the shrine of the statue)

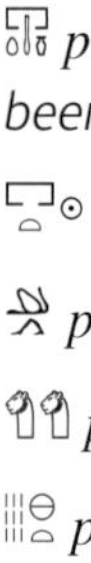 *pr.t-ḫrw t3 ḥnq.t a voice offering, bread and beer* (typical part of the offering formula)

pr.t growing (winter, a season)

pḥ to reach, to come to

pḥtj strength

psḏ.t the ennead (subsidiary gods surrounding the main deity of a temple)

f

 =f he; him; his; when following a noun in the dual, the form changes to  *=fj*

 *f3j to carry*

 *fḫ to leave* (*r for*)*; to loosen, to give up*

m

 *m in, at, out of, from, as; while*;  *m-ʿ from*;  *m-b3ḥ in front of*, also written ;  *m-ẖnw in, within*, also written  and  *m-ḫt after; behind*

 *m who?, what?*

 *m m3w.t as something new*; also written [illegible]

 *m3 to see*; duplicating stem in some forms *m33*

 *m3ʿ true; just person*; also written [illegible]; regularly used in [illegible] *m3ʿ-ḫrw justified*, also written  *M3ʿ.t Ma'at* (goddess of justice), *order*; also written [illegible] and [illegible] and

 mj like; [illegible] *r mjt.t jry in the same way*

 *mw water*

mw.t mother

mnw monument

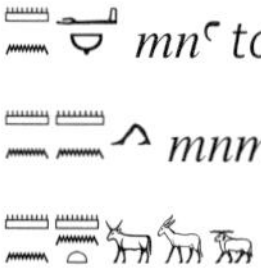 *mnʿ to nurse*

mnmn to shake

mnmn.t flock

 *mnnw fortress*

mnḫ.t linen

mnṯ.w Mentu (Bedouin group living in the Sinai)

 *Mn-ḫpr-Rʿ Stp-n-Rʿ Enduring-is-the-manifestation-of-Ra Whom-Ra-has-chosen* (name of king Thutmosis III)

 *mr canal*

see under *jmj-r3 overseer*

 *mrj to love*; [illegible] *mry beloved of*, also written [illegible]; *mrw.t love*; [illegible] *n mrw.t in order that*, also written [illegible]

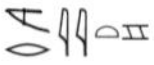 *mry.t shore*

 *mḥ to fill*

msj to give birth; *msy n born to*

msʿ crew, troop

 *m=k Look, …, Behold, …* (at the beginning of a main clause); feminine form [illegible] *m=ṯ*, plural form [illegible] *m=ṯn*

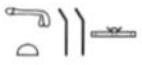 *mtj to witness, to give witness for*

 *mtj-n-zꜣ.w overseer of the phyles*

mdw jꜣw staff of old age

mḏr to resist

n

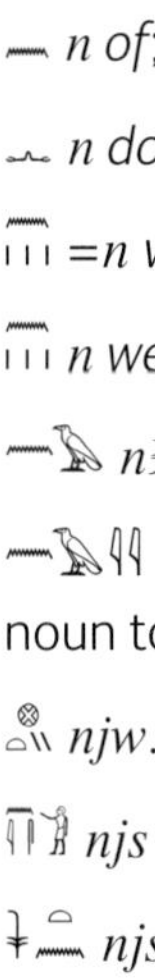 *n of*; feminine form  *n.t*, plural form  *n.w*

n do not, did not, not

=n we, us, our (attached pronoun)

n we, us (weak pronoun)

nꜣ the (used in the popular language)

nꜣy= used with attached pronoun before a noun to express possession

njw.tj local; also written 

njs prayer

njswt king; also written ; in titles and formulas usually written in an abbreviated form as ; NB: Outside titles and formulas the hieroglyph  does not mean *njswt king*, but is the sound sign *sw*; *njswt-bjt king of Upper and Lower Egypt* (a royal title);  *njswy.t kingship*, also written  and

 *nwy water*

nb every

nb lord; also written with a classifier ;  *nb.tj Two Ladies* (a royal title)

nbw gold

nfr good, perfect; perfectly

nfrw beauty, perfection

nm who?

nn this

nn not; not existent; without (before an infinitive)

Nnj Neni (name of a male individual)

nh.t shelter

 *nḥy request*

nḥm to protect

nḥḥ eternity

nḥsj Nubian

nḫt strong; also written 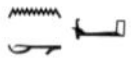 and  and 

ns.t throne

nsr.t uraeus (the cobra placed in front of kings, queens and deities)

nšnn raging

ntj which; feminine form  *ntt*, plural form *ntjw*;  *r nt.t (to the effect) that* (introduces the content of a message)

ntf he

nts she; also written 

ntsn they; also written 

ntk you (masculine singular)

ntṯ you (feminine singular); also written 

ntṯn you (plural); also written 

nṯr god;  *nṯrj divine*

nḏtj to protect

r

 *r to, towards; in order to; more than*

rꜣ mouth; spell; language;  *rꜣ-pw or* (follows the two terms it is connecting);  *rꜣ-pr temple*

rwd to grow; to be strong; to be firm; also written  and 

rwd.t strength

Rꜥ Ra (the sun god); also written  and 

rꜥ nb every day

rmṯ people

rn name; also written 

rnpj to rejuvenate; *rnp.t year*; *rnp.t-zp regnal year*

rḫ to learn; when used in the stative *rḫ* means *to know*

rdj to give; to cause that; after negations also *to not permit that*

rsj southern

rqj enemy

Rṯnw Syria; also written

h

h3j to come down, to go down; also written

h3w matters, belongings

h3w nearness; *m h3w near* (literally *in the nearness of*)

hp law

ḥ

ḥ3.t front; *ẖr ḥ3.t previously* (literally *under the forefront*)

ḥ3tj heart (exact difference between *jb* and *ḥ3tj* not clear)

ḥjḥj to search for

ḥw.t enclosure; *ḥw.t-k3 ka-chapel*; *Ḥw.t-M3ʿ.t Hut-Ma'at* (name of place whose exact location is not known)

ḥwj to smite

ḥʿw body

ḥʿpj inundation

ḥb festival

ḥf3w snake

ḥm Majesty

ḥm husband; *ḥm.t wife*

ḥr face

ḥr on; about; because of; while (before an infinitive); before attached pronouns usually written *ḥr=*; *ḥr nt.t for, because* (introduces a reason); *ḥrj upper*; also written ; *ḥrj.t-jb sanctuary*

ḥrj to travel on land

Ḥrw Horus (falcon god; divine equivalent of reigning king; a royal title); *Ḥrw-nbw Golden Horus* (a royal title)

Ḥḥ Semna (name of a site south of the Second Cataract)

ḥzj to travel

ḥzj to praise; *ḥzy the praised ones*; *ḥzw.t praise*

ḥtp to go down (said of the sun); *to be happy; offering; peace*; *m ḥtp safe*; *ḥtpt offering*

ḥḏ bright

ḥq3 ruler; also written ; *ḥq3-ḫ3s.t* Hyksos

ḥknw praise

ḫ

ḫ.t thing

ḫ.t wood

ḫ3s.t foreign land

ḫʿj to appear

ḫʿ.w crowns

ḫpr to happen, to grow up; *ḫprw manifestation*; *ḫpr.t occurrence, event*

ḫpš strength

ḫft according; *ḫft ntt because*; *ḫft jrj accordingly*

ḫm to not know, to ignore

ḫnt front; *ḫntj foremost*; *Ḫntj-jmn.tjw Khentamentiu* (epithet of Osiris, literally *Foremost-of-Westerners*; the Westerners are the dead)

 *ḫntj to sail upstream (= to sail south)*

 *ḫr to* (e.g. come *to* somebody); *under* (in dates)

 *ḫrw foe*

 *ḫrw voice*;  *ḫrw fj …, he said*

 *ḫrp to guide*

 *ḫsbd lapis lazuli*

 *ḫtj to inscribe*

 *ḫdj to sail downstream (= to sail north)*

ẖ

 *ẖ.t belly*

 *ẖnw royal residence*; see also under *m* for *m-ẖnw in, within*

 *H̱nmw Khnumu* (ram-headed god; also a personal name)

 *H̱rty Kherty* (an earth god; also a personal name)

 *ẖrd.w children*

 *ẖzj wretched*

 *ẖr under* (usually in the sense of *loaded under*)

z

 *z3 son*; in affiliations also written ;  *Z3-H̱rty Za-Kherty* (*Son-of-Kherty*, name of male individual);  *z3.t daughter*;  *Z3.t-Ḥw.t-rw Zat-Hathor* (*Daughter-of-Hathor*, name of female individual);  *Z3.t-H̱nmw Zat-Khnum* (*Daughter-of-Khnum*, name of female individual);  *Z3.t-H̱rty Zat-Kherty* (*Daughter-of-Kherty*, name of female individual)

 *zj man*;  *Zj-n-Wsr.t Senwosret* (*Man-of-the-strong-one*, name of male individual)

 *zm3 to unite* (*m with*)

 *znj to pass; ḥr by*

 *zẖr to cover*

 *zš to write, to inscribe*

 *Zkr Sokar* (name of a male deity)

s

, *=s she, it; her; its*

 *s.t throne, place*

 *s3 back*

 *sj she, it; her*; also written

 *sw he, it; him*

 *s:w3j to pass; ḥr by*

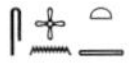 *swn.t trade*; *jrj swn.t to trade*

 *s:wsḫ to make broad, to extend*

[illegible] *swt however*; often not translated

[illegible] *s:wḏ3 jb to inform; message*; *r* or *ḥr about*

[illegible] *s:ʿnḫ to keep alive, to make live*

[illegible] *s:ʿḥʿ to erect*

[illegible] *Sbk Sobek*

[illegible] *sp3.t district*

[illegible] *spr to get* (*r to*), *to approach*

[illegible] *Spdw Soped* (a deity)

[illegible] *sfn to be mild* (*n with*)

[illegible] *=sn they; them; their*; also written [illegible] and [illegible] and [illegible]

[illegible] *sn brother*; [illegible] *sn.t sister*

[illegible] *sn-t3 to pray*; literally *to kiss the ground*

[illegible] *sqr to strike down*

[illegible] *sm3 to kill*

[illegible] *s:m3ʿ to put in order*

[illegible] *sm3r to eat*

[illegible] *s:mn to make enduring, to establish*; also written [illegible]

[illegible] *s:mnḫ to embellish*

snb health; healthy; to be healthy

snmḥ prayer

snṯr incense; also written

snḏw fearful

s:nḏm to dwell

s:rwd to establish, to make firm; also written

s:ḥtpj to satisfy; *S:ḥtp-jb-Rʿ* Sehetepibra (Who-makes-the-heart-of-Ra-happy, name of Amenemhet I)

s:ḥḏ to make bright, to illuminate

s:ḫpr to make exist, to bring to life

s:ḫr to make somebody fall, to smite

s:ẖkr to adorn

Sṯtjw 'Asiatics' (Bedouin from the Levant)

s:qb to make cool

sqd to travel

s:grḥ to pacify

st she, it; her; its

stj perfume; also written and

Stẖ Seth

st.t ray; also written

stꜣ to drag

sḏm to hear, to listen to; also written ; *sḏm-ʿš* servant

š

šꜣ field

šps noble; also written

šmw harvest (summer, a season)

šzp to receive

šs alabaster

šsꜣ skills

q

qn.t valour

qnj embrace

qrj thunder

qrs.t to bury; burial

qd to build

qd character

Qdm Qedem (name of a place, located perhaps in Syria)

g

gmj to find

gmgm to tremble

gr also

grg falsehood

grt moreover

grg falsehood; also written

gs side; half; *gs.wj shore*

k

=k you; your (masculine singular)

kꜣ ka-soul

kꜣ bull; also written

kꜣ So, … (introduces a new thought)

kꜣj boat

Kꜣš Kush (Upper Nubia); also written *Kš*

Kpnj Byblos (a town in modern Lebanon)

kfj to hide

Km.t Egypt

Kš Kush; see under *Kꜣš*

t

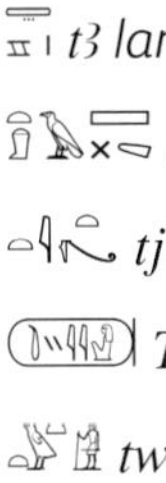

tꜣ land

tꜣš border; also written 

tj.t image

Ty Tiy (name of wife of Amenhotep III)

twt statue; suitable, fitting; also written  and 

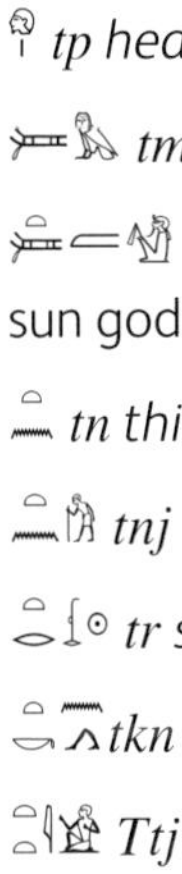

tp head;  *tp on;*  *tp-m before*

tm not

Tm Atum (name of the primeval sun god)

tn this; see also under *ṯn*

tnj to grow old

tr season; time

tkn to approach

Ttj Teti (name of a male individual)

ṯ

=ṯ you; your (feminine singular); also written

tꜣ the;  *tꜣy=* used with attached pronouns before feminine nouns to express possession

ṯw you (masculine singular); also written 

ṯn you (feminine singular); also written 

=ṯn you; your (plural); also written  and  and 

d

 *dꜣr to smite*

 dj to give; to cause that; also written ; after negations also *to not permit that; dj jb ḥnt to pay attention to;*  *dj ʿnḫ mj Rʿ ḏ.t given life like Ra forever*

 *dwꜣ to praise; praise*

 *dp.t ship*

 *dmj to touch*

 *dr to repel*

 *dhn to appoint*

ḏ

 *ḏ.t eternity*

 *ḏꜣj to travel*

 *ḏw mountain*

 *ḏw evil;*  *ḏw.t the evil*

 *ḏʿ storm*

 *ḏfꜣ food*

 *ḏfꜣ to clean*

 *ḏsr sacred*

 *Ḏdw Busiris* (a cult place for Osiris located in the Delta)

 *ḏd to speak;*  *ḏd mdw speaking words;*  *ḏd.w n=f called* (literally *to whom is (also) said*)

Sign list explanations

The following list includes the signs used in this course. The codes A1, G4, etc. refer to the standard list of hieroglyphs compiled by Alan Gardiner in his *Egyptian Grammar* (third edition 1955). The explanation includes a description of each sign and its uses, as: picture sign in transliteration and translation, sound sign and CLASSIFIER. Have a look at this example:

O 1 plan of building; *pr house; pr*; BUILDING, LOCATION

The sign has the code O 1; it depicts the plan of a building; as a picture sign it is transliterated *pr* and translated as *house*; it can also stand for the sounds *pr* in any other word; and it is used as a mute classifier to say that the preceding word is a building or location. Not all signs can be used in all the three ways: for example, A13 represents a captive and is used only as a classifier of words meaning CAPTIVE. In some cases, additional explanations of how a sign is used in specific words or phrases are given.

A Men and their activities

A 1 seated man; *=j I*; MALE PERSON; *wj I, me*; *jnk I*; PEOPLE

A 2 man with hand to mouth; ACTIVITY WITH MOUTH; *j O!*, …

A 4 man praying; *jꜣw to praise*; WORSHIP, HIDDEN

A9 man carrying basket; *ꜣtp to load*; *fꜣj* to carry; *kꜣ.t work*; CARRYING

A 12 soldier; *mšꜥ crew*; *troop*; *soldier*; SOLDIER, ARMY

A 13 captive; ENEMY

A 14 man with blood streaming out of his head; DIE, ENEMY

A 15 man falling; *ḫr to fall*; FALL

A 17 seated child, hand to mouth; *ẖrd child*; *nnj*; YOUNG, CHILD; *snmḥ prayer*; *snḏm to dwell*

A 19 old man with stick; *jꜣw old*; *smsw old*; *wr old, oldest*; OLD, LEANING

A 22 statue; STATUE

A 24 man striking with stick; *nḫt strong*; FORCE, EFFORT

A 26 man beckoning; CALL; *j Oh*

A 30 man praying; *jꜣw to praise*; *dwꜣ to praise*; PRAYING

A 35 man building a wall; *qd to build*; BUILDING

A 40 seated god; *=j I*; GOD

A 41 seated king; *=j I*; KING

A 51 noble man with flagellum; *šps noble*; *to be noble*; *=j I*; NOBLE

A 52 seated noble with flail; NOBLE

A 53 mummy; MUMMY, STATUE, FORM, LIKENESS

B Women and their activities

B 1 seated woman; *=j I*; det FEMALE PERSON; PEOPLE

B 4 woman giving birth; *msj to give birth*; BIRTH

C Anthropomorphic deities

C 10 goddess with feather; *Mꜣʿ.t Ma'at* (goddess of justice); GODDESS MA'AT

C 11 god with elevated arms and year symbol on head; *ḥḥ million*; GOD HEH

D Parts of the human body

D1 head; *tp head*; *ḏꜣḏꜣ head*; *tp*; HEAD, BEHIND, FORWARD

D 2 face; *ḥr face*; *ḥr*

D 4 eye; *jrj.t eye*; *jr*; SEE (see also U3)

D 6 eye with paint; EYE

D 8 eye enclosed; *ʿn*

D13 part of eye painting; EYEBROW

D 17 part or eye painting; *tjt image*; IMAGE

D 19	𓂉	nose and eye; *fnḏ nose*; *ḫnt*; SMELL, FACE, KISS, FRIENDLY
D 21	𓂋	mouth; *r3 mouth, spell*; *r*
D 27	𓂑	breast; *mnḏ breast*; BREAST, FEEDING
D 28	𓂓	arms; *k3 ka-soul*; *k3*
D 32	𓂘	two arms embracing; EMBRACING
D 34	𓂚	arms holding mace and buckler; *ʿḥ3 to fight*
D 35	𓂜	arms in gesture of negation; *n*; NEGATION; 𓂜𓈖 *nn* (unit 16)
D 36	𓂝	forearm; *ʿ arm*; *ʿ*; ACTIVITY (see also G20)
D 37	𓂞	arm with triangular loaf; *dj to give, to cause*; *jmj give!, cause!*; *dj*
D 40	𓂡	arm with stick; *nḫt strong*; FORCE, EFFORT
D 45	𓂦	arm with *nḥbt*; *ḏsr sacred*; SACRED
D 46	𓂧	hand; *ḏr.t hand*; *d*
D 50	𓂭	finger; *ḏbʿ finger*; *ḏbʿ ten thousand*
D 52	𓂸	phallus; *mt*; MALE
D 53	𓂺	phallus with liquid pouring out; *b3ḥ* in 𓅓𓅡𓄿 *m-b3ḥ before, in the presence of*; PHALLUS, MALE
D 54	𓂻	walking legs; *jwj to come*; *nmt.t step*; GOING
D 58	𓃀	foot; *bw place*; *b*
D 60	𓃂	leg + water pouring out of pot; *wʿb pure, to be pure*

E Mammals

E 1	𓃒	ox; *k3 ox*; OX
E 7	𓃘	ass; ASS
E 8	𓃙	calf; *jb calf*; *jb*; CALF

E 9	newborn bubalis; *jw*
E 10	bearded ram; *Ḫnmw Khnumu* (a god); *b3 ram*; RAM
E 20	Seth animal; *Stẖ Seth* (a god); CHAOS
E 21	Seth animal; *Stẖ Seth* (a god); CHAOS
E 23	lion; *m3j lion*; *rw*
E 29	gazelle; GAZELLE; *šs3 skills*
E 34	hare; *wn*

F Parts of mammals

F 1	head of ox; *k3 ox*
F 3	head of hippopotamus; *3t* in *3.t occasion*
F 4	forepart of lion; *ḥ3t front*; *ḥ3t*; *ḥ3tj-ʿ prince, governor*
F 9	head of leopard; *pḥtj strength*
F 12	jackal head on standard; *wsr*
F 13	horns of ox; *wp*
F 20	tongue; *ns tongue*; *jmj-r3 overseer*; *ns*; TONGUE
F 21	ear of ox; *sḏm to hear*; *jdnw proxy*; *msḏr* ear; LISTEN
F 22	hindquarters of lion; *pḥ*
F 23	foreleg of ox; *ḫpš strength*; FORELEG
F 25	leg of ox; *wḥm.t hoof*; *wḥm*
F 26	skin of goat; *ẖn.t animal skin*; *ẖn*
F 27	cow's skin; *st*; MAMMAL
F 29	cow's skin pierced by arrow; *stj to shoot*; *st*

F 31	three hides; *ms*
F 32	animal's belly with udder; *ẖ.t belly*; *ẖ*
F 34	heart; *jb heart*; HEART
F 35	heart and windpipe; *nfr*
F 36	lung and windpipe; *zmꜣ windpipe*; *zmꜣ*
F 39	backbone with one end; *jmꜣḫ* in *jmꜣḫw/jmꜣḫy revered*; BACK
F 40	backbone with two ends of spine; *ꜣw*
F 42	rib; *spr*
F 51	piece of flesh; FLESH, SELF

G Birds

G 1	vulture; *ꜣ* (can replace G 4)
G 4	buzzard; *tjw* (can replace G 1)
G 5	falcon; *Ḥrw Horus*; for see G8; for see R 13
G 7	falcon on standard; *=j I*; GOD, KING
G 8	falcon on collar; *Ḥrw-nbw Golden Horus* (royal title)
G 14	vulture; *mwt*; *mt*; *nr*
G 16	vulture and cobra on baskets; *nb.tj Two Ladies* (royal title)
G 17	owl; *m*; also *m*; *m=k Look, …*; *jmj-rꜣ overseer*
G 20	owl + forearm; *m*
G 21	guinea fowl; *nḥ*
G 25	crested ibis; *ꜣḫ akh-soul*; *ꜣḫ*
G 28	black ibis; *gm*

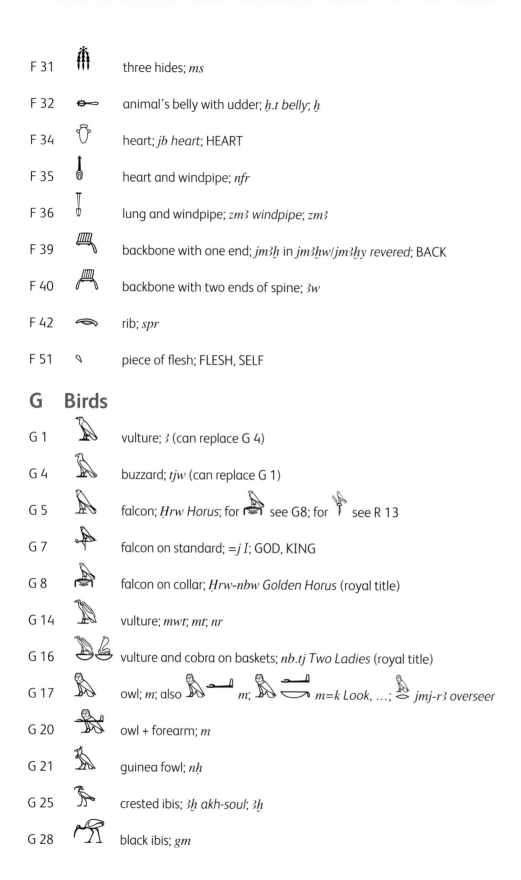

G 29 jabiru; *bꜣ ba-soul*; *bꜣ*

G 36 swallow; *wr*

G 37 sparrow; *nḏs small*; BAD, SMALL

G 38 goose; *gb goose*; *gb*; *zꜣ*; BIRD

G 40 pintail duck flying; *pꜣ* (used interchangeably with G 41)

G 41 pintail duck landing; *ṯn*; *ḫn* (can replace G 40; often used with T14 as classifier)

G 42 fattened bird; FOOD; *ḏfꜣ to clean* (mixed up with *ḏfꜣ food*)

G 43 quail; *w*

G 54 plucked goose; *snḏ*

H Parts of birds

H 1 head of pintail duck; *ꜣpd bird, fowl*; BIRD

H 2 head of crested bird; *mꜣꜥ*, *pꜣq*, *wšm*

H 6 feather; *mꜣꜥ.t justice, order*; *šw*

H 8 egg; *zꜣ son, daughter*; in *ꜣs.t Isis*

I Reptiles

I 3 crocodile; *msḥ crocodile*; *Sbk Sobek*; *jtj ruler*

I 6 skin of crocodile; *km*

I 8 tadpole; *ḥfn one hundred thousand*

I 9 horned viper; *f*

I 10 cobra; *ḏ.t cobra*; *ḏ*

I 12 erect cobra; COBRA, FEMALE DEITY

I 14 snake; SNAKE

K Fish and parts of fish

K1 bulti fish; *jn*

L Invertebrates and lesser animals

L 1 scarab; *ḫprr scarab*; *ḫpr*

L 2 bee; *bjt*; *njswt-bjt king of Upper and Lower Egypt* (royal title)

M Plants

M 3 branch of a tree; *ḫ.t wood*; *ḫt*; WOOD

M 4 palm rib; *rnp.t year*; *rnp*; *rnp.t-zp regnal year* (in dates)

M 5 palm rib + *t*; *tr time, season*; *tr*

M 6 palm rib + *r*; *tr time, season*; *tr*

M 8 pond with lotus flowers; *šꜣ pond*; *šꜣ*; *ꜣḫ.t inundation* (name of a season)

M 12 lotus flower; *ḫꜣ thousand*; *ḫꜣ*

M 13 papyrus stem; *wꜣḏ papyrus*; *wꜣḏ*; *wḏ*; *wꜣḏ*

M 17 reed; *j*; *y*

M 18 reed with walking legs; *jyj to come*

M 20 field with reed; *sḫt field*; *sm*; FIELD

M 22 rush; *nḫb*; often in *nn*

M 23 rush; *sw*; abbreviation for *njswt king* only in compound terms

M 24 rush with *r*; *rsj south*; *rs*

M 29 pod; *nḏm convenient, sweet*; *nḏm*

M 32 rhizome; *rd*

M 36 bundle of flax; *ḏr*

M 40		bundle of reeds; *jz*
M 42		blossom; *wn*; *qq*; *jmj*
M 44		spine; *spd pointed*; *Spd Soped* (a god); *spd*

N Sky, earth, water

N 1		sky; *p.t heaven, sky*; *ḥr*; SKY, UPPER
N 5		sun disc; *Rꜥ Ra*; SUN, DAY, TIME;  *zꜣ-Rꜥ son of Ra* (royal title)
N 8		sun with rays; *wbn to rise*; *ḥnmm.t human beings*; SUNLIGHT
N 10		moon; *psḏntjw new moon*; *psḏ.t ennead*; *psḏ*
N 11		crescent moon; *jꜥḥ moon*; *ꜣbd month* (in dates)
N 14		star; *sbꜣ star*; *dwꜣ to praise*; *wnw.t hour, hourly*; *wnw.t priesthood*; *sbꜣ*; *dwꜣ*; STAR
N 16		land with three grains of sand; *tꜣ land*
N 17		strip of land; *tꜣ land*; ENDLESS LAND;  *ḏ.t eternity*
N 18		land; *jw island*
N 21		short piece of land; *jdb riverbank*; LAND
N 23		canal; LAND
N 24	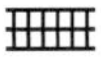	land with canals; *spꜣ.t district*; DISTRICT
N 25		hills; *ḫꜣs.t foreign country*; *ḫꜣs*; DESERT, FOREIGN COUNTRY
N 26		valley between eastern and western mountain; *ḏw mountain*; *ḏw*
N 27		sun between eastern and western mountain; *ꜣḫ.t horizon*
N 28		sun rays over hill; *ḫꜥ*
N 29		slope of mountain; *q*

N 31	path with shrubs; *wꜣj.t road*; *ḥr on*; *wꜣj*; ROAD, POSITION
N 33	grain of sand; SAND; PLURAL
N 35	waterline; *n*; LIQUID; *mw water*; *m-ḫnw inside*
N 36	canal; *mr canal*; *mr*; CANAL, RIVER (can replace N 37)
N 37	pond; *š pond*; *š* (can replace N 36)
N 41	well filled with water; *ḥm*; LAKE, CANAL

O Buildings and parts of buildings

O 1	plan of building; *pr house*; *pr*; BUILDING, LOCATION
O 3	plan of building + loaf + vessel; *pr.t-ḫrw tꜣ ḥnq.t voice offering bread and beer*
O 4	plan of house; *h*
O 6	plan of enclosure; *ḥwt*
O 10	enclosure + falcon; *Ḥw.t-Ḥrw Hathor*
O 15	enclosure with signs for *wsḫ.t* inscribed; *wsḫ.t broad hall*
O 26	stela; STELA
O 27	columned hall; HALL
O 29	column; *ꜥꜣ column*; *ꜥꜣ*; also used in vertical position
O 34	door bolt; *s door bolt*; *z*; *s*
O 35	door bolt + walking legs; *zj to go away*; *zbj to send away*; *zj*
O 36	plan of a wall with bastions; *jnb wall*; see also A35
O 38	corner; *qnb.t council*; CORNER
O 39	slab; *jnr stone*; STONE

O 42 fence; *šzp*; *sšp*

O 49 village with crossroads; *njw.t town*; TOWN, PLACE

O 50 threshing floor; *zp*; *rnp.t-zp regnal year* (in dates)

P Ships

P 1 boat on water; *dp.t boat*; SHIP

P 5 sail; *ṯꜣw sail*; SAILING, WIND

P 6 mast; *ꜥḥꜥ*

P 8 oar; *ḫrw*; OAR; *mꜣꜥ-ḫrw justified*

Q Furniture

Q 1 seat; *s.t seat, throne*; *st*; *ḥtm*; *Wsjr Osiris*

Q 2 portable seat; *Wsjr Osiris*

Q 3 stool; *p*

Q 6 coffin; *qrs coffin, burial*; BURIAL

R Temple furniture and sacred emblems

R 4 loaf on mat; *ḥtp to offer*; *ḥtp*

R 5 censer; *kꜣp* fumigate; *kp*, *kꜣp*; FUMIGATE; *Kpnj Byblos*

R 7 bowl with smoke; *snṯr incense*; INCENSE

R 8 cloth wound on pole; *nṯr god*; *nṯr*; GOD

R 11 pillar; *ḏd djed-pillar*; *ḏd*; *Ḏdw Busiris*

R 13 falcon on western standard; *jmn.t west*

R 14 western standard; *jmn.t west, right*

R 15 eastern standard; *jꜣbt.t east, left*

R 19 was-sceptre with feather; *Wꜣs.t Thebes*

S Crowns

S 3 red crown; *n*; *dšr.t Red Crown*

S 12 collar with beads; *nbw gold*; *Ḥrw-nbw Golden Horus* (royal title)

S 22 shoulder knot; *sṯ*

S 27 piece of tissue; *mnḫ.t linen*

S 28 cloth with fringe and folded cloth; CLOTH, COVERING

S 29 folded cloth; *s*, *z*; *ʿnḫ wḏꜣ snb* (*ʿ.w.s.*) *life, prosperity, health (l.p.h.)*

S 34 sandal strap; *ʿnḫ*; *ʿnḫ sandal strap*

S 38 crook; *ḥqꜣ*; *ḥqꜣ heqa-sceptre*

S 40 was-sceptre; *wꜣs was-sceptre*; *Wꜣs.t Thebes*; *wꜣs*; *ḏʿm*

S 42 aba-sceptre; *sḫm to have power*; *ḫrp control*; *ʿbꜣ aba-sceptre*; *ʿbꜣ*; *sḫm*; CONTROL

S 43 staff; *mdw medu-stick*; *mdw*; *ḏd-mdw speaking words*

T Warfare, hunting, butchery

T 3 mace; *ḥḏ mace*; *ḥḏ*; SMITING

T 8 dagger; *tp*

T 11 arrow; *sšr arrow*; *sẖr to cover*; *sjn*; *swn/sjn*; ARROW

T 12 bow string; *rwd hard, firm, strong*; *rwḏ*; *rd*; *ꜣr*

T 14 throw-stick; THROWING, FOREIGN PEOPLE

T 18 crook with package including a knife; *šms*

T 21 harpoon; *wꜥ one, single, alone*; *wꜥ*

T 22 arrowhead; *sn*

T 28 butcher's block; *ẖr* (different from W 11)

T 34 butcher's knife; *nm knife*; *nm*

U Agriculture

U 1 sickle; *mꜣ sickle*; *mꜣ*; SICKLE, BENT

U 3 sickle + human eye; *mꜣ to see*

U 4 sickle + socle; *mꜣꜥ true*

U 6 hoe; *mr*; CULTIVATE

U 15 sledge; *tm*

U 17 pick and basin; *grg to found*; *grg*

U 19 adze; *nw*

U 21 adze on a piece of wood; *stp*

U 22 chisel; *mnḫ*; CHISEL

U 23 chisel; *ꜣb*; *mr*

U 28 fire drill; *ḏꜣ*; abbreviation of *wḏꜣ health*, see S29

U 30 potter's kiln; *tꜣ kiln*; *tꜣ*

U 32 pestle and mortar; *smn*; ESTABLISH, POUND

U 33 pestle; *tj.t pestle*; *tj*; *t*

U 36 launderer's club; *ḥmww washer*; *ḥm*; *ḥm=f His Majesty*

V Ropes and baskets

V 1	rope; *št hundred*; *šn*; ROPE, ENCIRCLING (different from Z 7)
V 2	coil of robe and door bolt; *sṯꜣ*; PULLING
V 4	lasso; *wꜣ*
V 6	cord, ends pointing upwards; *šs rope*; *šs*; *šsr*; CORD; *šs mnḫ.t linen and alabaster*
V 10	cartouche; surrounds names of kings and queens; NAME
V 12	string; *fḫ to loosen*; *ʿrq*; BINDING, LOOSEN
V 13	rope with straps; *ṯ*
V 15	rope with straps + walking legs; *jṯj to seize*
V 16	looped cord; *zꜣ*
V 17	rolled up shelter of papyrus; *zꜣ protection*; *zꜣ*
V 20	hobble; *mḏw ten*
V 22	whip; *mḥ*
V 24	cord wound around stick; *wḏ*
V 26	spool with thread; *ʿḏ reel*; *ʿd*, *ʿḏ*; REEL
V 28	wick; *ḥ*
V 29	swab; *sk*; *wꜣḥ*; WARD OFF
V 30	basket; *nb.t basket*; *nb* (for translation with *lord* or *every, any*; see Unit 3)
V 31	basket with handle; *k*
V 39	tie; *tj.t Isis knot*; *Stḫ Seti* (royal name)

W Vessels

W 4 — bowl of alabaster + pavilion; *ḥb feast*

W 9 — vessel with handle; *ẖnm*

W 10 — beaker; *wsḫ.t breadth*; *wsḫ; sḫw*; *jꜥb*; *ḫnt*; BEAKER

W 11 — stand; *ns.t throne*; *g*; RED POT (different from T28)

W 14 — vessel; *ḥz hes-vessel*; *ḥz*

W 15 — water pot with water pouring from it; *qb cool*; *qbḥ libation, to libate*; COOL, LIBATION

W 17 — vessels in rack; *ḫnt*

W 19 — milk jug carried in a net; *mj*; MILK POT

W 24 — bowl; *nw*; *qd*; *m-ḫnw inside*; *jnk I*

W 25 — bowl + walking legs; *jnj to bring, to fetch*

X Bread and cake

X 1 — loaf; *tꜣ bread*; *t*; *jt father* in titles and formulae

X 6 — round loaf of bread; BREAD

X 8 — loaf; *dj to give, to cause*; *dj*

Y Writing, games, music

Y 1 — papyrus scroll; *mḏꜣ.t papyrus scroll;* ABSTRACT

Y 3 — writing equipment; *zš scribe*; *to write, to inscribe*

Y 5 — game board; *mn*

Z Strokes and hieratic signs

Z 1 — single stroke; often indicates use of previous sign as a picture sign; sometimes *=j I*

Z 2 — three strokes; *w*; PLURAL

Z 4	two strokes; *j*; DUAL
Z 5	stroke used in hieratic to replace complex or dangerous signs
Z 6	replacement stroke; *mwt death, to die*; DEATH
Z 7	hieroglyphic adaptation of the hieratic sign for the chicken quail; *w* (different from V1)
Z 9	cross; *swꜣ*; *sḏ*; *ḫbs*; *šbn*; *wp*; *wr*; BREAKING, SEPARATING, CROSSING, MOVING
Z11	two wooden planks; *jmj*; *wnm*

Aa Unclassified

Aa 1	placenta?; *ḫ*
Aa 2	*wḥꜣ*; BAD, DISGUSTING, SMELL
Aa 7	*sqr*
Aa 11	pedestal; *mꜣꜥ true*; *mꜣꜥ-ḫrw justified*
Aa 15	plinth; *m*; *jm*; *gs*
Aa 17	lid of a chest; *sꜣ*
Aa 20	*ꜥpr*
Aa 27	spindle; *nḏ*; often *nḏ*
Aa 28	builder's level; *qd*
Aa 30	decorative element; *ḫkr*

Sign list overview

A Men and their activities

1 2 3 4 5 6 7 8 9 10 11 12 13 14 15 16 17 18 19 20

21 22 23 24 25 26 27 28 29 30 31 32 33 34 35 36 37 38 39 40

41 42 43 44 45 46 47 48 49 50 51 52 53 54 55

B Women and their activities

1 2 3 4 5 6 7

C Deities in human form

1 2 3 4 5 6 7 8 9 10 11 12 17 18 19 20 (C 13–16 do not exist)

D Parts of the human body

1 2 3 4 5 6 7 8 9 10 11 12 13 14 15 16 17 18 19 20

21 22 23 24 25 26 27 28 29 30 31 32 33 34 35 36 37 38

39 40 41 42 43 44 45 46 47 48 49 50 51 52 53 54 55

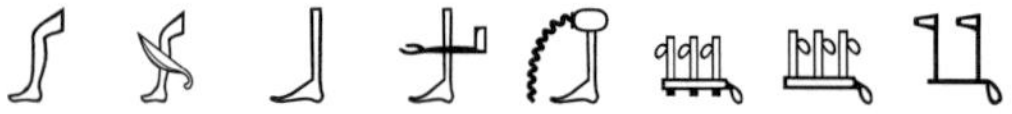

56 57 58 59 60 61 62 63

E Mammals

1 2 3 4 5 6 7 8 9 10 11 12 13 14 15

16 17 18 19 20 21 22 23 24 25 26 27 28 29 30

31 32 33 34

F Parts of mammals

1 2 3 4 5 6 7 8 9 10 11 12 13 14 15 16 17 18 19 20

21 22 23 24 25 26 27 28 29 30 31 32 33 34 35 36 37 38 39 40

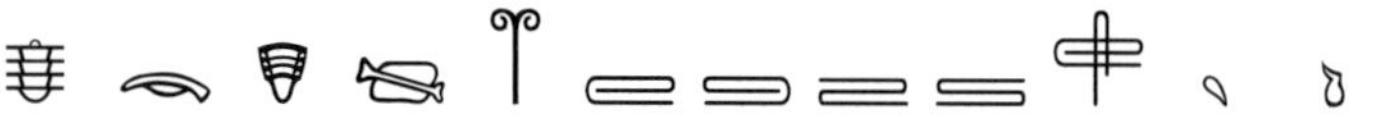

41 42 43 44 45 46 47 48 49 50 51 52

G Birds

1 2 3 4 5 6 7 8 9 10 11 12 13 14 15 16

17 18 19 20 21 22 23 24 25 26 27 28 29 30

31 32 33 34 35 36 37 38 39 40 41 42 43 44 45 46

47 48 49 50 51 52 53 54

H Parts of birds

1 2 3 4 5 6 7 8

I Amphibious animals, reptiles, etc.

1 2 3 4 5 6 7 8 9 10 11 12 13 14 15

K Fishes and parts of fishes

1 2 3 4 5 6 7

L Invertebrates and lesser animals

1 2 3 4 5 6 7

M Trees and plants

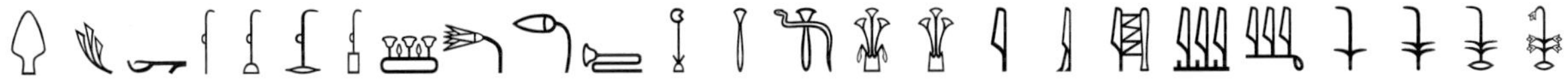

1 2 3 4 5 6 7 8 9 10 11 12 13 14 15 16 17 18 19 20 21 22 23 24 25

26 27 28 29 30 31 32 33 34 35 36 37 38 39 40 41 42

N Sky, earth, water

1 2 3 4 5 6 7 8 9 10 11 12 13 14 15 16 17 18 19 20

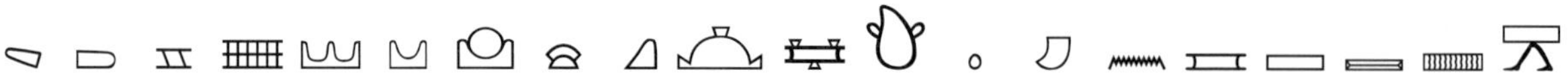

21 22 23 24 25 26 27 28 29 30 31 32 33 34 35 36 37 38 39 40

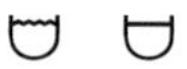

41 42

O Buildings and parts of buildings

1 2 3 4 5 6 7 8 9 10 11 12 13 14 15 16 17 18 19 20

21 22 23 24 25 26 27 28 29 30 31 32 33 34 35 36 37 38 39 40 41

42 43 44 45 46 47 48 49 50 51

P Ships and parts of ships

1 2 3 4 5 6 7 8 9 10 11

Q Domestic and funerary furniture

1 2 3 4 5 6 7

R Temple furniture and sacred emblems

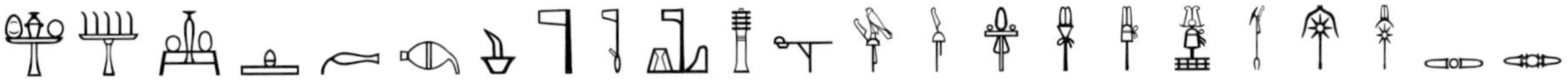

1 2 3 4 5 6 7 8 9 10 11 12 13 14 15 16 17 18 19 20 21 22 23

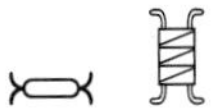

24 25

S Crowns, dress, staves, etc.

1 2 3 4 5 6 7 8 9 10 11 12 13 14 15 16 17 18 19 20

21 22 23 24 25 26 27 28 29 30 31 32 33 34 35 36 37 38 39 40

41 42 43 44 45 46 47 48

T Warfare, hunting, butchery

1 2 3 4 5 6 7 8 9 10 11 12 13 14 15 16 17 18 19 20 21 22 23

24 25 26 27 28 29 30 31 32 33 34 35

U Agriculture, crafts, production

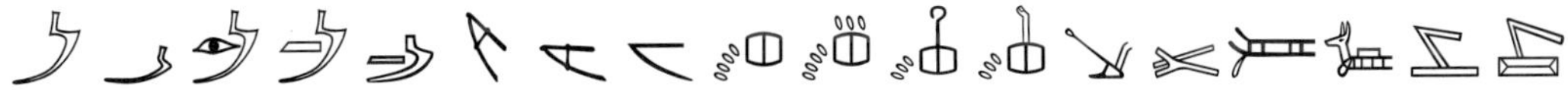

1 2 3 4 5 6 7 8 9 10 11 12 13 14 15 16 17 18

19 20 21 22 23 24 25 26 27 28 29 30 31 32 33 34 35 36 37 38 39 40 41

V Rope, fibre, baskets, bags, etc.

1 2 3 4 5 6 7 8 9 10 11 12 13 14 15 16 17 18 19 20 21 22

23 24 25 26 27 28 29 30 31 32 33 34 35 36 37 38

W Vessels of stone and earthenware

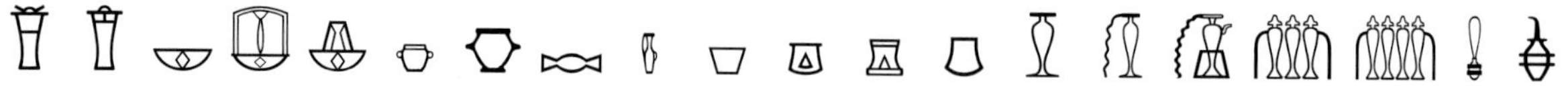

1 2 3 4 5 6 7 8 9 10 11 12 13 14 15 16 17 18 19 20

21 22 23 24 25

X Loaves and cakes

1 2 3 4 5 6 7 8

Y Writings, games, music

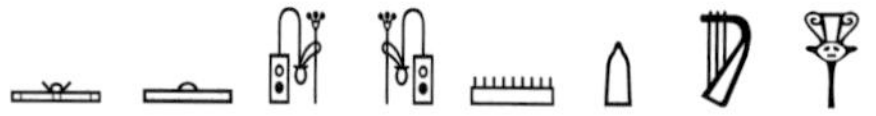

1 2 3 4 5 6 7 8

Z Strokes, signs derived from hieratic, geometrical figures

1 2 3 4 5 6 7 8 9 10 11

Aa Unclassified

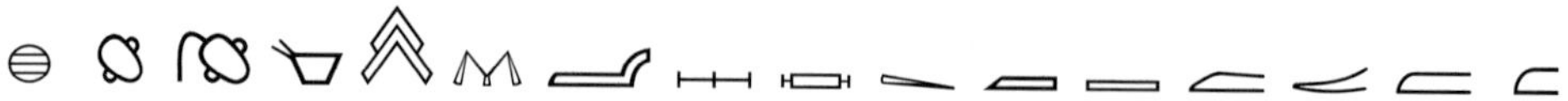

1 2 3 4 5 6 7 8 9 10 11 12 13 14 15 16

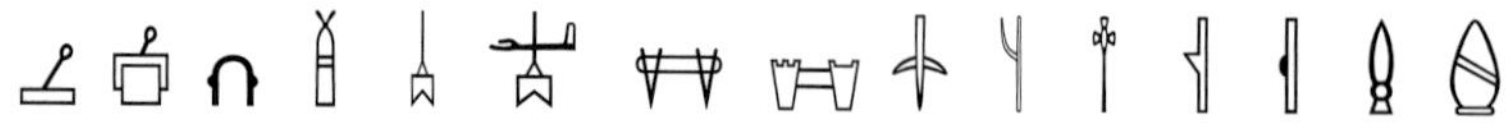

17 18 19 20 21 22 23 24 25 26 27 28 29 30 31

Credits

Cover: Inscription on spot UV, photo from P. E. Newbury 1893. *Beni Hasan I*, London: Paul Kegan, Tübner, Trench & Co.: Pl. 8.

Courtesy of The Egypt Exploration Society.

Pxiv: Map of Egypt and Near East. E. Petrocheilou (EP)

P8: Hieroglyph representing an owl. R. Bussmann (RB) and E. Petrocheilou (EP)

P8: Hieroglyph representing a viper. RB and EP

P8: Hieroglyph representing a cobra, RB and EP

P10: Photo of offering formula on stela UC14334. Photo: RB. Courtesy Petrie Museum of Egyptian Archaeology, UCL

P13: Stela UC14359, UCL Petrie Museum of Egyptian Archaeology. After H. M. Stewart 1979. *Egyptian Stelae, Reliefs and Paintings From the Petrie Collection II: Archaic to Second Intermediate Period*, pl. 30.3. Warminster: Aris & Phillips. Courtesy Oxbow books

P15: Block with cartouche of Ramses I, Abydos. Photo: RB

P16: Block with inscription of Thutmosis I, Elkab. Photo: RB

P17: Hieroglyph representing two arms. RB and EP

P17: Hieroglyph representing an offering mat. RB and EP

P20: Upper part of stela UC14441 showing family. Photo: RB Courtesy Petrie Museum of Egyptian Archaeology, UCL.

P23: Map of Abydos. EP

P24: Stela of Senwosret, BM EA 198, The British Museum. P. D. Scott-Moncrieff 1912. *Hieroglyphic texts from Egyptian stelae, etc., in the British Museum*, Part 2, pl. 28. London, British Museum Press. Courtesy British Museum Press

P30: Hieroglyph representing a seated man. RB and EP

P30: Hieroglyph representing a seated woman. RB and EP

P30: Hieroglyph representing a goose. RB and EP

P30: Hieroglyph representing a vulture. RB and EP

P32: Photo of rock inscription from Serabit el-Khadim. Courtesy Bonn University

P35: Rock inscription of Sahura. A. H. Gardiner, E. Peet 1917. *The Inscriptions of Sinai I*, pl. 5. London: Egypt Exploration Fund. Courtesy Egypt Exploration Society and Chicago University Press

P43: Rock inscription of Niuserre. A. H. Gardiner, E. Peet 1917. *The Inscriptions of Sinai I*, pl. 6. London: Egypt Exploration Fund. Courtesy Egypt Exploration Society and Chicago University Press

P44: Hieroglyph representing a falcon. RB and EP

P44: Hieroglyph representing a bee. RB and EP

P46: Photo of temples of Karnak. RB

P49: Map of Thebes. EP

P50: "Israel Stela", CG 34025, Egyptian Museum Cairo. W. M. F. Petrie 1896. *Six temples at Thebes*, pl. 12. London: Quartich.

P58: Hieroglyph representing an eye. RB and EP

P58: Hieroglyph representing a seated god. RB and EP

P60: Khnumhotep and officials. P. E. Newbury 1893. *Beni Hasan I*, pl. 30. London: Paul Kegan, Tübner, Trench & Co. Courtesy Egypt Exploration Society

P63: Rock tombs at Beni Hassan. Photo: RB

P64: Autobiography of Khnumhotep. P. E. Newbury 1893. *Beni Hasan I*, pl. 25. London: Paul Kegan, Tübner, Trench & Co. Courtesy Egypt Exploration Society

P70: Cemetery and floodplain at Beni Hassan. Photo: RB

P71: Hieroglyph representing a palette and reed. RB and EP

P71: Hieroglyph representing a seated noble. RB and EP

P71: Hieroglyph representing a vulture. RB and EP

P71: Hieroglyph representing a chicken quail. RB and EP

P74: Royal titles of Mentuhotep III from Armant. Mond, R, Myers, O. H. 1940. *Temples of Armant: A preliminary survey*, pl. 94. London: Egypt Exploration Society. Courtesy Egypt Exploration Society

P79: Marriage scarab of Amenhotep III, UC12259. Photo: Courtesy Petrie Museum of Egyptian Archaeology, UCL

P86: Photo of obelisk of Thutmosis III in Istanbul. Photo: Shutterstock

P88: Hieroglyph representing a bull. RB and EP

P88: Hieroglyph representing a swallow. RB and EP

P90: First Cataract at Aswan. Photo: RB

P93: Rock inscriptions on Sehel island. Photo: RB

P94: Rock inscription of Senwosret III. Gasse, A., Rondot, V. 2007. *Les inscriptions de Séhel*, p. 457 (SHE 147). Cairo: Institut français d'archéologie orientale. Courtesy Institut français d'archéologie orientale, Cairo

P101: Stela of Amenhotep II from Amada. Lepsius, K. R. 1849-1858. *Denkmaeler aus Aegypten und Aethiopien*, Abtheilung III, Blatt 65. Berlin: Nicolai

P103: Hieroglyph representing a rack of flasks. RB and EP

P103: Hieroglyph representing a falling man. RB and EP

P103: Hieroglyph representing a road. RB and EP

P104: Photo of ear stela from Harageh, UC14543. Photo: Petrie Museum of Egyptian Archaeology, UCL.

P108: Settlement at Deir el-Medina. Photo: G. Miniaci

P108: Photo of stela BM EA 444, The British Museum. M. L. Bierbrier 1982. *Hieroglyphic texts from Egyptian stelae, etc., in the British Museum*, Part 10, pl. 69. London: British Museum Press. Courtesy British Museum Press.

P116: Hieroglyph representing a praying man. RB and EP

P116: Hieroglyph representing an ear. RB and EP

P116: Hieroglyph representing a heart. RB and EP

P116: Hieroglyph representing a foreleg of lion. RB and EP

P118: Akhenaten and family worshiping sun disk. Davies, N. de G. 1906, *The rock tombs of el Amarna IV: The tombs of Penthu, Mahu, and others*, pl. 31. London: Egypt Exploration Fund. Courtesy Egypt Exploration Society

P122: Map of Amarna. EP

P130: Hymn to the Aten. N. de G. Davis 1908. *The Rock Tombs of El Amarna VI: Tombs of Parennefer and Ay*, pl. 25. London: Egypt Exploration Fund. Courtesy Egypt Exploration Society

P130: Hieroglyph representing a harpoon. EP

P130: Hieroglyph representing a lasso. EP

P132: Scene showing weighing of heart. Naville, E. 1886, *Das aegyptische Todtenbuch der XVIII. bis XX. Dynastie I: Text und Vignetten*, pl. 136. Berlin: Asher & Co

P136: Spell 125 in cursive hieroglyphs. Naville, E. 1886, *Das aegyptische Todtenbuch der XVIII. bis XX. Dynastie I: Text und Vignetten*, pl. 133. Berlin: Asher & Co

P141: Stela of Amenemheb. Petrie, W. M. F. Walker, J. F. 1909. *The palace of Apries (Memphis II)*, pl. 25. London: Quartich

P143: Hieroglyph representing a bird. RB and EP

P143: Hieroglyph representing a feather. RB and EP

P146: Wall scene "Opening the shrine". A. H. Gardiner 1933. *Sethos 1: The Temple of Sethos I at Abydos.* Volume 1: The Chapels of Osiris, Isis and Horus, frontispiz. Chicago: The Oriental Institute, University of Chicago; London: Egypt Exploration Society. Courtesy Egypt Exploration Society and Chicago University Press

P150: Plan of temple of Seti I, Abydos. EP

P151: Wall scene, burning incense before Osiris. A. H. Gardiner 1933. *Sethos 1: The Temple of Sethos I at Abydos.* Volume 1: The Chapels of Osiris, Isis and Horus, pl. 6. Chicago: The Oriental Institute, University of Chicago; London: Egypt Exploration Society. Courtesy Egypt Exploration Society and Chicago University Press

P159: Wall scene, burning incense before Isis. A. H. Gardiner 1933. *Sethos 1: The Temple of Sethos I at Abydos.* Volume 1: The Chapels of Osiris, Isis and Horus, pl. 19. Chicago: The Oriental Institute, University of Chicago; London: Egypt Exploration Society. Courtesy Egypt Exploration Society and Chicago University Press

P161: Hieroglyph representing a hare. RB and EP

P161: Hieroglyph representing a standard. RB and EP

P162: Figurines and objects found scattered around the „Ramessum box". J. E. Quibell 1898. *The Ramesseum* and W. Spiegelberg 1898. *And, The Tomb of Ptah-hetep*, pl. 3. London: B. Quartich

P174: Hieroglyph representing a bird. RB and EP

P174: Hieroglyph representing a goat skin. RB and EP

P174: Hieratic word for "to find". Darwing: RB. After V. S. Golenischeff 1913. Les papyrus hiératiques No. 1115, 1116A et 1116B de l'Ermitage imperial à St. Pétersbourg, pl. 3, St. Petersburg: Direction de l'Érmitage imperial

P174: Hieratic word for "residence". Drawing: RB. After V. S. Golenischeff 1913. Les papyrus hiératiques No. 1115, 1116A et 1116B de l'Ermitage imperial à St. Pétersbourg, pl. 5, St. Petersburg: Direction de l'Érmitage imperial

P176: Ibsha from Beni Hassan. P. E. Newbury 1893. *Beni Hasan I*, pl. 28. London: Paul Kegan, Tübner, Trench & Co. Courtesy Egypt Exploration Society

P184: Punt reliefs. Mariette, A. 1877. *Deir-el-Bahari: documents topographiques, historiques et ethnographiques recueillis dans ce temple*, pl. 5. Leipzig: Hinrichs

P187: Hieroglyph representing a scarab. RB and EP

P187: Hieroglyph representing a back part of lion. RB and EP

P190: Scribe, scale and administrators. P. E. Newbury 1893. *Beni Hasan I*, pl. 29. London: Paul Kegan, Tübner, Trench & Co. Courtesy Egypt Exploration Society

P193: Map of Lahun. EP

P194: Mery's Transfer of deed of Mery in hieroglyphs, UC 32037. S. Quirke, M. Collier 2004. *The UCL Lahun Papyri: Religious, Literary, Legal, Mathematical and Medical*, p. 100. Oxford: Archaeopress. Courtesy Archaeopress, Stephen Quirke and Mark Collier

P205: Letter in hieroglyphs, UC32199. S. Quirke, M. Collier 2002. *The UCL Lahun Papyri: Letters*, p. 96. Oxford: Archaeopress. Courtesy Archaeopress, Stephen Quirke and Mark Collier

P206: Hieroglyph representing a flying dug. RB and EP

P206: Hieroglyph representing a bird. RB and EP

P208: Drawing of landscape at Semna. Lepsius, LD. K. R. Lepsius, *Denkmäler aus Ägypten und Äthiopien*, Abtheilung II, Blatt 112.

P210: Map of Semna. EP

P211: Small Semna stela. Meurer, G. 1996. *Nubier in Ägypten bis zum Beginn des Neuen Reiches: Zur Bedeutung der Stele Berlin 14753*, Taf. 1 Berlin: Achet. Drawing by C. Müller 1996. Courtesy Achet, G. Meurer and C. Müller-Hazenbos

P218: Large Semna stela. Lepsius, *Denkmäler aus Ägypten und Äthiopien*, Abtheilung II, Blatt 136h

P219: Detail of large Semna stela

P220: Hieroglyph representing a oven. RB and EP

P220: Hieroglyph representing a sledge. RB and EP

Notes

Notes

Notes

Teach Yourself® is dedicated to promoting and advancing the learning of the world's languages – popular and rare, modern and ancient – by providing innovative and effective content for all levels, learning styles and lifestyles. Our courses are ideal for learners studying on their own or with a tutor. They can also be used in the classroom. Our courses, available in over 65 languages, are continuously updated, include modern methodologies, and are written by teachers and academics at the top of their fields. Download the Teach Yourself Library app or visit library.teachyourself.com to access our growing library of online resources. Teach Yourself language courses are tried and tested at universities across the globe.

If you are interested in using ***Complete Middle Egyptian*** in your classroom please contact us at ***learningsolutions@teachyourself.com***. We would be happy to work with you directly to provide a learning solution that fits your and your learners' needs.